New Technologies for Personalized Medicine in Head and Neck Oncologic and Reconstructive Surgery

New Technologies for Personalized Medicine in Head and Neck Oncologic and Reconstructive Surgery

Editors

Mark L. Urken
Carlos Navarro Cuéllar
José Luis Cebrián-Carretero

MDPI

Basel • Beijing • Wuhan • Barcelona • Belgrade • Novi Sad • Cluj • Manchester

Editors
Mark L. Urken
Icahn School of Medicine at Mount Sinai
New York
USA

Carlos Navarro Cuéllar
Hospital Gregorio Marañón
Madrid
Spain

José Luis Cebrián-Carretero
University Hospital La Paz
Madrid
Spain

Editorial Office
MDPI AG
Grosspeteranlage 5
4052 Basel, Switzerland

This is a reprint of articles from the Special Issue published online in the open access journal *Journal of Clinical Medicine* (ISSN 2077-0383) (available at: https://www.mdpi.com/journal/jcm/special_issues/Personalized_Head_Neck_Surgery).

For citation purposes, cite each article independently as indicated on the article page online and as indicated below:

Lastname, A.A.; Lastname, B.B. Article Title. *Journal Name* **Year**, *Volume Number*, Page Range.

ISBN 978-3-7258-1981-2 (Hbk)
ISBN 978-3-7258-1982-9 (PDF)
doi.org/10.3390/books978-3-7258-1982-9

Contents

Journal of
Clinical Medicine

MDPI

Editorial

New Technologies for Personalized Medicine in Head and Neck Oncologic and Reconstructive Surgery

José Luis Cebrián Carretero [1,*] and Carlos Navarro Cuéllar [2]

1 Department of Oral and Maxilofacial Surgery, Hospital Universitario La Paz, Universidad Autónoma de Madrid, IDIPAZ, 28046 Madrid, Spain
2 División of Oral and Maxillofacial Surgery, Hospital General Universitario Gregorio Marañón, Universidad Complutense de Madrid, 28007 Madrid, Spain; cnavarrocuellar@gmail.com
* Correspondence: josel.cebrian@salud.madrid.org

Citation: Cebrián Carretero, J.L.; Navarro Cuéllar, C. New Technologies for Personalized Medicine in Head and Neck Oncologic and Reconstructive Surgery. *J. Clin. Med.* **2022**, *11*, 4261. https://doi.org/10.3390/jcm11154261

Received: 30 June 2022
Accepted: 18 July 2022
Published: 22 July 2022

The search for standardized protocols has been a constant concern in Head and Neck Reconstructive Surgery. Nevertheless, the concept of personalization has emerged as a possibility to adjust these protocols to a single individual. This customization of the treatments has been extensively used in medical disciplines for decades and in the last five to ten years, has been incorporated to Surgery.

The aim of this Special Issue, **"New Technologies for Personalized Medicine in Head and Neck Oncologic and Reconstructive Surgery"**, is to offer a particular view of the implications of personalized surgery and customization in the Head and Neck area.

The skill of reconstructive surgery has traditionally been considered to be learning curve dependent. Until recently, overall success in craniofacial reconstruction has relied primarily on the use of 2D imaging modalities, and microsurgical reconstructions of the facial skeleton were performed "freehand" and reconstruction plates were manually adapted during surgery.

The use of computer-assisted surgery (CAS) and navigation technology in head and neck oncology was first described in 1995 by A. Wagner [1].

Virtual surgical planning (VSP), design, modeling (CAD-/CAM: computer assisted design, computer assisted manufacturing) and surgical navigation techniques have contributed during the last years to simplify and improve the accuracy of this specific type of surgery [2–4]. These technologies have gained significant acceptance in oncologic applications. In the area of reconstructive surgery, it provides many benefits, since the surgical precision required to restore facial symmetry, appearance, and function is a complex challenge and the three-dimensional (3D) position is difficult to control, especially in extensive bony defects [5–11].

Virtual surgical planning and computer-aided design (CAD) allows preplanning of the oncologic resection, flap dimensions, and osteotomies in the bone flap [12]. Computer-aided manufacturing (CAM) cutting guides allow surgeons to accurately perform planned resections and osteotomies, which has improved the precision, accuracy, and reliability of the results of bone resections and reconstructions [4,9,13,14]. Surgical navigation has improved reliability and outcomes by providing real-time feedback to the surgeon [4].

VSP began to be used in bone flaps and is now also used in soft tissue flaps for precise localization of the skin perforators of the flap and in ablative virtual surgery to enhance the localization of the soft tissue flaps. In the latter, it is used for precise localization of the skin perforators of the flap and in ablative virtual surgery to establish the reconstructive needs and the most appropriate flap thickness for each reconstruction.

The reconstructive benefits of CAD-CAM implementation include:

1. It enables preoperative visualization of the patient's individual anatomic features [9,15].
2. It simplifies the osteotomies during tumor ablation in oncologic patients [9].
3. It improves reconstructive accuracy [5,7–9].

4. It improves the osteosynthesis of the bone segments for reconstruction [8].
5. It increases the precision of the bone contact surfaces of the flap and the remnant bone, achieving a better aesthetic contour and lower complication rates [5,8].
6. It allows for preoperative visualization of reconstructive limitations and possible complications [9].
7. It increases the possibilities of obtaining clear resection margins, because the surgeon has a 3D visualization of the lesion and an understanding of the future bone defect and the immediate reconstructive plan, thus enhancing the decrease in local recurrence rates [2].
8. It decreases intraoperative time, specifically the decrease in the ischemic time of the microsurgical flap, better reliability in the results and the simplicity of use of this approach [5,8,9,11,14].
9. With surgical navigation, the time needed to identify the perforating vessels can be reduced [4,16,17].
10. Improvement in the predictability of the results, improving patient satisfaction, which means lower total cost (due to shorter surgical time, shorter hospital stay, and lower complication rates) that can potentially offset the technological costs [5,8,9,14].

In recent years, different "In House" navigation systems have been implemented for the placement of dental implants by means of dynamic navigation techniques in oncologic patients. This dynamic navigation technique allows placing the implants with sub-millimeter precision since the apical linear deviation is less than 1 mm and the angular deviation is less than 3°. The result is increased precision and accuracy in implant placement and prosthetic rehabilitation.

On the other hand, the main disadvantages of virtual surgery planning are: (1) increased costs, often due to the need for an external digital laboratory; (2) the surgical delay involved in surgical planning and obtaining the different models and cutting guides, which can delay the beginning of treatment in oncologic patients.

Currently, the introduction of 3D technology and its use in Virtual Planning, Navigation, and Custom-Made prosthesis, have opened several debates.

One of the most important is related to the precision and accuracy of these methods. As the main challenge in the reconstructive surgery of this region is to achieve optimal function and aesthetics, despite its complex three-dimensional (3D) anatomy, it seems that these new technical possibilities are indicated to approach Head and Neck pathology [17].

In this sense, the disadvantage of conventional techniques lies in trying to reconstruct a complex 3D structure by 2D imaging and planning. For complex cases, it can be time-consuming, and unreliable. The use of 2D techniques can negatively influence both the functional and esthetic outcomes [18]. It seems that personalized planning and modeling **optimize aesthetic outcomes and functional rehabilitation** [19].

Another important aspect is related to the **delay of treatment** when we use these techniques. The pretreatment interval is defined as the time from diagnosis to the beginning of treatment and can be influenced by the patient, the health system, and the disease. The expansion of this time can compromise the prognosis, since during this time interval the tumor can multiply and metastasize [20]. Planning and personalized prosthesis manufacturing could increase this period. During the last five years, producers have made a big effort to reduce this interval to no more than two weeks and in selected cases, in-house could potentially reduce the time by 24 h [21].

Another issue is related to the risk of achieving **free margins** in the resection when it is virtually planned. Several studies conclude that cancer patients can be safely treated via primary reconstruction with the help of virtual planning and guided surgery. It could be related to the fact that it is easier to be more aggressive while operating on an image than on an actual body [22].

On the other hand, the reduction in operating time is another factor that has several implications related to a better outcome for the patient and reducing overall costs. There is a long-established principle that correlates the acquisition of new technologies with increased costs, but this is not totally true if we take into account the biological costs related to increased operating time and prolonged hospitalization [23,24].

Finally, it is important to highlight how the implementation of all these new technologies improves the quality of life of patients. For this reason, it is necessary to carry out quality of life studies that relate the personalized treatment of patients and its results on their quality of life.

In the following years, we expect a **severe economic crisis** that will put some pressure on health systems around the world to reduce costs, and improving the quality of treatments.

In the present Issue, we will analyze the impact of personalization in Craniofacial Surgery. We have invited the most prominent authors who have experience in this field of knowledge, to offer deep insight into the panorama of the use of new technologies.

Funding: This research received no external funding.

Conflicts of Interest: The authors declare no conflict of interest.

References

1. Wagner, A.; Ploder, O.; Enislidis, G.; Truppe, M.; Ewers, R. Virtual image guided navigation in tumor surgery—Technical innovation. *J. Cranio-Maxillofac. Surg.* **1995**, *23*, 271–273. [CrossRef]
2. Abbate, V.; Orabona, G.D.A.; Solari, D.; Bonavolontà, P.; Iaconetta, G.; Califano, L. Mandibular Surgical Navigation: An Innovative Guiding Method. *J. Craniofacial Surg.* **2017**, *28*, 2122–2126. [CrossRef] [PubMed]
3. Dupret-Bories, A.; Vergez, S.; Meresse, T.; Brouillet, F.; Bertrand, G. Contribution of 3D printing to mandibular reconstruction after cancer. *Eur. Ann. Otorhinolaryngol. Head Neck Dis.* **2017**, *135*, 133–136. [CrossRef]
4. Pietruski, P.; Majak, M.; Światek-Najwer, E.; Żuk, M.; Popek, M.; Mazurek, M.; Świecka, M.; Jaworowski, J. Navigation-guided fibula free flap for mandibular reconstruction: A proof of concept study. *J. Plast. Reconstr. Aesthetic Surg.* **2019**, *72*, 572–580. [CrossRef] [PubMed]
5. Rodby, K.A.; Turin, S.; Jacobs, R.J.; Cruz, J.F.; Hassid, V.J.; Kolokythas, A.; Antony, A.K. Advances in oncologic head and neck reconstruction: Systematic review and future considerations of virtual surgical planning and computer aided design/computer aided modeling. *J. Plast. Reconstr. Aesthetic Surg.* **2014**, *67*, 1171–1185. [CrossRef] [PubMed]
6. Shen, S.-Y.; Yu, Y.; Zhang, W.-B.; Liu, X.-J.; Peng, X. Angle-to-Angle Mandibular Defect Reconstruction With Fibula Flap by Using a Mandibular Fixation Device and Surgical Navigation. *J. Craniofacial Surg.* **2017**, *28*, 1486–1491. [CrossRef]
7. Chan, A.; Sambrook, P.; Munn, Z.; Boase, S. Effectiveness of computer-assisted virtual planning, cutting guides and pre-engineered plates on outcomes in mandible fibular free flap reconstructions over traditional freehand techniques: A systematic review protocol. *JBI Database Syst. Rev. Implement. Rep.* **2019**, *17*, 2136–2151. [CrossRef]
8. Naros, A.; Weise, H.; Tilsen, F.; Hoefert, S.; Naros, G.; Krimmel, M.; Reinert, S.; Polligkeit, J. Three-dimensional accuracy of mandibular reconstruction by patient-specific pre-bent reconstruction plates using an "in-house" 3D-printer. *J. Cranio-Maxillofacial Surg.* **2018**, *46*, 1645–1651. [CrossRef]
9. Dean-Ferrer, A.; Pastor, D.; Lopez-Cedrún, J. Planificación virtual de los colgajos óseos, Atlas de Procedimientos y Técnicas Quirúrgicas. *Editor. Panam.* **2018**, *125*, 955–959.
10. Modabber, A.; Rauen, A.; Ayoub, N.; Möhlhenrich, S.; Peters, F.; Kniha, K.; Hölzle, F.; Raith, S. Evaluation of a novel algorithm for automating virtual surgical planning in mandibular reconstruction using fibula flaps. *J. Cranio-Maxillofac. Surg.* **2019**, *47*, 1378–1386. [CrossRef]
11. Yu, Y.; Zhang, W.; Wang, Y.; Liu, X.; Guo, C.; Peng, X. A Revised Approach for Mandibular Reconstruction with the Vascularized Iliac Crest Flap Using Virtual Surgical Planning and Surgical Navigation. *J. Oral Maxillofac. Surg.* **2016**, *74*, 1285.e1–1285.e11. [CrossRef] [PubMed]
12. Alassaf, M.H.; Li, W.; Joshi, A.S.; Hahn, J.K. Computer-based planning system for mandibular reconstruction. *Stud. Health Technol. Inform.* **2014**, *196*, 6–10. [PubMed]
13. Bernstein, J.; Daly, M.; Chan, H.; Qiu, J.; Goldstein, D.; Muhanna, N.; de Almeida, J.R.; Irish, J. Accuracy and reproducibility of virtual cutting guides and 3D-navigation for osteotomies of the mandible and maxilla. *PLoS ONE* **2017**, *12*, e0173111.
14. Ayoub, N.; Ghassemi, A.; Rana, M.; Gerressen, M.; Riediger, D.; Hölzle, F.; Modabber, A. Evaluation of computer-assisted mandibular reconstruction with vascularized iliac crest bone graft compared to conventional surgery: A randomized prospective clinical trial. *Randomized Control. Trial* **2014**, *15*, 114. [CrossRef] [PubMed]
15. Shenaq, D.; Matros, E. Virtual planning and navigational technology in reconstructive surgery. *J. Surg. Oncol.* **2018**, *118*, 845–852. [CrossRef]
16. Antúnez-Conde, R.; Salmerón, J.I.; Díez-Montiel, A.; Agea, M.; Gascón, D.; Sada, Á.; Navarro Cuellar, I.; Tousidonis, M.; Ochandiano, S.; Arenas, G.; et al. Mandibular Reconstruction with Fibula Flap and Dental Implants through Virtual Surgical Planning and Three Different Techniques: Double-Barrel Flap, Implant Dynamic Navigation and CAD/CAM Mesh with Iliac Crest Graft. *Front. Oncol.* **2021**, *11*, 719712. [CrossRef]

17. Del Castillo Pardo de Vera, J.L.; Pampín Martínez, M.; Guiñales Díaz de Cevallos, J.; Rodriguez Arias, J.P.; Cebrián Carretero, J.L. Precise modification of surgical and positioning guides for temporomandibular joint prosthesis. *Br. J. Oral Maxillofac. Surg.* **2022**, *60*, 855–858. [CrossRef]
18. Powcharoen, W.; Yang, W.F. Computer-Assisted versus Conventional Freehand Mandibular Reconstruction with Fibula Free Flap: A Systematic Review and Meta-Analysis. *Plast. Reconstr. Surg.* **2019**, *144*, 1417–1428. [CrossRef]
19. Bao, T.; He, J.; Yu, C.; Zhao, W.; Lin, Y.; Wang, H.; Liu, J.; Zhu, H. Utilization of a pre-bent plate positioning surgical guide system in precise mandibular reconstruction with a free fibula flap. *Oral Oncol.* **2017**, *75*, 133–139. [CrossRef]
20. Ford, P.J.; Farah, C.S. Early detection and diagnosis of oral cancer: Strategies for improvement. *J. Cancer Policy* **2013**, *1*, e2–e7. [CrossRef]
21. Orabona, G.D.A.; Abbate, V.; Maglitto, F.; Bonavolontà, P.; Salzano, G.; Romano, A.; Reccia, A.; Committeri, U.; Iaconetta, G.; Califano, L. Low-cost, self-made CAD/CAM-guiding system for mandibular reconstruction. *Surg. Oncol.* **2018**, *27*, 200–207. [CrossRef] [PubMed]
22. Goetze, E.; Moergel, M.; Gielisch, M.; Kämmerer, P.W. Safety of resection margins in CAD/CAM-guided primarily reconstructed oral squamous cell carcinoma—A retrospective case series. *Oral Maxillofac. Surg.* **2019**, *23*, 459–464. [CrossRef] [PubMed]
23. Cheng, H.; Clymer, J.W.; Chen BP, H.; Sadeghirad, B.; Ferko, N.C.; Cameron, C.G.; Hinoul, P. Prolonged operative duration is associated with complications: A systematic review and meta-analysis. *J. Surg. Res.* **2018**, *229*, 134–144. [CrossRef] [PubMed]
24. Wilde, F.; Hanken, H.; Probst, F.; Schramm, A.; Heiland, M.; Cornelius, C.-P. Multicenter study on the use of patient-specific CAD/CAM reconstruction plates for mandibular reconstruction. *Int. J. Comput. Assist. Radiol. Surg.* **2015**, *10*, 2035–2051. [CrossRef]

Journal of
Clinical Medicine

MDPI

Review

The Exoscope in Neurosurgery: An Overview of the Current Literature of Intraoperative Use in Brain and Spine Surgery

Nicola Montemurro [1,*], Alba Scerrati [2], Luca Ricciardi [3] and Gianluca Trevisi [4]

1 Department of Neurosurgery, Azienda Ospedaliera Universitaria Pisana (AOUP), University of Pisa, 56100 Pisa, Italy
2 Department of Neurosurgery, Sant'Anna University Hospital, 44124 Ferrara, Italy; scrlba@unife.it
3 Department of NESMOS, Neurosurgery, Sant'Andrea Hospital, "Sapienza" University of Rome, 00189 Rome, Italy; ricciardi.lu@gmail.com
4 Department of Neurosurgery, Presidio Ospedaliero Santo Spirito, 65124 Pescara, Italy; trevisi.gianluca@gmail.com
* Correspondence: nicola.montemurro@unipi.it

Abstract: Background: Exoscopes are a safe and effective alternative or adjunct to the existing binocular surgical microscope for brain tumor, skull base surgery, aneurysm clipping and both cervical and lumbar complex spine surgery that probably will open a new era in the field of new tools and techniques in neurosurgery. Methods: A Pubmed and Ovid EMBASE search was performed to identify papers that include surgical experiences with the exoscope in neurosurgery. PRISMA guidelines (Preferred Reporting Items for Systematic Reviews and Meta-analyses) were followed. Results: A total of 86 articles and 1711 cases were included and analyzed in this review. Among 86 papers included in this review 74 (86%) were published in the last 5 years. Out of 1711 surgical procedures, 1534 (89.6%) were performed in the operative room, whereas 177 (10.9%) were performed in the laboratory on cadavers. In more detail, 1251 (72.7%) were reported as brain surgeries, whereas 274 (16%) and 9 (0.5%) were reported as spine and peripheral nerve surgeries, respectively. Considering only the clinical series (40 studies and 1328 patients), the overall surgical complication rate was 2.6% during the use of the exoscope. These patients experienced complication profiles similar to those that underwent the same treatments with the OM. The overall switch incidence rate from exoscope to OM during surgery was 5.8%. Conclusions: The exoscope seems to be a safe alternative compared to an operative microscope for the most common brain and spinal procedures, with several advantages that have been reached, such as an easier simplicity of use and a better 3D vision and magnification of the surgical field. Moreover, it offers the opportunity of better interaction with other members of the surgical staff. All these points set the first step for subsequent and short-term changes in the field of neurosurgery and offer new educational possibilities for young neurosurgery and medical students.

Keywords: exoscope; high-definition 3D exoscope; augmented reality; intraoperative visualization; neurosurgery; brain tumor; virtual reality; spine; neuronavigation

Citation: Montemurro, N.; Scerrati, A.; Ricciardi, L.; Trevisi, G. The Exoscope in Neurosurgery: An Overview of the Current Literature of Intraoperative Use in Brain and Spine Surgery. *J. Clin. Med.* **2022**, *11*, 223. https://doi.org/10.3390/jcm11010223

Academic Editor: Morgan Broggi

Received: 27 November 2021
Accepted: 30 December 2021
Published: 31 December 2021

1. Introduction

The surgical microscope has represented a basic tool in neurosurgery since the late 1960s, and it continues to be critically essential in the microsurgical treatment of brain and spine pathologies [1–8]. Advances in digital imaging, WiFi internet connections, screen technology and optics have led to the development of extracorporeal telescopes, also known as exoscopes, which represent valuable alternatives to traditional OMs for surgical magnification [6,9,10]. The use of the microscope requires that surgeons look directly through the surgical microscopic objective lenses to visualize the target area; however, it seems that this "face-to-machine" interface has been overcome due to the introduction and use of new digital 3-dimensional (3D) imaging exoscopes [2].

As widely reported in microsurgery and minimally invasive procedures, the pursuit of highly detailed images and techniques has been providing both valuable clinical results and patient satisfaction [11]. The technology of exoscopes has continuously changed over the years, and these devices are often updated in their software and hardware. Exoscopes have been the latest addition to the neurosurgeons' armamentarium, acting as a bridge between OMs and endoscopes [12]. The development of the 3D exoscope represents a marvel of technological innovation in modern surgical practice, which continues to renew itself year by year, from the first 3D High Definition (HD) visualization exoscope to the most recent 3D 4K exoscope. Furthermore, these modern exoscopes are embedded with light filters for 5-aminolevulinic acid (5-ALA) and indocyanine video-angiography, pneumatic arms, adjustable operative settings, multiscreen output, longer focus distance, and greater magnification powers [13,14].

3D exoscopes are novel high-definition digital camera systems that are able to deliver intense light and magnification to the deepest areas of the surgical field, allowing the surgeon to see, through 3D glasses and a 3D monitor, critical neural and vascular structures as well as tissue differentiation with high magnification. A surgeon's position is not limited to the microscope' oculars, while freedom in movements during surgery, a higher comfort rate, a lower fatigue after longer procedures have been already reported in using an exoscope [9,15–18]. In neurosurgery, supports for various digitized information are essential for improving operative grades, as neurosurgeons could benefit from a new surgeon's eye that visualizes the operative field with integration of others medical information [10,17].

Exoscopes, as well as other modern devices, require specific training, although the learning curve is very short when compared to other neurosurgical systems such as operative microscopes (OM) and endoscopes [5–7,19]. Siller et al. [5] reported no significant differences among patients who underwent surgery with OM or exoscope for lumbar posterior decompression (LPD) and anterior cervical discectomy and fusion (ACDF). Similarly, Muhammad et al. [7] reported results in cranial surgery comparable to the OM with better visual quality and greater comfort for the surgeon. The exoscope system is a safe and effective alternative or adjunct to the existing binocular OM for brain tumor, skull base surgery, aneurysm clipping and vascular microanastomosis, both cervical and lumbar complex spine surgery [5–8,10,20–25]. The exoscope provides the surgeon with a comfortable, high-resolution visualization without compromising surgical exposure and patient safety. The integrated features like the lock-on-target and waypoints together with the footswitch allow the surgeon to efficiently place the camera and to return to saved positions, even hands-free. All these functions in combination with the digital visualization are convenient and ergonomic compared to OM, even when the surgeon has to see into the situs using extreme angles. To date, several exoscopic systems are available for neurosurgical use. VITOM® (Karl Storz, Tuttlingen, Germany), ORBEYE™ (Olympus, Tokyo, Japan), Modus V™ (Synaptive Medical, Toronto, ON, Canada), Kinevo 900 (Carl Zeiss Meditec AG, Jena, Germany), BrainPath® (Nico Corporation, Indianapolis, IN, US) and Aeos® (Aesculap, Tüttlingen, Germany) are the most commonly used, with different technical, software and hardware characteristics, but with the same goal [7,15,26–30]. As the exoscope will probably open a new era in the field of new tools and techniques in neurosurgery, as the OM did in the 1960s, this review aims to investigate about the use of the exoscope in preclinical and clinical neurosurgical settings, the most common neurosurgical procedures performed with the exoscope, as well as the impact of exoscope on surgical outcome and workflow, reporting operative complications, surgical procedures switched from exoscope to OM, and advantages and disadvantages compared to the microscope.

2. Materials and Methods

2.1. Literature Search

A Pubmed and Ovid EMBASE search was performed to identify papers that include surgical experiences with the exoscope in neurosurgery. PRISMA guidelines (Preferred Reporting Items for Systematic Reviews and Meta-analyses) were followed [31]. The key words "exoscope", "exoscopic visualization", "neurosurgery", "brain", "spine" and "cadaver lab" were used in both "AND" and "OR" combinations. The key words and the detailed search strategy are reported in Table 1.

Table 1. Search syntax.

PubMed Search Accessed on 5 July 2021 (108 Articles)	Embase Search Accessed on 5 July 2021 (106 Articles)
(exoscope OR exoscopic visualization) AND (neurosurgery OR brain OR spine OR cadaver lab)	('exoscope' OR 'exoscopic visualization') AND ('neurosurgery' OR 'brain' OR 'spine' OR 'cadaver lab')

The inclusion criteria were the following: case series or case report reporting clinical data and neurosurgical intraoperative experiences with exoscope (both 2D and 3D visualization, as well 3D 4K definition) in brain and spine surgery as well as laboratory experiences in the field of neurosurgery. Exclusion criteria were the following: (1) studies published in languages other than English with no available English translations, (2) review articles, (3) studies with insufficient data, (4) studies not related with this topic.

2.2. Data Collection

From each study, we extracted the following data: (1) number of neurosurgical procedures performed using the exoscope divided by cerebral (tumor and vascular), spinal and peripheral nerve pathology as well as laboratory experiences; (2) exoscope manufacturer and/or model; (3) visualization mode setting; (4) operative complications and surgical procedures switched from the exoscope to OM; (5) advantages and disadvantages identified by authors (video image quality, surgical field, handling, surgical ergonomics, educational usefulness, depth perception, operative time and/or workflow, operative team involvement).

2.3. Outcomes

The primary objective of this review was to examine the most common neurosurgical procedures performed with the use of the exoscope and to identify surgical workflows, operative complications during the use of the exoscope and surgical procedures switched from the exoscope to the OM. The secondary objective was to report the most common advantages and disadvantages identified by authors (video image quality, surgical field, handling, surgical ergonomics, educational usefulness, depth perception, operative time and/or workflow, operative team involvement) to highlight strengths and weaknesses of this new technology.

3. Results

The database search yielded 208 articles. After the removal of duplicates, 108 articles were eligible for screening. A total of 86 articles met the selection criteria [3–10,13,15,16,19,21,23,25–30,32–97]. The search flow diagram is shown in Figure 1.

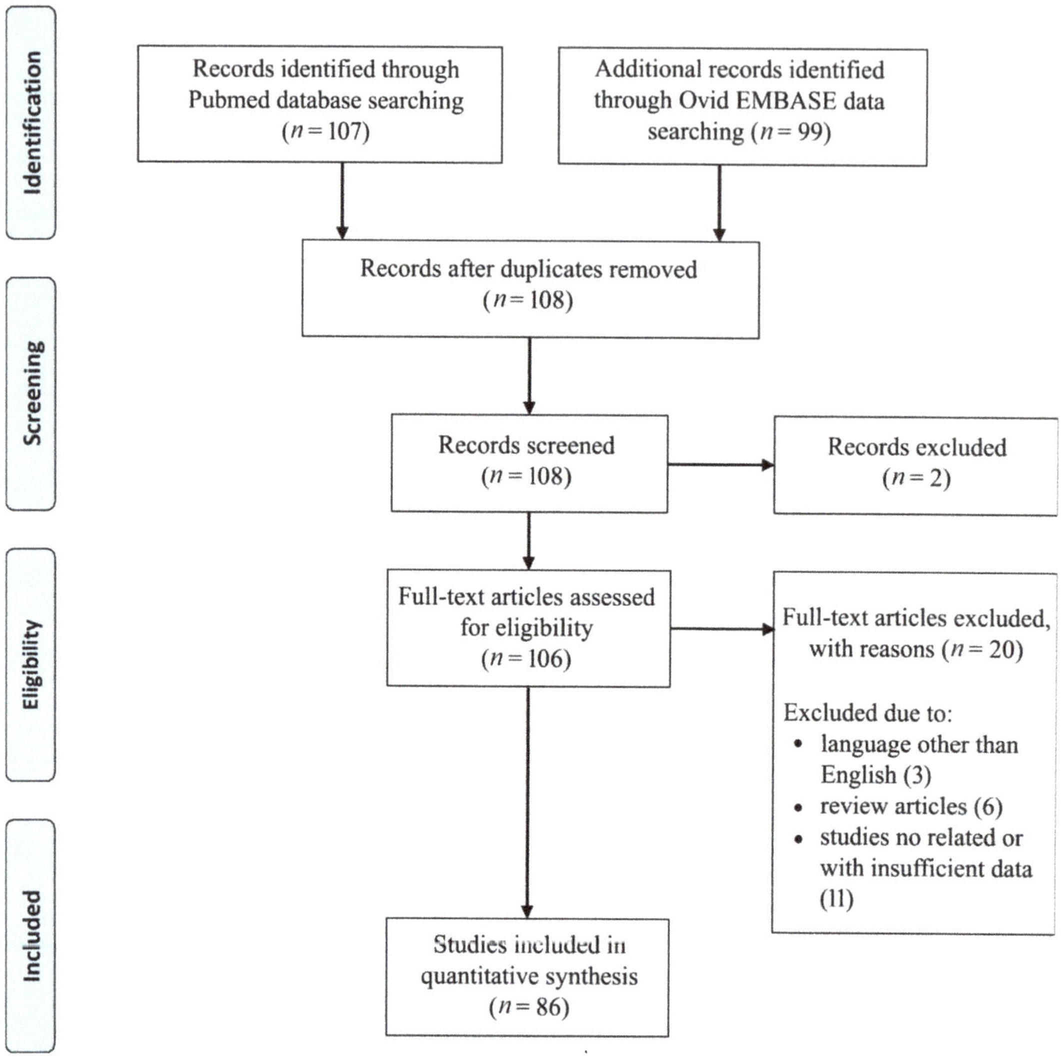

Figure 1. PRISMA flow diagram.

3.1. Demographic and Number of Neurosurgical Procedures Performed Using Exoscope

Studies included in our review are summarized in Table 2. A total of 86 articles and 1711 cases were included and analyzed in this review [3–10,13,15,16,19,21,23,25–30,32–97]. Among 86 papers included in the review 74 (86%) were published in the last 5 years, showing an increasing interest in the use of the exoscope in the operating room in neurosurgery. Out of 1711 surgical procedures, 1534 (89.6%) were performed on human beings in the operative room, whereas 177 (10.9%) were performed in the laboratory on cadavers. A total of 1251 (72.7%) were reported as brain surgeries, whereas 274 (15.9%) and nine (0.5%) were reported as spine and peripheral nerve surgeries, respectively. From this review of the literature, more than 311 gliomas, 171 brain metastasis and 97 meningioma and 244 pituitary adenomas were resected by using the exoscope. One hundred intracerebral hemorrhage (ICH) and 24 neurovascular conflicts were treated by using the exoscope. In spine surgery, 64 cervical disease, 189 lumbar pathologies and 12 spine tumors were reported. A total of 48 papers (55.8%) reported their experience with a 3D HD exoscope, of which 15 used a K4 monitor, reporting the use of a 4K HD exoscope in 17.4% of the papers. Excluding the 10 papers that report laboratory experiences, 21 papers (27.6%) resulted in single case reports, 12 papers (15.8%) were small series (with ≤5 patients treated) and 43 papers (56.6%) were clinical studies with a mean of 32.8 patients and a median of 18 patients. Most common exoscope manufacturers and/or models resulted VITOM® (Karl Storz, Tuttlingen, Germany) and ORBEYE® (Olympus, Tokyo, Japan), which were used and reported in 36% and in 23.3% of these review papers, respectively. Modus V™ (Synaptive Medical, Toronto, ON, Canada), BrainPath® (Nico Corporation, Indianapolis, IN, USA) and Kinevo 900 (Carl Zeiss Meditec AG, Jena, Germany) exoscopes were used in 9.3%, 7% and 3.5% of papers reported in this review. Tables 2 and 3 show all details about cranial and spine/peripheral nerve surgical procedures. Table 4 shows laboratory experiences with an exoscope.

Table 2. Summary of cranial studies included in the review.

Authors	Year	Neurosurgical Procedures		Total	Exoscope Manufacturer and/or Model	Visualization Mode Setting
		Tumor (n°)	Vascular and Others Disease (n°)			
Gildenberg & Labuz [32]	1997	glioma (17), metastasis (1)	-	18	N/A	-
Mamelak et al. [34]	2010	glioma (3), HMG (1), meningioma (3), LGG (1), pituitary adenoma (1)	vagus nerve stimulator (1)	10	HDXO-SCOPE, Karl Storz	HD 2D
Mamelak et al. [36]	2012	germinoma (1)	-	1	VITOM®	HD 2D
Belloch et al. [37]	2014	GBM (15), AA (2), metastasis (3), LGG (3)	-	23	HDXO-SCOPE, Karl Storz	HD 2D
Birch et al. [38]	2014	pineocytoma (3), germinoma (1), lipoma (1)	-	5	HDXO-SCOPE, Karl Storz	HD 2D
Piquer et al. [39]	2014	GBM (23), AA (2), metastasis (3), LGG (2)	-	30	VITOM®	HD 2D
Ritsma et al. [40]	2014	-	ICH (1)	1	Mi SPACE	HD 2D
Parihar et al. [41]	2016	meningioma (5), glioma (4), HMG (1), metastasis (1), schwannoma (3), neurocytoma (1), medulloblastoma (1), craniopharyngioma (1)	ICH (3), colloid cyst (1), arachnoid cyst (1), abscess (2), trigeminal neuralgia (1)	25	VITOM®	HD 2D
Scranton et al. [42]	2016	-	cavernoma (2)	2	N/A	HD 2D
Bauer et al. [43]	2017	-	ICH (18)	18	BrainPath®	HD 2D
Day [44]	2017	GBM (15), AA (4), ependymoma (2), neurocytoma (1), LGG (1), metastasis (20)	ICH (6)	49	BrainPath®	HD 2D
Gonen et al. [45]	2017	astrocytoma (56), meningioma (40), metastasis (33), schwannoma (5), epidermoid/dermoid cyst (3), paraganglioma (2), craniopharyngioma (1), pituitary adenoma (1), miscellaneous (8)	aneurysms (7), AVM (5), dAVF (1), ICH (20), trigeminal neuralgia (7), hemifacial spasm (1), arachnoid cysts (2), Chiari I (1), infection (3), colloid cyst (4)	200	ROVOT-m	HD 2D
Jackson et al. [46]	2017	GBM (3), AA (3), metastasis (1), lymphoma (2)	demyelinating disease (2)	11	VITOM®	HD 2D

Table 2. *Cont.*

Authors	Year	Neurosurgical Procedures		Total	Exoscope Manufacturer and/or Model	Visualization Mode Setting
		Tumor (n°)	Vascular and Others Disease (n°)			
Krishnan et al. [47]	2017	-	anastomosis (3), AVF (1), ICH (1)	3	VITOM®	HD 2D
Labib et al. [48]	2017	-	ICH (39)	39	Mi SPACE	HD 2D
Nagata et al. [50]	2017	-	hemifacial spasm (2)	2	ORBEYE®	HD 2D
Oertel & Burkhardt [51]	2017	metastasis (3), lymphoma (1)	trigeminal neuralgia (1)	5	VITOM®	HD 3D
Rossini et al. [52]	2017	meningioma (1)	-	1	VITOM®	HD 3D
Weiner & Placantonakis [53]	2017	JPA (1)	-	1	VITOM®	HD 3D
Beez et al. [54]	2018	astrocytoma (2)	myelomeningocele closure (1)	3	VITOM®	HD 3D
Gassie et al. [55]	2018	GBM (24), AA (6), metastasis (14), lymphoma (2)	cavernoma (2), demyelinating disease (2)	50	VITOM®	HD 2D
Griessenauer et al. [56]	2018	-	ICH (5)	5	BrainPath®	HD 2D
Iyer & Chaichana [57]	2018	GBM (11), AA (3)	-	14	VITOM®	HD 2D
Khalessi et al. [58]	2018	meningioma (1), glioma (1)	clipping (4), cavernoma (3), AVM (2), endarterectomy (1), CSDH (1), cyst (1), Chiari I (1)	17	ORBEYE®	HD 3D
Klinger et al. [59]	2018	-	aneurysm (1)	1	Modus V™	HD 3D
Mampre et al. [60]	2018	metastasis (11), HMG (2)	cavernoma (2)	15	VITOM®	HD 2D
Sindelar et al. [8]	2018	-	ICH (1)	1	BrainPath®	HD 2D
Takahashi et al. [61]	2018	meningioma (5), pituitary adenoma (1), GBM (1), HMG (2), metastasis (1), craniopharyngioma (1)	Moyamoya disease (2), congenital dermal sinus (1)	14	ORBEYE®	HD 2D
Akbari et al. [62]	2019	metastasis (4), GBM (3), LGG (2), AA (1)	-	10	VITOM®	HD 2D
Angileri et al. [4]	2019	-	cavernoma + HMG (1)	1	VITOM®	HD 3D
Bakhsheshian et al. [63]	2019	metastasis (25)	-	25	BrainPath®	HD 3D
Garneau et al. [16]	2019	schwannoma (4)	temporal lobe encephalocele (2)	6	Modus V™	HD 2D
Li Ching Ng & Di Ieva [66]	2019	-	MVD (1)	1	VITOM®	HD 3D
Muhammad et al. [7]	2019	schwannoma (1), meningioma (3)	-	4	Modus V™	HD 3D
Murai et al. [67]	2019	meningioma (3), schwannoma (3), pituitary adenoma (1), GBM (1)	clipping (3), bypass (2), carotid endarterectomy (2), ICH (3)	18	ORBEYE®	3D 4K
Nossek et al. [68]	2019	-	bypass (5)	5	ORBEYE®	3D 4K
Smith et al. [69]	2019	-	skull base (11)	11	ORBEYE® (10), VITOM® (1)	HD 3D
Ahmad et al. [9]	2020	-	microvascular anastomosis (12)	12	ORBEYE®	HD 3D

Table 2. *Cont.*

Authors	Year	Neurosurgical Procedures		Total	Exoscope Manufacturer and/or Model	Visualization Mode Setting
		Tumor (*n*°)	Vascular and Others Disease (n°)			
Baron et al. [10]	2020	GBM (28)	-	28	Modus V™	HD 3D
Burkhardt et al. [71]	2020	metastasis (3), LGG (1), AA (1), GBM (2), meningioma (1), subependymoma (1), lymphoma (1)	cavernoma (1), ICH (1), aneurysm (2), CSF leak (1), trigeminal neuralgia (1)	16	VITOM®	HD 3D
Chakravarthi et al. [72]	2020	hypothalamic mass (1)	-	1	Kinevo 900	HD 3D
Chen et al. [73]	2020	schwannoma (39)	-	39	VITOM®	HD 2D
Doglietto et al. [76]	2020	GBM (1)	-	1	ORBEYE®	3D 4K
Eichberg et al. [30]	2020	GBM (13), metastasis (19), glioma (8)	cavernoma (7), colloid cyst (4), other (5)	56	BrainPath®	HD 2D
Fuse et al. [3]	2020	meningioma (1)	-	1	VITOM®	HD 2D
Garneau et al. [77]	2020	-	temporal lobe encephalocele (1)	1	Modus V™	HD 3D
Khatri et al. [78]	2020	craniopharyngioma (1)	-	1	N/A	-
Kleshchova et al. [79]	2020	endodermal cyst (1)	-	1	N/A	-
Ligas et al. [80]	2020	-	hemifacial spasm (1)	1	N/A	-
Lin et al. [81]	2020	meningioma (4)	-	4	VITOM®	HD 3D
Patel et al. [84]	2020	-	bypass (1)	1	N/A	-
Roethe et al. [85]	2020	GBM (9), meningioma (6), LGG (4), metastasis (3), AA (3)	cavernoma (1), trigeminal neuralgia (1), CSF fistula (1)	28	Kinevo 900	3D 4K
Silverstein et al. [87]	2020	-	aneurysm (1)	1	ORBEYE®	HD 3D
Amoo et al. [90]	2021	metastasis (5), meningioma (4), GBM (5), schwannoma (1), craniopharyngioma (1)	AVM (1), hemifacial spasm (1)	18	ORBEYE®	3D 4K
Marenco-Hillembrand et al. [92]	2021	metastasis (8), LGG (4), GBM (3)	-	15	N/A	-
Muscas et al. [27]	2021	meningioma (4), cranial nerve tumors (2), glioma (3), choroid plexus papilloma (1)	aneurysm (1), colloid cyst (1), neurovascular conflict (1), ethmoidal fistula (1)	14	ORBEYE®	3D 4K
Muto et al. [93]	2021	metastasis (5)	-	5	VS3 Iridium	HD 3D
Rennert et al. [94]	2021	GBM (1)	ICH (1)	2	VITOM®	HD 3D
Rösler et al. [26]	2021	GBM (6), pituitary adenoma (1), meningioma (1), craniopharyngioma (1), LGG (4), lymphoma (1), metastasis (3), HMG (1), hemangioma (1)	ICH (1), epilepsy (6), trigeminal neuralgia (1)	27	ORBEYE®	3D 4K
Rotermund et al. [95]	2021	pituitary adenoma (239), craniopharyngioma (12), meningioma (7), chordoma (4), metastasis (2)	other (32)	296	ORBEYE®	3D 4K
Shimizu et al. [96]	2021	meningioma (5), schwannoma (4)	trigeminal neuralgia (2), hemifacial spasm (3)	14	ORBEYE®	3D 4K

Table 2. *Cont.*

Authors	Year	Neurosurgical Procedures		Total	Exoscope Manufacturer and/or Model	Visualization Mode Setting
		Tumor (*n*°)	Vascular and Others Disease (n°)			
Strickland et al. [97]	2021	-	AVM (1)	1	N/A	-
Wali et al. [21]	2021	-	aneurysm (1)	1	ORBEYE®	3D 4K
Yoon et al. [25]	2021	metastasis (3), meningioma (3), GBM (4), HMG (1)	-	11	VOMS-100 (5), VITOM® (6)	3D 4K

2d, 2 dimensional; 3D 4K, 3 dimensional 4K high-definition; AA, anaplastic astrocytoma; AVM, arteriovenous malformation; CSF, cerebrospinal fluid; CSDH, chronic subdural hematoma; dAVF, arteriovenous fistula; GBM, glioblastoma multiforme; HD, high definition; HMG, hemangioblastomas; ICH, intracerebral hemorrhage; N/A, not available; JPA, juvenile pilocytic astrocytoma; LGG, low-grade glioma; MVD, microvascular decompression.

Table 3. Summary of spine/peripheral nerve studies included in the review.

Authors	Year	Neurosurgical Procedures		Total	Exoscope Manufacturer and/or Model	Visualization Mode Setting
		Spine (n°)	Peripheral (n°)			
Mamelak et al. [34]	2010	ACDF (2), epidural abscess (1), lumbar discectomy (3)	-	6	HDXO-SCOPE, Karl Storz	HD 2D
Shirzadi et al. [19]	2012	LPD (11), TLIF (13)	-	24	VITOM®	HD 2D
Parihar et al. [41]	2016	neurofibroma (4), meningioma (1), ACDF (4), corpectomy (2), tuberculosis (1), lumbar discectomy (2)	-	14	VITOM®	HD 2D
Krishnan et al. [47]	2017	LPD (7), cervical foraminotomy (2), ACDF (1)	schwannoma (2), microneurorrhaphy (1)	13	VITOM®	HD 2D
Oertel & Burkhardt [51]	2017	ACDF (2), cervical laminectomies (2), TLIF (2), extradural tumor (1), LPD (1), lumbar discectomy (3)	-	11	VITOM®	HD 3D
Khalessi et al. [58]	2018	ACDF (1), disc herniation (2)	-	3	ORBEYE®	HD 3D
De Divitiis et al. [6]	2019	tumor (5)	-	5	VITOM®	HD 3D
Kwan et al. [65]	2019	ACDF (4), cervical corpectomy (1), cervical laminectomies (3), LPD (2)	-	10	ORBEYE®	HD 3D
Muhammad et al. [7]	2019	CPD (1), ACDF (1), disc herniation (2)	-	4	Modus V™	HD 3D
Murai et al. [67]	2019	LDP (3)	neurolysis (1)	4	ORBEYE®	3D 4K
Ariffin et al. [15]	2020	decompression (18), discectomy (17), TLIF (28), OLIF (6)	-	69	Kinevo 900	3D 4K
Barbagallo & Certo [70]	2020	ACDF (2)	-	2	VITOM®	HD 3D
Burkhardt et al. [71]	2020	ACDF (4), cervical laminectomies (1), metastasis (1), lumbar decompression (4), TLIF (1), disc herniation (5), dAVF (1), angiolipoma (1)	-	18	VITOM®	HD 3D
D'Ercole et al. [75]	2020	ALIF (9)	-	9	VITOM®	HD 3D
Oren et al. [82]	2020	disc herniation (1)	-	1	ORBEYE®	3D 4K
Roethe et al. [85]	2020	LPD (1)	-	1	Kinevo 900	3D 4K
Siller et al. [5]	2020	LDP (40), ACDF (20)	-	60	VITOM®	HD 3D
Teo et al. [29]	2020	fracture (2), meningioma (1), disc herniation (5)	-	8	Modus V™	HD 3D

Table 3. *Cont.*

Authors	Year	Neurosurgical Procedures		Total	Exoscope Manufacturer and/or Model	Visualization Mode Setting
		Spine (n°)	Peripheral (n°)			
Vetrano et al. [88]	2020	-	schwannoma (2)	2	ORBEYE®	3D 4K
Visocchi et al. [89]	2020	CVJ pathologies (6)	-	6	VITOM® (3), ORBEYE® (3)	3D 4K
Kim et al. [91]	2021	disc herniation (1)	-	1	N/A	-
Rösler et al. [26]	2021	ACDF (1), metastasis (1), tumor (1), schwannoma (2), LPD (4)	schwannoma (2), peripheral nerve (1)	12	ORBEYE®	3D 4K

3D 4K, 3 dimensional 4K high-definition; ACDF, anterior cervical discectomy and fusion; ALIF, anterior lumbar interbody fusion; CPD, cervical posterior decompression; CVJ, craniovertebral junction; HD, high definition; LPD, lumbar posterior decompression; OLIF, oblique lateral interbody fusion; TLIF, transforaminal lumbar interbody fusion.

Table 4. Summary of laboratory studies included in the review.

Authors	Year	Laboratory Neurosurgical Procedures (n°)	Total	Exoscope Manufacturer and/or Model	Visualization Mode Setting
Mamelak et al. [33]	2008	craniotomy (4)	4	HDXO-SCOPE, Karl Storz	HD 2D
Di Ieva et al. [35]	2012	suboccipital approach (20)	20	VITOM®	HD 2D
Moisi et al. [49]	2017	craniotomy (6)	6	Modus V™	HD 2D
Sack et al. [13]	2018	craniotomy (5)	5	ORBEYE®	HD 3D
Herlan et al. [64]	2019	pterional approach (6)	6	FA Aesculap	HD 3D
Crosetti et al. [74]	2020	dissection (4)	4	VITOM®	HD 3D
Hafez et al. [23]	2020	bypass anastomosis (100)	100	VITOM®	HD 3D
Pafitanis et al. [83]	2020	micro sutures (10), anastomoses (5)	15	Modus V™	HD 3D
Rubini et al. [86]	2020	skull base (12)	12	VITOM®	HD 3D
Hafez et al. [28]	2021	bypass (5)	5	AEOS	3D 4K

3D 4K, 3 dimensional 4K high-definition; HD, high definition.

3.2. Evaluation of Exoscopic Surgical Procedures

Excluding case reports and considering clinical series reporting surgical complications, 40 studies and 1328 patients were assessed, reporting an overall surgical complication rate of 2.6% during the use of the exoscope. These patients experienced complication profiles similar to those that underwent the same treatments with the OM. Similarly, 21 clinical series with a total of 891 patients reported an overall switch incidence rate from exoscope to OM during surgery of 5.8% (52 cases). A total of 30 articles reported a qualitative comparison between the exoscope and the OM, while a total of 12 papers reported a quantitative, concrete and prospective comparison between one or more common features of the exoscope with the OM. The video image quality, 3D visualization and surgical filed with exoscopes were rated superior to similar to those of OMs in all papers. The comfort level of surgeon's posture during surgery, the educational usefulness, and the operative team involvement with the exoscope were assessed as superior compared to OM. Otherwise, depth perception was rated to be similar or inferior to the OM. Workflow and operative time were evaluated as equal or slightly higher than those of OMs. Table 5 shows all details.

Table 5. Summary of evaluation exoscopic surgical procedures studies.

Authors	Year	Patients (n°)	Operative complications (%)	Surgical Procedures Switched from Exoscope to OM (%)	Video Image Quality	Surgical Field	Handling	Surgical Ergonomics	Educational Usefulness	Depth Perception	Operative Time and/or Workflow	Operative Team Involvement
Mamelak et al. [34]	2010	16	0	Nd	+	+		+	+			+
Shirzadi et al. [19]	2012	24	0	Nd	=						=	
Belloch et al. [37]	2014	23	0	Nd			+	+				
Birch et al. [38]	2014	5	20	Nd		=					=	
Piquer et al. [39]	2014	30	0	Nd	+	+		+				
Parihar et al. [41]	2016	39	0	0	=			+		−		
Bauer et al. [43]	2017	18	0	Nd		=	=					
Day [44]	2017	49	8.2	Nd		+	+					
Gonen et al. [45]	2017	200	0	0	+	+						+
Jackson et al. [46]	2017	11	0	0	+	+						
Krishnan et al. [47]	2017	18	Nd	0	+	+	+			−	−	
Labib et al. [48]	2017	39	7.7	Nd	+	+						
Oertel & Burkhardt [51]	2017	16	0	0	=	=	+	+		=		+
Iyer & Chaichana [57]	2018	14	0	Nd	+	+	+					
Khalessi et al. [58]	2018	18	0	Nd	+	+	+	+		=		+
Mampre et al. [60]	2018	15	0	Nd	+	+						
Bakhsheshian et al. [63]	2019	25	4	0	+	+						
Garneau et al. [16]	2019	6	0	0	+	+		+		−	−	+
Herlan et al. [64]	2019	6	NA	Nd	+	=		+		=		
Kwan et al. [65]	2019	10	0	Nd	+	+	+	+	+			+
Muhammad et al. [7]	2019	8	0	0	+	+		+		−		
Murai et al. [67]	2019	22	0	18.2%	+			+	+			
Smith et al. [69]	2019	11	0	36.4%	=	=		+	+			+
Ahmad et al. [9]	2020	22	0	Nd	+	+	+	+			=	
Ariffin et al. [15]	2020	69	5.8	Nd	+	+	+	+	+	+		+
Baron et al. [10]	2020	28	3.6	Nd	+	+						
Burkhardt et al. [71]	2020	34	Nd	17.6%	=/+	=/+				−		
Chen et al. [73]	2020	39	30.8	Nd		=		+			=	+
Eichberg et al. [30]	2020	56	8.9	Nd	=	=		=				

Table 5. *Cont.*

Authors	Year	Patients (n°)	Operative complications (%)	Surgical Procedures Switched from Exoscope to OM (%)	Video Image Quality	Surgical Field	Handling	Surgical Ergonomics	Educational Usefulness	Depth Perception	Operative Time and/or Workflow	Operative Team Involvement
Hafez et al. [23]	2020	100	NA	Nd	=	+			+			
Pafitanis et al. [83]	2020	15	NA	Nd	=	=						
Roethe et al. [85]	2020	29	6.9	3.4%	−	=	=	+			=	
Siller et al. [5]	2020	60	0	0	−	=	=	+	+	−	=	+
Teo et al. [29]	2020	8	0	Nd	=/+	=/+			=/+			
Visocchi et al. [89]	2020	6	0	Nd	+	+						
Amoo et al. [90]	2021	18	0	0	=			+	+			+
Muscas et al. [27]	2021	14	0	57.1%	+	+		+				+
Muto et al. [93]	2021	5	0	0	=	=						
Rösler et al. [26]	2021	39	0	69.2%	+			+		−		
Rotermund et al. [95]	2021	296	0	0	+	+	+	+			=	
Shimizu et al. [96]	2021	14	0	0		+		+				
Yoon et al. [25]	2021	11	9.1	18.2%	=	+		+	+		−	

+, superior compared to OM; =, similar compared to OM; −, inferior compared to OM; NA, not applicable; Nd, not available.

4. Discussion

There were over 1524 surgeries that reported using an exoscope: 1251 (72.7%) on brain, whereas 274 (15.9%) and 9 (0.5%) on spine and peripheral nerves, respectively. Among these, more than 311 were gliomas, 171 were brain metastasis and 97 were meningioma and 244 were pituitary adenoma, 100 resulted ICH and 24 were neurovascular conflicts. Similarly in spine, 64 cervical and 189 lumbar pathologies were treated with the use of exoscope in the operative room, as well as 12 spine tumors were reported.

The development of surgical magnification and neurosurgery progressed on separate paths until the 1960s, when the merging of these two innovations led to the rapid growth of cerebral surgery [98–101]. From that time, intraoperative technological advances improved, and the OM and endoscope allowed complete resection of glioma and other intraventricular and pituitary tumors, neurovascular and spine diseases, under magnification with good lighting and through minimally invasive approaches [12,15,16,45,47,57,58,60,95,102,103].

Neuronavigation, ultrasound, intraoperative magnetic resonance imaging (MRI) and/or computed tomography (CT) scan, robotic technology, augmented reality and awake surgery increased the ability of the neurosurgeon to perform safe and maximal tumor resection [12,102,104–110]. Exoscopes launched a new era in the field of neurosurgery. These exoscopes are designed to provide high-resolution 3D imaging of the structure of tissue, blood vessels and other features to enable more accurate surgery and, including a display video, allow for simultaneous surgical team viewing. Exoscopes represent the next generation of operative imaging, helping the neurosurgeon to operate in a more ergonomic sitting position, facilitating the surgery team and reducing surgeon fatigue by reducing the amount of time practitioners would have to view the images through a microscope eyepiece. These systems work to bridge the gap between OM and endoscopes by combining the form factor of the endoscope with the image quality of the microscope [43,49,78,94]. Some disadvantages of exoscopic visualization were reported, especially in the early 2D exoscope, such as a limited applicability in deep seated cranial pathologies and tissue identification in case of bleeding, a magnification of deep-seated pathologies and above all the lack of stereopsis. All of these disadvantages seem to be solved with new 3D exoscopes, which however led to headache and nausea in very few cases due to the use of polarized glasses [19,41,51,52]. Furthermore, these devices still have usage limitations due to their high cost and to the impossibility, at the moment, to use 5-ALA fluorescence for tumor resection. A major advantage of the exoscope is the shared 3D view for all participants in the procedure [28,67,95]. The possibility to look at the same time in the same monitor allows more than one surgeon to operate and improves efficiency by sharing information with all surgical staff. Although Takahashi and colleagues [61] reported that assistant surgeons could sometimes experience a rotated view of the monitor; in this case the use of two or more 3D monitors in the operative room can solve this problem.

One of the characteristics ascribed to exoscopes is that they are superior to a conventional OM in terms of ergonomic features both in brain and spine surgery [37,39,49,52,67,69,90–92,94–97,111–115], as the ergonomic handling and the ease of intraoperative positioning of the device were found to be beneficial. Second, 3D monitors lead to an improved involvement of the co-surgeon and the scrub nurse during the procedure, and although some authors were satisfied with the high-resolution 3D digital images during surgery [52,60,68,73], others were not satisfied with the visual quality. In spine surgery, when two neurosurgeons are operating facing each other, the use of 2 monitors each positioned in front of each surgeon allows extreme freedom of movement and modification of the surgical corridor [89]. The important aspect of the exoscope monitor is that the surgeon, assistant and nurse all see the same image with the same quality and the exoscope does not interfere with communication and allows all surgical staff to feel more involved in the surgical procedure [7]. By increasing the visualization of anatomic details helps to identify the different layers and the tumor-nerve interface, and exoscopes can be useful also for peripheral nerve sheath tumors to preserve functional fascicles achieving gross-total resection [88].

Exoscopic tools seem to shift from cortical cranial tumor surgery to deep-seated brain tumors, as exoscope technology has progressively improved during the last few years, with results in terms of clinical outcome and surgical complications similar to conventional OM [85]. Hafez and colleagues [23] reported the largest comparative and laboratory series with the use of the exoscope and OM and showed that both methods are effective in doing bypass suturing, whereas the suturing time was less using the microscope and stitch distribution was better using the exoscope. Among brain tumors, Gonen and colleagues [45] reported the largest series of glioma resection (56 patients) using the exoscope, accounting for 44 cases of high-grade gliomas and 12 of low-grade gliomas and reporting just one (1.8%) perioperative complication (hemorrhage within the resection bed) in a patient with glioblastoma multiforme. Similarly, Gassie et al. [55], Piquer et al. [39], Day [44] and Eichberg et al. [30] reported that 30, 25, 22 and 12 patients, respectively, underwent surgical resection for glioma using different exoscopes. Overall postoperative surgical complications with permanent motor deficit range from 0% to 8% [30,39,44,55]. Rotermund et al. [95] reported the largest series of patients underwent transsphenoidal surgery for pituitary adenoma (239 patients), reporting that no serious episodes or minor complications occurred based on the usage of the exoscope, as well as no significant differences regarding the duration of surgery, complications or extent of resection compared to conventional microscopy. Chen et al. [73] reported a total of 81 patients received tumor resection through the retrosigmoid approach with either an exoscope (39 patients) or an OM (42 patients). Patients in the two groups had comparable tumor location ($p = 0.439$) and Koos grading ($p = 0.867$). There were significant differences in the duration of surgery ($p = 0.172$), the extent of tumor resection ($p = 0.858$), facial function ($p = 0.838$) and hearing ability ($p = 1.000$). Gonen et al. [45], Khalessi et al. [58], Ahmad et al. [9] had a total of 35 patients with neurovascular pathologies (aneurysms, arteriovenous malformations, cavernomas) who underwent surgery with an exoscope, reporting an overall good outcome and only 2.8% postoperative complications. In particular, Ahmad et al. [9] reported 12 microvascular anastomosis, reporting no difference in operative time ($p = 0.714$), ischemia time ($p = 0.972$), or microsurgical complications ($p = 1$) between the ORBEYE and conventional microscopy groups.

Regarding 3D visualization, Ricciardi et al. [14] in a previous review comparing exoscopes and microscopes found that image quality, optical power and magnification of the exoscope were rated at least equivalent to the microscope. In addition, exoscopes are also able to allow the surgeons to quickly switch from a micro to a macro vision and vice versa, when necessary, to explore all corners of the surgical field and to keep an eye on any bleeding [35,39,52]. Nevertheless, at present exoscopes have some limitations. Burkhardt et al. [71] reported that in 5 out of 10 cases (50%) of cranial surgery, a switch to the OM was necessary, due to the need to use 5-ALA fluorescence guided visualization in two cases and because the illumination of the depth of the operative field was not sufficient in 3 cases. Lin et al. [81] obtained gross total resection in all four cases of intraventricular meningiomas, reporting no intraoperative complications nor conversion to microscopic or open approach. Ridge et al. [116] and Teo et al. [29] highlighted the role of the exoscope in reducing the risk of infection exposure to the surgical team during the COVID-19 pandemic [117–119].

The use of the exoscope has been largely reported with a variety of different exoscope models used also in spinal surgery [5,7,15,26,29,41,71,89]. Ariffin et al. [15] submitted an interesting series of minor to major surgical spine procedures in 69 patients using the exoscope, reporting only four cases (5.8%) of dural tear as surgical complications and no postoperative neurological deficits. Similarly, Siller et al. [5] (40 patients undergoing lumbar posterior decompression (LPD) and 20 patients undergoing anterior cervical discectomy and fusion (ACDF), showing no intraoperative complications by using the exoscope, and reported similar results in outcome compared to controls in whom an OM was used. According to the attending surgeon, the intraoperative handling of the instruments was rated to be comparable to that of the OM, while the comfort level of the surgeon's posture intraoperatively (especially during "undercutting" procedures) was rated as superior [15].

Otherwise, Burkhardt et al. [71], including 16 cranial and 18 spinal surgical procedures in their paper, reported some intraoperative difficulties and that one spinal and five cranial procedures switched to OM or the endoscope for the following reasons: poor illumination (four cases), tissue identification (one case), and the need for fluorescence imaging (one case).

This review shows how a such large number of published papers and patients underwent brain and spinal surgery with the exoscope, showing the simplicity of use, the total safety for the patient, the good 3D vision and magnification of the surgical field and the opportunity of better interaction with other members of the surgical staff. All these points set the first step for subsequent and short-term changes in the field of neurosurgery and offer new educational possibilities for young neurosurgery and medical students. This review has some limitations. First, this review is susceptible to changes over the short term, as exoscopes were increasingly used in recent years and therefore an increasing number of papers will be published in the near future, and because technology and science advance incessantly. Second, this review aims to show the advantages and disadvantages of a new tool used in neurosurgery, reporting surgical experiences of different authors and summarizing the current literature, without drawing unique technical conclusions, as we believe it is still too early at this moment. Future clinical studies and reviews are needed to demonstrate if exoscopes will change the neurosurgical sciences.

5. Conclusions

Exoscopes have been used constantly in an increasing number of surgical procedures all around the world, suggesting that they could ultimately replace the OM in the future and represent the beginning of a new era of intraoperative visualization in neurosurgery. A 3D exoscope seems to be a safe alternative compared to the OM for most common brain and spinal procedures, with several advantages that have been reached. This review confirmed the role of the exoscope as a new tool that can help surgeons during surgery and even replace the OM in the near future due to several aspects: a better ergonomic posture of the surgeons during surgical procedures, the possibility to improve neurosurgical education, and in creating a better and effective operational team involvement. The quality of images and 3D 4K videos in most recent exoscopes has been increasingly improved in recent years, although at the moment the most reported drawback remains the slight lack of depth perception. The exoscope itself can be considered a useful educational tool in neurosurgery. As with other adaptations of new technology, it will take some time for systems to be tweaked and the pros and cons of different approaches to be better appreciated. More research needs to be done. A short learning curve is mandatory.

Author Contributions: Conceptualization, N.M. and L.R.; methodology, N.M. and A.S.; validation, N.M. and A.S.; data curation, N.M.; writing—original draft preparation, N.M.; writing—review and editing, N.M., L.R. and G.T.; supervision, N.M. and G.T. All authors have read and agreed to the published version of the manuscript.

Funding: This research received no external funding.

Institutional Review Board Statement: Not applicable.

Informed Consent Statement: Not applicable.

Acknowledgments: We thank Federica Tataranni for her English revision.

Conflicts of Interest: The authors declare no conflict of interest.

References

1. Kriss, T.C.; Kriss, V.M. History of the operating microscope: From magnifying glass to microneurosurgery. *Neurosurgery* **1998**, *42*, 899–907. [CrossRef] [PubMed]
2. Langer, D.J.; White, T.G.; Schulder, M.; Boockvar, J.A.; Labib, M.; Lawton, M.T. Advances in intraoperative optics: A brief review of current exoscope platforms. *Oper. Neurosurg.* **2020**, *19*, 84–93. [CrossRef] [PubMed]

3. Fuse, Y.; Watanabe, T.; Shintai, K.; Kishida, Y.; Nagatani, T.; Seki, Y. Non-brain-exposure exoscopic and endoscopic volume reduction surgery for benign meningioma en plaque in an elderly patient: A case report. *NMC Case Rep. J.* **2020**, *7*, 233–236 [CrossRef] [PubMed]
4. Angileri, F.F.; Esposito, F.; Scibilia, A.; Priola, S.M.; Raffa, G.; German, A. Exoscope-guided (VITOM 3D) single-stage removal of supratentorial cavernous angioma and hemangioblastoma: 3-dimensional operative video. *Oper. Neurosurg.* **2019**, *17*, E164–E165. [CrossRef]
5. Siller, S.; Zoellner, C.; Fuetsch, M.; Trabold, R.; Tonn, J.C.; Zausinger, S. A high-definition 3D exoscope as an alternative to the operating microscope in spinal microsurgery. *J. Neurosurg. Spine* **2020**, *33*, 705–714. [CrossRef]
6. De Divitiis, O.; D'avella, E.; Denaro, L.; Somma, T.; Sacco, M.; D'avella, D. Vitom 3D: Preliminary experience with intradural extramedullary spinal tumors. *J. Neurosurg. Sci.* **2019**, *2*, 1–4. [CrossRef]
7. Muhammad, S.; Lehecka, M.; Niemelä, M. Preliminary experience with a digital robotic exoscope in cranial and spinal surgery: A review of the Synaptive Modus V system. *Acta Neurochir.* **2019**, *161*, 2175–2180. [CrossRef]
8. Sindelar, B.D.; Patel, V.; Chowdhry, S.; Bailes, J.E. A case report in hemorrhagic stroke: A complex disease process and requirement for a multimodal treatment approach. *Cureus* **2018**, *10*, e2976. [CrossRef]
9. Ahmad, F.I.; Mericli, A.F.; DeFazio, M.V.; Chang, E.I.; Hanasono, M.M.; Pederson, W.C.; Kaufman, M.; Selber, J.C. Application of the ORBEYE three-dimensional exoscope for microsurgical procedures. *Microsurgery* **2020**, *40*, 468–472. [CrossRef]
10. Baron, R.B.; Lakomkin, N.; Schupper, A.J.; Nistal, D.; Nael, K.; Price, G.; Hadjipanayis, C.G. Postoperative outcomes following glioblastoma resection using a robot-assisted digital surgical exoscope: A case series. *J. Neurooncol.* **2020**, *148*, 519–527. [CrossRef]
11. Barkun, J.S.; Aronson, J.K.; Feldman, L.S.; Maddern, G.J.; Strasberg, S.M.; Altman, D.G.; Barkun, J.S.; Blazeby, J.M.; Boutron, I.C.; Campbell, W.B.; et al. Evaluation and stages of surgical innovations. *Lancet* **2009**, *374*, 1089–1096. [CrossRef]
12. Raheja, A.; Mishra, S.; Garg, K.; Katiyar, V.; Sharma, R.; Tandon, V.; Goda, R.; Suri, A.; Kale, S.S. Impact of different visualization devices on accuracy, efficiency, and dexterity in neurosurgery: A laboratory investigation. *Neurosurg. Focus* **2021**, *50*, E18. [CrossRef]
13. Sack, J.; Steinberg, J.A.; Rennert, R.C.; Hatefi, D.; Pannell, J.S.; Levy, M.; Khalessi, A.A. Initial experience using a high-definition 3-dimensional exoscope system for microneurosurgery. *Oper. Neurosurg.* **2018**, *14*, 395–401. [CrossRef]
14. Ricciardi, L.; Chaichana, K.L.; Cardia, A.; Stifano, V.; Rossini, Z.; Olivi, A.; Sturiale, C.L. The exoscope in neurosurgery: An innovative "point of view". A systematic review of the technical, surgical and educational aspects. *World Neurosurg.* **2019**, *124*, 136–144. [CrossRef]
15. Ariffin, M.H.M.; Ibrahim, K.; Baharudin, A.; Tamil, A.M. Early Experience, setup, learning curve, benefits, and complications associated with exoscope and three-dimensional 4K hybrid digital visualizations in minimally invasive spine surgery. *Asian Spine J.* **2020**, *14*, 59–65. [CrossRef]
16. Garneau, J.C.; Laitman, B.M.; Cosetti, M.K.; Hadjipanayis, C.; Wanna, G. The use of the exoscope in lateral skull base surgery: Advantages and limitations. *Otol. Neurotol.* **2019**, *40*, 236–240. [CrossRef]
17. Nishiyama, K. From Exoscope into the next generation. *J. Korean Neurosurg. Soc.* **2017**, *60*, 289–293. [CrossRef]
18. Corsalini, M.; Di Venere, D.; Sportelli, P.; Magazzino, D.; Ripa, C.; Cantatore, F.; Cagnetta, G.; De Rinaldis, C.; Montemurro, N.; De Giacomo, A.; et al. Evaluation of prosthetic quality and masticatory efficiency in patients with total removable prosthesis: Study of 12 cases. *Oral Implantol.* **2018**, *11*, 230–240.
19. Shirzadi, A.; Mukherjee, D.; Drazin, D.G.; Paff, M.; Perri, B.; Mamelak, A.N.; Siddique, K. Use of the video telescope operating monitor (VITOM) as an alternative to the operating microscope in spine surgery. *Spine* **2012**, *37*, E1517–E1523. [CrossRef]
20. Ricciardi, L.; Mattogno, P.P.; Olivi, A.; Sturiale, C.L. Exoscope era: Next technical and educational step in microneurosurgery. *World Neurosurg.* **2019**, *128*, 371–373. [CrossRef]
21. Wali, A.R.; Kang, K.M.; Rennert, R.; Santiago-Dieppa, D.; Khalessi, A.A.; Levy, M. First-in-human clinical experience using high-definition exoscope with intraoperative indocyanine green for clip reconstruction of unruptured large pediatric aneurysm. *World Neurosurg.* **2021**, *151*, 52. [CrossRef]
22. Dawley, T.; Schulder, M. Commentary: First-in-man clinical experience using a high-definition 3-dimensional exoscope system for microneurosurgery. *Oper. Neurosurg.* **2019**, *16*, E161–E162. [CrossRef]
23. Hafez, A.; Elsharkawy, A.; Schwartz, C.; Muhammad, S.; Laakso, A.; Niemelä, M.; Lehecka, M. Comparison of conventional microscopic and exoscopic experimental bypass anastomosis: A technical analysis. *World Neurosurg.* **2020**, *135*, e293–e299. [CrossRef]
24. Perrini, P.; Montemurro, N.; Caniglia, M.; Lazzarotti, G.; Benedetto, N. Wrapping of intracranial aneurysms: Single-center series and systematic review of the literature. *Br. J. Neurosurg.* **2015**, *29*, 785–791. [CrossRef]
25. Yoon, W.S.; Lho, H.W.; Chung, D.S. Evaluation of 3-dimensional exoscopes in brain tumor surgery. *J. Korean Neurosurg. Soc.* **2021**, *64*, 289–296. [CrossRef]
26. Rösler, J.; Georgiev, S.; Roethe, A.L.; Chakkalakal, D.; Acker, G.; Dengler, N.F.; Prinz, V.; Hecht, N.; Faust, K.; Schneider, U.; et al. Clinical implementation of a 3D4K-exoscope (Orbeye) in microneurosurgery. *Neurosurg. Rev.* **2021**, *18*, 1–9. [CrossRef]
27. Muscas, G.; Battista, F.; Boschi, A.; Morone, F.; Della Puppa, A. A Single-center experience with the olympus ORBEYE 4K-3D exoscope for microsurgery of complex cranial cases: Technical nuances and learning curve. *J. Neurol. Surg. Part A Cent. Eur. Neurosurg.* **2021**, *82*, 484–489. [CrossRef]

28. Hafez, A.; Haeren, R.H.L.; Dillmann, J.; Laakso, A.; Niemelä, M.; Lehecka, M. Comparison of operating microscope and exoscope in a highly challenging experimental setting. *World Neurosurg.* **2021**, *147*, e468–e475. [CrossRef] [PubMed]
29. Teo, T.H.L.; Tan, B.J.; Loo, W.L.; Yeo, A.K.S.; Dinesh, S.K. Utility of a high-definition 3D digital exoscope for spinal surgery during the COVID-19 pandemic. *Bone Jt. Open* **2020**, *1*, 359–363. [CrossRef] [PubMed]
30. Eichberg, D.G.; Di, L.; Shah, A.H.; Luther, E.M.; Jackson, C.; Marenco-Hillembrand, L.; Chaichana, K.L.; Ivan, M.E.; Starke, R.M.; Komotar, R.J. Minimally invasive resection of intracranial lesions using tubular retractors: A large, multi-surgeon, multi-institutional series. *J. Neurooncol.* **2020**, *149*, 35–44. [CrossRef] [PubMed]
31. Moher, D.; Shamseer, L.; Clarke, M.; Ghersi, D.; Liberati, A.; Petticrew, M.; Shekelle, P.; Stewart, L.A.; PRISMA-P Group. Preferred reporting items for systematic review and meta-analysis protocols (PRISMA-P) 2015 statement. *Syst. Rev.* **2015**, *4*, 1. [CrossRef]
32. Gildenberg, P.L.; Labuz, J. Stereotactic craniotomy with the exoscope. *Stereotact. Funct. Neurosurg.* **1997**, *68*, 64–71. [CrossRef]
33. Mamelak, A.N.; Danielpour, M.; Black, K.L.; Hagike, M.; Berci, G. A high-definition exoscope system for neurosurgery and other microsurgical disciplines: Preliminary report. *Surg. Innov.* **2008**, *15*, 38–46. [CrossRef]
34. Mamelak, A.N.; Nobuto, T.; Berci, G. Initial clinical experience with a high-definition exoscope system for microneurosurgery. *Neurosurgery* **2010**, *67*, 476–483. [CrossRef]
35. Di Ieva, A.; Komatsu, M.; Komatsu, F.; Tschabitscher, M. Endoscopic telovelar approach to the fourth ventricle: Anatomic study. *Neurosurg. Rev.* **2012**, *35*, 341–348. [CrossRef]
36. Mamelak, A.N.; Drazin, D.; Shirzadi, A.; Black, K.L.; Berci, G. Infratentorial supracerebellar resection of a pineal tumor using a high definition video exoscope (VITOM®). *J. Clin. Neurosci.* **2012**, *19*, 306–309. [CrossRef]
37. Belloch, J.P.; Rovira, V.; Llácer, J.L.; Riesgo, P.A.; Cremades, A. Fluorescence-guided surgery in high grade gliomas using an exoscope system. *Acta Neurochir.* **2014**, *156*, 653–660. [CrossRef]
38. Birch, K.; Drazin, D.; Black, K.L.; Williams, J.; Berci, G.; Mamelak, A.N. Clinical experience with a high definition exoscope system for surgery of pineal region lesions. *J. Clin. Neurosci.* **2014**, *21*, 1245–1249. [CrossRef]
39. Piquer, J.; Llácer, J.L.; Rovira, V.; Riesgo, P.; Rodriguez, R.; Cremades, A. Fluorescence-guided surgery and biopsy in gliomas with an exoscope system. *Biomed Res. Int.* **2014**, *2014*, 207974. [CrossRef]
40. Ritsma, B.; Kassam, A.; Dowlatshahi, D.; Nguyen, T.; Stotts, G. Minimally Invasive Subcortical Parafascicular Transsulcal Access for Clot Evacuation (Mi SPACE) for Intracerebral Hemorrhage. *Case Rep. Neurol. Med.* **2014**, *2014*, 102307. [CrossRef]
41. Parihar, V.; Yadav, Y.R.; Kher, Y.; Ratre, S.; Sethi, A.; Sharma, D. Learning neuroendoscopy with an exoscope system (video telescopic operating monitor): Early clinical results. *Asian J. Neurosurg.* **2016**, *11*, 421–426. [CrossRef]
42. Scranton, R.A.; Fung, S.H.; Britz, G.W. Transulcal parafascicular minimally invasive approach to deep and subcortical cavernomas: Technical note. *J. Neurosurg.* **2016**, *125*, 1360–1366. [CrossRef]
43. Bauer, A.M.; Rasmussen, P.A.; Bain, M.D. Initial single-center technical experience with the brainpath system for acute intracerebral hemorrhage evacuation. *Oper. Neurosurg.* **2017**, *13*, 69–76. [CrossRef]
44. Day, J.D. Transsulcal parafascicular surgery using brain path® for subcortical lesions. *Neurosurgery* **2017**, *64*, 151–156. [CrossRef]
45. Gonen, L.; Chakravarthi, S.S.; Monroy-Sosa, A.; Celix, J.M.; Kojis, N.; Singh, M.; Jennings, J.; Fukui, M.B.; Rovin, R.A.; Kassam, A.B. Initial experience with a robotically operated video optical telescopic-microscope in cranial neurosurgery: Feasibility, safety, and clinical applications. *Neurosurg. Focus* **2017**, *42*, E9. [CrossRef]
46. Jackson, C.; Gallia, G.L.; Chaichana, K.L. Minimally invasive biopsies of deep-seated brain lesions using tubular retractors under exoscopic visualization. *J. Neurol. Surg. A Cent. Eur. Neurosurg.* **2017**, *78*, 588–594. [CrossRef]
47. Krishnan, K.G.; Schöller, K.; Uhl, E. Application of a compact high-definition exoscope for illumination and magnification in high-precision surgical procedures. *World Neurosurg.* **2017**, *97*, 652–660. [CrossRef]
48. Labib, M.A.; Shah, M.; Kassam, A.B.; Young, R.; Zucker, L.; Maioriello, A.; Britz, G.; Agbi, C.; Day, J.D.; Gallia, G.; et al. The safety and feasibility of image-guided brainpath-mediated transsulcul hematoma evacuation: A multicenter study. *Neurosurgery* **2017**, *80*, 515–524. [CrossRef]
49. Moisi, M.D.; Hoang, K.; Tubbs, R.S.; Page, J.; Fisahn, C.; Paulson, D.; Jeyamohan, S.; Delashaw, J.; Hanscom, D.; Oskouian, R.J.; et al. Advancement of surgical visualization methods: Comparison study between traditional microscopic surgery and a novel robotic optoelectronic visualization tool for spinal surgery. *World Neurosurg.* **2017**, *98*, 273–277. [CrossRef]
50. Nagata, Y.; Watanabe, T.; Nagatani, T.; Takeuchi, K.; Chu, J.; Wakabayashi, T. The multiscope technique for microvascular decompression. *World Neurosurg.* **2017**, *103*, 310–314. [CrossRef]
51. Oertel, J.M.; Burkhardt, B.W. Vitom-3D for exoscopic neurosurgery: Initial experience in cranial and spinal procedures. *World Neurosurg.* **2017**, *105*, 153–162. [CrossRef] [PubMed]
52. Rossini, Z.; Cardia, A.; Milani, D.; Lasio, G.B.; Fornari, M.; D'Angelo, V. VITOM 3D: Preliminary experience in cranial surgery. *World Neurosurg.* **2017**, *107*, 663–668. [CrossRef] [PubMed]
53. Weiner, H.L.; Placantonakis, D.G. Resection of a pediatric thalamic juvenile pilocytic astrocytoma with whole brain tractography. *Cureus* **2017**, *9*, e1768. [CrossRef] [PubMed]
54. Beez, T.; Munoz-Bendix, C.; Beseoglu, K.; Steiger, H.J.; Ahmadi, S.A. First clinical applications of a high-definition three-dimensional exoscope in pediatric neurosurgery. *Cureus* **2018**, *10*, e2108. [CrossRef]
55. Gassie, K.; Wijesekera, O.; Chaichana, K.L. Minimally invasive tubular retractor-assisted biopsy and resection of subcortical intra-axial gliomas and other neoplasms. *J. Neurosurg. Sci.* **2018**, *62*, 682–689. [CrossRef]

56. Griessenauer, C.; Medin, C.; Goren, O.; Schirmer, C.M. Image-guided, minimally invasive evacuation of intracerebral hematoma: A matched cohort study comparing the endoscopic and tubular exoscopic systems. *Cureus* **2018**, *10*, e3569. [CrossRef]
57. Iyer, R.; Chaichana, K.L. Minimally invasive resection of deep-seated high-grade gliomas using tubular retractors and exoscopic visualization. *J. Neurol. Surg. A Cent. Eur. Neurosurg.* **2018**, *79*, 330–336. [CrossRef]
58. Khalessi, A.A.; Rahme, R.; Rennert, R.C.; Borgas, P.; Steinberg, J.A.; White, T.G.; Santiago-Dieppa, D.R.; Boockvar, J.A.; Hatefi, D.; Pannell, J.S.; et al. First-in-man clinical experience using a high-definition 3-dimensional exoscope system for microneurosurgery. *Oper. Neurosurg.* **2019**, *16*, 717–725. [CrossRef]
59. Klinger, D.R.; Reinard, K.A.; Ajayi, O.O.; Delashaw, J.B., Jr. Microsurgical clipping of an anterior communicating artery aneurysm using a novel robotic visualization tool in lieu of the binocular operating microscope: Operative video. *Oper. Neurosurg.* **2018**, *14*, 26–28. [CrossRef]
60. Mampre, D.; Bechtle, A.; Chaichana, K.L. Minimally invasive resection of intra-axial posterior fossa tumors using tubular retractors. *World Neurosurg.* **2018**, *119*, e1016–e1020. [CrossRef]
61. Takahashi, S.; Toda, M.; Nishimoto, M.; Ishihara, E.; Miwa, T.; Akiyama, T.; Horiguchi, T.; Sasaki, H.; Yoshida, K. Pros and cons of using ORBEYE™ for microneurosurgery. *Clin. Neurol. Neurosurg.* **2018**, *174*, 57–62. [CrossRef]
62. Akbari, S.H.A.; Sylvester, P.T.; Kulwin, C.; Shah, M.V.; Somasundaram, A.; Kamath, A.A.; Beaumont, T.L.; Rich, K.M.; Chicoine, M.R. Initial experience using intraoperative magnetic resonance imaging during a trans-sulcal tubular retractor approach for the resection of deep-seated brain tumors: A case series. *Oper. Neurosurg.* **2019**, *16*, 292–301. [CrossRef]
63. Bakhsheshian, J.; Strickland, B.A.; Jackson, C.; Chaichana, K.L.; Young, R.; Pradilla, G.; Chen, J.W.; Bailes, J.; Zada, G. Multicenter investigation of channel-based subcortical trans-sulcal exoscopic resection of metastatic brain tumors: A retrospective case series. *Oper. Neurosurg.* **2019**, *16*, 159–166. [CrossRef]
64. Herlan, S.; Marquardt, J.S.; Hirt, B.; Tatagiba, M.; Ebner, F.H. 3D exoscope system in neurosurgery-comparison of a standard operating microscope with a new 3d exoscope in the cadaver lab. *Oper. Neurosurg.* **2019**, *17*, 518–524. [CrossRef]
65. Kwan, K.; Schneider, J.R.; Du, V.; Falting, L.; Boockvar, J.A.; Oren, J.; Levine, M.; Langer, D.J. Lessons learned using a high-definition 3-dimensional exoscope for spinal surgery. *Oper. Neurosurg.* **2019**, *16*, 619–625. [CrossRef]
66. Li Ching Ng, A.; Di Ieva, A. How I do it: 3D exoscopic endoscope-assisted microvascular decompression. *Acta Neurochir.* **2019**, *161*, 1443–1447. [CrossRef]
67. Murai, Y.; Sato, S.; Yui, K.; Morimoto, D.; Ozeki, T.; Yamaguchi, M.; Tateyama, K.; Nozaki, T.; Tahara, S.; Yamaguchi, F.; et al. Preliminary clinical microneurosurgical experience with the 4K3-dimensional microvideoscope (ORBEYE) system for microneurological surgery: Observation study. *Oper. Neurosurg.* **2019**, *16*, 707–716. [CrossRef]
68. Nossek, E.; Schneider, J.R.; Kwan, K.; Kulason, K.O.; Du, V.; Chakraborty, S.; Rahme, R.; Faltings, L.; Ellis, J.; Ortiz, R.; et al. Technical aspects and operative nuances using a high-definition 3-dimensional exoscope for cerebral bypass surgery. *Oper. Neurosurg.* **2019**, *17*, 157–163. [CrossRef]
69. Smith, S.; Kozin, E.D.; Kanumuri, V.V.; Barber, S.R.; Backous, D.; Flávio Nogueira, J.; Lee, D.J. Initial experience with 3-dimensional exoscope-assisted transmastoid and lateral skull base surgery. *Otolaryngol. Head Neck. Surg.* **2019**, *160*, 364–367. [CrossRef]
70. Barbagallo, G.M.V.; Certo, F. Three-dimensional, high-definition exoscopic anterior cervical discectomy and fusion: A valid alternative to microscope-assisted surgery. *World Neurosurg.* **2019**, *130*, e244–e250. [CrossRef]
71. Burkhardt, B.W.; Csokonay, A.; Oertel, J.M. 3D-exoscopic visualization using the VITOM-3D in cranial and spinal neurosurgery. What are the limitations? *Clin. Neurol. Neurosurg.* **2020**, *198*, 106101. [CrossRef]
72. Chakravarthi, S.S.; Lyons, L.; Bercu, M.; Singer, J.A. Minimally invasive parafascicular surgical approach for the management of a pediatric third ventricular ependymoma: Case report and review of literature. *World Neurosurg.* **2020**, *141*, 311–317. [CrossRef]
73. Chen, X.; Gao, X.L.; Chai, Y.; Shi, M.M.; Zhang, J.N.; Yue, S.Y. Use of a compact high-definition two-dimensional exoscope in surgical treatment of large vestibular schwannoma. *Chin. Med. J.* **2020**, *133*, 1292–1297. [CrossRef]
74. Crosetti, E.; Arrigoni, G.; Manca, A.; Fantini, M.; Caracciolo, A.; Sardanapoli, F.; Succo, G. VITOM-3D assisted neck dissection via a retroauricular approach (RAND-3D): A preclinical investigation in a cadaver lab. *Acta Otorhinolaryngol. Ital.* **2020**, *40*, 343–351. [CrossRef]
75. D'Ercole, M.; Serchi, E.; Zanello, M.; Tufo, T.; Sturiale, C. Clinical application of a high definition three-dimensional exoscope in anterior lumbar interbody fusion: Technical note. *Int. J. Spine Surg.* **2020**, *14*, 1003–1008. [CrossRef]
76. Doglietto, F.; Belotti, F.; Panciani, P.; Poliani, P.L.; Fontanella, M.M. High-definition 3-dimensional exoscope for 5-ALA glioma surgery: 3-dimensional operative video. *Oper. Neurosurg.* **2020**, *18*, E82. [CrossRef]
77. Garneau, J.C.; Laitman, B.M.; Cosetti, M.K.; Hadjipanayis, C.; Wanna, G.B. Repair of a temporal bone encephalocele with the surgical exoscope. *Otol. Neurotol.* **2020**, *41*, 561. [CrossRef] [PubMed]
78. Khatri, D.; Wagner, K.; Ligas, B.; Higbie, C.; Langer, D. Excision of a retrochiasmatic craniopharyngioma by transcallosal, interforniceal approach with exoscope assistance: 2-dimensional operative video. *Oper. Neurosurg.* **2020**, *19*, E411. [CrossRef]
79. Kleshchova, O.; White, T.G.; Kwan, K.; Chiluwal, A.; Anderson, T.A.; Langer, D.J. Resection of a posterior fossa endodermal cyst with exoscopic assistance: 2-dimensional operative video. *Oper. Neurosurg.* **2020**, *18*, E173–E174. [CrossRef]
80. Ligas, B.; Khatri, D.; Higbie, C.; Wagner, K.; Langer, D. Hemifacial spasm due to bony stenosis of the internal auditory meatus: Look beyond the loop. *World Neurosurg.* **2020**, *137*, 179–182. [CrossRef]

81. Lin, M.; Bakhsheshian, J.; Strickland, B.; Rennert, R.C.; Chu, R.M.; Chaichana, K.L.; Zada, G. Exoscopic resection of atrial intraventricular meningiomas using a navigation-assisted channel-based trans-sulcal approach: Case series and literature review. *J. Clin. Neurosci.* **2020**, *71*, 58–65. [CrossRef] [PubMed]
82. Oren, J.; Kwan, K.; Schneider, J.; Levine, M.; Langer, D. Minimally invasive navigated foraminal discectomy via contralateral approach using a 3-dimensional 4k high-definition exoscope: 2-dimensional operative video. *Oper. Neurosurg.* **2020**, *19*, E188. [CrossRef] [PubMed]
83. Pafitanis, G.; Hadjiandreou, M.; Alamri, A.; Uff, C.; Walsh, D.; Myers, S. The Exoscope versus operating microscope in microvascular surgery: A simulation non-inferiority trial. *Arch. Plast. Surg.* **2020**, *47*, 242–249. [CrossRef] [PubMed]
84. Patel, N.V.; Ligas, B.; Gandhi, S.; Ellis, J.; Ortiz, R.; Costantino, P.; Qato, K.; Langer, D.J. Internal maxillary to middle cerebral artery bypass using an anterior tibial artery graft, performed using a 3-dimensional exoscope: 2-dimensional operative video. *Oper. Neurosurg.* **2020**, *19*, E187. [CrossRef]
85. Roethe, A.L.; Landgraf, P.; Schröder, T.; Misch, M.; Vajkoczy, P.; Picht, T. Monitor-based exoscopic 3D4k neurosurgical interventions: A two-phase prospective-randomized clinical evaluation of a novel hybrid device. *Acta Neurochir.* **2020**, *162*, 2949–2961. [CrossRef]
86. Rubini, A.; Di Gioia, S.; Marchioni, D. 3D exoscopic surgery of lateral skull base. *Eur. Arch. Otorhinolaryngol.* **2020**, *277*, 687–694. [CrossRef]
87. Silverstein, J.W.; Ellis, J.A.; Langer, D.J. Loss of motor evoked potentials due to carotid artery retraction in an exoscopic clipping of a basilar tip aneurysm. *Neurodiagn. J.* **2020**, *60*, 289–299. [CrossRef]
88. Vetrano, I.G.; Acerbi, F.; Falco, J.; D'Ammando, A.; Devigili, G.; Nazzi, V. High-definition 4K 3D exoscope (ORBEYETM) in peripheral nerve sheath tumor surgery: A preliminary, explorative, pilot study. *Oper. Neurosurg.* **2020**, *19*, 480–488. [CrossRef]
89. Visocchi, M.; Mattogno, P.P.; Ciappetta, P.; Barbagallo, G.; Signorelli, F. Combined transoral exoscope and OArm-assisted approach for craniovertebral junction surgery: Light and shadows in single-center experience with improving technologies. *J. Craniovertebr. Junction Spine* **2020**, *11*, 293–299.
90. Amoo, M.; Henry, J.; Javadpour, M. Beyond magnification and illumination: Preliminary clinical experience with the 4K 3D ORBEYE™ exoscope and a literature review. *Acta Neurochir.* **2021**, *163*, 2107–2115. [CrossRef]
91. Kim, M.; Wainwright, J.; Stein, A.; Hanft, S. Posterior transdural approach for a calcified thoracic intradural disc herniation using a 3-dimensional exoscope: 2-dimensional operative video. *Oper. Neurosurg.* **2021**, *21*, E44–E45. [CrossRef]
92. Marenco-Hillembrand, L.; Suarez-Meade, P.; Chaichana, K.L. Bur hole-based resections of intrinsic brain tumors with exoscopic visualization. *J. Neurol. Surg. A Cent. Eur. Neurosurg.* **2021**, *82*, 105–111. [CrossRef]
93. Muto, J.; Mine, Y.; Nakagawa, Y.; Joko, M.; Kagami, H.; Inaba, M.; Hasegawa, M.; Lee, J.Y.K.; Hirose, Y. Intraoperative real-time near-infrared optical imaging for the identification of metastatic brain tumors via microscope and exoscope. *Neurosurg. Focus* **2021**, *50*, E11. [CrossRef]
94. Rennert, R.C.; Khani, M.; Thomas, K.; Morris, T.W.; Rodriguez, A.; Day, J.D. Transsulcal parafascicular brain path-assisted approach to subcortical lesions: 2-dimensional operative video. *Surg. Neurol. Int.* **2021**, *17*, 107.
95. Rotermund, R.; Regelsberger, J.; Osterhage, K.; Aberle, J.; Flitsch, J. 4K 3-dimensional video microscope system (orbeye) for transsphenoidal pituitary surgery. *Acta Neurochir.* **2021**, *163*, 2097–2106. [CrossRef]
96. Shimizu, T.; Toyota, S.; Nakagawa, K.; Murakami, T.; Mori, K.; Kishima, H.; Taki, T. Retrosigmoid approach in the supine position using ORBEYE: A consecutive series of 14 cases. *Neurol. Med. Chir.* **2021**, *61*, 55–61. [CrossRef]
97. Strickland, B.A.; Brunswick, A.; Zada, G. Exoscopic to endoscopic channel-based trans-sulcal resection of a third ventricular cavernous malformation: Technical case illustration. *World Neurosurg.* **2021**, *148*, 66. [CrossRef]
98. Yaşargil, M.G.; Krayenbühl, H. The use of the binocular microscope in neurosurgery. *Bibl. Ophthalmol.* **1970**, *81*, 62–65.
99. Uluç, K.; Kujoth, G.C.; Başkaya, M.K. Operating microscopes: Past, present, and future. *Neurosurg. Focus* **2009**, *27*, E4. [CrossRef]
100. Perrini, P.; Montemurro, N.; Iannelli, A. The contribution of Carlo Giacomini (1840–1898): The limbus Giacomini and beyond. *Neurosurgery* **2013**, *72*, 475–482. [CrossRef]
101. Hayden, M.G.; Lee, M.; Guzman, R.; Steinberg, G.K. The evolution of cerebral revascularization surgery. *Neurosurg. Focus* **2009**, *26*, E17. [CrossRef]
102. Zebian, B.; Vergani, F.; Lavrador, J.P.; Mukherjee, S.; Kitchen, W.J.; Stagno, V.; Chamilos, C.; Pettorini, B.; Mallucci, C. Recent technological advances in pediatric brain tumor surgery. *CNS Oncol.* **2017**, *6*, 71–82. [CrossRef]
103. Montemurro, N.; Fanelli, G.N.; Scatena, C.; Ortenzi, V.; Pasqualetti, F.; Mazzanti, C.M.; Morganti, R.; Paiar, F.; Naccarato, A.G.; Perrini, P. Surgical outcome and molecular pattern characterization of recurrent glioblastoma multiforme: A single-center retrospective series. *Clin. Neurol. Neurosurg.* **2021**, *207*, 106735. [CrossRef]
104. Rahman, M.; Murad, G.J.; Bova, F.; Friedman, W.A.; Mocco, J. Stereotactic radiosurgery and the linear accelerator: Accelerating electrons in neurosurgery. *Neurosurg. Focus* **2009**, *27*, E13. [CrossRef]
105. Montemurro, N.; Condino, S.; Cattari, N.; D'Amato, R.; Ferrari, V.; Cutolo, F. Augmented reality-assisted craniotomy for parasagittal and convexity en plaque meningiomas and custom-made cranio-plasty: A preliminary laboratory report. *Int. J. Environ. Res. Public Health* **2021**, *18*, 9955. [CrossRef]
106. Shurkhay, V.A.; Goryaynov, S.A.; Aleksandrova, E.V.; Spallone, A.; Potapov, A.A. Navigation systems in neurosurgery. *Vopr Neirokhirurgii Im NN Burdenko* **2016**, *80*, 107–114. [CrossRef]

107. Condino, S.; Montemurro, N.; Cattari, N.; D'Amato, R.; Thomale, U.; Ferrari, V.; Cutolo, F. Evaluation of a wearable AR platform for guiding complex craniotomies in neurosurgery. *Ann. Biomed Eng.* **2021**, *49*, 2590–2605. [CrossRef]
108. Trevisi, G.; Roujeau, T.; Duffau, H. Awake surgery for hemispheric low-grade gliomas: Oncological, functional and methodological differences between pediatric and adult populations. *Child's Nerv. Syst.* **2016**, *32*, 1861–1874. [CrossRef]
109. Montemurro, N.; Herbet, G.; Duffau, H. Right cortical and axonal structures eliciting ocular deviation during electrical stimulation mapping in awake patients. *Brain Topogr.* **2016**, *29*, 561–571. [CrossRef]
110. Perrini, P.; Gambacciani, C.; Martini, C.; Montemurro, N.; Lepori, P. Anterior cervical corpectomy for cervical spondylotic myelopathy: Reconstruction with expandable cylindrical cage versus iliac crest autograft. A retrospective study. *Clin. Neurol. Neurosurg.* **2015**, *139*, 258–263. [CrossRef]
111. Lavé, A.; Gondar, R.; Demetriades, A.K.; Meling, T.R. Ergonomics and musculoskeletal disorders in neurosurgery: A systematic review. *Acta Neurochir.* **2020**, *162*, 2213–2220. [CrossRef] [PubMed]
112. Canseco, J.A.; Schroeder, G.D.; Patel, P.D.; Grasso, G.; Chang, M.; Kandziora, F.; Vialle, E.N.; Oner, F.C.; Schnake, K.J.; Dvorak, M.F.; et al. Regional and experiential differences in surgeon preference for the treatment of cervical facet injuries: A case study survey with the AO spine cervical classification validation group. *Eur. Spine J.* **2021**, *30*, 517–523. [CrossRef] [PubMed]
113. Mavrovounis, G.; Meling, T.R.; Lafuente, J.; Fountas, K.N.; Demetriades, A.K. Postural ergonomics and work-related musculoskeletal disorders in neurosurgery: Lessons from an international survey. *Acta Neurochir.* **2021**, *163*, 1541–1552. [CrossRef] [PubMed]
114. Schroeder, G.D.; Canseco, J.A.; Patel, P.D.; Divi, S.N.; Karamian, B.A.; Kandziora, F.; Vialle, E.N.; Oner, F.C.; Schnake, K.J.; Dvorak, M.F.; et al. Establishing the injury severity of subaxial cervical spine trauma: Validating the hierarchical nature of the ao spine subaxial cervical spine injury classification system. *Spine* **2021**, *46*, 649–657. [CrossRef] [PubMed]
115. Montemurro, N.; Santoro, G.; Marani, W.; Petrella, G. Posttraumatic synchronous double acute epidural hematomas: Two craniotomies, single skin incision. *Surg. Neurol. Int.* **2020**, *11*, 435. [CrossRef] [PubMed]
116. Ridge, S.E.; Shetty, K.R.; Lee, D.J. Heads-up surgery: Endoscopes and exoscopes for otology and neurotology in the era of the COVID-19 pandemic. *Otolaryngol. Clin. N. Am.* **2021**, *54*, 11–23. [CrossRef]
117. Montemurro, N. Intracranial hemorrhage and COVID-19, but please do not forget "old diseases" and elective surgery. *Brain Behav. Immun.* **2021**, *92*, 207–208. [CrossRef]
118. Gordon, S.A.; Deep, N.L.; Jethanamest, D. Exoscope and personal protective equipment use for otologic surgery in the era of COVID-19. *Otolaryngol. Head Neck Surg.* **2020**, *163*, 179–181. [CrossRef]
119. Haldeman, S.; Nordin, M.; Tavares, P.; Mullerpatan, R.; Kopansky-Giles, D.; Setlhare, V.; Chou, R.; Hurwitz, E.; Treanor, C.; Hartvigsen, J.; et al. Distance management of spinal disorders during the COVID-19 pandemic and beyond: Evidence-based patient and clinician guides from the global spine care initiative. *JMIR Public Health Surveill.* **2021**, *7*, e25484. [CrossRef]

Journal of
Clinical Medicine

MDPI

Article

Surgical Navigation in Mandibular Reconstruction: Accuracy Evaluation of an Innovative Protocol

Davide Sozzi [1,*], Andrea Filippi [1,2], Gabriele Canzi [3], Elena De Ponti [4], Alberto Bozzetti [1] and Giorgio Novelli [1]

1 O.U. Maxillofacial Surgery, Department of Medicine and Surgery, School of Medicine, ASST-Monza, San Gerardo Hospital, University of Milano-Bicocca, Via Pergolesi 33, 20900 Monza, Italy; andreafilippimd@gmail.com (A.F.); alberto.bozzetti@unimib.it (A.B.); nove.gio@gmail.com (G.N.)
2 Post-Graduate School of Maxillofacial Surgery, Department of Medicine and Surgery, University of Milan, Via Festa del Perdono 7, 20122 Milan, Italy
3 Maxillofacial Surgery Unit, Emergency Department, ASST-GOM Niguarda, Niguarda Hospital, Piazza Ospedale Maggiore 3, 20162 Milan, Italy; gabriele.canzi@ospedaleniguarda.it
4 Department of Medical Physics, ASST-Monza, San Gerardo Hospital, University of Milano-Bicocca, Via Pergolesi 33, 20900 Monza, Italy; elena.deponti@unimib.it
* Correspondence: davide.sozzi@unimib.it

Abstract: Abstract**Aim**: the purpose of this work is to present an innovative protocol for virtual planning and surgical navigation in post-oncological mandibular reconstruction through fibula free flap. In order to analyze its applicability, an evaluation of accuracy for the surgical protocol has been performed. **Methods**: 21 patients surgically treated for mandibular neoplasm have been included in the analysis. The Brainlab Vector Vision 3.0® software for surgical navigation has been used for preoperative surgical planning and intra-operative navigation. A post-operative accuracy evaluation has been performed matching the position of mandibular landmarks between pre-operative and post-operative CT scans. **Results**: the maximal discrepancy observed was included between −3.4 mm and +3.2 mm, assuming negative values for under correction and positive values for overcorrection. An average grade of accuracy included between 0.06 ± 0.58 mm and 0.43 ± 0.68 mm has been observed for every mandibular landmark examined, except for mandibular angles that showed a mean discrepancy value included between 1.36 ± 1.73 mm and 1.46 ± 1.02 mm when compared to preoperative measurements. **Conclusion**: a satisfying level of accuracy has been observed in the protocol presented, which appears to be more versatile if compared to closed custom-made systems. The technique described may represent a valid option for selected patients, but it cannot be considered for routine activity because of the complexity of the method, the mobility of the jaw, the necessity of surgical navigator and the long surgical learning curve that is required.

Keywords: mandibular reconstruction; fibula flap; virtual surgical planning; surgical navigation; computer-assisted surgery; oral cancer

Citation: Sozzi, D.; Filippi, A.; Canzi, G.; De Ponti, E.; Bozzetti, A.; Novelli, G. Surgical Navigation in Mandibular Reconstruction: Accuracy Evaluation of an Innovative Protocol. *J. Clin. Med.* **2022**, *11*, 2060. https://doi.org/10.3390/jcm11072060

Academic Editors: Carlos Navarro Cuéllar, José Luis Cebrián-Carretero and Mark L. Urken

Received: 20 February 2022
Accepted: 4 April 2022
Published: 6 April 2022

1. Introduction

Mandibular reconstruction has been a major challenge for a long time and it is still characterized by considerable complexity, due to the peculiar anatomical morphology and the central role of the jaw in face functions and aesthetics [1,2]. The main field of application for mandibular reconstruction is represented by oncological pathology (benign and malignant), which can involve bone and soft tissue, requiring massive mandibular resections in order to guarantee radicality. Further issues come from complementary radiotherapy, which may induce fibrosis and vascular damage, worsening the functional outcomes [3,4].

Reconstructive surgery underwent a huge development during the last 40 years thanks to the introduction of new surgical techniques, technologies and materials, which converted a highly disfiguring surgery into an effective surgery for both therapeutic and aesthetic purposes [1,5].

The osteocutaneous fibula free flap with titanium implants fixation currently represents one of the best reconstructive options for mandibular defects because of its versatility, the massive portion of bone available and the possibility of being prosthetically rehabilitated [6–13]. A fundamental requirement in order to obtain a good morphological reconstruction is represented by the respect of individual dental occlusion and condyle-glenoid relationship through the accurate shaping of fixation plate that will keep the bone in the correct position.

The evolution of technologies led to the introduction of virtual surgical planning which, through CAD-CAM systems, provides an important aid to the surgeon in both ablative and reconstructive surgical steps [14–17]. Surgical navigation represents a valid and useful technique for the correct reconstruction of facial middle third, which is represented by non-motile bones; nevertheless, its use in mandibular reconstruction is limited by bone movements that reduce the accuracy of the method [18–21].

The aim of this study is to evaluate the accuracy of an innovative surgical protocol in mandibular post-oncological reconstruction in order to implement reconstructive outcomes and define the limits of the technique: this work analyzes a single-center experience in computer-assisted planning associated to surgical navigation for one-stage oncological mandibular resection and reconstruction through osteocutaneous fibula free flap.

2. Materials and Methods

2.1. Sample Selection

This study analyzes 21 patients affected by oral-mandibular neoplasms (both benign and malignant), 9 female and 12 male, with a mean age of 45.9 ± 15.0 years (range 17–65); a mean age of 33.3 years was observed in the group with benign tumor (range 17–65), while a mean age of 53.8 years was observed in patients with malignant diagnosis (range 36–65).

Every patient has been treated through the same protocol of virtual planning and surgical navigation developed by the Unit of Maxillofacial Surgery of San Gerardo Hospital in Monza—Milano-Bicocca University (Italy) between January 2010 and September 2018. Within the sample, 13 patients were affected by malignant neoplasms (11 squamous carcinomas, one synovial sarcoma and one adenoid-cystic carcinoma); eight patients of the whole sample were affected by benign neoplasm (6 ameloblastomas, one odontogenic keratocyst and one giant cell granuloma).

Every patient underwent hemi-mandibulectomy and one-stage reconstruction through free fibula flap. In this case, 14 patients have been treated by resection of ascending and horizontal mandibular branches, with a 2-segments fibular reconstruction; four patients have been treated through the same resection and a double barrel reconstruction; three patients required even partial symphysis resection and a 3-segments fibular reconstruction.

All surgical procedures included in the analysis have been performed by the same team, with the same two senior surgeons cooperating during both resective and reconstructive steps.

2.2. Virtual Planning

The first step in surgical planning is represented by the realization of a dental splint, which has the function to stabilize the dental arches and to incorporate the radiopaque marker points for surgical navigation. The splint should be acquired in centric occlusion and it has to be thin enough to allow the correct interfacing of dental cusps and thick enough to maintain integrity during surgical procedure.

The dental splint plays a fundamental role because it contains the fiducial marker points used for surgical navigation and it keeps the mandible in the correct position: the mobility of the mandible during the pre-operative CT scanning and during the intra-operative surgical navigation would make the technique unusable. It is necessary to identify the marker points' position before surgery and this position must be kept unchanged during every step of the protocol (Figure 1).

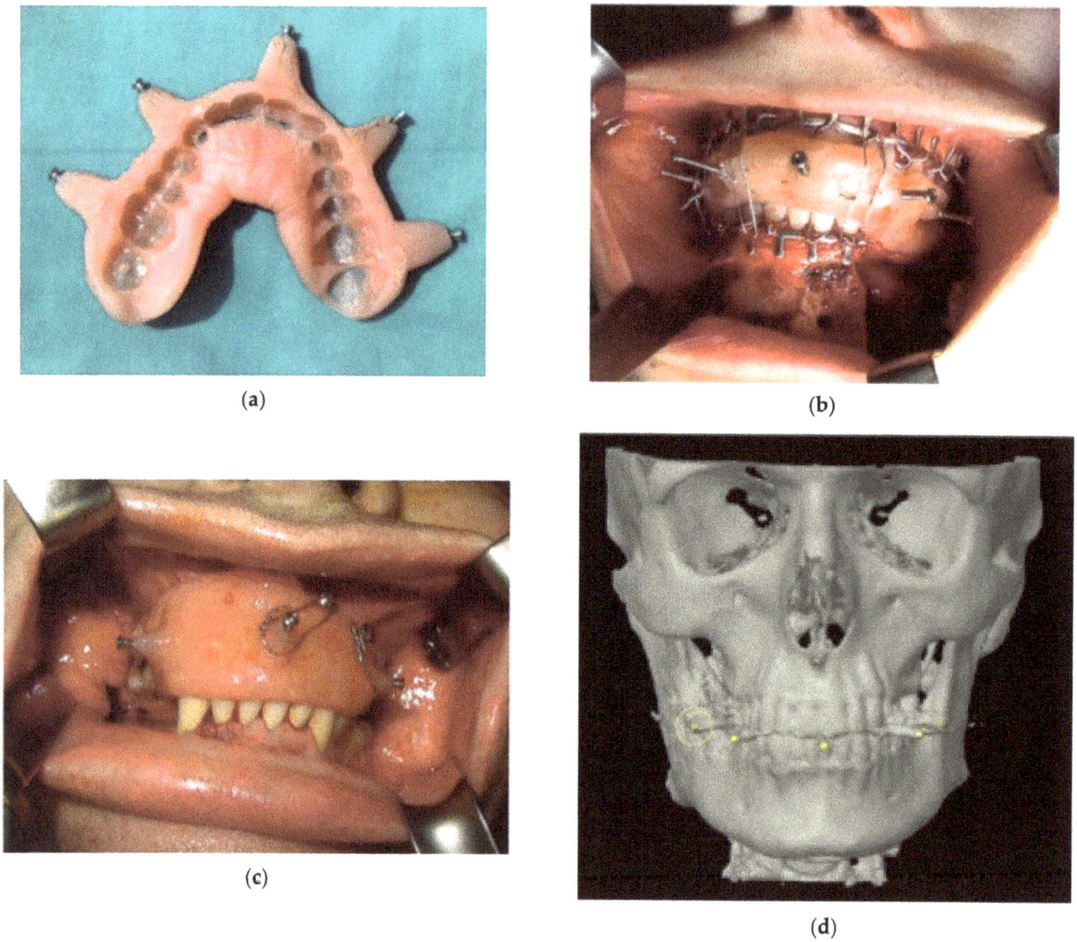

Figure 1. (**a–d**): The dental splint is manufactured in order to include the fiducial markerpoints and to maintain a rigid intermaxillary fixation.

Dental splints, created with cold sterilizable acrylic resin, can be modeled on dental arches plaster models (indirect technique) or straight on patient's dental arches (direct technique). The markers applied on the splint are represented by titanium screws with hexagonal engagement (1.5 mm diameter and 2.0 mm depth). In order to obtain a good spatial reference, it is necessary to place at least five orthogonal marker points in an easy-to-reach position during the entire surgical procedure. The dental splint is then sterilized through gamma-irradiation for the intraoperative use.

The second step of virtual planning is represented by the acquisition of high resolution CT scans of facial bones and lower limbs angio-CT, which have to be elaborated in DICOM (Digital Imaging and Communications in Medicine) format.

Lower limbs angio-CT has a dual purpose: the evaluation of lower limbs vascular anatomy and the structural analysis of the fibular bone for virtual planning.

The facial CT scan must be acquired while the patient is wearing the dental splint and, to ensure maximal accuracy during the virtual planning phase, our protocol provides a laser scan of the dental arches surface, which is lately elaborated and integrated to previously acquired data, reducing scattering artifacts that can be encountered in CT images.

Images are then imported in the planning software and converted into STL (Standard Triangulation Language) format, which allows to elaborate an accurate 3D model that can be manipulated in order to simulate the surgical resection. After that, the virtual 3D fibula is segmented and modeled through the same software in order to replenish the mandibular continuity (Figure 2).

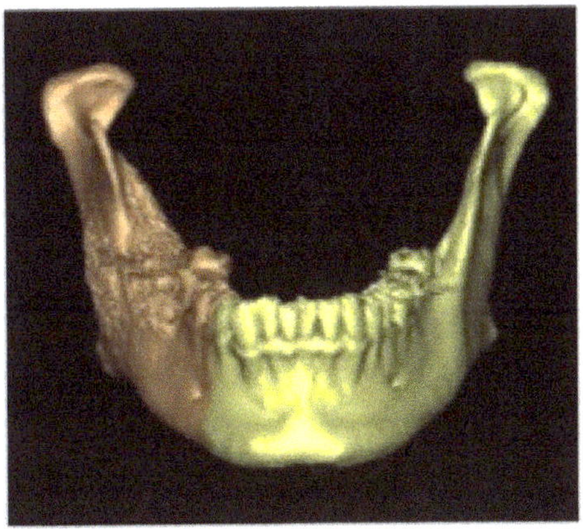

(a)

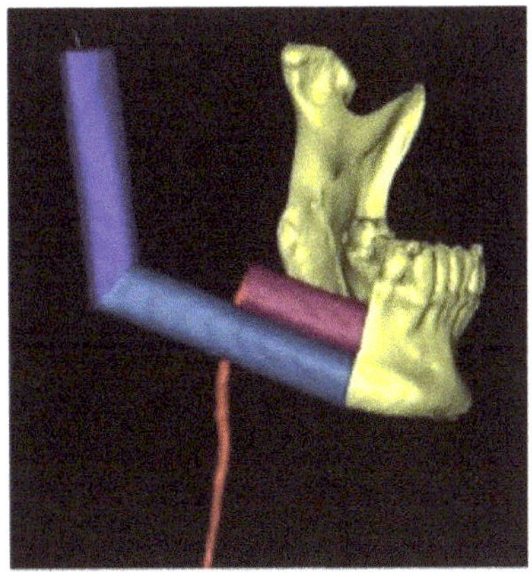

(b)

Figure 2. (**a**,**b**): Virtual surgical planning on CT images.

2.3. 3D Model Printing and Plate Shaping

The final model of the "new" mandible is printed through a 3D-printer using thermoplastic powders and it is used as template for reconstructive titanium plate shaping (Figure 3).

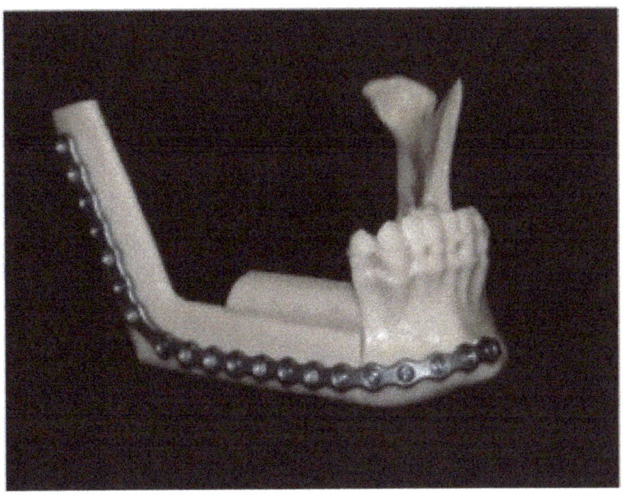

Figure 3. The titanium plate is shaped on 3D printed model.

2.4. Pre-Surgical Navigation: 3D Model Registration

CT images and virtual planning data are imported to the Brainlab Vector Vision 3.0® software for surgical navigation and every marker point position is then identified on the CT images to make triangulation possible.

The Dynamic Reference Frame (DRF) system is attached to the 3D mandible model: it is represented by a tripod on which are fixed some luminous reflectors, that are detected by the infrared camera of the surgical navigator and permit the identification of the spatial position of the 3D model. The DRF system can guarantee high accuracy of surgical navigation even in a mobile body region, such as the patient's head.

The position of the screw holes previously realized on the 3D model is then recorded, as well as the lines of resection that are expected to be followed in the ablative surgical step (Figure 4).

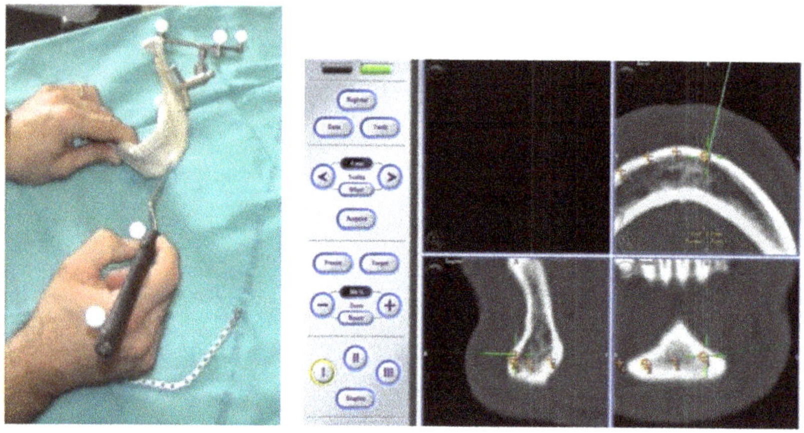

(a) (b)

Figure 4. (**a**,**b**): Through preoperative surgical navigation of the 3D model, the position of the screw holes is recorded.

2.5. Intra-Operative Surgical Navigation

The intra-operative surgical navigation begins with the positioning of the DRF system tripod on patient's skull and the subsequent placing of the dental splint on patient's dental arches; marker points position on dental splint is then recorded and matched with CT scans previously loaded.

In this phase every surgical instrument should be recorded using a dedicated calibration tool which recognizes type, dimensions and characteristics of the different surgical instruments.

The mandibular bone is exposed and, before performing the resection, the screw holes for reconstruction plate are realized with a recorded drill, whose bit position can be identified live on CT images in order to place the screws in the exact programmed location (Figure 5). The mandibular resection is then performed respecting the programmed margins, following the oncological safety principle.

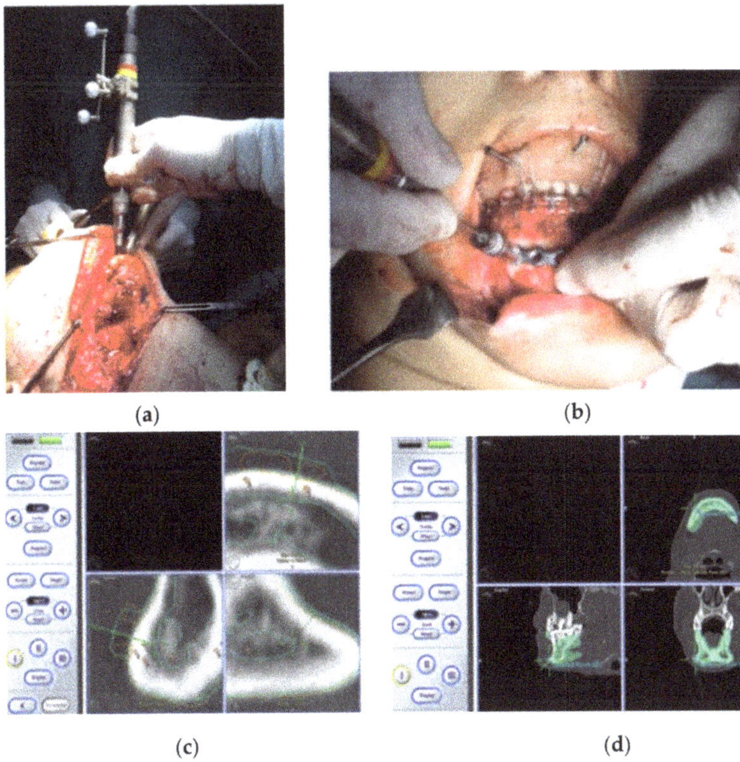

Figure 5. (**a–d**): The fibula flap is inset and fixed through a recorded drill and surgical navigation.

Once the pathological bone segment has been removed, the reconstruction plate should be placed, matching the position of the holes made with the positions previously programmed. Simultaneously, a second surgical team performs the fibula flap harvesting [6]. When flap preparation is complete, the planned osteotomies are performed and the fibular bone is shaped with the aid of the 3D plaster model.

The modeled bone is then inset onto the receiving site, precisely adapting it to the shape of the titanium plate, which works as rigid template for the final modeling of the reconstructive bone. A final check of the bone and plate position is made to guarantee a good matching between the virtual planning and the new mandible. Lastly, the flap is revascularized performing microsurgical anastomoses with the most fitting cervical-facial vessels.

2.6. Post-Operative Evaluation

The post-operative evaluation is based on the overlap of post-operative CT images with the pre-operative virtual planning images through the Plasticad 3DIEMME 2015® software, realizing tridimensional virtual STL models and analyzing the matching between the overlapped models; the difference in millimeters for specific structures is then calculated (Figure 6).

In this work, the post-operative CT scan has been acquired within 15 days from surgery and the correspondence analysis focused on the residual mandible, assuming a value equal to 0 in case of perfect overlap and match, a negative value in case of undercorrection and a positive value in case of overcorrection. The virtual model overlap should be analyzed in all spatial planes.

The anatomical structures that have been used for the overlap analysis are: left condyle (sagittal and coronal projection), right condyle (sagittal and coronal projection), mandibular midline (sagittal and coronal projection), left mandibular angle (sagittal and coronal projection) and right mandibular angle (sagittal and coronal projection).

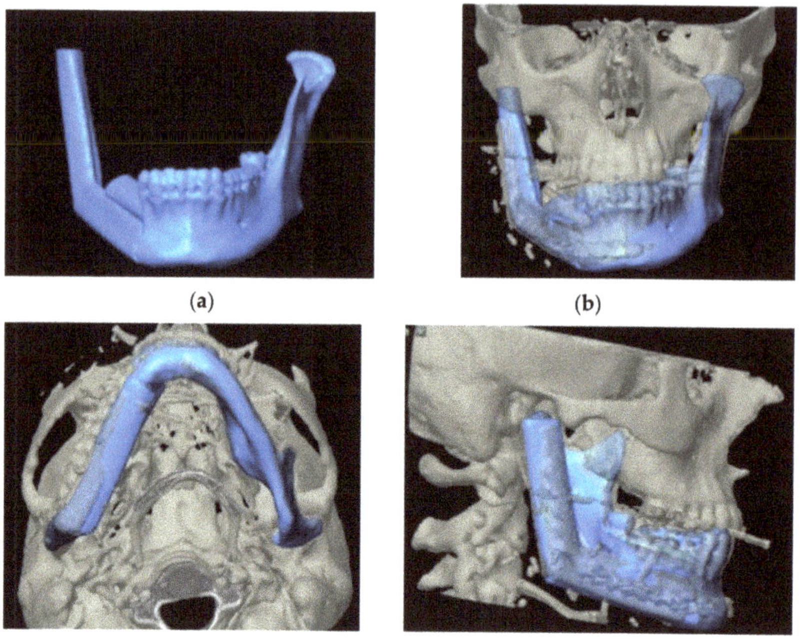

(a) (b) (c) (d)

Figure 6. (**a**–**d**): Preoperative images of surgical planning and postoperative CT images are overlapped and positional discrepancies are measured.

2.7. Statistical Analysis

The surgical data and image measures were retrospectively collected and analyzed. The parameters of evaluation have been obtained calculating the difference in millimeters between post-operative and pre-operative position of reference points. The statistical analysis has been performed through the Stata 9.0® software (Stata Corporation College Station, TX, USA). Mean and median of every parameter have been calculated.

The distribution of the values has been verified through indexes of symmetry (*Skewness Index*), shape (*Kurtosi Index*) and global normality.

All variables measuring accuracy were characterized by Gaussian distribution, except for the parameter "*right mandibular angle in coronal projection*", which resulted asymmetrical. This fact confirmed that mean was the correct indicator to represent all the observations, except for "*right mandibular angle in coronal projection*", for which median and Wilcoxon sum rank test was used.

The normal data distribution enabled to use the parametric Student's *t*-test for the comparison of the means of all the other parameters evaluated.

The second step of data analysis has been led evaluating the matching between the treated side for each patient and the offset value showing the least accuracy, examining differences related to the side of the surgical site.

Lastly, it has been checked whether the average of the individual measured parameters significantly deviated from zero, which represents the absolute perfection of the surgical outcome, separately considering patients operated on left-hand and right-hand side. This analysis was performed applying the Student's *t*-test.

The level of significance used for the study of the associations described was assumed for a p value < 0.05.

3. Results

The quantitative features of accuracy parameter have been displayed through a box plot in order to evaluate the distribution of the parameters (Figure 7). The box plot analysis showed a Gaussian distribution of the results, except for "right mandibular angle in coronal projection", which revealed a highly asymmetrical distribution. An overcorrective tendency has been observed for the parameters "right condyle (sagittal and coronal projection)", "midline (sagittal and coronal projection)", "left angle in coronal projection" and "right angle in coronal projection"; an undercorrective tendency has been observed instead for "left angle in sagittal projection" and "right angle in sagittal projection".

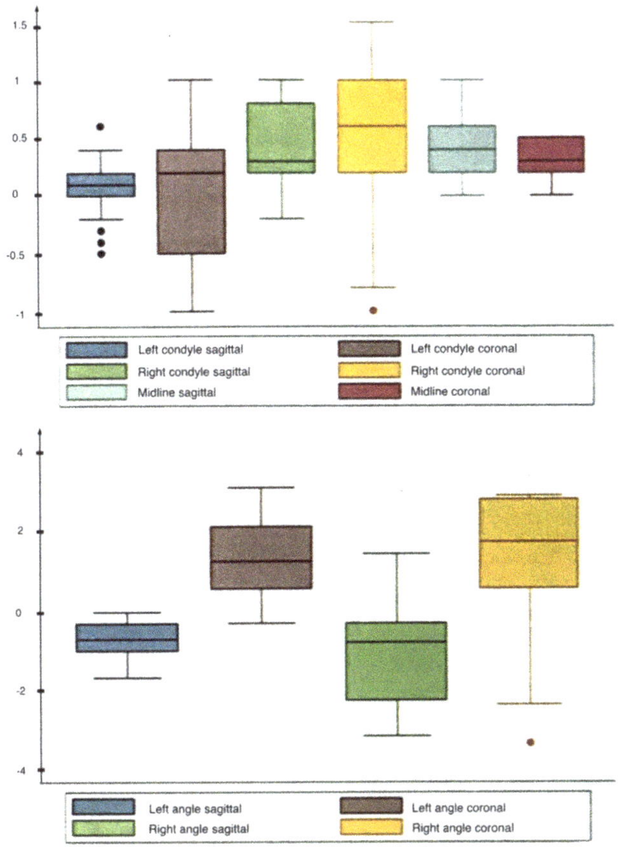

Figure 7. Landmarks box plot: the box represents the interquartile range between Q1 and Q3, the continuous line inside the box represents the median, the continuous line outside the box shows the global range of parameters distribution and the dots represent outliers.

A global error between −3.4 mm and +3.2 mm has been observed in the entire examination, with a higher grade of discrepancy documented for the mandibular angles position (Table 1).

Table 1. Mean and median values of difference (in mm) between pre-operative and post-operative position of every mandibular marker point, measured on TC images.

MARKERPOINTS	MEAN ± SD (Range)	MEDIAN (95%CI)
Left condyle sagittal (mm)	0.07 ± 0.28 (−0.5; 0.6)	0.1 (0.0:0.2)
Left condyle coronal (mm)	0.06 ± 0.58 (−1.0; 1.0)	0.2 (−0.5; 0.4)
Right condyle sagittal (mm)	0.4 ± 0.38 (−0.2; 1.0)	0.3 ± (0.2; 0.7)
Right condyle coronal (mm)	0.43 ± 0.68 (−1.0; 1.5)	0.6 (0.2; 1.0)
Midline sagittal (mm)	0.45 ± 0.30 (0.0; 1.0)	0.4 (0.2; 0.6)
Midline coronal (mm)	0.29 ± 0.17 (0.0; 0.5)	0.3 (0.2; 0.5)
Left angle sagittal (mm)	−0.7 ± 0.48 (−1.7; 0.0)	−0.7 (−1.0; −0.3)
Left angle coronal (mm)	1.46 ± 1.02 (−0.3; 3.2)	1.3 (0.6; 2.1)
Right angle sagittal (mm)	−1.07 ± 1.42 (−3.2; 1.5)	−0.8 (−2.2; −0.3)
Right angle coronal (mm)	1.36 ± 1.73 (−3.4; 3.0)	1.8 (0.7; 2.8)

In order to detect significant differences of accuracy between patients treated on right and left-hand sides, the mean values of every marker point have been compared through Student's *t*-test (Table 2).

Table 2. Comparison of mandibular marker points through Student's *t*-test for patients treated on right-hand and left-hand side.

MARKERPOINTS	LEFT (n = 7) Mean ± SD (Range) *Median* (95% CI)	RIGHT (n = 14) Mean ± SD (Range) *Median* (95% CI)	p Value Student's t-Test * Wilcoxon Sum Rank Test
Left condyle sagittal (mm)	0.23 ± 0.21 *0.2 (−0.1; 0.4)*	−0.01 ± 0.29 *0.0 (−0.3; 0.2)*	0.030
Left condyle coronal (mm)	0.01 ± 0.51 *0.2 (−0.3; 0.4)*	0.08 ± 0.63 *0.2 (−0.5; 0.7)*	0.409
Right condyle sagittal (mm)	0.63 ± 0.28 *0.6 (0.3; 0.9)*	0.28 ± 0.38 *0.3 (−0.1; 0.5)*	0.022
Right condyle coronal (mm)	0.53 ± 0.68 *0.8 (0.2; 1.0)*	0.39 ± 0.70 *0.5 (−0.3; 1.0)*	0.332
Midline sagittal (mm)	0.43 ± 0.41 *0.3 (0.1; 1.0)*	0.46 ± 0.25 *0.4 (0.2; 0.6)*	0.404
Midline coronal (mm)	0.30 ± 0.18 *0.3 (0.2; 0.5)*	0.29 ± 0.17 *0.3 (0.1; 0.5)*	0.432
Left angle sagittal (mm)	−1.21 ± 0.31 *−1.2 (−1.5; −0.9)*	−0.44 ± 0.31 *−0.3 (−0.7; −0.2)*	<0.0001
Left angle coronal (mm)	2.29 ± 1.19 *2.6 (2.2; 3.0)*	1.04 ± 0.62 *1.1 (0.5; 1.5)*	0.002
Right angle sagittal (mm)	−0.44 ± 0.35 *−0.5 (−0.8; −0.3)*	−1.39 ± 1.65 *−1.8 (−2.9; −0.1)*	0.078
Right angle coronal (mm)	0.77 ± 0.62 *0.6 (0.4; 1.2)*	1.65 ± 2.04 *2.4 (1.5; 2.9)*	0.023 *

Every value of the column was calculated through Student's *t*-test, except the last value (Right angle coronal) which was calculated through Wilcoxon Sum Rank Test (that's the reason of *).

Accuracy parameters have been finally compared with "zero", which is considered as the condition of perfect matching between preoperative and postoperative marker points' position. Once again, the Student's *t*-test has been used for this analysis (Tables 3 and 4).

Table 3. Comparison between mean values of marker points measure and "zero" for patients treated on left-hand side. p value < 0.5 has been considered significant.

MARKERPOINTS	LEFT (n = 7) Mean ± SD	p Value Student's t-Test
Left condyle sagittal (mm)	0.23 ± 0.21	0.026
Left condyle coronal (mm)	0.01 ± 0.51	0.943
Right condyle sagittal (mm)	0.63 ± 0.28	0.001
Right condyle coronal (mm)	0.53 ± 0.68	0.086
Midline sagittal (mm)	0.43 ± 0.41	0.033
Midline coronal (mm)	0.30 ± 0.18	0.005
Left angle sagittal (mm)	−1.21 ± 0.31	<0.0001
Left angle coronal (mm)	2.29 ± 1.19	0.002
Right angle sagittal (mm)	−0.44 ± 0.35	0.016
Right angle coronal (mm)	0.77 ± 0.62	0.016

Table 4. Comparison between mean values of marker points measure and zero for patients treated on right-hand side. p value < 0.5 has been considered significant.

MARKERPOINTS	RIGHT (n = 14) Mean ± SD	p Value Student's t-Test
Left condyle sagittal (mm)	−0.01 ± 0.29	0.854
Left condyle coronal (mm)	0.08 ± 0.63	0.648
Right condyle sagittal (mm)	0.28 ± 0.38	0.016
Right condyle coronal (mm)	0.39 ± 0.70	0.061
Midline sagittal (mm)	0.46 ± 0.25	<0.0001
Midline coronal (mm)	0.29 ± 0.17	<0.0001
Left angle sagittal (mm)	−0.44 ± 0.31	<0.0001
Left angle coronal (mm)	1.04 ± 0.62	<0.0001
Right angle sagittal (mm)	−1.39 ± 1.65	0.008
Right angle coronal (mm)	1.65 ± 2.04	0.010

No perfect matching has been observed for both treated sides (examined separately) and the highest discrepancy has been detected for mandibular angles in coronal projection: 2.29 ± 1.19 mm for left-hand side and 1.65 ± 2.04 mm for right-hand side.

4. Discussion

Free flaps represent the gold standard for post-oncological mandibular reconstruction and the fibula flap, with its reliable vascular pedicle and its reduced donor site morbidity, provides an adequate quantity of bicortical bone that is suitable for dental rehabilitation [6,10–14,22–27]. While "*free-hand*" techniques are characterized by operator-dependent outcomes and by less accuracy in condylar repositioning and individual occlusion restoration [14,22], the introduction of Computer-Assisted Surgery (CAS) techniques led to more accurate reconstructions and to a shorter length of surgery [14,17,28,29].

A further evolution of techniques is represented by the integration of Computer-Assisted Design (CAD) and Computer-Assisted Manufacturing (CAM): the CAD-CAM technique has led to the introduction of *Patient-Specific Mandible Reconstruction Plates* (*PSMPs*) and surgical cutting guides [15,30,31]. Although this process provides a high grade of accuracy in bone reconstruction and it is widely used [32], it should be considered that such a rigid system may lead to various issues when dealing with malignant tumors that may require to modify the resection width.

Maxillofacial surgical navigation has been firstly introduced in 1994 by Hassfeld for the treatment of skull base tumors [33] and then it has been successfully applied to orbit, temporal bone, zygomatic bone, and maxillary bone [20,34–40]; all these sites are characterized by immobility. The surgical navigation of the mandible was considered difficult and impractical because of the jaw mobility: in 2011 Bell et al. elaborated a protocol of virtual planning and surgical navigation for maxillary and mandibular bone reconstruction coming to the conclusion that mandibular surgical navigation is not superior to the method with CAD-CAM models, but rather it introduces more complexity and increased surgical time [41]. Considering the current limits of CAD-CAM techniques, related to the rigidity of the system and the need of involving qualified engineers in the preoperative steps, we decided to exploit our experience with surgical navigation in treatment of upper and middle third of the skull in order to elaborate a new protocol of integration between virtual surgery simulation (VSS) and surgical navigation, evaluating its accuracy [30–32,38–40]. Every step of our protocol has been performed by physicians, with no need of further professional figures.

The main problem of surgical navigation of the jaw is represented by the mobility of the mandibular bone and the consequent difficulty in placing and identifying the fiducial marker points [41–44].

Wu et al. (2016), Zhang el al. (2016) and Shan et al. (2016) described the use of a custom-made dental splint to improve stability and reproducibility of inter-maxillary fixation during the different phases. Marker points were placed, in form of titanium screws, on maxillary bone and were not integrated to the dental splint [18,32,42].

Within this background, we elaborated a protocol that provides the use of a dental splint on which radiopaque fiducial marker points are built-in. The splint and mandible positions must necessarily be the same during the phase of CT images acquisition and the surgical phase, in order to ensure a perfect matching between patient and radiological data. In order to obtain spatial stability, the mandible and the splint are maintained in the same position during the whole surgical procedure through the use of inter-maxillary rigid fixation.

Basic importance for the realization of the procedure is represented by the precision of the dental splint and the 3D model, which is made through a *laser sintering* technique and has to perfectly match with the dental splint. We elaborated an intra-oral laser scan system for both the dental arches that produces DICOM format images, which are superimposed to high resolution CT images of the skull bone; this system ensures high accuracy for the virtual and 3D sintered models, significantly reducing the scattering artifacts.

The use of a dental splint with built-in markers points allows the maintenance of a stable and reproducible maxillary-mandibular centric occlusion and to acquire easy access to the marker points during both the planning and surgical phases, with high accuracy and a systematic method-related error lower than 1 mm [20].

We consider that splint-linked marker points are a valuable tool for surgical navigation of the jaw because of the low invasiveness and the high accessibility; these marker points also allow the surgeon to obtain a stable inter-maxillary fixation even after the oncological resection.

Further surgical navigation methods have been previously described [19,32,42–44]: some Authors suggested the use of an inter-maxillary fixation without dental splint, with lower accuracy and reproducibility of the procedure. Casap et al. in 2008 and Abbate et al. in 2017 introduced the positioning of the DRF system directly on the mandible, opposite to the lesion side, obtaining a good matching between the post-operative outcome and the virtual planning; although this method may represent a valid alternative to the use of inter-maxillary fixation, it is characterized by some important disadvantages, such as the long time required for the procedure, the possibility of screws loosening on the DRF system and the size of the space occupied by the device in the operative field [19,44].

In our experience, the application of the DRF system on the patient's skull appears to be the most adequate solution in combination with the use of a dental splint and intra-operative inter-maxillary fixation.

The main aim of this work was to assess the accuracy of an innovative protocol analyzing the position of reference point on CT pre-operative and post-operative images.

No flap failure has been observed in the sample studied. The post-operative clinical evaluation showed a satisfactory functional outcome, with restoration of the jaw symmetry and dental-skeletal occlusion; the mutual position of condyle in the glenoid cavity led to an adequate mandible mobility in all patients.

The accuracy assessment has been performed, as already proposed by Roser et al., by overlapping post-operative CT images and virtual planning data, and then comparing the position of reference point [22]. The reference points that have been selected for the overlapping analysis are: left condyle, right condyle, midline, left mandibular angle and right mandibular angle (in sagittal and coronal projection). These points have been identified because of the aesthetic and functional relevance in mandibular reconstruction: the condyle position is essential to prevent malocclusion, mobility defects, chronic pain and temporomandibular ankylosis; the midline position is important for symmetry and occlusion; mandibular angles are highly relevant for facial aesthetics and masticatory load distribution.

The surgical navigation system showed a systematic error lower than 1 mm after the correct registration of marker points, coinciding with literature data [18,45]. In the analysis of postoperative measures negative values have been associated to undercorrection, while positive values represent overcorrection.

The means of the accuracy assessment parameters showed a lower precision in the angles repositioning, with a mean between 1.36 ± 1.73 mm and 1.46 ± 1.02 mm (Table 1). We consider this outcome as an acceptable one because this difference in the mandibular district has no adverse clinical implications, with a good aesthetic and functional result.

We observed a higher accuracy for the rest of the reference points analyzed, averaging between 0.06 ± 0.58 mm and 0.43 ± 0.68 mm (Table 1).

Our results agree with literature data, which show a mean overlapping precision between 1 and 3 mm [42]. Wu et al. analyzed the accuracy of mandibular angles repositioning observing a mean result of 1.92 ± 0.97 mm [18]. Zhang et al. proposed a protocol for surgical navigation in mandibular reconstruction through the use of iliac crest free flap and reported a mean difference in condyle positioning of 1.45 ± 0.50 mm [32].

All studied parameters did not show correlation with the treated side of the jaw, confirming the absence of significant systematic errors of the procedure deriving from the side of the surgical site.

The comparison between mean and median values of the studied parameters divided by side of surgical site showed a condyle overcorrection trend in sagittal projection for patients treated on left-hand side (left condyle p value = 0.030 and right condyle p value = 0.022), an angle undercorrection trend in sagittal projection (left angle p value < 0.0001 and right angle p value = 0.078) and an angle overcorrection trend in coronal projection (left angle p value = 0.002 and right angle p value = 0.023) (Table 2). This trend may be induced by the presence of the reconstructive titanium plate, which produces a slight thickness and induces a higher overlapping difference value in coronal projection. The sagittal undercorrection may be explained instead by the morphology of the reconstructive bone, which turns out to be more edgy and less uniform.

The comparison between the means of single parameters and the "*zero*" value, intended as the perfect overlap and then the theoretical perfect reconstruction, showed that the accuracy of our protocol, although not achieving perfection, turns out to be highly satisfying.

The difference in overlap for midline in sagittal projection may be explained again by the presence of the reconstructive plate, considering the value of the difference that is equal to 0.43 ± 0.41 mm (p value = 0.033) for left-hand side and 0.46 ± 0.25 mm (p value < 0.0001) for right-hand side (Tables 3 and 4).

This study has been performed on a 21 patients sample, which appears to be a relevant and conspicuous number when compared to international scientific literature [18,19]; nevertheless, the absolute number of the sample examined is exiguous and does not permit the obtainment of a satisfying statistical significance. Further studies on larger samples should be performed in the future with the aim of confirming and validating the results.

Although virtual planning and surgical navigation may present several advantages for reconstruction accuracy and length of surgery, it is mandatory to highlight that pre-operative surgical planning and 3D model production require a massive use of time and resources.

A further advantage of surgical navigation, which emerged from this study and was also asserted by Wu et al., concerns the versatility of the technique, that can be adapted to the margins of resection required by clinical condition, leading to an accurate reconstruction even in case of resection modifications [18]. This element shows important relevance when dealing with cancer patients, since the necessity of widened resections may occur in order to achieve a correct treatment from an oncological point of view.

One of the main limits of this protocol is represented by the relevant time necessary for pre-operative virtual planning and registration, which is highly augmented if compared to free-hand techniques. Another simple but basic limit of this technique is represented by the need of the surgical navigator, which nowadays is not used by every hospital facility.

An important practical limit of the method is represented by very bulky tumor mass and edentulous patients: a correct placing of the dental splint and a stable inter-maxillary fixation cannot be obtained in these patients.

Surgical navigation requires a long and complex learning curve, implying a reduced diffusion of the method. Moreover, "Computer-Assisted Surgery" techniques, virtual planning and surgical navigation represent an important aid for the surgeon but do not replace the personal experience, which retains its essentiality.

5. Conclusions

The protocol of virtual planning and surgical navigation elaborated by our team represents an innovation for mandibular reconstruction and showed high standards of accuracy.

Virtual planning simulates the surgical phase in order to obtain highly predictable and reproducible outcomes; it constitutes the basis of the surgical navigation. The real time guide offered by this technique reduces the margin of error compared to free-hand techniques, length of surgery is reduced and, furthermore, surgical navigation allows the surgeon to modify ongoing the resection and reconstruction dimensions.

The proposed virtual planning and surgical navigation protocol showed high accuracy and good applicability, but it should be emphasized that it requires massive pre-surgical time of application and a long learning curve for the surgeon.

Even if it should be reserved for selected cases, this protocol may represent a valid alternative surgical option for mandibular reconstruction, leading to satisfactory outcomes with reduction of the length of surgery.

Author Contributions: D.S., design, acquisition, analysis, writing, revising; A.F., acquisition, analysis, writing, revising; G.C., design, writing, revising; E.D.P., design, writing, revising; A.B., design, writing, revising; G.N., design, acquisition, revising. All authors have read and agreed to the published version of the manuscript.

Funding: This research received no external funding.

Institutional Review Board Statement: No ethical approval was obtained because of the observational and retrospective nature of the study.

Informed Consent Statement: Patient consent was waived because of the retrospective nature of the study. No patient can be identified in this work.

Data Availability Statement: The data that support the findings of this study are available on request from the corresponding author. The data are not publicly available due to ethical and privacy restriction.

Conflicts of Interest: The authors certify that there is no conflict of interest with any financial organization regarding the material discussed in the manuscript.

References

1. Bak, M.; Jacobson, A.S.; Buchbinder, D.; Urken, M.L. Contemporary reconstruction of the mandible. *Oral Oncol.* **2010**, *46*, 71–76. [CrossRef] [PubMed]
2. Ferreira, J.J.; Zagalo, C.M.; Oliveira, M.L.; Correia, A.M.; Reis, A.R. Mandible reconstruction: History, state of the art and persistent problems. *Prosthet. Orthot. Int.* **2015**, *39*, 182–189. [CrossRef] [PubMed]
3. Schliephake, H.; Hausamen, J.E. An overview of the principles of reconstructive surgery. In *Maxillofacial Surgery*, 2nd ed.; Ward Booth, P., Schendel, S.A., Hausamen, J.E., Eds.; Churchill Livingtone: St. Louis, MI, USA, 2007; pp. 535–548.
4. Wilik, R.M. Bony reconstruction of the jaws. In *Peterson's Principles of Oral an Maxillofacial Surgery*, 2nd ed.; Miloro, M., Ed.; BC Decker: Hamilton, ON, Canada, 2004; pp. 783–801.
5. Goh, B.T.; Lee, S.; Tideman, H.; Stoelinga, P.J. Mandibular reconstruction in adults: A review. *Int. J. Oral Maxillofac. Surg.* **2008**, *37*, 597–605. [CrossRef] [PubMed]
6. Hidalgo, D.A. Fibula free flap: A new method of mandible reconstruction. *Plast. Reconstr. Surg.* **1989**, *84*, 71–79. [CrossRef]
7. Hidalgo, D.A.; Pusic, A.L. Free-flap mandibular reconstruction: A 10-year follow-up study. *Plast. Reconstr. Surg.* **2002**, *110*, 438–449, discussion 450–451. [CrossRef]
8. Yim, K.K.; Wei, F.C. Fibula osteoseptocutaneous flap for mandible reconstruction. *Microsurgery* **1994**, *15*, 245–249. [CrossRef]
9. Brown, J.S.; Lowe, D.; Kanatas, A.; Schache, A. Mandibular reconstruction with vascularised bone flaps: A systematic review over 25 years. *Br. J. Oral Maxillofac. Surg.* **2017**, *55*, 113–126. [CrossRef]
10. Lodders, J.N.; Leusink, F.K.J.; Ridwan-Pramana, A.; Winters, H.A.H.; Karagozoglu, K.H.; Dekker, H.; Forouzanfar, T.; Schulten, E.A.J.M. Long-term outcomes of implant-based dental rehabilitation in head and neck cancer patients after reconstruction with the free vascularized fibula flap. *J. Craniomaxillofac. Surg.* **2021**, *49*, 845–854. [CrossRef]
11. Sozzi, D.; Novelli, G.; Silva, R.; Connelly, S.T.; Tartaglia, G.M. Implant rehabilitation in fibula-free flap reconstruction: A retrospective study of cases at 1–18 years following surgery. *J. Craniomaxillofac. Surg.* **2017**, *45*, 1655–1661. [CrossRef]
12. Zavattero, E.; Ramieri, G.; Agrò, G.; Fasolis, M.; Garzino-Demo, P.; Borbon, C. Implant Dental Rehabilitation of Fibula-Free Flap Reconstructed Jaws. *J. Craniofac. Surg.* **2021**, *32*, e134–e136. [CrossRef]
13. Kumar, V.V.; Jacob, P.C.; Ebenezer, S.; Kuriakose, M.A.; Kekatpure, V.; Baliarsing, A.S.; Al-Nawas, B.; Wagner, W. Implant supported dental rehabilitation following segmental mandibular reconstruction—Quality of life outcomes of a prospective randomized trial. *J. Craniomaxillofac. Surg.* **2016**, *44*, 800–810. [CrossRef]
14. Zhang, L.; Liu, Z.; Li, B.; Yu, H.; Shen, S.G.; Wang, X. Evaluation of computer-assisted mandibular reconstruction with vascularized fibular flap compared to conventional surgery. *Oral Surg. Oral Med. Oral Pathol. Oral Radiol.* **2016**, *121*, 139–148. [CrossRef]
15. Wilde, F.; Hanken, H.; Probst, F.; Schramm, A.; Heiland, M.; Cornelius, C.P. Multicenter study on the use of patient-specific CAD/CAM reconstruction plates for mandibular reconstruction. *Int. J. Comput. Assist. Radiol. Surg.* **2015**, *10*, 2035–2051. [CrossRef]
16. Mascha, F.; Winter, K.; Pietzka, S.; Heufelder, M.; Schramm, A.; Wilde, F. Accuracy of computer-assisted mandibular reconstructions using patient-specific implants in combination with CAD/CAM fabricated transfer keys. *J. Craniomaxillofac. Surg.* **2017**, *45*, 1884–1897. [CrossRef]
17. Succo, G.; Berrone, M.; Battiston, B.; Tos, P.; Goia, F.; Appendino, P.; Crosetti, E. Step-by-step surgical technique for mandibular reconstruction with fibular free flap: Application of digital technology in virtual surgical planning. *Eur. Arch. Otorhinolaryngol.* **2015**, *272*, 1491–1501. [CrossRef]
18. Wu, J.; Sun, J.; Shen, S.G.; Xu, B.; Li, J.; Zhang, S. Computer-assisted navigation: Its role in intraoperatively accurate mandibular reconstruction. *Oral Surg. Oral Med. Oral Pathol. Oral Radiol.* **2016**, *122*, 134–142. [CrossRef]
19. Abbate, V.; Orabona, G.D.A.; Solari, D.; Bonavolontà, P.; Iaconetta, G.; Califano, L. Mandibular Surgical Navigation: An Innovative Guiding Method. *J. Craniofac. Surg.* **2017**, *28*, 2122–2126. [CrossRef]
20. Hohlweg-Majert, B.; Schön, R.; Schmelzeisen, R.; Gellrich, N.C.; Schramm, A. Navigational maxillofacial surgery using virtual models. *World J. Surg.* **2005**, *29*, 1530–1538. [CrossRef]
21. Yu, H.; Shen, S.G.; Wang, X.; Zhang, L.; Zhang, S. The indication and application of computer-assisted navigation in oral and maxillofacial surgery-Shanghai's experience based on 104 cases. *J. Craniomaxillofac. Surg.* **2013**, *41*, 770–774. [CrossRef]
22. Roser, S.M.; Ramachandra, S.; Blair, H.; Grist, W.; Carlson, G.W.; Christensen, A.M.; Weimer, K.A.; Steed, M.B. The accuracy of virtual surgical planning in free fibula mandibular reconstruction: Comparison of planned and final results. *J. Oral Maxillofac. Surg.* **2010**, *68*, 2824–2832. [CrossRef]
23. Wang, L.Y.; Du, H.M.; Zhang, G.; Tang, W.; Liu, L.; Jing, W.; Long, J. The application of digital surgical diagnosis and treatment technology: A promising strategy for surgical reconstruction of craniomaxillofacial defect and deformity. *Med. Hypotheses* **2011**, *77*, 1004–1005. [CrossRef]

24. Sink, J.; Hamlar, D.; Kademani, D.; Khariwala, S.S. Computer-aided stereolithography for presurgical planning in fibula free tissue reconstruction of the mandible. *J. Reconstr. Microsurg.* **2012**, *28*, 395–403. [CrossRef]
25. He, Y.; Zhu, H.G.; Zhang, Z.Y.; He, J.; Sader, R. Three-dimensional model simulation and reconstruction of composite total maxillectomy defects with fibula osteomyocutaneous flap flow-through from radial forearm flap. *Oral Surg. Oral Med. Oral Pathol. Oral Radiol. Endod.* **2009**, *108*, e6–e12. [CrossRef]
26. Lyons, A.J.; James, R.; Collyer, J. Free vascularised iliac crest graft: An audit of 26 consecutive cases. *Br. J. Oral Maxillofac. Surg.* **2005**, *43*, 210–214. [CrossRef]
27. Muñoz Guerra, M.F.; Gías, L.N.; Rodríguez Campo, F.J.; Díaz González, F.J. Vascularized free fibular flap for mandibular reconstruction: A report of 26 cases. *J. Oral Maxillofac. Surg.* **2001**, *59*, 140–144. [CrossRef]
28. Hendra, F.N.; Van Cann, E.M.; Helder, M.N.; Ruslin, M.; de Visscher, J.G.; Forouzanfar, T.; de Vet, H.C.W. Global incidence and profile of ameloblastoma: A systematic review and meta-analysis. *Oral Dis.* **2020**, *26*, 12–21. [CrossRef]
29. Moratin, J.; Horn, D.; Metzger, K.; Ristow, O.; Flechtenmacher, C.; Engel, M.; Hoffmann, J.; Freier, K.; Freudlsperger, C. Squamous cell carcinoma of the mandible—Patterns of metastasis and disease recurrence in dependence of localization and therapy. *J. Craniomaxillofac. Surg.* **2020**, *48*, 1158–1163. [CrossRef]
30. Wilde, F.; Cornelius, C.P.; Schramm, A. Computer-Assisted Mandibular Reconstruction using a Patient-Specific Reconstruction Plate Fabricated with Computer-Aided Design and Manufacturing Techniques. *Craniomaxillofac. Trauma Reconstr.* **2014**, *7*, 158–166. [CrossRef]
31. Wilde, F.; Winter, K.; Kletsch, K.; Lorenz, K.; Schramm, A. Mandible reconstruction using patient-specific pre-bent reconstruction plates: Comparison of standard and transfer key methods. *Int. J. Comput. Assist. Radiol. Surg.* **2015**, *10*, 129–140. [CrossRef]
32. Zhang, W.B.; Yu, Y.; Wang, Y.; Mao, C.; Liu, X.J.; Guo, C.B.; Yu, G.Y.; Peng, X. Improving the accuracy of mandibular reconstruction with vascularized iliac crest flap: Role of computer-assisted techniques. *J. Craniomaxillofac. Surg.* **2016**, *44*, 1819–1827. [CrossRef] [PubMed]
33. Hassfeld, S.; Mühling, J.; Zöller, J. Intraoperative navigation in oral and maxillofacial surgery. *Int. J. Oral Maxillofac. Surg.* **1995**, *24 Pt 2*, 111–119, (In English and German). [CrossRef]
34. Hassfeld, S.; Mühling, J. Computer assisted oral and maxillofacial surgery–a review and an assessment of technology. *Int. J. Oral Maxillofac. Surg.* **2001**, *30*, 2–13. [CrossRef] [PubMed]
35. Austin, R.E.; Antonyshyn, O.M. Current applications of 3-d intraoperative navigation in craniomaxillofacial surgery: A retrospective clinical review. *Ann. Plast. Surg.* **2012**, *69*, 271–278. [CrossRef] [PubMed]
36. Bell, R.B. Computer planning and intraoperative navigation in cranio-maxillofacial surgery. *Oral Maxillofac. Surg. Clin. N. Am.* **2010**, *22*, 135–156. [CrossRef]
37. Yu, H.; Shen, G.; Wang, X.; Zhang, S. Navigation-guided reduction and orbital floor reconstruction in the treatment of zygomatic-orbital-maxillary complex fractures. *J. Oral Maxillofac. Surg.* **2010**, *68*, 28–34. [CrossRef]
38. Novelli, G.; Tonellini, G.; Mazzoleni, F.; Sozzi, D.; Bozzetti, A. Surgical navigation recording systems in orbitozygomatic traumatology. *J. Craniofac. Surg.* **2012**, *23*, 890–892. [CrossRef]
39. Novelli, G.; Tonellini, G.; Mazzoleni, F.; Bozzetti, A.; Sozzi, D. Virtual surgery simulation in orbital wall reconstruction: Integration of surgical navigation and stereolithographic models. *J. Craniomaxillofac. Surg.* **2014**, *42*, 2025–2034. [CrossRef]
40. Novelli, G.; Gramegna, M.; Tonellini, G.; Valente, G.; Boni, P.; Bozzetti, A.; Sozzi, D. Orbital Osteoblastoma: Technical Innovations in Resection and Reconstruction Using Virtual Surgery Simulation. *Craniomaxillofac. Trauma Reconstr.* **2016**, *9*, 271–276. [CrossRef]
41. Bell, R.B.; Weimer, K.A.; Dierks, E.J.; Buehler, M.; Lubek, J.E. Computer planning and intraoperative navigation for palatomaxillary and mandibular reconstruction with fibular free flaps. *J. Oral Maxillofac. Surg.* **2011**, *69*, 724–732. [CrossRef]
42. Shan, X.F.; Chen, H.M.; Liang, J.; Huang, J.W.; Zhang, L.; Cai, Z.G.; Guo, C. Surgical navigation-assisted mandibular reconstruction with fibula flaps. *Int. J. Oral Maxillofac. Surg.* **2016**, *45*, 448–453. [CrossRef]
43. Heiland, M.; Habermann, C.R.; Schmelzle, R. Indications and limitations of intraoperative navigation in maxillofacial surgery. *J. Oral Maxillofac. Surg.* **2004**, *62*, 1059–1063. [CrossRef]
44. Casap, N.; Wexler, A.; Eliashar, R. Computerized navigation for surgery of the lower jaw: Comparison of 2 navigation systems. *J. Oral Maxillofac. Surg.* **2008**, *66*, 1467–1475. [CrossRef]
45. Widmann, G.; Keiler, M.; Zangerl, A.; Stoffner, R.; Longato, S.; Bale, R.; Puelacher, W. Computer-assisted surgery in the edentulous jaw based on 3 fixed intraoral reference points. *J. Oral Maxillofac. Surg.* **2010**, *68*, 1140–1147. [CrossRef]

Journal of
Clinical Medicine

MDPI

Article

Mechanical Fatigue Performance of Patient-Specific Polymer Plates in Oncologic Mandible Reconstruction

Julian Lommen [1], Lara Schorn [1,*], Christoph Sproll [1], Norbert R. Kübler [1], Luis Fernando Nicolini [2], Ricarda Merfort [2], Ayimire Dilimulati [2], Frank Hildebrand [2], Majeed Rana [1] and Johannes Greven [2]

1 Department of Oral-, Maxillofacial and Facial Plastic Surgery, University Hospital Düsseldorf, Moorenstr. 5, 40225 Dusseldorf, Germany; julian.lommen@med.uni-duesseldorf.de (J.L.); christoph.sproll@med.uni-duesseldorf.de (C.S.); kuebler@med.uni-duesseldorf.de (N.R.K.); rana@med.uni-duesseldorf.de (M.R.)

2 Department of Orthopedics, Trauma and Reconstructive Surgery, RWTH Aachen University Hospital, Pauwelsstreet 30, 52074 Aachen, Germany; lnicolini@ukaachen.de (L.F.N.); rmerfort@ukaachen.de (R.M.); ayimire.dilimulati@alumni.fh-aachen.de (A.D.); fhildebrand@ukaachen.de (F.H.); jgreven@ukaachen.de (J.G.)

* Correspondence: lara.schorn@med.uni-duesseldorf.de; Tel.: +49-211-18189

Abstract: Mandible defects are conventionally reconstructed using titanium plates. However, titanium causes metallic artifacts which impair radiological imaging. This study aims at evaluating mechanical fatigue of radiolucent fiber-reinforced polyetheretherketone (f-PEEK), polyetheretherketone (PEEK), polyetherketoneketone (PEKK), and polyphenylsulfone (PPSU) polymer plates for mandible reconstruction. A total of 30 plates (titanium [n = 6], f-PEEK [n = 6], PEEK [n = 6], PEKK [n = 6], PPSU [n = 6]) were implanted in synthetic mandibulectomized polyurethane mandibles. Servo-pneumatic mechanical testing with cyclic application of 30–300 N at 3 Hz was conducted. Bite forces were 70% on the unresected and 30% on the resected side. Total number of cycles was set to 250,000. Testing was aborted in case of plate or screw failure. Axial load to failure was tested with a speed of 1 mm/s. Kruskal–Wallis and Dunn's post hoc tests were used. Titanium, f-PEEK, and PEEK showed no failure in fatigue testing and PPSU ($p < 0.001$) failed against titanium, f-PEEK, PEEK, and PEKK. Titanium allowed the highest load to failure compared to f-PEEK ($p = 0.049$), PEEK ($p = 0.008$), PEKK ($p < 0.001$), and PPSU ($p = 0.007$). f-PEEK, PEEK, and PEKK withstood expected physiological bite force. Although titanium plates provided the highest fatigue strength, f-PEEK and PEEK plates showed no failure over 250,000 chewing cycles indicating sufficient mechanical strength for mandible reconstruction.

Keywords: reconstruction plate; segmental mandibulectomy; polymer plate; mechanical properties; polyetheretherketone; polyetherketoneketone; polyphenylsulfone; computer-aided design (CAD); computer-aided manufacturing (CAM)

Citation: Lommen, J.; Schorn, L.; Sproll, C.; Kübler, N.R.; Nicolini, L.F.; Merfort, R.; Dilimulati, A.; Hildebrand, F.; Rana, M.; Greven, J. Mechanical Fatigue Performance of Patient-Specific Polymer Plates in Oncologic Mandible Reconstruction. *J. Clin. Med.* **2022**, *11*, 3308. https://doi.org/10.3390/jcm11123308

Academic Editors: Mark L. Urken, Carlos Navarro Cuéllar and José Luis Cebrián-Carretero

Received: 20 May 2022
Accepted: 7 June 2022
Published: 9 June 2022

1. Introduction

Surgical treatment of patients with oral squamous cell carcinoma (OSCC) often requires substantial osseous resection including segmental mandibulectomy when medullary bone infiltration is diagnosed [1]. In those cases, surgical reconstruction of the mandible is commonly conducted by implantation of rigid titanium reconstruction plates to restore the mandibular continuity. These plates can be conventionally bent intraoperatively or patient-specifically and offer a high degree of mechanical stability [2]. Computer-aided designing of patient-specific titanium implants (PSI) using precise selective laser melting techniques improves postoperative masticatory function, esthetics, and quality of life in patients [3]. Due to sophisticated fitting accuracy, the use of PSI in mandibular reconstruction is widely accepted [4]. However, titanium plates cause significant streak and blooming artifacts in computer tomography (CT) images thwarting thorough radiological assessment of implant surrounding tissues [5]. This phenomenon disadvantageously affects postoperative radiological tumor follow-up as well as adjuvant radiotherapy strongly dependent on a high-resolution, artifact-free planning CT [6]. Furthermore, titanium implants cause a radiation dose enhancement affecting the immediate surrounding tissues [7].

As a counterpart to this, it could be shown that various types of polymer reconstruction plates consisting of polyetheretherketone (PEEK), polyetherketoneketone (PEKK), polyphenylsulfone (PPSU), and polyethylene (PE) cause significantly fewer artifacts in CT images leading to better image quality [5]. Because bite forces after segmental mandibulectomy remain limited, presumably frangible polymer reconstruction materials have become of enormous scientific interest [8]. With this background, even glass fiber-reinforced composite plates which have been shown to provide less fatigue strength and stiffness compared to titanium plates might be an option for mandibular reconstructions [9]. The polyaromatic semi-crystalline PEEK is a tough, rigid, and biocompatible osteosynthesis material widely used in cranioplasty and facial reconstructive surgery [10,11]. PEKK is an elastic polymer with good shock absorbance properties and mechanical strength, whereas PPSU is a heat-resistant and stable polymer [12,13]. There are no scientific data on the biomechanical strength of PEEK, carbon fiber-reinforced polyetheretherketone (f-PEEK), PEKK, and PPSU used as reconstruction plates after segmental mandibulectomy.

Consequently, the aim of the present study was to evaluate mechanical fatigue of patient-specific PEEK, f-PEEK, PEKK, and PPSU reconstruction plates compared to titanium plates. We hypothesize that polymer plates endure a comparable number of cycles until failure providing sufficient stability to withstand expected physiological bite forces after segmental mandibulectomy.

2. Materials and Methods

2.1. Test Specimens

A total number of 30 synthetic polyurethane mandibles (SYNBONE®, Zizers, Switzerland) with the model number 8950 were used in this study. As described by numerous other studies these mandibles have a striking resemblance to human bone and are as similar as possible to the original anatomical shape [9,14–16]. All mandibles used in this study were standardized models from the same lot number. None of the mandibles had missing teeth prior to segmental mandibulectomy.

2.2. Plates and Screws

Titanium (Ti6Al4V ELI (Grade 23), SLM Solutions, Lübeck, Germany), PEEK (VESTAKEEP® i4 3DF T, Evonik, Essen, Germany), f-PEEK (TECAFIL PEEK MT CF 30, Ensinger, Seewalchen, Austria), PEKK (PEKK Filament, Kumovis, Munich, Germany), and PPSU (Veriva® PPSU, Solvay, Hanover, Germany) reconstruction plates were used in this trial (Figure 1). All plates are identical in design and dimensions and only differ in the used material. For rigid fixation, all plates contained four screw holes on both sides of the defect marked as positions 1–8 (Figure 1). Plate thickness was 3.0 mm for all plates. Bicortical self-retaining titanium screws with a diameter of 2.7 mm and a 2.2 × 105 mm drill without stop were used for plate fixation. For respective screw parameters see Table 1.

2.3. Virtual Planning, Shaping, and Manufacturing of Reconstruction Plates

ATOS Core 135 MV135 scanner (GOM GmbH, Braunschweig, Germany) was used for computer-aided design and manufacturing (CAD/CAM) of titanium, PEEK, f-PEEK, PEKK, and PPSU plates. Segmentation, 3D reconstruction, and virtual planning was conducted using the software Individual Patient Solution, IPS Gate® (KLS Martin Group®, Tuttlingen, Germany) (Figure 2). The 3D virtual model was subsequently converted to stereolithography (STL) image files using Mimics 21.0© (Materialise NV, Belgium). Webinar-based (Microsoft© Teams, Redmond, WA, USA) virtual surgery between surgeons and engineers from KLS Martin© defined defect size of segmental mandibulectomy (Figure 2). Dimensions of titanium and polymer plates were defined using Geomagic© Freeform Plus© (3D Systems©, Rock Hill, SC, USA) (Figure 2). Titanium plates were manufactured using an additive selective laser melting (SLM) procedure. f-PEEK, PEEK, PEKK, and PPSU plates were manufactured using additive fused filament fabrication (FFF). Resection guides were laser-sintered from polyamide (PA 2200).

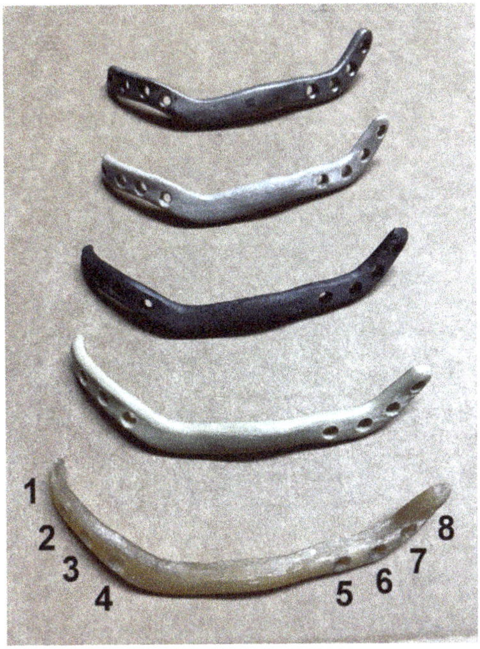

Figure 1. Display of the five different plates used for defect bridging. All plates in this trial are identical in design and dimensions. From top: titanium, polyetheretherketone (PEEK), fiber-reinforced polyetheretherketone (f-PEEK), polyetherketoneketone (PEKK), and polyphenylsulfone (PPSU). The numbers 1–8 symbolize the different drilling holes for implant orientation and selection of the required screw length.

Table 1. List of all screw types, positions and respective lengths.

Screw Type	Position	Screw Length (mm)
Ø 2.7 mm, locking (bicortical)	1	17
Ø 2.7 mm, locking (bicortical)	2	17
Ø 2.7 mm, locking (bicortical)	3	15
Ø 2.7 mm, locking (bicortical)	4	17
Ø 2.7 mm, locking (bicortical)	5	13
Ø 2.7 mm, locking (bicortical)	6	11
Ø 2.7 mm, locking (bicortical)	7	11
Ø 2.7 mm, locking (bicortical)	8	9

2.4. Plate Fixation to Test Specimens

For segmental mandibulectomy individualized polyamide resection-guides and rotating burrs were utilized. The first and second molar as well as premolar teeth were resected. No plate prepositioning before resection was conducted. For plate fixation, bicortical self-retaining titanium screws specifically positioned according to the plate design were used (Figure 3).

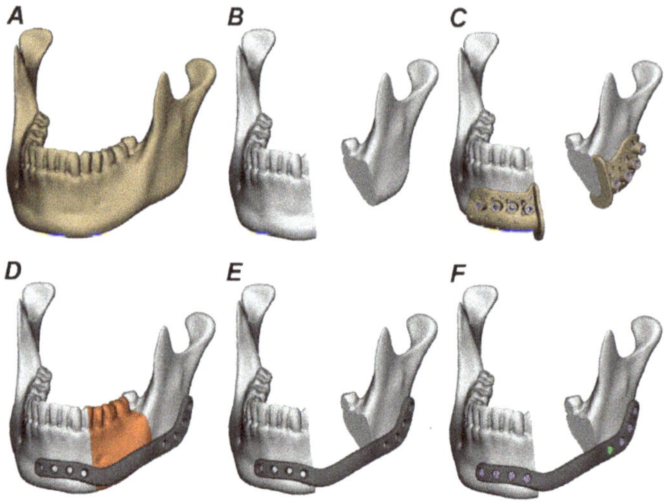

Figure 2. Segmentation, 3D reconstruction, and virtual planning of the mandibular defect size and plate design. (**A–C**), Digital image of the scanned polyurethane mandible before and after defining the defect size and planning the positioning of the resection guides. (**D–F**), Assessment of the adequate dimensions for patient-specific titanium and polymer plates using the medical modeling software (Geomagic© Freeform Plus© from 3D Systems ©, Rock Hill, SC, USA).

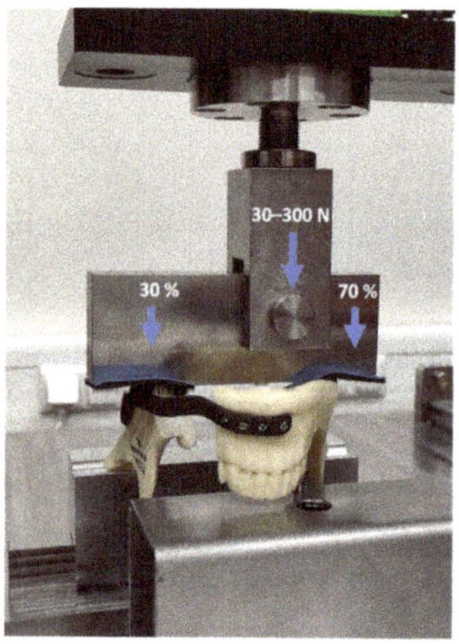

Figure 3. Display of servo-hydraulic mechanical testing with a MTS Bionix (Eden Prairie, MN, USA) testing machine. Cyclical loading of bite forces between 30 and 300 N with distribution of 30% of maximum force on the resected and 70% on the unresected side of the mandible.

2.5. Mechanical Testing

Based on prior studies simulating bite forces after segmental mandibulectomy controlled application of 300 N in the premolar region of the mandibles was conducted [17]. As current literature suggests bite forces were set to 70% on the unresected and 30% on the resected side of the specimen using a see-saw device [16]. Fatigue mechanical testing was carried out with a custom-made servo pneumatic test stand (DynaMess, Stolberg, Germany) with cyclical application of bite forces of up to 300 N. The force applied on the specimen was controlled and recorded by a force transducer that provides a maximum error of 1% relative to the target value. Fixation of mandibles in the testing machine is displayed in Figure 3. The minimum preload force of 30 N was set for practical reasons to prevent dislocation of the mandibles. Frequency was adjusted to 3 Hz. The total number of cycles was set to 250,000 (and 500,000 for titanium) which roughly represents the amount of chewing cycles per year [16] and was recorded at a frequency of 100 Hz [18]. Testing was stopped in case of plate or screw failure or significant deformation of osteosynthesis materials; cycles were then recorded up to the point of failure. If 250,000 cycles of fatigue loading were completed without failure, the bone–implant construct was exposed to axial load to failure compression testing with a testing speed of 1 mm/s [19].

2.6. Statistical Analysis

Statistical analyses were conducted using Microsoft Excel© (Microsoft Corporation, Redmond, WA, USA) and IBM© SPSS© Statistics (Version 22, IBM GmbH, Ehningen, Germany). Levene's test was used to assess homogeneity of variance. Kruskal Wallis test and Wilcoxon signed-rank test were used for comparative analyses between groups. Post-hoc Bonferroni analysis was done using Dunn's test. A p-value < 0.05 was considered statistically significant.

3. Results

3.1. Fatigue Test

In total 29 plates were tested in the fatigue test over the course of 250,000 cycles to analyze plate failure. All titanium, f-PEEK, and PEEK plates (n = 6) showed no signs of failure after completion of 250,000 cycles. There was no statistical difference between these three plate materials. Of all tested PEKK plates (n = 6), five showed no signs of failure and one plate broke after 25,701 cycles. All PPSU plates (n = 5) broke during testing after as little as 6 cycles and lasting a maximum of 110,997 cycles before failure. Since all five PPSU plates broke quite early, the last PPSU plate was spared for use in load to failure testing. Statistical differences were found between PPSU and titanium ($p < 0.001$), f-PEEK ($p < 0.001$), PEEK ($p < 0.001$), and PEKK ($p < 0.001$) plates. A summary of the results of the fatigue test is given in Table 2 and Figure 4.

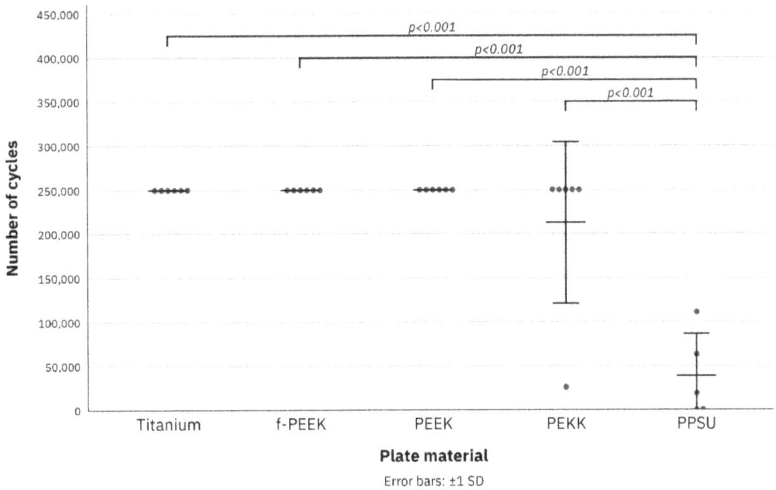

Figure 4. Boxplot diagram of the results of fatigue test for titanium, fiber-reinforced polyetheretherketone (f-PEEK), polyetheretherketone (PEEK), polyetherketoneketone (PEKK) and polyphenylsulfone (PPSU) plates over the course of 250,000 cycles. Error bars: ±1 standard deviation. Jitter display for numbers of the same value.

Table 2. Results of the fatigue test. N/A: Plate used in load to failure test.

Plate Number	Plate Material	Number of Cycles	Plate Failure	Screw Failure
1	Titanium	250,000	No	No
2	Titanium	250,000	No	No
3	Titanium	250,000	No	No
4	Titanium	250,000	No	No
5	Titanium	250,000	No	No
6	Titanium	250,000	No	No
1	f-PEEK	250,000	No	No
2	f-PEEK	250,000	No	No
3	f-PEEK	250,000	No	No
4	f-PEEK	250,000	No	No
5	f-PEEK	250,000	No	No
6	f-PEEK	250,000	No	No
1	PEEK	250,000	No	No
2	PEEK	250,000	No	No
3	PEEK	250,000	No	No
4	PEEK	250,000	No	No
5	PEEK	250,000	No	No
6	PEEK	250,000	No	No
1	PEKK	250,000	No	No
2	PEKK	25,701	Yes	No
3	PEKK	250,000	No	No
4	PEKK	250,000	No	No
5	PEKK	250,000	No	No
6	PEKK	250,000	No	No
1	PPSU	285	Yes	No
2	PPSU	6	Yes	No
3	PPSU	19,011	Yes	No
4	PPSU	63,075	Yes	No
5	PPSU	110,997	Yes	No
6	PPSU	N/A	N/A	N/A

3.2. *Load to Failure Test*

None of the six titanium plates broke in a load to failure test to a maximum force of 1500 N. One titanium plate was tested at a maximum force of 2281 N with no signs of failure of the plate but failure of the specimen. f-PEEK plates broke at a maximum force of 443 N and PEEK plates broke at a maximum force of 545 N. PEKK plates broke at a maximum force of 440 N with one plate already breaking over the course of the fatigue test. Since five PPSU plates already broke in the fatigue test only one PPSU plate could be tested in the load to failure test. PPSU broke at a maximum force of 326 N. Statistical differences were found between PPSU and titanium ($p = 0.007$), PEKK and titanium ($p < 0.001$), PEKK and f-PEEK (0.046), PEEK and titanium ($p = 0.008$), and f-PEEK and titanium ($p = 0.049$). A summary of the results of the load to failure test is given in Table 3 and Figure 5.

Table 3. Results of the load to failure test. N/A: Plate broke in fatigue test.

Plate Number	Plate Material	Maximum Force (N)
1	Titanium *	2281
2	Titanium **	1500
3	Titanium **	1500
4	Titanium **	1500
5	Titanium **	1500
6	Titanium **	1500

Table 3. *Cont.*

Plate Number	Plate Material	Maximum Force (N)
1	f-PEEK	443
2	f-PEEK	711
3	f-PEEK	733
4	f-PEEK	679
5	f-PEEK	684
6	f-PEEK	709
1	PEEK	698
2	PEEK	565
3	PEEK	586
4	PEEK	601
5	PEEK	554
6	PEEK	545
1	PEKK	440
2	PEKK	N/A
3	PEKK	509
4	PEKK	545
5	PEKK	545
6	PEKK	458
1	PPSU	N/A
2	PPSU	N/A
3	PPSU	N/A
4	PPSU	N/A
5	PPSU	N/A
6	PPSU	326

* Failure of the polyurethan mandible. ** Maximum force was set to 1500 N, no failure occurred.

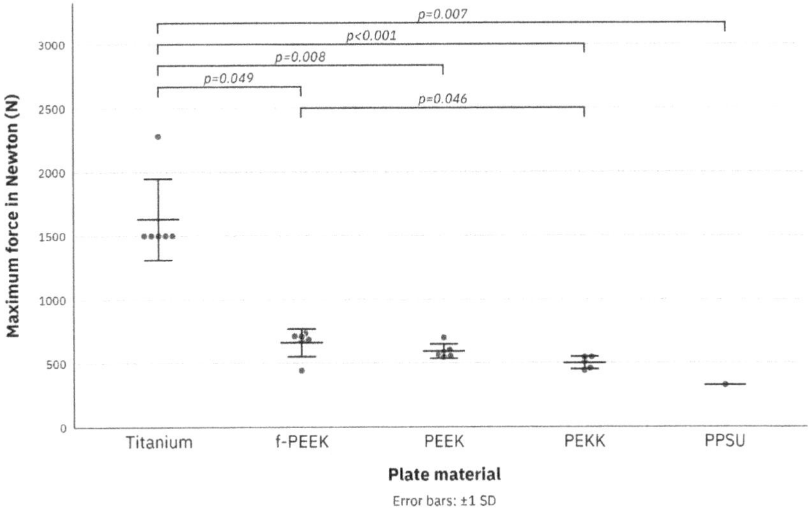

Figure 5. Boxplot diagram of the results of load to failure test for titanium, fiber-reinforced polyetheretherketone (f-PEEK), polyetheretherketone (PEEK), polyetherketoneketone (PEKK), and polyphenylsulfone (PPSU) plates for maximum force of 2500 Newton [N]. Error bars: ±1 standard deviation. Jitter display for numbers of the same value.

4. Discussion

The use of durable patient-specific titanium plates for reconstruction of the mandible in patients with OSCC is common practice. A recent study found that CAD/CAM titanium reconstruction plates provide higher fatigue strength compared to miniplates and higher stiffness compared to manually bend reconstruction plates [14]. Despite their conventional use in oncological head and neck reconstruction, metallic artifact formation in CT and MRI scans as well as impediments in radiation dose calculations in adjuvant radiation therapy remain a serious medical problem [20,21]. In the wake of scientific efforts to counter these problems, polymer materials are increasingly being investigated as possible substitutes. Just recently it was shown that the polymer materials PEEK, PEKK, PPSU, and PE cause significantly fewer artifacts in CT imaging when used as mandible reconstruction plates compared to titanium tested on human cadavers [5].

However, this alone does not justify their application as interchangeable plates in reconstructive surgery as only few studies have evaluated the biomechanical properties of such polymers. A recent study found that despite glass fiber-reinforced composite (GFRC) reconstruction plates providing less stiffness compared to CAD/CAM titanium plates, primary stability for mandible reconstruction with an osseous free flap is sufficient [9]. The results of the present study show that carbon fiber reinforced PEEK plates provide comparable fatigue strength under cyclic chewing forces. This is a very promising result since the average time for adequate bone union of a vascularized osseous fibula flap was found to be 21.3 weeks in another recent study [22]. Under this scientific assumption, polymer plates in mandible reconstruction would only need to provide primary stability for approximately 6 months until sturdy bone union is achieved. As the study by Schupp et al., (2007) suggests, the number of annual chewing cycles with considerable bite forces is estimated to be 250,000 [16,23]. Therefore, the results of the present study indicate that f-PEEK and PEEK reconstruction plates offer sufficient fatigue strength and stiffness to endure regular bite forces at least over the course of one year. Since maximum bite forces of adult men and women are reported to be 284.90 N and 304.96 N respectively, the presented data show that not only f-PEEK and PEEK but also PEKK plates withstood simulated physiological bite forces [24]. Reduced bites forces after segmental mandibulectomy and the small proportion of patients being fully prosthodontically rehabilitated in the long-term warrant consideration of polymer plates as possible future alternatives for titanium plates [1]. However, the data of the presented study only evaluated fatigue strength of polymer plates in one defect location of the body of the mandible. In the future, it is advisable to also test fatigue strength of polymer plates bridging larger mandibular defects, especially when the midline is crossed. Since time of postoperative radiation therapy in tumor patients at advanced clinical stage should ideally not exceed 6 weeks, mechanical properties of f-PEEK and PEEK plates presumably suffice [25]. In case of a two-stage surgical approach, prolonged plate stability becomes particularly important to prevent plate fracture before reconstruction with a bone graft. When plates are combined with an osseous free flap, a sufficient time frame for primary stability and bone union also appears likely. Some studies suggest stiffness being the most important aspect of stability of osteosynthesis materials [26]. All screws and plates in the presented study were of locking-type which further increases mechanical stiffness. None of the inserted screws in this study broke. However, interaction between polymer locking plates and titanium locking screws needs to be regarded as weaker compared to fully-titanium components. There are studies indicating that overly stiff CAD/CAM titanium plates could obstruct bone union by preventing a certain amount of bone fragment movement which is considered beneficial [14,27]. Therefore, hypothetically, the weaker polymer plates may support ossification of bone grafts to a certain extent. However, it needs to be clarified that the present study did not evaluate bone union or interfragmentary movement—a strong predictor of pseudarthrosis—of a bone graft fixated with polymer plates. Insertion of a bone graft after segmental mandibulectomy may stabilize the anterior and posterior bony ends and possibly deceases torque of the reconstruction plate [28]. This might further increase fatigue strength of polymer plates and should be tested in future trials.

At this time, it remains scientifically unclear which factors positively influence bone healing after segmental mandibulectomy. Since all titanium and polymer plates in the present study were manufactured with identical dimensions and inserted with the same type of screw, system comparability of results is high. However, the described individual manufacturing of patient-specific polymer plates poses the disadvantage that plates cannot be adjusted during surgery. Therefore, precise preoperative planning is a key factor for an excellent outcome. It has been indicated that plate thickness might be a relevant factor for soft tissue complications such as plate exposure [29]. The study by Rendenbach et al., (2019) used 2-mm thick GFRC plates in their tests [9]. This is slightly thinner than the 3-mm polymer plates used in the present study. Since conventional CAD/CAM titanium plates typically show a thickness between 2 and 3 mm, it seems unlikely that the polymer materials will cause a drastic increase in soft tissue complications even though this has not yet been investigated. The presented data have their limitations as they have not been tested under in vivo conditions. Patient gender, age, comorbidities as well as soft tissue management have not been evaluated in this study. Moreover, the number of residual teeth in patients with OSCC prior to surgery varies. As the dentition is a strong predictor for expected residual bite forces after segmental mandibulectomy, it is likely that numerous patients present with lower bite forces compared to the forces tested in this study [30]. Consequently, polymer plate fracture especially in combination with a bone graft might be less likely in vivo.

In considering the immediate scientific future, recent studies have focused on tissue engineering procedures based on the release of growth factors from polymer materials to improve bone healing [31,32]. The use of bone morphogenetic protein-2 (rhBMP-2) with a collagen carrier was shown to provide good osseous regeneration even without concomitant bone materials [33]. The study group of the present trial previously showed that insoluble bovine collagenous bone matrices have a better release kinetic of the model protein fluorescein conjugated bovine serum albumin (FITC-BSA) when coated with medium molecular size polymers [34]. Such coatings might also be possible for polymer reconstruction plates of the mandible shown in the present study. It remains to be seen how such polymer plates perform in vivo.

5. Conclusions

CAD/CAM titanium reconstruction plates still provide a higher fatigue strength compared to f-PEEK, PEEK, PEKK, and PPSU polymers. However, f-PEEK and PEEK plates showed no failure over the simulated 250,000 chewing cycles certifying sufficient maximal mechanical strength and durability under cyclic physiological load for mandible reconstruction. Future trials need to assess interaction between the polymers and soft tissues on a molecular level.

Author Contributions: Conceptualization, J.L., L.S., and N.R.K.; methodology, J.G., J.L., R.M.; software, M.R., J.L.; validation, L.F.N.; formal analysis, A.D., J.L.; investigation, A.D.; resources, J.G.; data curation, A.D.; writing—original draft preparation, J.L.; writing—review and editing, J.L., J.G., C.S., R.M., L.F.N.; visualization, J.G., J.L., R.M.; supervision, F.H., N.R.K.; project administration, C.S. All authors have read and agreed to the published version of the manuscript.

Funding: This research received no external funding.

Institutional Review Board Statement: Not applicable.

Informed Consent Statement: Not applicable.

Data Availability Statement: Not applicable.

Acknowledgments: We thank Frank Reinauer, Veit Irion, and Adem Aksu from KLS Martin Group for their support in designing and manufacturing implants and screws.

Conflicts of Interest: The authors declare no conflict of interest. The funders had no role in the design of the study; in the collection, analyses, or interpretation of data; in the writing of the manuscript, or in the decision to publish the results.

References

1. Sproll, C.K.; Holtmann, H.; Schorn, L.K.; Jansen, T.M.; Reifenberger, J.; Boeck, I.; Rana, M.; Kübler, N.R.; Lommen, J. Mandible handling in the surgical treatment of oral squamous cell carcinoma: Lessons from clinical results after marginal and segmental mandibulectomy. *Oral Surg. Oral Med. Oral Pathol. Oral Radiol.* **2020**, *129*, 556–564. [CrossRef] [PubMed]
2. Möllmann, H.L.; Apeltrath, L.; Karnatz, N.; Wilkat, M.; Riedel, E.; Singh, D.D.; Rana, M. Comparison of the Accuracy and Clinical Parameters of Patient-Specific and Conventionally Bended Plates for Mandibular Reconstruction. *Front. Oncol.* **2021**, *11*, 719028. [CrossRef] [PubMed]
3. Vignesh, U.; Mehrotra, D.; Howlader, D.; Singh, P.K.; Gupta, S. Patient Specific Three-Dimensional Implant for Reconstruction of Complex Mandibular Defect. *J. Craniofacial Surg.* **2019**, *30*, e308–e311.
4. Toto, J.M.; Chang, E.I.; Agag, R.; Devarajan, K.; Patel, S.A.; Topham, N.S. Improved operative efficiency of free fibula flap mandible reconstruction with patient-specific, computer-guided preoperative planning. *Head Neck* **2015**, *37*, 1660–1664. [CrossRef] [PubMed]
5. Lommen, J.; Schorn, L.; Sproll, C.; Haussmann, J.; Kübler, N.R.; Budach, W.; Rana, M.; Tamaskovics, B. Reduction of CT Artifacts Using Polyetheretherketone (PEEK), Polyetherketoneketone (PEKK), Polyphenylsulfone (PPSU), and Polyethylene (PE) Reconstruction Plates in Oral Oncology. *J. Oral Maxillofac. Surg.* **2022**, in press. [CrossRef]
6. Bojechko, C.; Hua, P.; Sumner, W.; Guram, K.; Atwood, T.; Sharabi, A. Adaptive replanning using cone beam CT for deformation of original CT simulation. *J. Med. Radiat. Sci.* **2021**, *69*, 267–272. [CrossRef]
7. Friedrich, R.E.; Todorovic, M.; Heiland, M.; Scheuer, H.A.; Krüll, A. Scattering effects of irradiation on surroundings calculated for a small dental implant. *Anticancer Res.* **2012**, *32*, 2043–2046.
8. Maurer, P.; Pistner, H.; Schubert, J. Computer assisted chewing power in patients with segmental resection of the mandible. *Mund Kiefer Gesichtschir.* **2006**, *10*, 37–41. [CrossRef]
9. Rendenbach, C.; Steffen, C.; Sellenschloh, K.; Heyland, M.; Morlock, M.M.; Toivonen, J.; Moritz, N.; Smeets, R.; Heiland, M.; Vallittu, P.K.; et al. Patient specific glass fiber reinforced composite versus titanium plate: A comparative biomechanical analysis under cyclic dynamic loading. *J. Mech. Behav. Biomed. Mater.* **2019**, *91*, 212–219. [CrossRef]
10. Zhang, J.; Tian, W.; Chen, J.; Yu, J.; Zhang, J.; Chen, J. The application of polyetheretherketone (PEEK) implants in cranioplasty. *Brain Res. Bull.* **2019**, *153*, 143–149. [CrossRef]
11. Panayotov, I.V.; Orti, V.; Cuisinier, F.; Yachouh, J. Polyetheretherketone (PEEK) for medical applications. *J. Mater. Sci. Mater. Med.* **2016**, *27*, 118. [CrossRef] [PubMed]
12. Alqurashi, H.; Khurshid, Z.; Syed, A.U.Y.; Rashid Habib, S.; Rokaya, D.; Zafar, M.S. Polyetherketoneketone (PEKK): An emerging biomaterial for oral implants and dental prostheses. *J. Adv. Res.* **2021**, *28*, 87–95. [CrossRef] [PubMed]
13. Díez-Pascual, A.M.; Díez-Vicente, A.L. Effect of TiO(2) nanoparticles on the performance of polyphenylsulfone biomaterial for orthopaedic implants. *J. Mater. Chem. B* **2014**, *2*, 7502–7514. [CrossRef] [PubMed]
14. Rendenbach, C.; Sellenschloh, K.; Gerbig, L.; Morlock, M.M.; Beck-Broichsitter, B.; Smeets, R.; Heiland, M.; Huber, G.; Hanken, H. CAD-CAM plates versus conventional fixation plates for primary mandibular reconstruction: A biomechanical in vitro analysis. *J. Craniomaxillofac. Surg.* **2017**, *45*, 1878–1883. [CrossRef]
15. Steiner, T.; Raith, S.; Scherer, E.; Mücke, T.; Torsiglieri, T.; Rohleder, N.H.; Eder, M.; Grohmann, I.; Kesting, M.; Bier, H.; et al. Which kind of frontal mandibulotomy is the smartest? A biomechanical study. *J. Craniomaxillofac. Surg.* **2015**, *43*, 199–203. [CrossRef]
16. Schupp, W.; Arzdorf, M.; Linke, B.; Gutwald, R. Biomechanical testing of different osteosynthesis systems for segmental resection of the mandible. *J. Oral Maxillofac. Surg.* **2007**, *65*, 924–930. [CrossRef]
17. Slagter, A.P.; Bosman, F.; van der Glas, H.W.; van der Bilt, A. Human jaw-elevator muscle activity and food comminution in the dentate and edentulous state. *Arch. Oral Biol.* **1993**, *38*, 195–205. [CrossRef]
18. Nicolini, L.F.; Kobbe, P.; Seggewiß, J.; Greven, J.; Ribeiro, M.; Beckmann, A.; Da Paz, S.; Eschweiler, J.; Prescher, A.; Markert, B.; et al. Motion preservation surgery for scoliosis with a vertebral body tethering system: A biomechanical study. *Eur. Spine J.* **2022**, *31*, 1013–1021. [CrossRef]
19. Brandes, L.L.; Nicolini, L.F.; Greven, J.; Lichte, P.; Stopinski, T.T.; Sattler, M.; Hildebrand, F.; Pishnamaz, M. Biomechanical Performance of BoneHelix(®) Compared with Elastic Stable Intramedullary Nailing (ESIN) in a Pediatric Tibia Fracture Model. *Life* **2021**, *11*, 1189. [CrossRef]
20. Radzi, S.; Cowin, G.; Robinson, M.; Pratap, J.; Volp, A.; Schuetz, M.A.; Schmutz, B. Metal artifacts from titanium and steel screws in CT, 1.5T and 3T MR images of the tibial Pilon: A quantitative assessment in 3D. *Quant. Imaging Med. Surg.* **2014**, *4*, 163–172.
21. Kovacs, D.G.; Rechner, L.A.; Appelt, A.L.; Berthelsen, A.K.; Costa, J.C.; Friborg, J.; Persson, G.F.; Bangsgaard, J.P.; Specht, L.; Aznar, M.C. Metal artefact reduction for accurate tumour delineation in radiotherapy. *Radiother. Oncol.* **2018**, *126*, 479–486. [CrossRef] [PubMed]
22. Liu, S.; Tao, S.; Tan, J.; Hu, X.; Liu, H.; Li, Z. Long-term follow-up of fibular graft for the reconstruction of bone defects. *Medicine* **2018**, *97*, e12605. [CrossRef] [PubMed]
23. Bates, J.F.; Stafford, G.D.; Harrison, A. Masticatory function-a review of the literature: (II) Speed of movement of the mandible, rate of chewing and forces developed in chewing. *J. Oral Rehabil.* **1975**, *2*, 349–361. [CrossRef] [PubMed]
24. Takaki, P.; Vieira, M.; Bommarito, S. Maximum bite force analysis in different age groups. *Int. Arch. Otorhinolaryngol.* **2014**, *18*, 272–276. [PubMed]

25. Franco, R.; de Matos, L.L.; Kulcsar, M.A.V.; de Castro-Júnior, G.; Marta, G.N. Influence of time between surgery and postoperative radiation therapy and total treatment time in locoregional control of patients with head and neck cancer: A single center experience. *Clinics* **2020**, *75*, e1615. [CrossRef]
26. Henschel, J.; Tsai, S.; Fitzpatrick, D.C.; Marsh, J.L.; Madey, S.M.; Bottlang, M. Comparison of 4 Methods for Dynamization of Locking Plates: Differences in the Amount and Type of Fracture Motion. *J. Orthop. Trauma* **2017**, *31*, 531–537. [CrossRef]
27. Trainotti, S.; Raith, S.; Kesting, M.; Eichhorn, S.; Bauer, F.; Kolk, A.; Lethaus, B.; Hölzle, F.; Steiner, T. Locking versus nonlocking plates in mandibular reconstruction with fibular graft–a biomechanical ex vivo study. *Clin. Oral Investig.* **2014**, *18*, 1291–1298. [CrossRef]
28. Park, S.M.; Lee, J.W.; Noh, G. Which plate results in better stability after segmental mandibular resection and fibula free flap reconstruction? Biomechanical analysis. *Oral Surg. Oral Med. Oral Pathol. Oral Radiol.* **2018**, *126*, 380–389. [CrossRef]
29. Brown, J.S.; Lowe, D.; Kanatas, A.; Schache, A. Mandibular reconstruction with vascularised bone flaps: A systematic review over 25 years. *Br. J. Oral Maxillofac. Surg.* **2017**, *55*, 113–126. [CrossRef]
30. Okuyama, K.; Michi, Y.; Mizutani, M.; Yamashiro, M.; Kaida, A.; Harada, K. Clinical study on mandibular fracture after marginal resection of the mandible. *Oral Surg. Oral Med. Oral Pathol. Oral Radiol.* **2016**, *121*, 461–467. [CrossRef]
31. Vallittu, P.K.; Närhi, T.O.; Hupa, L. Fiber glass-bioactive glass composite for bone replacing and bone anchoring implants. *Dent. Mater.* **2015**, *31*, 371–381. [CrossRef] [PubMed]
32. Seto, I.; Marukawa, E.; Asahina, I. Mandibular reconstruction using a combination graft of rhBMP-2 with bone marrow cells expanded in vitro. *Plast. Reconstr. Surg.* **2006**, *117*, 902–908. [CrossRef] [PubMed]
33. Herford, A.S.; Boyne, P.J. Reconstruction of mandibular continuity defects with bone morphogenetic protein-2 (rhBMP-2). *J. Oral Maxillofac. Surg.* **2008**, *66*, 616–624. [CrossRef] [PubMed]
34. Lommen, J.; Schorn, L.; Landers, A.; Holtmann, H.; Berr, K.; Kübler, N.R.; Sproll, C.; Rana, M.; Depprich, R. Release kinetics of the model protein FITC-BSA from different polymer-coated bovine bone substitutes. *Head Face Med.* **2019**, *15*, 27. [CrossRef]

Journal of
Clinical Medicine

MDPI

Article

Virtual Surgical Planning and Customized Subperiosteal Titanium Maxillary Implant (CSTMI) for Three Dimensional Reconstruction and Dental Implants of Maxillary Defects after Oncological Resection: Case Series

Jose Luís Cebrián Carretero [1], José Luis Del Castillo Pardo de Vera [1,*], Néstor Montesdeoca García [2], Pablo Garrido Martínez [2], Marta María Pampín Martínez [1], Iñigo Aragón Niño [1], Ignacio Navarro Cuéllar [3] and Carlos Navarro Cuéllar [3]

1 Oral and Maxillofacial Surgery Department, Hospital La Paz, Paseo de la Castellana, 261, 28046 Madrid, Spain
2 Oral and Maxillofacial Surgery Department, Hospital La Luz, 28003 Madrid, Spain
3 Oral and Maxillofacial Surgery Department, General Universitario HLA Moncloa, Avenida de Valladolid, 83, 28008 Madrid, Spain
* Correspondence: jldelcastillopardo@gmail.com

Citation: Cebrián Carretero, J.L.; Del Castillo Pardo de Vera, J.L.; Montesdeoca García, N.; Garrido Martínez, P.; Pampín Martínez, M.M.; Aragón Niño, I.; Navarro Cuéllar, I.; Navarro Cuéllar, C. Virtual Surgical Planning and Customized Subperiosteal Titanium Maxillary Implant (CSTMI) for Three Dimensional Reconstruction and Dental Implants of Maxillary Defects after Oncological Resection: Case Series. *J. Clin. Med.* **2022**, *11*, 4594. https://doi.org/10.3390/jcm11154594

Academic Editor: Mieszko Wieckiewicz

Received: 4 July 2022
Accepted: 31 July 2022
Published: 6 August 2022

Abstract: Maxillectomies cause malocclusion, masticatory disorders, swallowing disorders and poor nasolabial projection, with consequent esthetic and functional sequelae. Reconstruction can be achieved with conventional approaches, such as closure of the maxillary defect by microvascular free flap surgery or prosthetic obturation. Four patients with segmental maxillary defects that had been reconstructed with customized subperiosteal titanium maxillary implants (CSTMI) through virtual surgical planning (VSP), STL models and CAD/CAM titanium mesh were included. The smallest maxillary defect was 4.1 cm and the largest defect was 9.6 cm, with an average of 7.1 cm. The reconstructed maxillary vertical dimension ranged from 9.3 mm to 17.4 mm, with a mean of 13.17 mm. The transverse dimension of the maxilla at the crestal level was attempted to be reconstructed based on the pre-excision CT scan, and these measurements ranged from 6.5 mm in the premaxilla area to 14.6 mm at the posterior level. All patients were rehabilitated with a fixed prosthesis on subperiosteal implants with good esthetic and functional results. In conclusion, we believe that customized subperiosteal titanium maxillary implants (CSTMI) are a safe alternative for maxillary defects reconstruction, allowing for simultaneous dental rehabilitation while restoring midface projection. Nonetheless, prospective and randomized trials are required with long-term follow-up, to assess its long-term performance and safety.

Keywords: subperiosteal maxillary implants; 3D reconstruction; oral rehabilitation

1. Introduction

The maxilla is a very important structure in the osseous structure of the face. Large maxillary defects secondary to trauma, congenital malformations and tumor resections cause serious bone and soft tissue defects, with consequent esthetic and functional sequelae [1]. Maxillectomy causes malocclusion, disorders of mastication, swallowing, speech and a deficient nasolabial projection and, consequently too of the midfacial center [2]. Its reconstruction requires independence of the oral, nasal and orbital cavities to achieve a functional reconstruction and bone restoration, as well as soft tissue support, which is a real challenge for the reconstructive surgeon [3,4].

Among the options employed during the last decades, the use of conventional techniques such as regional flaps (fascia and temporal muscle), prosthetic obturators, prostheses supported on zygomatic implants and the use of microvascularized flaps stand out [5,6]. However, the sealing of the maxillary defect by means of soft parts does not solve the problem of masticatory function, the use of prosthetic obturators [7] causes social and psychological problems for the patient that alter his quality of life and, sometimes, the use of zygomatic implants does not provide sufficient anchorage and stability in the prostheses [8].

For this reason, in recent years, reconstruction using microvascularized free flaps has become the technique of choice, since it allows for immediate reconstruction with a fairly predictable result and sometimes allows the placement of osseointegrated dental implants. The ultimate goal of reconstruction is to allow optimal dental rehabilitation [1–3].

The functions of the oral cavity depend on several factors, these being the volumetric reconstruction of the maxillary defect and the type of tissue used in the reconstruction (taking into account that sometimes if postoperative radiotherapy is required, the tissues lose stability and harden, which can hinder the placement and retention of a prosthesis), so that the placement of implants in the bone flaps are increasingly used to achieve adequate oral rehabilitation [5,9].

The most commonly used vascularized free flaps are the fibula flap, the antebrachial flap, iliac crest flap, rectus abdominis muscle flap, inferior abdominal artery perforator flap and the anterolateral thigh perforator flap. Among those that provide bone that could allow the placement of dental implants, they sometimes do not provide sufficient bone height to restore the maxillary ridge [10]. This discrepancy, as occurs in mandibular reconstruction, causes great difficulty in implant placement, causing overloading of the implants, with the risk of loss of the functional and esthetic result in the medium/long term. Therefore, a reconstruction is required that allows an adequate volumetric restitution for the optimal function of the implant-supported structure.

Subperiosteal implants were developed in Sweden at the beginning of the 1940s. Positioning these implants in the patient was very difficult and could cause a range of complications. In recent years, the digital revolution has meant a paradigm shift in the world of oral and maxillofacial surgery.

The purpose of this study was to evaluate the outcomes of the three-dimensional reconstruction of segmental maxillary defects with customized subperiosteal titanium maxillary implants (CSTMI) through virtual surgical planning (VSP), STL models and CAD/CAM titanium mesh [11]. STLs (stereolithographic models) are the files that include the three-dimensional information of the anatomical models; CAD/CAM (Computer-Aided Design and Manufacturing) is the process of three-dimensional design and fabrication of titanium mesh in a patient-specific manner through computer design and additive manufacturing via 3D printing.

2. Materials and Methods

2.1. Patients

To address the research purpose, the investigators performed a retrospective study, including patients with segmental maxillary oncological defects that had been reconstructed with a subperiosteal titanium maxillary implant at Hospital General Universitario La Paz (Madrid, Spain) between 2018 and 2021. Four oncologic patients were diagnosed with maxillary squamous cell carcinoma (Table 1).

Due to the difficulty or impossibility of bone reconstruction of the maxilla with the conventional techniques of bone grafting, microsurgical reconstruction or osteogenic distraction, all patients had previously used a removable dental prosthesis.

2.2. Preoperative Planning

Virtual surgical planning (VSP), stereolithographic models (STL) and a custom-made titanium meshes (CAD/CAM) (Avinent®, Madrid, Spain) were designed prior to surgery to enable both vertical and horizontal reconstruction of the maxillary defect. The surgery was planned with the help of high-resolution computed tomography using 0.5 mm thin slices, and plaster models were used to plan the optimal position of the dental crowns.

Table 1. Descriptive variables in all patients.

Gender Age (Years)	Diagnosis	Lenght of Defect (cm)	Vertical Reconstruction (mm)	Number of Implants	Radiotherapy	Functional Result	Aesthetic Result
M/59	Maxillary Squamous Cell Carcinoma	8.4	15.8	4	Yes	2	2
M/69	Maxillary Squamous Cell Carcinoma	6.3	10.2	6	Yes	2	2
F/65	Maxillary Squamous Cell Carcinoma	4.1	9.3	4	No	2	2
M/72	Maxillary Squamous Cell Carcinoma	9.6	17.4	6	No	2	2
Average		7.1	13.17				

The DICOM files obtained from the CBCT were imported into software to create three-dimensional (3D) models of the residual bone anatomy in each patient. Each file obtained was saved in STL format and then merged with the STL file obtained from the intraoral scanner and the diagnostic wax-up to improve all the patient's bone and dental information and achieve greater precision in the final result. This step made it possible to determine the ideal prosthetic emergence profile and to plan the position of the implants appropriately.

The next step was to design and define the shape and extent of the subperiosteal structure, taking into account the position of the prosthetic abutments and the remaining bone in each case. For this reason, the areas of greatest thickness and bone density were chosen for the location of the screws that would fix the structure, as well as the length of each screw in its specific position.

The final structure was exported in STL format to review and polish the edges and maximize the 3D quality of the design, making it ready for manufacturing.

2.3. Surgical Procedure

All procedures were performed under general anesthesia. A single injection of 2 g of amoxiclavulanic acid was administered intraoperatively. After infiltration with a local anesthetic and vasoconstrictor (articaine and 1:200.000 epinephrine), crestal incisions were performed to raise a mucoperiosteal flap to ensure adequate soft tissue coverage of the titanium implant.

Then, strict subperiosteal dissection of the alveolar ridge of the defect to be reconstructed and the adjacent areas including the remaining teeth was performed. After careful dissection with a periostotome and complete exposure of the maxillary defect, the maxillary implant was placed, ensuring a passive fit of the CSTMI on the bone surface. The CSTMI was fixed to the bone using 1.5 and 2 mm diameter screws of different lengths according to the previous virtual plan. The ends of the prosthetic connections emerged through small incisions in the flap. Finally, periosteal relaxing incisions were made in the periosteum to favor a correct mobilization of the flap, and the wound was sutured in a watertight fashion with resorbable sutures.

In the postoperative period, oral antibiotic therapy (amoxicillin/clavulanic acid 1 g/8 h) was prescribed for the first 7 days, along with analgesics, anti-inflammatory drugs and 0.12% chlorhexidine mouthwashes, two or three times a day, during the first week.

2.4. Prosthodontic Rehabilitation

Two weeks after the intervention, the stitches are removed and a provisional prosthesis is placed by the prosthodontist, milling the edges to avoid friction and mucosal injuries.

A month and a half after the operation, once the gum is completely healed, impressions are taken, and the fixed prosthesis is made in metal porcelain designed by CAD/CAM. All the prostheses were made in the clinic using the conventional protocol.

2.5. Follow-Up Visits

All patients were followed up periodically to detect any complications regarding soft tissue coverage, prosthetic complications or peri-implantitis or hardware failure (Table 1).

Esthetic results: An esthetic evaluation was performed by the patients to assess scores in facial symmetry, intraoral healing and maxillary projection. The results were classified with scores 0 ("poor"), 1 ("fair") and 2 ("good").

Functional results: All patients were rehabilitated with implant-supported fixed prostheses. Swallowing was evaluated and the results were classified with the following scores:

0 (liquid diet), 1 (soft diet) and 2 (normal diet). Speech articulation was assessed as intelligible speech and unintelligible speech.

3. Results

Four patients with segmental maxillary defects that had been reconstructed with customized subperiosteal titanium maxillary implants (CSTMI) through virtual surgical planning (VSP), STL models and CAD/CAM titanium mesh were included.

Due to the difficulty or impossibility of bone reconstruction of the maxilla with the conventional techniques of bone grafting, microsurgical reconstruction or osteogenic distraction, all patients had previously used a removable dental prosthesis.

The follow-up period was from 9 months to 3 years 2 months (averaging 1 year and 8 months). In all patients, the diagnosis was squamous cell carcinoma of the maxilla.

Microvascularized free graft reconstruction was attempted in three patients, but failed. In the remaining patient, a maxillary defect was reconstructed after oncological excision, as their general condition made microsurgical reconstruction inadvisable. The patients had an average age of 66.2 years. Three patients were men (75%), and one was a woman (25%). The smallest maxillary defect was 4.1 cm and the largest defect was 9.6 cm, with an average of 7.1 cm (Table 1).

Two patients received previous radiotherapeutic treatment (50%), and subperiosteal implant placement was delayed up to 2 years in these radiated cases and was only one year after excision in the two non-irradiated cases. The reconstructed maxillary vertical dimension ranged from 9.3 mm to 17.4 mm, with a mean of 13.17 mm. The transverse dimension of the maxilla at the crestal level was attempted to be reconstructed based on the pre-excision CT scan, and these measurements ranged from 6.5 mm in the premaxilla area to 14.6 mm at the posterior level.

All patients evolved uneventfully, and there were no infection signs or soft tissue dehiscence, and the oral mucosa healed perfectly without recessions or ulcers. The immediate postoperative period was painless in all patients, with only slight discomfort.

All implants were perfectly adjusted to the planned position, as confirmed by postoperative CBCT. At the end of the follow-up period, none of the patients had pain or soft tissue or prosthetic part problems. The biocompatibility of the patients with the materials used was good, and no complications were found in the soft tissues, the maxillary bone, the implants or the dental prostheses (Table 1).

No exposure of the titanium mesh was observed, and in none of the patients was the particulate bone graft used. All patients were rehabilitated with a fixed implant prosthesis.

All patients reported a good esthetic result. In terms of functional results, speech articulation was evaluated as intelligible language in all patients. All patients reported a regular diet.

4. Case Presentation

A 45-year-old male patient came to our department with mobility of teeth in the premaxilla and associated palatal lesion (Figure 1A,B). After histological and radiological studies, a diagnosis of maxillary squamous cell carcinoma was made. Tumor resection with segmental maxillectomy and clear margins and immediate reconstruction with a three-segment fibula flap was performed (Figure 1C,D).

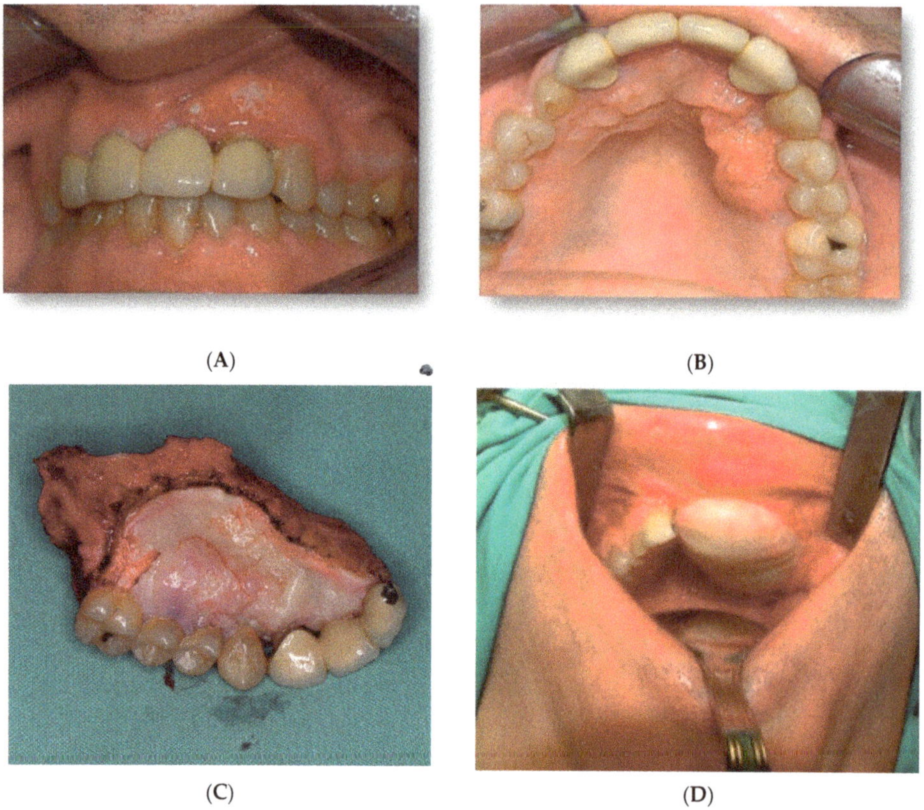

Figure 1. Intraoral view. (**A**,**B**) Maxillary squamous cell carcinoma with mobility of teeth. (**C**) Resection piece after excision of the tumour. (**D**) Microvascularized fibula flap.

He underwent surgery two years later due to contralateral recurrence and was treated with another fibula flap and radiotherapy in another institution (Figure 2A). He came to our department because he had problems with implants, which were subsequently removed. (Figure 2B,C).

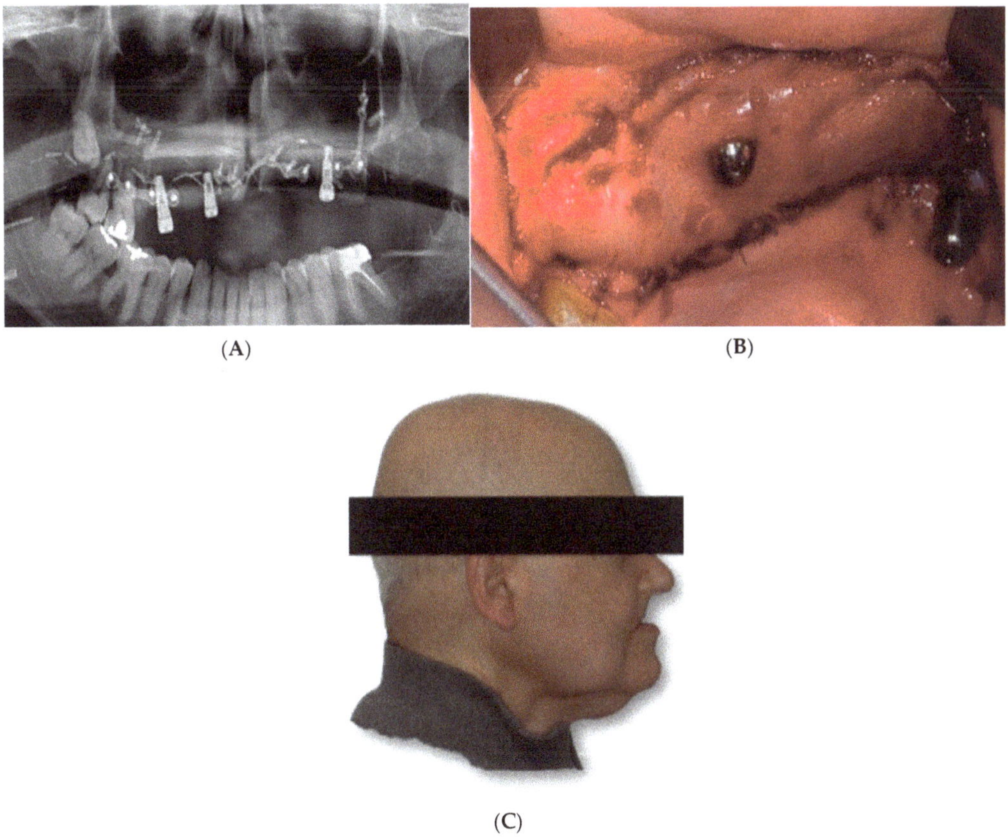

Figure 2. Bilateral fibula flap. (**A**) Ortopantomography showing both fibula flaps and the dental implants. (**B**) Intraoral view. (**C**) Clinical picture. Lack of maxillary projection.

Two and a half years after the beginning of the treatment, a volumetric reconstruction and dental rehabilitation of the maxillary defect by means of a custom-made subperiosteal titanium maxillary implant were proposed.

The DICOM data obtained from the CBCT were extracted and imported into software, where the residual anatomy of the patient's bone was reconstructed in 3D (Mimics®, Materialise, Leuven, Belgium), and the file was saved as an STL. In this phase, care was taken to best define the cortical walls of the residual bone (Figure 3A,C). The best position for the fixation screw was also evaluated.

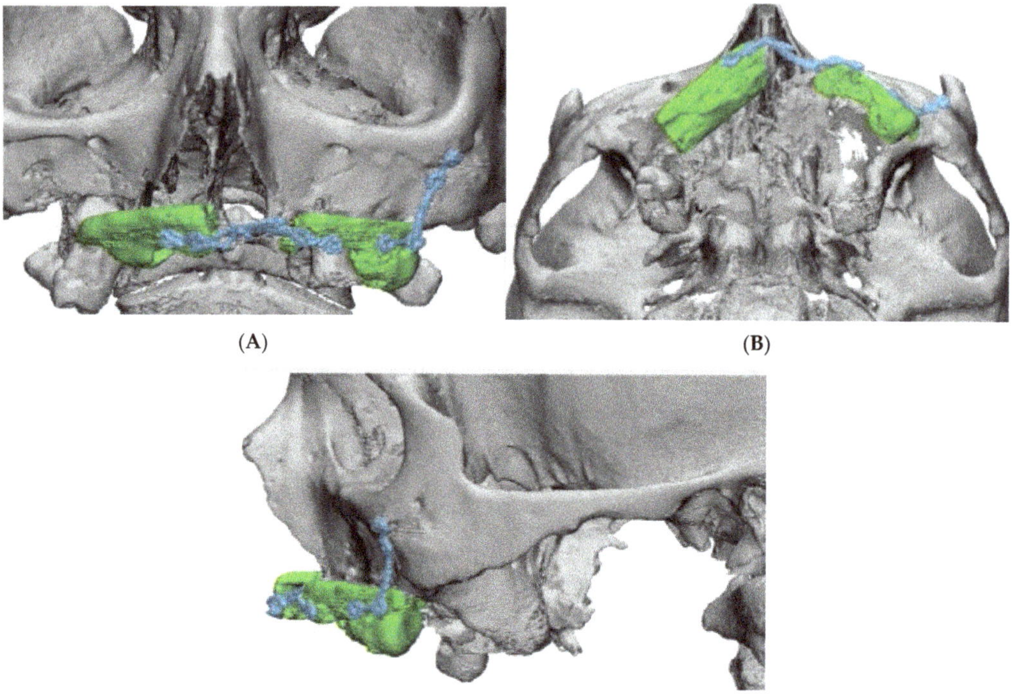

(A) (B) (C)

Figure 3. 3D reconstruction of the residual bone of the fibula flaps. (**A**) Frontal view. (**B**). Basal view. (**C**) Lateral view.

Virtual planning (Materialise Mimics v22.0®, Materialise Iberia NV, Barcelona, Spain) was performed for placement of a customized prosthesis. The 3D reconstruction was then aligned with the STL files obtained from the intraoral scan of the patient´s arch, and with the diagnostic wax-up. This helped define the optimal prosthetic emergence profile and allowed a proper design of the subperiosteal implant (Figure 4).

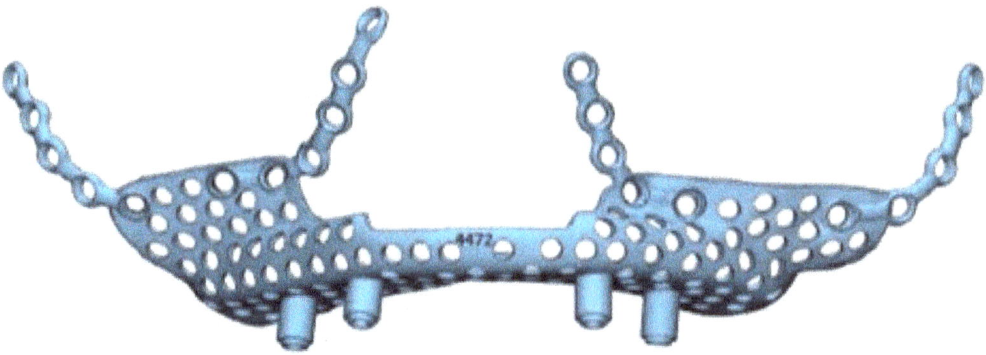

Figure 4. A 3D proper design of the subperiosteal implant.

The implant was manufactured by Avinent®, Avinent Implant System, Barcelona, Spain, in sintered titanium with four subperiosteal implants with a universal external connection of 4.1 mm width. In addition to the structure, we used a 3D model of the patient's maxilla and a replica of the structure to serve as a reference for the surgery (Figure 5).

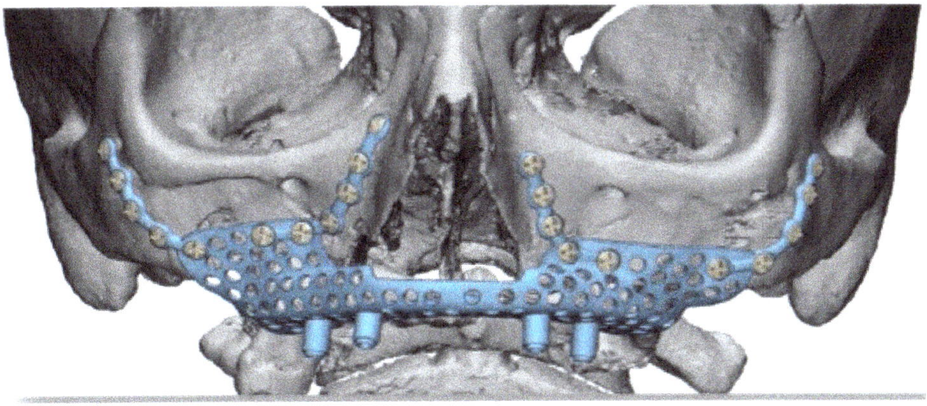

Figure 5. Virtual planning for placement of a customised prosthesis.

The surgery was performed under general anesthesia and nasotracheal intubation. After local infiltration with a vasoconstrictor, a crestal incision was made extending towards posterior sectors, and a careful detachment of the periosteum, both in the vestibule and in the palatal area, allowed the placement of the custom-made structure without interference. The subperiosteal implant was placed in the planned area to check its correct adaptation to the bone, without forcing its positioning, and finally it was fixed to the remaining nasomaxillary bone and zygomaticomaxillary buttress by means of osteosynthesis screws predetermined in length according to the bone thickness in each area (Figure 6).

Figure 6. The customised prosthesis was positioned, which was fixed into the nasomaxillary and zygomaticomaxillary buttresses.

Two weeks after surgery, under local anesthesia, the attached gingiva was incised on each of the implant abutments, which were covered by the gingiva, and by means of straight and 30° pilates, a provisional prosthesis was made, which the patient used during the first 2 months. After this period, impressions were taken with an open tray for the definitive prosthesis. A metal framework was built in CAD/CAM milled cobalt–chrome and covered with feldspar ceramic (Figure 7A,C).

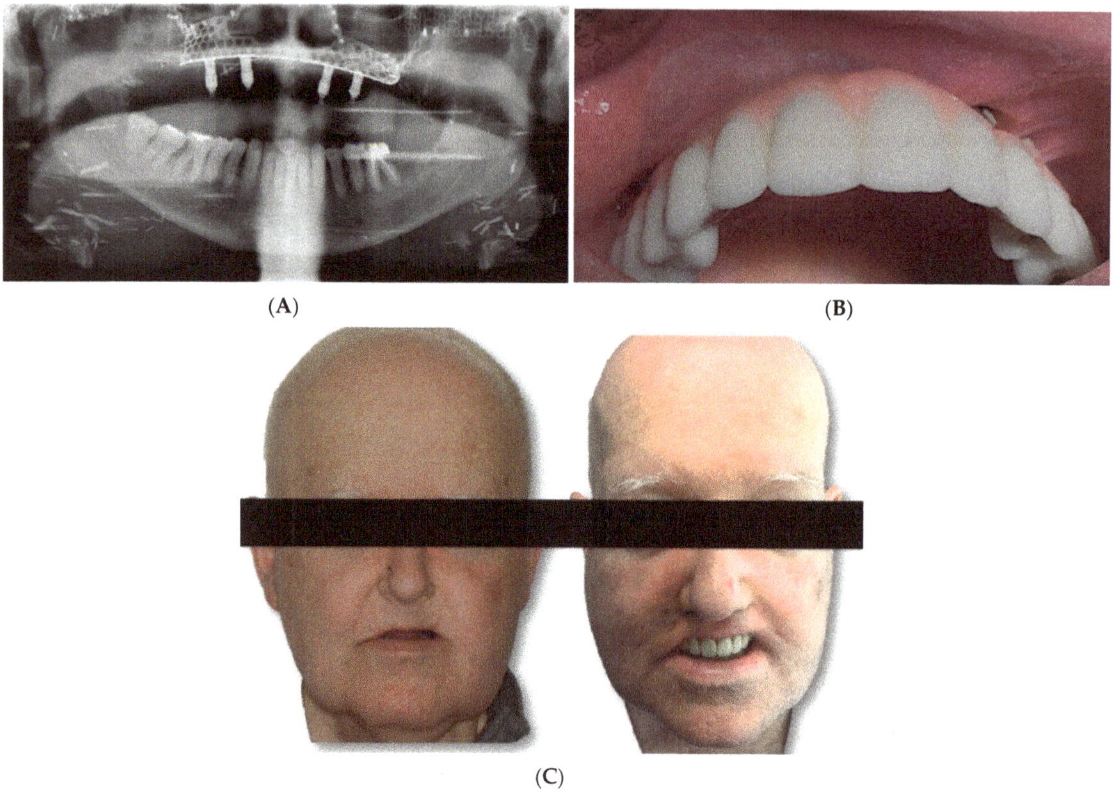

Figure 7. 3D reconstruction of the residual bone of the fibula flaps. (**A**) Ortopantomography showing the subperiostal implant. (**B**) Definitive prostheses. (**C**) Before and after of the definitive prosthesis.

5. Discussion

Dental rehabilitation after oncological surgical treatment is of utmost importance and should be planned from the beginning [12,13]. Generally, endosseous implants can reliably be placed in fibula flap (FFF) primarily (immediately at the time of fibula harvest) or secondarily (delayed by 6–12 months), with comparable safety and outcome profile [14]. The most common complications associated are peri-implantitis and marginal bone loss. Nonetheless, the main drawback of the FFF bone is the lack of vertical height for implant placement

Another option is zygoma implants, combining autologous soft tissue reconstruction with zygomatic implant-supported rehabilitation. They provide a predictable support for prosthetic rehabilitation of the maxilla and can be placed at the time of ablative surgery [12]. However, occasionally, zygoma implants cannot be placed due to insufficient bone support, requiring excellent surgical skills. In addition, complications such as infection at the implant tip, tissue retraction, communication between the oral cavity and the maxillary sinus, extraoral fistulation and intra-orbital abscesses can occur [15].

On the other hand, microsurgical reconstruction of maxillary defects is complex and entails a high risk of [15,16]. Some patients may not be fit for microsurgical reconstruction due to poor basal status. In such patients, an alternative to accomplish adequate oral rehabilitation is to design patient-specific subperiosteal implants.

In recent years, the advent of titanium 3D printing and 3D planning software have made reconsideration of the subperiosteal implant concept possible. The design of a subperiosteal implant is performed with a high degree of accuracy for each patient [17]. Thus, the concept of a 'high-tech' subperiosteal implant has been reborn.

Recently, Mommaerts introduced an innovative device for an additively manufactured subperiosteal implant (AMSJI®, CADskills, Gent, Belgium) that uses modern computer-aided design and manufacturing (CAD/CAM) technology [18] to provide an alternative implant option for dental rehabilitation in patients with extreme jawbone atrophy, which could be used for the rehabilitation of extended post-resection defects [13]. The major advantage of the subperiosteal implant is that it allows for immediate masticatory, esthetic and phonetic function [18].

Several papers have reported on the stability and osseointegration of the AMSJI at the wings and basal frame. In the study by Van den Borre et al., 15 patients who received bilateral AMSJI implantation in the maxilla were analyzed. Minor atrophy was seen at the alveolar ridge, but minimal atrophy was detected under the fixation wing. Patients showed a mean resorption at the alveolar ridge of 0.33 mm (SD 0.76 mm) and 0.08 (SD 0.33) mm at the wings and basal frame on the underlying zygo-maxillary bone one year post loading [17].

In a retrospective clinical study, Cerea et al. presented an analogue–digital technique for fabricating custom-made subperiosteal implants for both the maxilla and the mandible. In total, 70 partially or completely edentulous patients were included. At the two-year follow-up, the implant survival rate was 95.8%. The rate of prosthetic complications amounted to 8.9%. The authors concluded that the application of custom-made titanium subperiosteal implants can represent a safe alternative to conventional bone regeneration [19].

De Moor et al. [15] used finite element analysis to perform a biomechanical evaluation of the subperiosteal implant for the maxilla in a Cadwood and Howell class V patient. The simulations showed a stable and safe performance during average occlusal forces. However, they stated that further resorption of the residual ridge might cause fatigue of the implant, and thus, they recommend a close follow-up of bone quality in these patients. Additionally, the results showed that the arms experienced higher stresses compared to the rest of the implant, so future optimization should be driven towards the strengthening of the arms to improve stability. They concluded that this type of device is completely safe to use and is considered the best solution for edentulous patients with Cadwood and Howell class V–VIII bone resorption [15]. These results could be extrapolated and applied in cases of maxillary reconstruction in oncological patients.

The subperiosteal implant is a valuable and interesting alternative to major microsurgical reconstruction requiring composite bone free flaps, to bone grafting and to zygoma implants. Mastication can be provided immediately with one surgical intervention, and donor site morbidity is diminished, reducing complications and costs. With the new advances in virtual surgical planning and CAD/CAM technologies, specific subperiosteal implants with an optimal and accurate design can be manufactured.

The current digital fabrication procedure reduces the number of surgical sessions and patients' discomfort. Additionally, customization makes the fit of the implant very accurate, which might ultimately reduce the number of intraoperative complications, increase the safety of the surgical procedure and improve the confidence of the surgeon.

The ability to keep the fixation screws outside the maxillary sinus is also another major benefit of the subperiosteal implant in patients with chronic or silent sinusitis [18,19]. There is also the possibility to disconnect each post from the basal structure using a diamond burr under local anesthesia in cases of peri-implantitis without jeopardizing masticatory function, all while retaining the same prosthesis [19,20].

However, its efficiency still needs to be proven in the long term. Several reviews have, however, also reported on complications such as infections, early and late implant exposure, bone resorption, fistulation and implant mobility, leading to implant failure [17].

Prospective and more extensive studies are needed to assess its efficiency and safety and draw more conclusions. One new modification currently being evaluated by Mommaerts involves placing all the connecting arms under the palatal gingiva [18].

The main complications and problems could be related to material fatigue, poor osseointegration, implant exposure and mobility, peri-implantitis and length of the connection pillars used [21,22]. Randomized and prospective clinical trials are needed to assess the long-term performance of these devices.

6. Conclusions

In conclusion, we believe that customized subperiosteal titanium maxillary implants (CSTMI) could be a safe alternative for maxillary defect reconstruction, allowing simultaneous dental rehabilitation while restoring midface projection. Recent reports and our experience show promising results in terms of functional and esthetic restoration. Nonetheless, prospective and randomized trials are required with long-term follow-up to assess its long-term performance and safety.

We have reviewed the article against The PROCESS 2020 Guideline: Updating Consensus Preferred Reporting Of CasESeries in Surgery (PROCESS) Guidelines [23].

Author Contributions: Conceptualization, J.L.C.C. and J.L.D.C.P.d.V.; methodology, J.L.D.C.P.d.V.; software, I.A.N.; validation, J.L.C.C., I.N.C. and J.L.D.C.P.d.V.; formal analysis, J.L.C.C.; investigation, J.L.D.C.P.d.V.; resources, J.L.C.C., J.L.D.C.P.d.V., N.M.G. and P.G.M.; data curation, M.M.P.M.; writing—original draft preparation, J.L.D.C.P.d.V. and M.M.P.M.; writing—review and editing, I.A.N.; visualization, I.N.C. and C.N.C.; supervision, J.L.D.C.P.d.V. and C.N.C.; project administration, J.L.C.C. All authors have read and agreed to the published version of the manuscript.

Funding: This research received no external funding.

Institutional Review Board Statement: The study was conducted according to the guidelines of the Declaration of Helsinki, is endorsed by the Hospital Ethics Committee at University Hospital La Paz, Madrid, Spain. Institutional Review Board Statement: All subjects gave their informed consent for inclusion before they participated in the study. The study as conducted in acco dance with the Declaration of Helsinki, and the protocol was approved by the Ethics Committee of Hospital La Paz (Project identification code: HULP PI-5180).

Informed Consent Statement: Informed consent was obtained from all subjects involved in the study.

Data Availability Statement: The data presented in this study are available on request from the corresponding author. The data are not publicly available due to data protection regulations.

Conflicts of Interest: The authors declare no conflict of interest.

References

1. Wijbenga, J.G.; Schepers, R.H.; Werker, P.M.; Witjes, M.J.; Dijkstra, P.U. A systematic review of functional outcome and quality of life following reconstruction of maxillofacial defects using vascularized free fibula flaps and dental rehabilitation reveals poor data quality. *J. Plast. Reconstr. Aesthetic Surg.* **2016**, *69*, 1024–1036. [CrossRef]
2. Barber, A.J.; Butterworth, C.J.; Rogers, S.N. Systematic review of primary osseointegrated dental implants in head and neck oncology. *Br. J. Oral Maxillofac. Surg.* **2011**, *49*, 29–36. [CrossRef] [PubMed]
3. Chuka, R.; Abdullah, W.; Rieger, J.; Nayar, S.; Seikaly, H.; Osswald, M.; Wolfaardt, J. Implant utilization and time to prosthetic rehabilitation in conventional and advanced fibular free flap reconstruction of the maxilla and mandible. *Int. J. Prosthodont.* **2017**, *30*, 289–294. [CrossRef]
4. Hidalgo, D.A. Fibula free flap: A new method of mandible reconstruction. *Plast. Reconstr. Surg.* **1989**, *84*, 71–79. [CrossRef]
5. Lenox, N.D.; Kim, D.D. Maxillary reconstruction. *Oral Maxillofac. Surg. Clin. North Am.* **2013**, *25*, 215–222. [CrossRef] [PubMed]
6. Breik, O.; Idle, M.; Martin, T.; Praveen, P.; Parmar, S. Three-Dimensional Computer-Assisted Surgical Planning and Manufacturing in Complex Maxillary Reconstruction. *Atlas Oral Maxillofac. Surg. Clin. North Am.* **2020**, *28*, 151–164. [CrossRef]
7. Numajiri, T.; Morita, D.; Nakamura, H.; Tsujiko, S.; Yamochi, R.; Sowa, Y.; Toyoda, K.; Tsujikawa, T.; Arai, A.; Yasuda, M.; et al. Using an In-House Approach to Computer-Assisted Design and Computer-Aided Manufacturing Reconstruction of the Maxilla. *J. Oral Maxillofac. Surg.* **2018**, *76*, 1361–1369. [CrossRef]
8. Ahmed, Z.U.; Flynn, J.; Riedel, E.R.; Huryn, J.M.; Rosen, E.B. Definitive maxillary obturator prosthesis: Timelines for fabrication and follow-up. *Spec. Care Dent.* **2020**, *40*, 315–319. [CrossRef] [PubMed]

9. Chou, P.Y.; Denadai, R.; Hallac, R.R.; Dumrongwongsiri, S.; Hsieh, W.C.; Pai, B.C.; Lo, L.J. Comparative Volume Analysis of Alveolar Defects by 3D Simulation. *J. Clin. Med.* **2019**, *8*, 1401. [CrossRef] [PubMed]
10. Bluebond-Langner, R.; Rodriguez, E.D. Application of skeletal buttress analogy in composite facial reconstruction. *Craniomaxillofac. Trauma Reconstr.* **2009**, *2*, 19–25. [CrossRef]
11. Navarro Cuéllar, C.; Tousidonis Rial, M.; Antúnez-Conde, R.; Ochandiano Caicoya, S.; Navarro Cuéllar, I.; Arenas de Frutos, G.; Sada Urmeneta, Á.; García-Hidalgo Alonso, M.I.; Navarro Vila, C.; Salmerón Escobar, J.I. Virtual Surgical Planning, Stereolitographic Models and CAD/CAM Titanium Mesh for Three-Dimensional Reconstruction of Fibula Flap with Iliac Crest Graft and Dental Implants. *J. Clin. Med.* **2021**, *10*, 1922. [CrossRef] [PubMed]
12. Glas, H.H.; Vosselman, N.; de Visscher, S.A.H.J. The use of 3D virtual surgical planning and computer aided design in reconstruction of maxillary surgical defects. *Curr. Opin. Otolaryngol. Head Neck Surg.* **2020**, *28*, 122–128. [CrossRef] [PubMed]
13. Vosselman, N.; Merema, B.J.; Schepman, K.P.; Raghoebar, G.M. Patient-specific sub-periosteal zygoma implant for prosthetic rehabilitation of large maxillary defects after oncological resection. *Int. J. Oral Maxillofac. Surg.* **2019**, *48*, 115–117. [CrossRef]
14. Patel, S.Y.; Kim, D.D.; Ghali, G.E. Maxillofacial Reconstruction Using Vascularized Fibula Free Flaps and Endosseous Implants. *Oral Maxillofac. Surg. Clin. North Am.* **2019**, *31*, 259–284. [CrossRef]
15. De Moor, E.; Huys, S.E.F.; van Lenthe, G.H.; Mommaerts, M.Y.; vander Sloten, J. Mechanical evaluation of a patient-specific additively manufactured subperiosteal jaw implant (AMSJI) using finite-element analysis. *Int. J. Oral Maxillofac. Surg.* **2022**, *51*, 405–411. [CrossRef] [PubMed]
16. Kumar, V.V.; Jacob, P.C.; Ebenezer, S.; Kuriakose, M.A.; Kekatpure, V.; Baliarsing, A.S.; Al-Nawas, B.; Wagner, W. Implant supported dental rehabilitation following segmental mandibular reconstruction- quality of life outcomes of a prospective randomized trial. *J. Cranio-Maxillofac. Surg.* **2016**, *44*, 800–810. [CrossRef]
17. Van den Borre, C.; Rinaldi, M.; De Neef, B.; Loomans, N.A.; Nout, E.; Van Doorne, L.; Naert, I.; Politis, C.; Schouten, H.; Klomp, G.; et al. Radiographic evaluation of bone remodeling after additively manufactured subperiosteal jaw implantation (Amsji) in the maxilla: A one-year follow-up study. *J. Clin. Med.* **2021**, *10*, 3542. [CrossRef]
18. Mommaerts, M.Y. Evolutionary steps in the design and biofunctionalization of the additively manufactured sub-periosteal jaw implant 'AMSJI' for the maxilla. *Int. J. Oral Maxillofac. Surg.* **2019**, *48*, 108–114. [CrossRef]
19. Mommaerts, M.Y. Additively manufactured sub-periosteal jaw implants. *Int. J. Oral Maxillofac. Surg.* **2017**, *46*, 938–940. [CrossRef]
20. Cerea, M.; Dolcini, G.A. Custom-Made Direct Metal Laser Sintering Titanium Subperiosteal Implants: A Retrospective Clinical Study on 70 Patients. *BioMed Res. Int.* **2018**, *2018*, 5420391. [CrossRef] [PubMed]
21. Ângelo, D.F.; Vieira Ferreira, J.R. The role of custom-made subperiosteal implants for rehabilitation of atrophic jaws—A case report. *Ann. Maxillofac. Surg.* **2020**, *10*, 507–511. [CrossRef] [PubMed]
22. Nguyen, T.M.; Caruhel, J.-B.; Khonsari, R.H. A subperiosteal maxillary implant causing severe osteolysis. *J. Stomatol. Oral Maxillofac. Surg.* **2018**, *119*, 523–525. [CrossRef] [PubMed]
23. Agha, R.A.; Sohrabi, C.; Mathew, G.; Franchi, T.; Kerwan, A.; O'Neill, N.; PROCESS Group. The PROCESS 2020 Guideline: Updating Consensus Preferred Reporting Of CasESeries in Surgery (PROCESS) Guidelines. *Int. J. Surg.* **2020**, *84*, 231–235. [CrossRef] [PubMed]

Journal of
Clinical Medicine

Article

Advances and Innovations in Ablative Head and Neck Oncologic Surgery Using Mixed Reality Technologies in Personalized Medicine

Nadia Karnatz, Henriette L. Möllmann *, Max Wilkat, Aida Parviz and Majeed Rana

Department of Oral and Maxillofacial Surgery, Heinrich Heine University Duesseldorf, 40225 Duesseldorf, Germany
* Correspondence: henriettelouise.moellmann@med.uni-duesseldorf.de

Abstract: The benefit of computer-assisted planning in head and neck ablative and reconstructive surgery has been extensively documented over the last decade. This approach has been proven to offer a more secure surgical procedure. In the treatment of cancer of the head and neck, computer-assisted surgery can be used to visualize and estimate the location and extent of the tumor mass. Nowadays, some software tools even allow the visualization of the structures of interest in a mixed reality environment. However, the precise integration of mixed reality systems into a daily clinical routine is still a challenge. To date, this technology is not yet fully integrated into clinical settings such as the tumor board, surgical planning for head and neck tumors, or medical and surgical education. As a consequence, the handling of these systems is still of an experimental nature, and decision-making based on the presented data is not yet widely used. The aim of this paper is to present a novel, user-friendly 3D planning and mixed reality software and its potential application for ablative and reconstructive head and neck surgery.

Keywords: mixed reality; head neck tumor; surgical navigation; three-dimensional visual output

Citation: Karnatz, N.; Möllmann, H.L.; Wilkat, M.; Parviz, A.; Rana, M. Advances and Innovations in Ablative Head and Neck Oncologic Surgery Using Mixed Reality Technologies in Personalized Medicine. *J. Clin. Med.* **2022**, *11*, 4767. https://doi.org/10.3390/jcm11164767

Academic Editors: Carlos Navarro Cuellar, José Luis Cebrián-Carretero and Mark L. Urken

Received: 29 July 2022
Accepted: 12 August 2022
Published: 16 August 2022

1. Introduction

Optimal visualization of medical data in the treatment planning and decision-making of head and neck tumors, which provides targeted information, forms the basis for interdisciplinary communication. However, it is crucial to meet the different professional requirements of the various disciplines. The radiologist requires 2D imaging of the highest quality in order to detect or diagnose pathologies [1,2]. The surgeon bases his therapeutic decisions, in addition to his clinical experience, largely on radiological cross-sectional imaging. This provides him with pre- and intraoperative information, which, however, is not available to the pathologist. Specialties such as radiation therapy or oncology often still require their own imaging for planning or monitoring their therapy [3–5]. These monodisciplinary approaches significantly complicate communication. For example, traditional 2D cross-sectional imaging still serves as the basis for diagnostic and therapeutic decisions, although 3D models are already being calculated from 2D cross-sectional images using segmentation and rendering techniques to visualize regions of interest. However, conventionally, these 3D models are still static renderings projected onto a 2D plane to be visualized on a 2D screen [6]. A milestone in medicine has been the generation of a digital interface between 2D radiological slice imaging and the 3D surgical environment in computer-assisted surgery using a multiplanar view with colored 3D volume rendering of patients' hard and soft tissue. By enabling the use of intraoperative computer-assisted navigation technology in the surgical site based on one or more imaging modalities. The optimized spatial orientation enables higher accuracy of surgical results as well as gentler surgical methods [7,8]. So far, this digital 2D/3D interface is still conditionally available to the surgeon. However, for adequate treatment of craniofacial tumors, computer-aided visualization and planning of 3D image data are necessary for all disciplines involved. For this purpose, an interdisciplinary image viewing interface would be required to visualize multimodal image data (computer tomography (CT), magnetic resonance imaging (MRI), cone beam-CT (CBCT), positron emission tomography (PET), PET/CT, and single photon emission computed tomography (SPECT)) for diagnostics, therapy planning, therapy sequence, treatment response, and search for distant metastasis or quality control [9,10]. Mixed reality (MR) technology, as a new tool in medicine and other disciplines, is a possible digital step in this direction. It is a new digital holographic visualization technology that allows virtual 3D objects to be created in space from radiological cross-sectional images, providing an immersive experience and possibilities for interactions with objects that would not be possible in a 2D environment. Therefore, MR merges the real world and virtual environments, creating a collective surrounding in which physical and digital objects are able to interact [11,12]. By combining the real world with the virtual world, medical data can be processed and visualized in real-time in a computer-generated environment [13].

Difficult-to-understand three-dimensional anatomy and geometry of the human skull require a high degree of spatial imagination, which is a difficult skill to acquire. With the help of MR technology, topographic considerations, complex structures, and pathological lesions can be visualized in a way that can be understood across disciplines by visualizing segmentation results with photo-realistic textures, trajectories, and annotations. In addition, the visualization of the 2D slice images in MR, which is still indispensable for the radiologist, is still possible and can be enriched with additional information such as tumor extension and safety distance for the surgeon, sampling locations for the pathologist, or infiltration of structures for the radiation therapist. Other computer-generated virtual viewing systems have been described in the literature, such as virtual reality (VR) and augmented reality (AR) [14,15]. In virtual reality, special software and hardware are used to simulate an artificial 3D environment that is completely detached from reality and creates an independent virtual environment. The disadvantage here is that the user cannot move freely in real space and is no longer aware of the real environment. AR extends a real environment (e.g., the surgical field) with computer-generated content. This provokes a 3D experience with a more integrated and sophisticated perspective of the patient's condition. Multiple data from different categories (such as preoperative and/or intraoperative MRI, CT, etc.) can simultaneously be captured [16–18].

However, AR only adds virtual objects as additional information to the real environment, while MR technology overlays synthetic content in the real environment, making interactions with the virtual objects possible. Therefore, AR and VR should be considered only as partial solutions, such as their use in teaching [19,20].

MR technology provides a specific, language-independent, and multidisciplinary tool to enable radiologists, surgeons, oncologists, radiation therapists, and pathologists to visualize radiological imaging in a way that meets mono- and interdisciplinary requirements.

2. Materials and Methods

The aim of this work was to demonstrate and establish a novel, user-friendly, all-in-one 3D planning and reviewing mixed reality software (Brainlab AG, Munich, Germany) for ablative and reconstructive head and neck surgery and to clinically evaluate it.

Since 2021, the possibilities of using mixed reality technology for ablative/reconstruction surgery have been investigated at the University Hospital Düsseldorf, Clinic for Oral and Maxillofacial Surgery.

The use of this immersive technology in the scope of this work can be divided into the following four categories:

1. 3D visualization in preoperative imaging and planning;
2. tumor board—decision making and quality control platform;
3. patient-specific information;
4. education/surgical training.

2.1. Mixed Reality Technologies

2.1.1. Hardware

One of the main challenges of mixed reality technology is to develop a user-friendly interface between the hardware and the user. In particular, the implementation of MR technology on a head-mounted display (HMD) allows the user to be mobile and independent of a workstation. Several hardware technologies are currently available for visualizing immersive mixed reality content. With handheld displays, the real environment can be captured through the use of cameras and linked to digital elements to add virtual content from any perspective. In the field of education and training, the use of handheld displays offers a promising addition to the possibilities used so far [21]. However, their use in surgery is not practical due to the manual positioning required still a lot is experimental nature. With HMDs capable of spatial computing and wireless transmission of the mixed reality content, surgeons can visualize the medical data and move freely in space. Sensors on the devices enable sensing of the physical environment for spatial computing used to automatically integrate holographic information into the real world [22,23]. Global Positioning System (GPS) for location, accelerometers, and ambient brightness meters can further support the mixed reality integration and can increase the immersiveness. Visual observations from cameras together with accelerometers and ambient brightness meters are used to track the head position and orientation in 6DoF. By continuous tracking of the environment and user position, mixed reality can create a more interactive and immersive experience. With special MR headsets already on the market, such as Google Glass, Microsoft HoloLens, or Magic Leap, digital content is projected in real-time on a small screen in front of the user's eyes [24]. Real-time data transmission and handheld controllers facilitate user interaction. Moreover, worth mentioning are projector-based mixed reality systems that map digital content by projecting it onto organic shapes [13].

2.1.2. Fundamentals of Visualization

For visualizing medical data in MR, DICOM (Digital Imaging and Communication in Medicine) datasets can be used, based upon which 3D models can be calculated automatically by algorithms and converted into polygons [25]. Rendering pipelines can then be employed to visualize the polygonal objects with appropriate textures on the HMDs. In order for the virtual objects to be congruent with the real environment in the user's field of view, their position, viewing direction, and viewing angle must be detected for a correct overlay. This also requires very high accuracy in the surface mapping of the environment and the continuous monitoring of the user's movement [26]. Thus, these registration steps are used to achieve alignment between physical and virtual information [27,28]. Various registration modalities such as cameras, inertial sensors, or mechanical systems are used in location technologies. Here, a trade-off between localization accuracy and complexity often has to be found. Mixed reality applications are mostly based on inside-out trackers attached to head-mounted displays. Since these trackers are based on visual features, degradation of image quality due to motion blur or illumination changes can lead to loss of location. Therefore, the combination of camera localization with other sensors such as inertial sensors can be performed [29,30]. Even the smallest deviations can lead to significant misregistration of virtual objects or so-called "jitter" effects [31,32]. Very high demands are placed on a medical system in terms of precision and reliability.

2.2. 3D Visualization in Preoperative Imaging and Planning

The 3D visualization of head and neck tumors requires a high degree of representational accuracy of medical data [33]. The extent of a tumor as well as infiltration and destruction of structures influence treatment decisions. Mixed reality technology can be helpful as a visual interface between tomographic examination and spatial representation for surgical planning. It provides radiologists and surgeons with a multimodal interactive user interface for data processing and an efficient way to navigate through tomographic data, enabling surgical planning tailored to the patient [34–36]. Combined with mixed reality technology, digital patient-specific models can be created with high precision, enabling individualized treatment planning [37]. After the patient was scheduled for complex tumor resection, 3D digital reconstruction was performed using preoperative cross-sectional imaging. CT and MRI scans were used as the basis for 3D visualization of the tumor, with CT imaging performed in x-mm slices after peripheral injection of a contrast agent and modern low-dose (0.2–0.5 mSv) protocols. MRI datasets were acquired in 0.8-mm slices, using a 1.5 Tesla MRI scanner. To create the spatial representation, the datasets were imported into the Brainlab Elements™ planning application (Brainlab AG, Munich, Germany) in the standard Digital Imaging and Communications in Medicine (DICOM) format. For reproducible orientation of the anatomical structures, a symmetrical view of the data is required for the three-dimensional reconstruction; therefore, the CT slice is aligned in all dimensions (axial, coronal, sagittal multiplanar view) according to the horizontal Frankfurt midsagittal planes. Automatic image fusion of the CT and MRI datasets makes the entire multimodal information available to the practitioner. The superimposition of soft tissue and hard tissue imaging thus allows the extent of the tumor, as well as its soft tissue as well as bony infiltration of adjacent structures to be visualized in three dimensions. This technique of multimodal rigid image registration is based on mutual information and uses features such as multiple resolutions, intensity rebinning, and scaling in parameter space [8]. With the help of the planning software, automated segmentation of the anatomical structures and target tumor tissue from the image datasets was performed. This is based on an atlas-based algorithm that derives appropriate congruences between the patient and atlas datasets [38]. Furthermore, by adding voxels, semi-automatic segmentation is possible to improve the delineation of critical structures—this was performed using the radiological scans as a mapping aid. Selective segmentation also allows simulation of resection boundaries or reconstructions. The time required to create a 3D reconstruction depends on the complexity of the case. Cases with complex pathology and anatomy require extensive discussions led by the treating surgeons, the more complex the case the higher the manual workup. In particular, poor radiologic scans require manual reprocessing in contrast to cases with high-quality radiologic scans [39]. To improve visualization, voxel regions can be assigned specific color and opacity values, or supporting parameters such as textures or annotations can be used to mark or graphically represent structures [40,41]. By transmitting the processed treatment plans over a wireless network to a head-mounted MR device with the appropriate viewer software (Magic Leap 1, Plantation, Florida, USA; Viewer version 5.3, Brainlab AG, Munich, Germany), it is possible to view the radiological data as well as their reconstructions as 3D holograms (see Figure 1).

The user is now able to manipulate the digital reconstructions to view patient anatomy and pathology from different perspectives. Through the additional planning of trajectories, the surgeon is now able, for example, to evaluate different possible accesses or biopsies preoperatively in 3D with high accuracy. For research purposes only, not released yet.

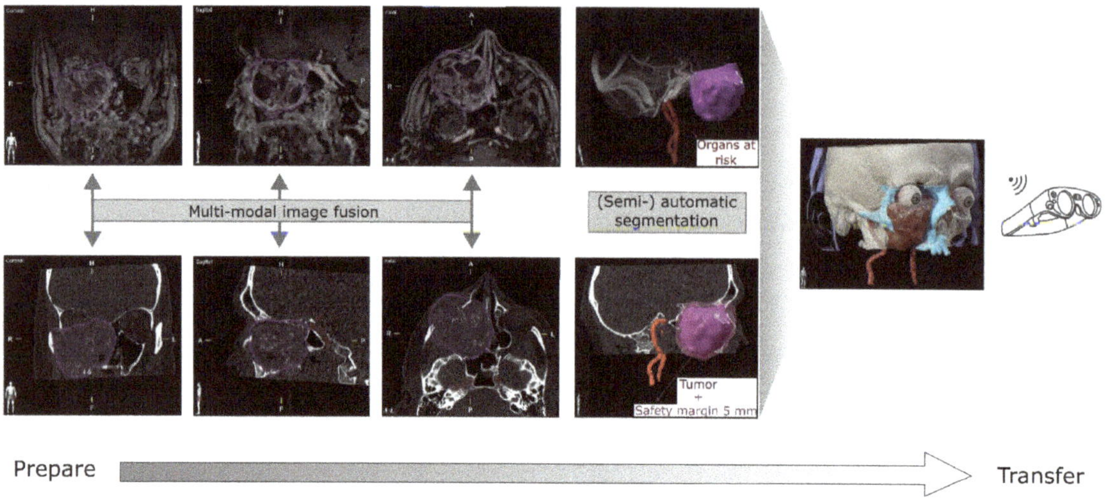

Figure 1. Planning steps for mixed reality visualizations. To fully leverage the potential of each imaging modality for surgical planning, the individual imaging series must be fused in a first step. Based on the resulting set of imaging data, the structures of interest can then be segmented automatically, or, in the case of pathological structures, semi-automatically and—if necessary—corrected manually. Due to the full integration of the mixed reality HMD (head-mounted-display) into the planning software, the segmented structures can then be transferred wirelessly to the devices and photo-realistically rendered.

2.3. *Tumor Board—Decision-Making and Quality Control Platform*

Considering the complexity of oncological care in the head and neck region, a multidisciplinary team is essential for diagnosis and therapy decisions. This team is composed of oral and maxillofacial plastic surgeons, ear, nose, and throat physicians, radiation therapists, oncologists, pathologists, and radiologists. Here, the actual purpose of the multidisciplinary tumor board is to provide a joint decision-making sensibility but also a platform for quality control of treatment in terms of adherence to guidelines and evaluation of therapeutic outcomes. This includes ensuring a correct diagnosis, especially staging and treatment planning, but also coordination of care and management of complications [42–44]. It has been shown that the demands of the visualization of data and findings on the part of the specialist disciplines are often divergent and that joint communication is not always easy and can therefore take up a lot of time [45,46]. By implementing mixed reality software in the multidisciplinary tumor board (MDT), it is possible to streamline and centralize the oncological care of head and neck tumors, as it provides a language-independent, patient-centered, and flexible virtual platform for visualizing all information. In addition, available system resources can be superimposed in MR.

Interaction with segmented objects, for example, repositioning of specific structures, can be an integral part of therapy planning and is already possible on desktop planning workstations. In order for a tumor board meeting to be held entirely in mixed reality, these functionalities must of course also be transferred to this format. The prototype software used in this work included this function and thus enabled the free-hand placement/movement of mixed reality objects such as anatomical structures or imported implants. In advance of the MR application during the tumor board, the segmentation of the tumor as well as the delineation of the safety distance should be performed by the radiologist and the surgeon, respectively. In particular, critical structures that make R0 resection difficult can be marked. With the help of 3D rendering and mixed reality, the information can now be shared with the individual participants of the multidisciplinary tumor board, thus providing a basis for discussion regarding treatment options. Especially in complex surgical cases, surgical interdisciplinary collaboration can be used to exchange information about the feasibility of the intervention or surgical approaches. The interaction with the hologram, however, also enables non-specialist disciplines or assistant physicians to gain a better understanding of the problem. Through virtual panels, the MDT radiologist is able to access individual 2D slice images without closing central information. This improves the user experience for all members of the MDT.

Mixed reality is leading the way in terms of surgical and pathology coordination. By integrating computer-assisted surgery datasets into the mixed reality environment, a three-dimensional (voxel-based) dataset allows matching with macroscopic assessment of the extent of a head and neck tumor. A major problem in tumor resection (without navigation) is the naming and exact assignment of the anatomical three-dimensional position of the specimens. Intraoperative navigation enables reliable marking and assignment of histological specimens. This data can be stored and transmitted in DICOM format to provide patient-specific tumor information. This allows the clinical extension to be compared with the radiological extension. Tumor mapping can be presented to MDT participants in 3D rendered form, including all anatomical structures so that decisions about tumor respectability do not rely solely on radiological imaging [8,47]. Another advantage is that this allows information to be shared that is otherwise only available to the treating surgeon. Decisions, critical issues, etc. can be documented using annotations and can be made available for post-operative discussion using mixed reality. Similarly, it should be possible for the pathologist to share pathology reports, staining, or other relevant microscopy results, or for the practitioner to share photorealistic representation of the patient's clinic in the MDT.

With the additional implementation of radiotherapy control, there is a decided basis for decision-making with regard to patient-specific therapy decisions in complex cases such as recurrences. Thus, using mixed reality technology, the room becomes a 3-dimensional shared computer screen with all members of the MDT, similar to an electronic medical record in real-time to share case information.

A special aspect of this is the remote collaboration feature, which allows tumor board participants to be virtually co-present through real-time data exchange. This virtual co-presence allows MDT meetings to be more efficient and by means of modern network technology, such as the 5G standard, an immersive environment can still be created and real-time communication via audio chat features can be enabled.

Especially for patients who are not treated at large tumor centers, this enables individualized patient therapy, as physicians can exchange information with colleagues from tumor centers at any time via the remote collaboration function. With regard to digitalization in medicine, with the help of mixed reality technology and the accompanying information platform, collaboration in large academic medical networks in the care of oncological care of head and neck tumors is conceivable. With the help of intercom functions and avatars, resources can be centralized. MDTs with MR technologies improve accessibility, especially for clinicians who are not on-site. This promotes better patient-specific care as well as control of quality measures.

2.4. Patient-Specific Information

Patient education not only serves to obtain informed consent from the patient prior to a surgical procedure but is also the basis for the exchange of information between physician and patient and should or can promote patient compliance during medical and rehabilitative treatment. However, informed consent can only be achieved if the patient is aware of the risks, the indication for the procedure, and the expected outcomes. Due to the complexity of surgical procedures in head and neck tumor surgery and increasingly shorter treatment times, information transfer is often difficult [48,49]. Nevertheless, ensuring adequate patient education regarding ethical and legal aspects is imperative. Thus, it has already been shown in the literature that increased patient satisfaction was achieved by adding additional information to the planned intervention in the form of paper-based or digital documents as well as audiovisual explanations [50]. However, an additional number of information sources also means a flood of information that may overwhelm the patient. Here, it is the physician's task to place the multitude of information in an adequate medical context to avoid patient uncertainty. Personal doctor-patient contact is and remains essential. It is therefore imperative to convey targeted information to the patient in a compact and comprehensible manner in a conversation. Here, mixed reality technology as a digital medium can combine the human and communicative aspects of an informative patient conversation and patient-specific information on treatment. In the following, the possible use of mixed reality technology is described in more detail, which can be used for "diagnosis description" and therapy planning in the context of an adequate doctor-patient relationship in individual patient education [51]. The viewer of the head-mounted device serves as a platform for the display of digital information and objects. Here, the physician and patient see the same virtual objects. By visualizing the volumetric data from the patient's own CT or MRI datasets in a 3D hologram, the patient is able to perceive his individual patient information and not just a description (see Figure 2).

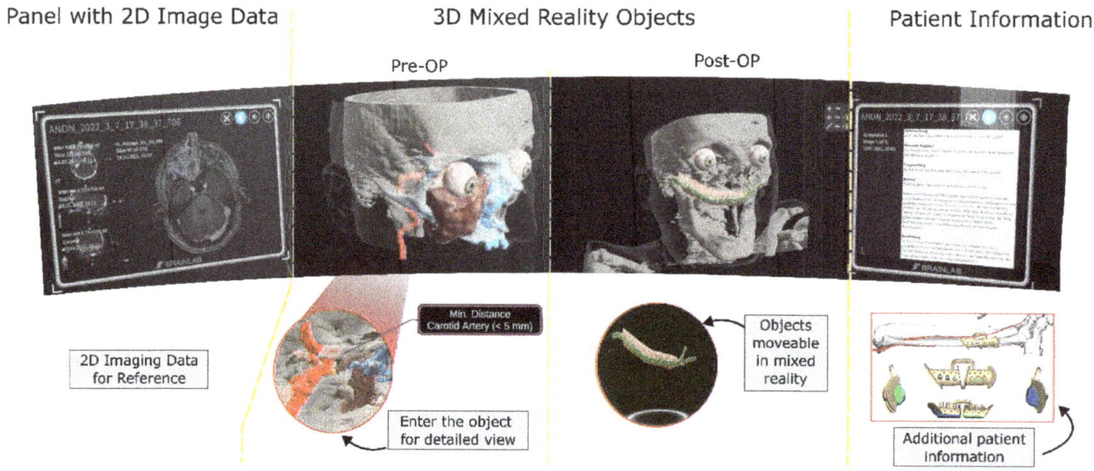

Figure 2. Capture of a mixed reality scene. Mixed reality has the ability to bundle all available information about the patient and make it accessible in a single, unified way. The conventional 2D images are still available and can also be examined in mixed reality. The 3D objects resulting from the 2D images can be interacted with, e.g., approaching the object can be used to understand anatomical positional relationships in detail. In addition, it is possible to integrate all other available patient information into the scene, for example radiological diagnoses, implant plans, or radiation therapy data. Kindly compiled by BrainLab.

The patient obtains the impression of looking into his own body, commonly referred to as his digital twin. Especially with regard to the complexity of head and neck tumors and the anatomy in this area, the patient is able to perceive his own disease for the first time, because he is not only shown a model of a head and neck tumor but his own tumor disease. By using annotations or segmented structures, the physician is able to explain patient-specific risks in addition to the general risks of a surgical procedure. This can significantly improve the understanding towards the extent of the surgery, possible postoperative complications, or functional limitations and help the patient accept them. Especially with regard to the importance of the safety distance of a head and neck tumor or the necessity of second or two-stage surgery, mixed reality technology is an adequate medium to explain these issues to the patient. The intuitive control of the system and the possibility of interaction with the virtual object allow doctors and patients to talk together about correlations or even alternatives. Thus, the patient is integrated into his patient education and not only "instructed". This collaborative interaction between doctor and patient does not limit the "traditional" aspects of a patient education session such as interpersonal communication. By combining the real world with the aid of optical see-through glasses with virtual objects, medical data can be visualized and discussed with the patient. Nevertheless, the doctor is always available as a present and personal contact person. In particular, by integrating Standard Triangle Language (STL)—files of reconstructions in the context of rehabilitation of tissue defects, MR technology can clarify the complexity of the interventions [52]. Virtual annotations up to complex, photorealistic renderings can enhance the quality of targeted informative doctor-patient discussions. Thus, there is the possibility of common ground between doctor and patient.

2.5. Medical Education and Surgical Training

Mixed reality-based technology can open up new ways to teach medical content. The use of immersive experiences to facilitate the teaching and learning of complex subject matter enables resource-efficient teaching of theoretical and practical content [53]. The application of different extended reality technologies, including VR, AR, and MR is applicable to educating students as well as training physicians [54]. For example, extended reality technologies are currently being used in orthopedic computer-assisted surgery (CAS) systems and training simulators to increase surgical accuracy, improve outcomes, and reduce complications [55,56]. The use of MR technology to visualize a patient case was performed as part of a lecture for undergraduate students. Data from a head and neck tumor patient was used for this purpose. In addition to segmenting the tumor, anatomical structures such as eyes and skull bones were visualized to give students an impression of the location and extent of the mass. These can be shown or hidden separately or in various combinations. As part of the hands-on application, the CT scan was also shown in a separate panel and enabled a direct reference between 3D objects and their underlying 2D data in mixed reality. Communication between students and lecturers is also facilitated by annotation and structural textures. This enabled the visualization of patient-specific pathologies in addition to teaching macroscopic anatomy. With the help of the head-mounted device worn by the lecturer and students, the virtual model of the patient data scan could be discussed. In addition, by using a camera integrated into the head-mounted device, a surgeon is able to stream real-time videos of patients into the lecture hall and using the remote collaboration audio chat feature is able to communicate with the lecturer and the student to discuss the case. Thus, such a session can be projected onto a screen via live stream and display the patient and its associated 3D holograms (see Figure 3).

Depending on the question, it was thus possible to explain to the students the connection between theoretical knowledge and practical application. A recent study by Bork et al. 2018 investigated the application of AR technology in anatomy teaching. Participant feedback showed clear benefits in three-dimensional imagination compared to established teaching methods. Interactive applications and overall learning experience were also identified as clear benefits [57]. Another field of application for MR technology is its use in problem-based learning. Macroscopic anatomical knowledge forms the basis of all surgical training and continuing education. In preparation for planning a patient-specific implant after resection of a head and neck tumor, subjects should learn orbital reconstruction using a simulation tool to demonstrate the basis and intersections with computer-assisted surgery. Future studies to quantitatively evaluate the learning outcome are already being planned.

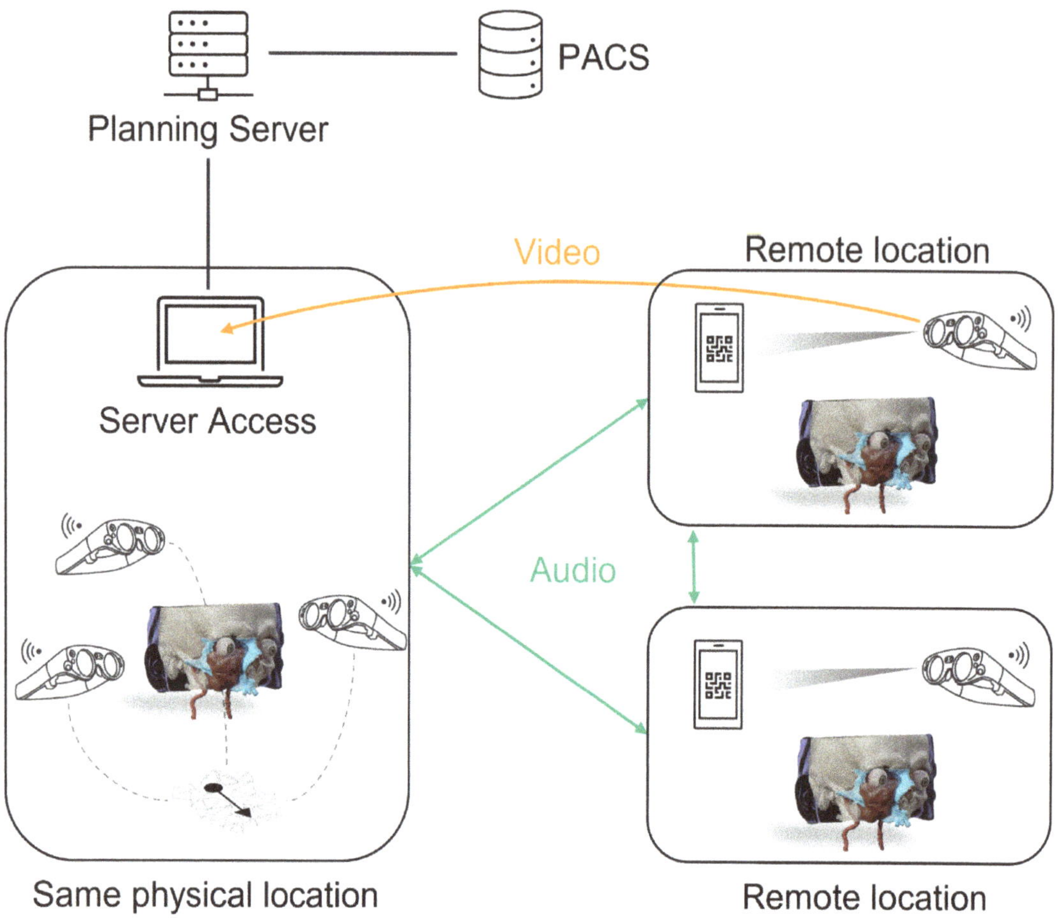

Figure 3. Schematic drawing of a (remote) mixed reality session. All required steps for the initial treatment planning are performed on a client PC, which accesses a server with the associated planning software installed. PACS integration facilitates access to the medical imaging data so that all information are directly available to the surgeon. Subsequently, multiple mixed reality HMDs at the same physical location as the client PC can connect to a joint session. Interaction with the virtual objects is synchronized in real-time, so that all participants see the same scenery from their viewpoints, thus enabling collaborative case discussions. Remote users can join the same mixed reality session by scanning a QR-code generated from and sent by the originator of the session to each remote participant. Bi-directional transmission of the audio signal enables communication across multiple locations via the HMD's integrated microphone and speakers. User input synchronization and spatial audio enable immersive mixed reality experiences. In order to transmit the views from one session to other locations, the HMDs can send the video signal, which captures the real world enriched with the virtual objects, to the other participants via an integrated camera. In this way, also people who are not wearing an HMD can be involved in the session. Kindly compiled by BrainLab.

3. Results

Based on our previous experimental experience, it has been shown that MR technology is a suitable and accurate method for the visualization and treatment planning of head and neck tumors. Accurate radiological imaging of pathologies is an obligatory requirement for complex craniofacial interventions. In all presented areas, image data suitable for MR technologies was obtained and successfully processed. The time required for the processing of image data sets for the corresponding application fields, including data transfer, automatic and manual object segmentation, trajectories, and additional annotations, is highly variable and dependent on the complexity of the case. In particular, the processing of data in the preparation of an MR-based tumor board requires significantly more time. Before mixed reality technology can be used efficiently, exact requirements as well as the problem definition for the application area must be defined. This includes the requirements of the network environment to enable real-time data transmission as well as the specific content of the application areas as follows: When using MR technology in patient information, the automatic segmentation of CT data scans is sufficient since the aim here is merely to visualize pathologies in order to find a basis in the context of the patient conversation. Additional annotations can be set during the conversation, and prior manual processing of the data is only necessary in complex cases. The extent to which this new type of MR technology leads to increased understanding on the part of the patient or possibly to excessive demands, still needs to be clarified. Another limitation is that paper-based explanations remain obligatory due to the legal framework, so no added value can be expected in terms of time expenditure. In particular, the use of MR technology in the tumor board can be decisive, but the demands on technology and digitization are highest here. A time-consuming preparation of the data in line with the specialties is absolutely necessary in order to create a basis for decision-making. In particular, the implementation of the different protocols of the participating disciplines as well as their visualization requires more detailed investigations. Here, the segmentation and 3D rendering of the radiological CT scans for 3D visualization in preoperative imaging and planning is the most proven, as many of the workflow steps are already automated here with the help of the planning software. Investigating the transfer of teaching content through mixed reality in terms of efficiency and effectiveness must also be part of further investigations. Nevertheless, the literature has already identified an advantage to using VR and AR technologies. This allows the repetition of learning techniques while saving resources. Simulation is an important aspect of training, yet technology is not yet able to simulate haptic aspects of an examination or intervention [53,58,59]. Qualitatively, improvements in visualization and understanding can be expected in all application areas, as well as the facilitation of interdisciplinary communication in the future [60,61]. Aspects of quality control after processing of preoperative, intraoperative, and postoperative data are also conceivable sub-areas of mixed reality technology, as all data and results can be visualized for follow-up control. However, all application areas have in common that, so far, no defined workflow has been agreed upon to implement guidelines and legal requirements in a professional manner as well as to enable effective and efficient use of this technology.

4. Discussion

Various studies in oral and maxillofacial surgery have addressed potential applications of mixed reality technology in the visualization and treatment planning of head and neck tumors [62–64]. In this work, possible application scenarios of the new technology could be demonstrated. Modern imaging techniques such as CT and MRI are able to visualize parameters such as tumor volume and extent with high accuracy thanks to further developments in the last decades. This has led to an improvement in the staging of head and neck tumors [2,3]. However, there is still a need for a digital interface between tomographic examination and spatial imaging for surgical planning. MR technology, as a multimodal interactive image analysis platform, can create digital patient-specific 3D holographic models with high precision from multimodal image data [35,36]. Thus, by integrating segmented datasets, 3D visualization of tumor extent and clearance distance has the potential to provide better information on resectability or postoperative functional limitations. At the same time, 3D visualization from tumor mapping for comparison of radiological imaging with clinical parameters is possible [65]. Mixed reality technology in oncologic head and neck surgery increases reliability by visualizing safety distances and thus protecting vital structures. It can also serve as a planning aid in radiotherapy planning and assist in the planning process [62,66]. For postoperative follow-up, it is a useful tool to correlate outlined tumor margins and transfer them to different image datasets to detect tumor recurrence or the outcome of adjuvant chemotherapy and radiotherapy to evaluate treatment outcomes. Furthermore, the implementation of MR in a multidisciplinary tumor board allows the creation of a language-independent, patient-centered, and flexible virtual platform for visualization of all information. Important aspects of pre-, intra-, and postoperative treatment planning and quality control of the treatment strategy can be visualized and shared. In addition, available system resources can be coordinated [67,68]. Adequate patient education must consider anatomical and functional aspects. In this regard, MR technology is a viable tool for illustration and patient risk education. The planning software segments the anatomical structures with the automatic atlas-based algorithm and provides specific information about the patient's clinical situation. The 3D visualization of the patient's own disease and a patient-specific preoperative simulation can assist the patient in making treatment decisions. Studies showed that visual representation of information significantly improves the understanding of explanations [48,50]. Augmented reality, virtual reality (VR), and mixed reality (MR) can enable the delivery of medical content without negatively impacting patients in various medical disciplines. Yet, financial resources can be conserved, or ethical and regulatory constraints can be avoided [53,58].

5. Conclusions

The ideal application of MR technology would be a mobile or head-mounted display that allows the physician or operator to visualize patient data within the field of view rather than using one or more screens. Manipulation, simulation, and 3D holographic visualization of data can enable an increase in surgical accuracy and improve patient safety by reducing procedure-related complications. The broad range of applications also allows use of patient information, potentially resulting in increased patient compliance. In addition, technologies such as MR open the doors for the integration of novel learning methods into conventional medical teaching, thus initiating a paradigm shift towards active, student-centered learning with the help of multimodal, complementary learning methods. However, there have been few prospective, randomized studies comparing the benefits of using mixed reality technology in clinical practice with established methods in head and neck tumor surgery. Regarding the advantages of MR, this technology can play a major role in advanced head and neck cancer treatment.

Author Contributions: Conceptualization, N.K. and M.R.; methodology N.K. and M.R.; validation, M.R. and N.K.; formal analysis, N.K.; investigation, N.K.; resources, M.W.; writing—original draft preparation, N.K. and M.R.; writing—review and editing, A.P., H.L.M. and M.R.; writing—revised the manuscript, H.L.M. and M.R.; visualization, N.K.; supervision, M.R.; project administration, M.R. All authors have read and agreed to the published version of the manuscript.

Funding: This work has been supported by the Ministry of Economic Affairs, Innovation, Digitalization and Energy of the State of North Rhine-Westphalia (MWIDE NRW) along with the Competence Center 5G.NRW under grant number 005-01903-0047.

Institutional Review Board Statement: The study was conducted in accordance with the Declaration of Helsinki, and approved by the Ethics Committee of the University Düsseldorf (protocol code 2022-1849 and date of approval 23 May 2022).

Informed Consent Statement: Written informed consent has been obtained from the patient to publish this paper.

Data Availability Statement: Not applicable.

Acknowledgments: We would like to thank Shufang Liu and Michael Schwerter (Brainlab AG) for their technical support.

Conflicts of Interest: The authors declare no conflict of interest.

References

1. Lell, M.; Mantsopoulos, K.; Uder, M.; Wuest, W.; Lell, M. Bildgebung der Kopf-Hals-Region. *Der Radiol.* **2016**, *56*, 181–201. [CrossRef] [PubMed]
2. Alberico, R.A.; Husain, S.H.S.; Sirotkin, I. Imaging in head and neck oncology. *Surg. Oncol. Clin. N. Am.* **2004**, *13*, 13–35. [CrossRef]
3. Abraham, J. Imaging for Head and Neck Cancer. *Surg. Oncol. Clin. N. Am.* **2015**, *24*, 455–471. [CrossRef]
4. Antoniou, A.J.; Marcus, C.; Subramaniam, R.M. Value of Imaging in Head and Neck Tumors. *Surg. Oncol. Clin. N. Am.* **2014**, *23*, 685–707. [CrossRef] [PubMed]
5. Sadick, M.; Schoenberg, S.O.; Hoermann, K.; Sadick, H. Aktuelle Standards und Fortschritte in der onkologischen Bildgebung von Kopf-Hals-Tumoren. *Laryngo-Rhino-Otol.* **2012**, *91*, S27–S47. [CrossRef] [PubMed]
6. Bittermann, G.; Scheifele, C.; Prokic, V.; Bhatt, V.; Henke, M.; Grosu, A.-L.; Schmelzeisen, R.; Metzger, M.C. Description of a method: Computer generated virtual model for accurate localisation of tumour margins, standardised resection, and planning of radiation treatment in head & neck cancer surgery. *J. Cranio-Maxillofac. Surg.* **2013**, *41*, 279–281. [CrossRef]
7. Edwards, S.P. Computer-Assisted Craniomaxillofacial Surgery. *Oral Maxillofac. Surg. Clin. N. Am.* **2010**, *22*, 117–134. [CrossRef]
8. Rana, M.; Essig, H.; Eckardt, A.M.; Tavassol, F.; Ruecker, M.; Schramm, A.; Gellrich, N.-C. Advances and Innovations in Computer-Assisted Head and Neck Oncologic Surgery. *J. Craniofacial Surg.* **2012**, *23*, 272–278. [CrossRef]
9. Tsetsos, N.; Poutoglidis, A.; Arsos, G.; Tsentemeidou, A.; Kilmpasanis, A.; Katsampoukas, D.; Fyrmpas, G. 18F-FDG-PET/CT interpretation pitfalls in patients with head and neck cancer. *Am. J. Otolaryngol.* **2022**, *43*, 103209. [CrossRef]
10. Bittermann, G.; Ermer, M.; Voss, P.; Duttenhoefer, F.; Zimmerer, R.; Schmelzeisen, R.; Metzger, M. Comparison of virtual and titanium clip marking of tumour resection margins for improved radiation planning in head and neck cancer surgery. *Int. J. Oral Maxillofac. Surg.* **2015**, *44*, 1468–1473. [CrossRef]
11. Tepper, O.M.; Rudy, H.L.; Lefkowitz, A.; Weimer, K.A.; Marks, S.M.; Stern, C.S.; Garfein, E.S. Mixed Reality with HoloLens: Where Virtual Reality Meets Augmented Reality in the Operating Room. *Plast. Reconstr. Surg.* **2017**, *140*, 1066–1070. [CrossRef] [PubMed]
12. Condino, S.; Turini, G.; Parchi, P.D.; Viglialoro, R.M.; Piolanti, N.; Gesi, M.; Ferrari, M.; Ferrari, V. How to Build a Patient-Specific Hybrid Simulator for Orthopaedic Open Surgery: Benefits and Limits of Mixed-Reality Using the Microsoft HoloLens. *J. Health Eng.* **2018**, *2018*, 5435097. [CrossRef] [PubMed]
13. Smith, R.T.; Clarke, T.J.; Mayer, W.; Cunningham, A.; Matthews, B.; Zucco, J.E. Mixed Reality Interaction and Presentation Techniques for Medical Visualisations. *Adv. Exp. Med. Biol.* **2020**, *1260*, 123–139. [CrossRef]
14. Hanna, M.G.; Ahmed, I.; Nine, J.; Prajapati, S.; Pantanowitz, L. Augmented Reality Technology Using Microsoft HoloLens in Anatomic Pathology. *Arch. Pathol. Lab. Med.* **2018**, *142*, 638–644. [CrossRef] [PubMed]
15. Hu, H.-Z.; Feng, X.-B.; Shao, Z.-W.; Xie, M.; Xu, S.; Wu, X.-H.; Ye, Z.-W. Application and Prospect of Mixed Reality Technology in Medical Field. *Curr. Med. Sci.* **2019**, *39*, 1–6. [CrossRef] [PubMed]
16. Bernardo, A. Virtual Reality and Simulation in Neurosurgical Training. *World Neurosurg.* **2017**, *106*, 1015–1029. [CrossRef]
17. Davids, J.; Manivannan, S.; Darzi, A.; Giannarou, S.; Ashrafian, H.; Marcus, H.J. Simulation for skills training in neurosurgery: A systematic review, meta-analysis, and analysis of progressive scholarly acceptance. *Neurosurg. Rev.* **2021**, *44*, 1853–1867. [CrossRef]
18. Cannizzaro, D.; Zaed, I.; Safa, A.; Jelmoni, A.J.M.; Composto, A.; Bisoglio, A.; Schmeizer, K.; Becker, A.C.; Pizzi, A.; Cardia, A.; et al. Augmented Reality in Neurosurgery, State of Art and Future Projections. A Systematic Review. *Front. Surg.* **2022**, *9*, 864792. [CrossRef]
19. Elsayed, M.; Kadom, N.; Ghobadi, C.; Strauss, B.; Al Dandan, O.; Aggarwal, A.; Anzai, Y.; Griffith, B.; Lazarow, F.; Straus, C.M.; et al. Virtual and augmented reality: Potential applications in radiology. *Acta Radiol.* **2020**, *61*, 1258–1265. [CrossRef]
20. Sutherland, J.; Belec, J.; Sheikh, A.; Chepelev, L.; Althobaity, W.; Chow, B.J.W.; Mitsouras, D.; Christensen, A.; Rybicki, F.J.; La Russa, D.J. Applying Modern Virtual and Augmented Reality Technologies to Medical Images and Models. *J. Digit. Imaging* **2019**, *32*, 38–53. [CrossRef]
21. Sparwasser, P.M.; Schoeb, D.; Miernik, A.; Borgmann, H. Augmented Reality und Virtual Reality im Operationssaal—Status Quo und Quo vadis. *Aktuel- Urol.* **2018**, *49*, 500–508. [CrossRef] [PubMed]
22. Fida, B.; Cutolo, F.; di Franco, G.; Ferrari, M.; Ferrari, V. Augmented reality in open surgery. *Updat. Surg.* **2018**, *70*, 389–400. [CrossRef] [PubMed]
23. Qian, L.; Song, T.; Unberath, M.; Kazanzides, P. AR-Loupe: Magnified Augmented Reality by Combining an Optical See-Through Head-Mounted Display and a Loupe. *IEEE Trans. Vis. Comput. Graph.* **2022**, *28*, 2550–2562. [CrossRef] [PubMed]
24. Reis, G.; Yilmaz, M.; Rambach, J.; Pagani, A.; Suarez-Ibarrola, R.; Miernik, A.; Lesur, P.; Minaskan, N. Mixed reality applications in urology: Requirements and future potential. *Ann. Med. Surg.* **2021**, *66*, 102394. [CrossRef]
25. Tang, R.; Ma, L.-F.; Rong, Z.-X.; Li, M.-D.; Zeng, J.-P.; Wang, X.-D.; Liao, H.-E.; Dong, J.-H. Augmented reality technology for preoperative planning and intraoperative navigation during hepatobiliary surgery: A review of current methods. *Hepatobiliary Pancreat. Dis. Int.* **2018**, *17*, 101–112. [CrossRef]
26. Cutolo, F.; Cattari, N.; Fontana, U.; Ferrari, V. Optical See-Through Head-Mounted Displays with Short Focal Distance: Conditions for Mitigating Parallax-Related Registration Error. *Front. Robot. AI* **2020**, *7*, 572001. [CrossRef]

27. Sakai, D.; Joyce, K.; Sugimoto, M.; Horikita, N.; Hiyama, A.; Sato, M.; Devitt, A.; Watanabe, M. Augmented, virtual and mixed reality in spinal surgery: A real-world experience. *J. Orthop. Surg.* **2020**, *28*, 2309499020952698. [CrossRef]
28. Fang, W.; Zheng, L.; Deng, H.; Zhang, H. Real-Time Motion Tracking for Mobile Augmented/Virtual Reality Using Adaptive Visual-Inertial Fusion. *Sensors* **2017**, *17*, 1037. [CrossRef]
29. Choi, I.; Kim, J.; Kim, D. A Target-Less Vision-Based Displacement Sensor Based on Image Convex Hull Optimization for Measuring the Dynamic Response of Building Structures. *Sensors* **2016**, *16*, 2085. [CrossRef]
30. Park, G.; Argyros, A.; Lee, J.; Woo, W. 3D Hand Tracking in the Presence of Excessive Motion Blur. *IEEE Trans. Vis. Comput. Graph.* **2020**, *26*, 1891–1901. [CrossRef]
31. Kim, M.; Jeon, C.; Kim, J. A Study on Immersion and Presence of a Portable Hand Haptic System for Immersive Virtual Reality. *Sensors* **2017**, *17*, 1141. [CrossRef] [PubMed]
32. Chen, K.B.; Ponto, K.; Tredinnick, R.D.; Radwin, R.G. Virtual exertions: Evoking the sense of exerting forces in virtual reality using gestures and muscle activity. *Hum. Factors* **2015**, *57*, 658–673. [CrossRef] [PubMed]
33. Kraeima, J.; Dorgelo, B.; Gulbitti, H.A.; Steenbakkers, R.J.H.M.; Schepman, K.P.; Roodenburg, J.L.N.; Spijkervet, F.K.L.; Schepers, R.H.; Witjes, M.J.H. Multi-modality 3D mandibular resection planning in head and neck cancer using CT and MRI data fusion: A clinical series. *Oral Oncol.* **2018**, *81*, 22–28. [CrossRef] [PubMed]
34. Liu, S.; Wang, H.; Wang, C.; Zhang, W.; Chen, G.; Hu, X. Intra-operative 3D hologram support with mixed reality technique based on CT-MRI fusion images: Operation guidance for brain brachytherapy. *J. Contemp. Brachytherapy* **2021**, *13*, 205–210. [CrossRef]
35. Mitani, S.; Sato, E.; Kawaguchi, N.; Sawada, S.; Sakamoto, K.; Kitani, T.; Sanada, T.; Yamada, H.; Hato, N. Case-specific three-dimensional hologram with a mixed reality technique for tumor resection in otolaryngology. *Laryngoscope Investig. Otolaryngol.* **2021**, *6*, 432–437. [CrossRef]
36. Saito, Y.; Sugimoto, M.; Imura, S.; Morine, Y.; Ikemoto, T.; Iwahashi, S.; Yamada, S.; Shimada, M. Intraoperative 3D Hologram Support with Mixed Reality Techniques in Liver Surgery. *Ann. Surg.* **2020**, *271*, e4–e7. [CrossRef]
37. Lu, L.; Wang, H.; Liu, P.; Liu, R.; Zhang, J.; Xie, Y.; Liu, S.; Huo, T.; Xie, M.; Wu, X.; et al. Applications of Mixed Reality Technology in Orthopedics Surgery: A Pilot Study. *Front. Bioeng. Biotechnol.* **2022**, *10*, 740507. [CrossRef]
38. Iglesias, J.E.; Sabuncu, M.R. Multi-atlas segmentation of biomedical images: A survey. *Med. Image Anal.* **2015**, *24*, 205–219. [CrossRef]
39. Pednekar, G.V.; Udupa, J.K.; McLaughlin, D.J.; Wu, X.; Tong, Y.; Simone, C.B.; Camaratta, J.; Torigian, D.A. Image Quality and Segmentation. *Proc. SPIE Int. Soc. Opt. Eng.* **2018**, *10576*, 622–628. [CrossRef]
40. Gehrsitz, P.; Rompel, O.; Schöber, M.; Cesnjevar, R.; Purbojo, A.; Uder, M.; Dittrich, S.; Alkassar, M. Cinematic Rendering in Mixed-Reality Holograms: A New 3D Preoperative Planning Tool in Pediatric Heart Surgery. *Front. Cardiovasc. Med.* **2021**, *8*, 633611. [CrossRef]
41. Wang, H.; Yushkevich, P.A. Multi-atlas Segmentation without Registration: A Supervoxel-Based Approach. *Med. Image Comput. Comput. Assist. Interv.* **2013**, *16*, 535–542. [CrossRef] [PubMed]
42. Jalil, R.; Akhter, W.; Lamb, B.; Taylor, C.; Harris, J.; Green, J.; Sevdalis, N. Validation of Team Performance Assessment of Multidisciplinary Tumor Boards. *J. Urol.* **2014**, *192*, 891–898. [CrossRef] [PubMed]
43. Lassalle, R.; Marold, J.; Schöbel, M.; Manzey, D.; Bohn, S.; Dietz, A.; Boehm, A. Entscheidungsprozesse im Tumorboard bei eingeschränkter Evidenzlage. *Laryngo-Rhino Otol.* **2013**, *93*, 237–243. [CrossRef] [PubMed]
44. Tschiesner, U.; Stier-Jarmer, M.; Strieth, S.; Singer, S.; Dietz, A.; Fietkau, R.; Wollenberg, B.; Mast, G.; Cieza, A.; Harréus, U.A. Entwicklung eines ICF-basierten Leitfadens für die Beurteilung funktioneller Aspekte bei Kopf-Hals-Tumoren. *Endoscopy* **2013**, *92*, 314–325. [CrossRef]
45. Freytag, M.; Herrlinger, U.; Hauser, S.; Bauernfeind, F.G.; Gonzalez-Carmona, M.A.; Landsberg, J.; Buermann, J.; Vatter, H.; Holderried, T.; Send, T.; et al. Higher number of multidisciplinary tumor board meetings per case leads to improved clinical outcome. *BMC Cancer* **2020**, *20*, 355. [CrossRef]
46. Kuhn, K.J.; Cloutier, J.; Boutin, R.D.; Steffner, R.; Riley, G. Soft tissue pathology for the radiologist: A tumor board primer with 2020 WHO classification update. *Skelet. Radiol.* **2020**, *50*, 29–42. [CrossRef]
47. Pfefferle, M.; Shahub, S.; Shahedi, M.; Gahan, J.; Johnson, B.; Le, P.; Vargas, J.; Judson, B.O.; Alshara, Y.; Li, Q.; et al. Renal biopsy under augmented reality guidance. *Proc. SPIE Int. Soc. Opt. Eng.* **2020**, *11315*, 113152W. [CrossRef]
48. Giampieri, M. Communication and informed consent in elderly people. *Minerva Anestesiol* **2012**, *78*, 236–242.
49. Grassi, L.; Caruso, R.; Costantini, A. Communication with Patients Suffering from Serious Physical Illness. *Adv. Psychosom. Med.* **2015**, *34*, 10–23. [CrossRef]
50. Arabul, M.; Kandemir, A.; Celik, M.; Alper, E.; Akpinar, Z.; Aslan, F.; Vatansever, S.; Unsal, B. Impact of an information video before colonoscopy on patient satisfaction and anxiety. *Turk. J. Gastroenterol.* **2012**, *23*, 523–529. [CrossRef]
51. Perrenoud, B.; Velonaki, V.-S.; Bodenmann, P.; Ramelet, A.-S. The effectiveness of health literacy interventions on the informed consent process of health care users: A systematic review protocol. *JBI Database Syst. Rev. Implement. Rep.* **2015**, *13*, 82–94. [CrossRef] [PubMed]
52. Ito, T.; Kawashima, Y.; Yamazaki, A.; Tsutsumi, T. Application of a virtual and mixed reality-navigation system using commercially available devices to the lateral temporal bone resection. *Ann. Med. Surg.* **2021**, *72*, 103063. [CrossRef] [PubMed]
53. Wish-Baratz, S.; Crofton, A.R.; Gutierrez, J.; Henninger, E.; Griswold, M.A. Assessment of Mixed-Reality Technology Use in Remote Online Anatomy Education. *JAMA Netw. Open* **2020**, *3*, e2016271. [CrossRef] [PubMed]

54. Kolecki, R.; Pręgowska, A.; Dąbrowa, J.; Skuciński, J.; Pulanecki, T.; Walecki, P.; van Dam, P.M.; Dudek, D.; Richter, P.; Proniewska, K. Assessment of the utility of Mixed Reality in medical education. *Transl. Res. Anat.* **2022**, *28*, 100214. [CrossRef]
55. Goh, G.S.; Lohre, R.; Parvizi, J.; Goel, D.P. Virtual and augmented reality for surgical training and simulation in knee arthroplasty. *Arch. Orthop. Trauma. Surg.* **2021**, *141*, 2303–2312. [CrossRef]
56. Teatini, A.; Kumar, R.P.; Elle, O.J.; Wiig, O. Mixed reality as a novel tool for diagnostic and surgical navigation in orthopaedics. *Int. J. Comput. Assist. Radiol. Surg.* **2021**, *16*, 407–414. [CrossRef]
57. Bork, F. Interactive augmented reality systems: Hilfsmittel zur personalisierten Patientenaufklärung und Rehabilitation. *Unfallchirurg* **2018**, *121*, 286–292. [CrossRef]
58. Barteit, S.; Lanfermann, L.; Bärnighausen, T.; Neuhann, F.; Beiersmann, C. Augmented, Mixed, and Virtual Reality-Based Head-Mounted Devices for Medical Education: Systematic Review. *JMIR Serious Games* **2021**, *9*, e29080. [CrossRef]
59. Hughes, C.; Stapleton, C.; Hughes, D.E.; Smith, E. Mixed reality in education, entertainment, and training. *IEEE Comput. Graph. Appl.* **2005**, *25*, 24–30. [CrossRef]
60. Cartucho, J.; Shapira, D.; Ashrafian, H.; Giannarou, S. Multimodal mixed reality visualisation for intraoperative surgical guidance. *Int. J. Comput. Assist. Radiol. Surg.* **2020**, *15*, 819–826. [CrossRef]
61. Zhu, L.-Y.; Hou, J.-C.; Yang, L.; Liu, Z.-R.; Tong, W.; Bai, Y.; Zhang, Y.-M. Application value of mixed reality in hepatectomy for hepatocellular carcinoma. *World J. Gastrointest. Surg.* **2022**, *14*, 36–45. [CrossRef] [PubMed]
62. Ayoub, A.; Pulijala, Y. The application of virtual reality and augmented reality in Oral & Maxillofacial Surgery. *BMC Oral Health* **2019**, *19*, 238. [CrossRef]
63. Kerner, K.F.; Imielinska, C.; Rolland, J.; Tang, H. Augmented Reality for teaching endotracheal intubation: MR imaging to create anatomically correct models. *AMIA Annu. Symp. Proc.* **2003**, *2003*, 888.
64. Tang, Z.-N.; Hu, L.-H.; Soh, H.Y.; Yu, Y.; Zhang, W.-B.; Peng, X. Accuracy of Mixed Reality Combined with Surgical Navigation Assisted Oral and Maxillofacial Tumor Resection. *Front. Oncol.* **2021**, *11*, 715484. [CrossRef]
65. Essig, H.; Rana, M.; Meyer, A.; Eckardt, A.M.; Kokemueller, H.; von See, C.; Lindhorst, D.; Tavassol, F.; Ruecker, M.; Gellrich, N.-C. Virtual 3D tumor marking-exact intraoperative coordinate mapping improve post-operative radiotherapy. *Radiat. Oncol.* **2011**, *6*, 159. [CrossRef]
66. Tarutani, K.; Takaki, H.; Igeta, M.; Fujiwara, M.; Okamura, A.; Horio, F.; Toudou, Y.; Nakajima, S.; Kagawa, K.; Tanooka, M.; et al. Development and Accuracy Evaluation of Augmented Reality-based Patient Positioning System in Radiotherapy: A Phantom Study. *Vivo* **2021**, *35*, 2081–2087. [CrossRef]
67. Hammer, R.D.; Fowler, D.; Sheets, L.R.; Siadimas, A.; Guo, C.; Prime, M.S. Digital Tumor Board Solutions Have Significant Impact on Case Preparation. *JCO Clin. Cancer Inform.* **2020**, *4*, 757–768. [CrossRef]
68. Hammer, R.D.; Prime, M.S. A clinician's perspective on co-developing and co-implementing a digital tumor board solution. *Health Inform. J.* **2020**, *26*, 2213–2221. [CrossRef]

Journal of
Clinical Medicine

MDPI

Article

Personalized Surgery Service in a Tertiary Hospital: A Method to Increase Effectiveness, Precision, Safety and Quality in Maxillofacial Surgery Using Custom-Made 3D Prostheses and Implants

Jorge Pamias-Romero [1,2], Joan Masnou-Pratdesaba [3], Manel Sáez-Barba [1,2], Alba de-Pablo-García-Cuenca [1,2], Sahyly Siurana-Montilva [4], Anna Sala-Cunill [5], Victòria Valls-Comamala [5], Rosa Pujol-Pina [2] and Coro Bescós-Atín [1,2,*]

[1] Oral and Maxillofacial Surgery Service, Hospital Universitari Vall d'Hebron, Vall d'Hebron Barcelona Hospital Campus, Passeig Vall d'Hebron 119-129, 08035 Barcelona, Spain
[2] New Technologies and Craniofacial Microsurgery, Vall d'Hebron Institut de Recerca (VHIR), Hospital Universitari Vall d'Hebron, Vall d'Hebron Barcelona Hospital Campus, Passeig Vall d'Hebron 119-129, 08035 Barcelona, Spain
[3] Radiology Department, Hospital Universitari Vall d'Hebron, Vall d'Hebron Barcelona Hospital Campus, Passeig Vall d'Hebron 119-129, 08035 Barcelona, Spain
[4] MRI Unit, Radiology Department, Hospital Universitari Vall d'Hebron, Vall d'Hebron Barcelona Hospital Campus, Passeig Vall d'Hebron 119-129, 08035 Barcelona, Spain
[5] Innovation, Quality and Processes Management, Hospital Universitari Vall d'Hebron, Vall d'Hebron Barcelona Hospital Campus, Passeig Vall d'Hebron 119-129, 08035 Barcelona, Spain
* Correspondence: cbescos@vhebron.net; Tel.: +34-932-746-179

Citation: Pamias-Romero, J.; Masnou-Pratdesaba, J.; Sáez-Barba, M.; de-Pablo-García-Cuenca, A.; Siurana-Montilva, S.; Sala-Cunill, A.; Valls-Comamala, V.; Pujol-Pina, R.; Bescós-Atín, C. Personalized Surgery Service in a Tertiary Hospital: A Method to Increase Effectiveness, Precision, Safety and Quality in Maxillofacial Surgery Using Custom-Made 3D Prostheses and Implants. *J. Clin. Med.* **2022**, *11*, 4791. https://doi.org/10.3390/jcm11164791

Academic Editor: Eng Ooi

Received: 14 July 2022
Accepted: 10 August 2022
Published: 16 August 2022

Abstract: Personalized surgery (PS) involves virtual planning (VP) and the use of 3D printing technology to design and manufacture custom-made elements to be used during surgery. The widespread use of PS has fostered a paradigm shift in the surgical process. A recent analysis performed in our hospital—along with several studies published in the literature—showed that the extensive use of PS does not preclude the lack of standardization in the process. This means that despite the widely accepted use of this technology, standard individual roles and responsibilities have not been properly defined, and this could hinder the logistics and cost savings in the PS process. The aim of our study was to describe the method followed and the outcomes obtained for the creation of a PS service for the Oral and Maxillofacial Surgery Unit that resolves the current absence of internal structure, allows for the integration of all professionals involved and improves the efficiency and quality of the PS process. We performed a literature search on the implementation of PS techniques in tertiary hospitals and observed a lack of studies on the creation of PS units or services in such hospitals. Therefore, we believe that our work is innovative and has the potential to contribute to the implementation of PS units in other hospitals.

Keywords: tertiary hospital; virtual planning; 3D printing; personalized surgery

1. Introduction

Advances in the field of personalized surgery (PS) involve a "paradigm shift" in the surgical process with respect to conventional surgery techniques. This entails changes in the way the surgical process is planned and performed, which in turn give rise to new workflows that not only involve doctors and surgeons but also engineers and technicians. All these professionals work in joint multidisciplinary teams.

PS involves virtual planning (VP) and the use of 3D printing technology for custom-made elements (known as CAD-CAM [computer-assisted design and computer-assisted manufacturing] technology). PS allows surgeons to develop a virtual surgical plan prior to surgery and to use custom-made surgical devices and surgical prostheses for each patient, with a goal of safer surgeries with more predictable outcomes [1–7].

PS also makes it possible to achieve complex reconstructions from a structural and geometrical point of view through the design and manufacture of custom-made prostheses and implants that perfectly fit a variety of anatomical defects. Therefore, PS has been widely used in several surgical disciplines, in particular in maxillofacial surgery, mostly for complex reconstructions and in relation to congenital and acquired craniomaxillofacial deformities [8–10].

In this sense, Lopez et al. describe their use of 3D printing for the treatment of craniomaxillofacial congenital anomalies, including craniosynostosis and microtia. The authors endorse the potential of 3D printing and CAD-CAM techniques for the design of unique scaffolds of any shape or size, offering a personalized approach to patient-specific skeletal defects. They underscore how powerful these techniques are when it comes to the design and reconstruction of complex anatomical sites, such as the ear, in people who suffer from microtia [10].

Day et al. present a series of more than 30 craniofacial defects treated at a tertiary craniofacial referral center using a combination of virtual surgical planning, 3D modelling and patient-specific custom implants. The treated defects were caused either by syndromes (Pierre Robin, Treacher Collins, Apert's, Pfeiffer, Crouzon) or by other conditions, including craniosynostosis, hemifacial microsomia, micrognathia, multiple facial clefts and trauma. The authors report excellent outcomes for these techniques and mention that complex deformities that require detailed analysis and precise reconstruction benefit the most from the use of advanced 3D techniques. On the basis of the obtained results, the authors conclude that modern 3D technology can potentially improve aesthetic and functional outcomes after complex craniofacial reconstruction, as it allows the surgeon to better analyze complex craniofacial deformities, precisely plan surgical correction with computer simulation of results, customize osteotomies, plan distractions and print custom implants as needed [8].

Other disciplines, such as neurosurgery, traumatology and orthopedic surgery, are increasingly using digital technology and 3D printing to help surgeons minimize human error and reduce surgical time. As published by several authors, the technique is highly reproducible, and it allows for the transfer of the virtually planned steps to the operating table [11,12].

Our hospital has been using PS since 2012, mostly in the Oral and Maxillofacial Surgery Service, and the number of patients treated with PS has increased over time. Although the technique is being used in the hospital on a regular basis, an internal analysis undertaken by the Management Department in the hospital (in collaboration with the professionals who were using PS in 2017) revealed several shortcomings, which are reported below.

First, a significant shortcoming was the lack of an internal structure to act as an "activity hub" and avoid the dispersion of the different professionals involved in the process. The lack of expert staff (engineers and technicians) to collaborate and provide cross-disciplinary interaction and know-how concentration in the PS process was also a concern. Another limitation was the lack of standardization in the PS process and that of indicators to allow for the proper evaluation and analysis of each step of the process. The abovementioned deficiencies resulted in considerable heterogeneity in the PS surgery process, which in turn caused duplicities in radiological tests, an increase in the time required for the diagnosis and planning of cases and potential delays in surgery scheduling. All these shortcomings were associated with unnecessary costs.

The objective of this article is to describe the PS Service we designed for our hospital, with the aim of correcting the identified drawbacks and undertaking the standardization of the PS process. It is our goal to resolve the lack of internal structure so that all professionals involved are coordinated and all resources and facilities are properly used in order to improve the efficiency and quality of the PS process.

2. Materials and Methods

We created a working group to analyze the shortcomings encountered in the internal analysis and to design a comprehensive PS service to avoid the identified limitations and provide the best PS solution for our hospital. The group published several internal documents regarding the creation of a service from the ground up, how the project would fit into national and European public policies and the suitability of the project for public procurement of innovative process solutions. The project was approved by the Hospital Management Unit and was awarded FEDER funds. Furthermore, a public procurement of innovative process solutions is currently underway [13].

We also wanted to determine and analyze how other tertiary hospitals in our country and in the rest of the world are handling the creation and management of PS services in order to learn from their success stories and from the problems they have encountered. To this end, we performed several literature reviews.

A literature review was performed in the PubMed database regarding the implementation of PS techniques within tertiary hospital centers, including 3D printing and the design of personalized prostheses. The keywords searched initially included personalized surgery, 3D printing and tertiary centers/hospitals, which yielded no results. In order to broaden the search, we added the keywords personalized surgery and 3D printing, which yielded 103 results. These results were then narrowed down by selecting inclusion criteria, including free full-text availability and publication within the last 10 years, leading to a total of 27 papers. Other publications were hand-picked among those articles obtained in different searches (using several keywords closely related to those listed above) performed over a few months.

Two of the papers were considered relevant to our proposed model of PS. These were an experimental study and a review of 3D-printed surgical implants in a clinical setting and their potential benefits. The authors discuss how 3D printing is commonly used for surgical training and preoperative planning, with very limited clinical applications, and they propose a wider use of these techniques within hospitals and clinics, demonstrating that "manufacturing surgical implants at the clinic with desktop three-dimensional printers can be feasible, effective and economical". Although this does not exactly reflect our proposed model, it supports the idea that innovative structural and technological advancements within healthcare clinics could be achieved by concentrating many of the involved professionals and procedures internally, leading to a faster and improved service [14,15].

As for the other papers, whereas some pioneering groups have described digital networks in navigation-guided surgery [16,17], we found no articles in which a comprehensive PS service was created from the ground up in a tertiary hospital. Therefore, we decided to perform a new, exhaustive review of the literature by means of a systematic review; our search criteria and strategy are detailed in Appendix A.

We found a total of 109 articles and read the title and abstract of each of them. None of the articles we found provided information on tertiary healthcare centers or hospitals where a PS unit had been created in order to integrate solutions related to PS in several surgical disciplines. Therefore, we consider our work to be innovative and to have the potential to assist other hospitals in their introduction of PS units so that this ever-growing technology can be effectively applied.

3. Results

3.1. Project Description

The model suggested for the PS service focuses on the creation of a new internal structure in the hospital; a 3D surgical planning and design laboratory (3D-LAB) will be the core of the project and will allow for the integration of all the stages of the PS process at Vall d'Hebron University Hospital (HUVH). The 3D-LAB laboratory will be in permanent contact with the industry (outside the hospital) to exchange information and the customized products that will be used during the PS process (Figure 1).

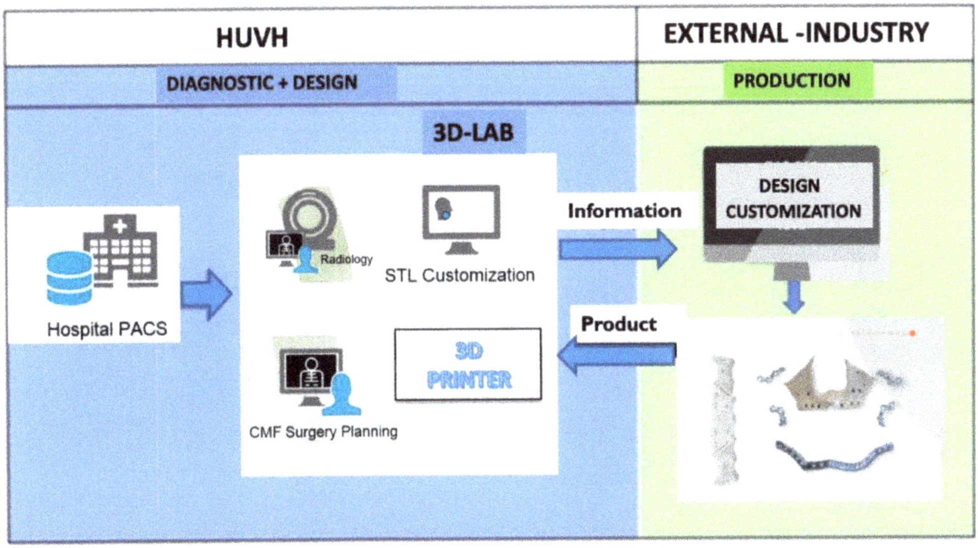

Figure 1. Laboratory of personalized surgery (PS) (3D-LAB).

3.2. 3D-LAB Internal Structure and Functional Specifications

The 3D-LAB will have several facilities in place to perform activities undertaken by a multidisciplinary team that will include surgeons, engineers and technicians.

The facilities are as follows: (1) diagnosis and planning software systems hosted on a central server that allows for direct data import from a corporate storage system (PACS: picture archiving and communication system) in DICOM format (digital imaging and communications in medicine); (2) data export standards (PDF reports and Excel and SPSS spreadsheets); (3) workstations; (4) a 3D printer for prototyping (resin 3D printers) and (5) a data recording system (REDCap database).

The 3D-LAB will be the core and coordinator of the global PS process. Several functions will be performed in the 3D-LAB throughout the process, including interaction with the industry (Figure 2). The functions are described below:

1. Radiological image import from PACS;
2. Processing and merging of images;
3. Diagnosis and planning using diagnosis and planning software;
4. 3D prototyping of the required elements for case diagnosis and planning, including resin surgical guides and models that could be required for the placement of CAD-CAM implants or for the use of pre-bent plates;
5. File generation in STL and DICOM formats containing the processed information to be exported to the industry, where the customized elements can be manufactured (using titanium or other materials). At this stage, we will establish online communication with the industry (website connection) to collaborate in the planning and design of the customized elements;
6. Collection of all the customized products that are manufactured outside the hospital (manufacturing outsourced to the industry). All products manufactured by the industry will be sent to the 3D-LAB office for the final stage of surgical treatment, making it possible to follow up on the delivery time for the various products and monitor the case traceability, materials and products throughout the process;
7. Evaluation of results using several established indicators;
8. Establishment of quality control parameters, including the following: delivery time, required regulations and certifications (quality, material biocompatibility and accuracy of measurement), accepted technologies and load/resistance validations; and

9. A communication and networking platform for all professionals involved and establishment of a training plan with respect to PS for all professionals.

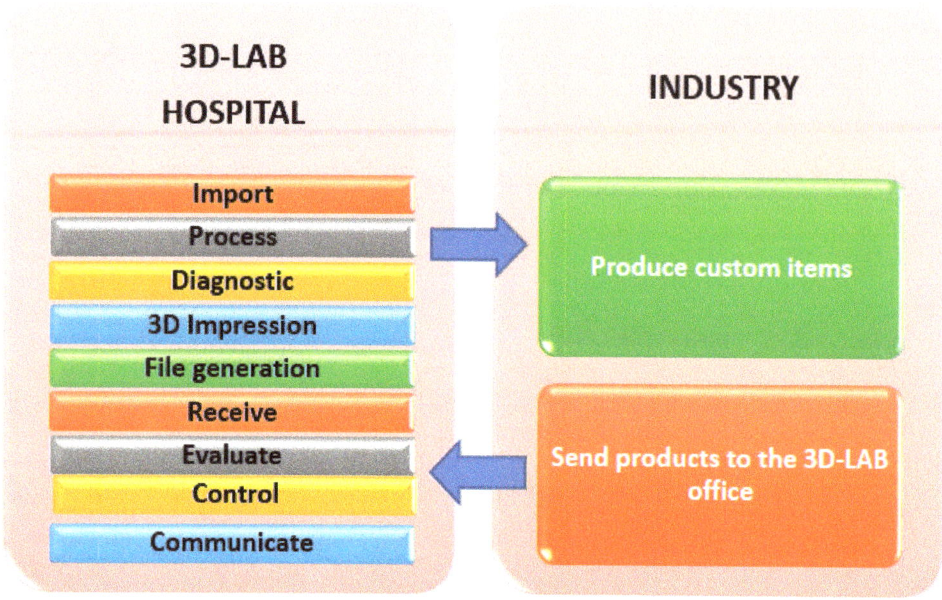

Figure 2. Stages of the personalized surgery (PS) process.

The manufacturing stage of customized elements will be outsourced to the industry. Customized elements will be manufactured according to the files created in and sent from the 3D-LAB office, using various manufacturing techniques and materials (mostly titanium or PEEK) according to the required surgery. Manufacturing will take place according to particular quality standards and certifications required for the products ordered.

The final surgical treatment in which the customized elements will be used and implanted will take place in HUVH operating rooms and will be performed by the same professionals who were involved in the PS process.

3.3. Evaluation of Result Indicators

Results will be evaluated using several kinds of indicators throughout the stages of the process (stages include diagnosis, planning and design, manufacturing, treatment and post-surgery). These are described in Table 1.

Indicators regarding the quality of service and patient safety will be evaluated all throughout the stages of the PS process. They will include diagnosis and planning time, delivery time for customized products, surgical time, ischemia time (when microsurgical techniques are used), surgical technique reversion, average length of ICU stay and hospital stay, postoperative complications and hospital readmission.

Precision indicators will be used to assess the precision of the surgical technique and that of the manufacturing process of the customized elements, whereas indicators with respect to the effectiveness of the technique will focus on functional evaluation and the quality of life (QoL) of patients; various validated tests and surveys will be completed by patients who undergo surgical interventions involving PS techniques.

Process indicators will be used to monitor compliance during the performance of various stages of the process. Compliance will be monitored using evaluation forms filled-out by the staff who work in the 3D-LAB office.

Table 1. Indicators for the evaluation of results of personalized surgery (PS).

Indicator Area	Indicator	Definition
Quality of service and patient safety	Customized planning and design time (*Planning and design stage*)	Average time period from the moment the patient is chosen for PS until the design stage is completed
	Delivery time of customized elements (*Manufacturing stage*)	Average manufacturing time from the moment information is sent to the industry until the product is received at the 3D-LAB office
	Surgical time (*Treatment stage*)	Average time from anesthetic induction to end of surgery
	Graft ischemia time (in the event of PS with a microvascularized graft) (*Treatment stage*)	Average time period between the moment the graft is detached from its vessel in the donor site and the moment the anastomosis in the receptor area has been completed and its functionality has been confirmed
	Change of surgical technique (*Treatment stage*)	Percentage of patients in whom we reverted to a conventional surgical technique out of the total of patients who underwent PS
	Average ICU stay (*Treatment stage*)	ICU stay (days) after intervention
	Average hospital stay (*Treatment stage*)	Average hospital stay until discharge after surgery
	Post-surgical complications (*Treatment stage*)	Percentage of patients who suffer complications that arise from PS out of the total number of patients treated with PS [18]
	Hospital readmission (*Treatment stage*)	Percentage of patients who are readmitted to hospital after discharge (48 h post surgery) for reasons related to the surgery out of the total number of discharged patients who underwent PS
Precision	Surgical precision	Degree of precision of the surgical technique (overlapping of pre- and post-surgical images).
	Precision of customized prosthetic elements	Fitting and alignment degree of customized prosthetic elements
Efficacy of the technique	Quality of life (QoL)	Quality of life (QoL) evaluation through tests and surveys [19]
Process	Process indicators	Monitoring of compliance with all stages throughout the process using evaluation forms, as well as monitoring of compliance with the design processes

Technical costs will also be quantified, including the time devoted to the process by professionals, surgical costs, costs of prostheses/implants and other general costs.

4. Discussion

The proposed model is based on the creation of a new in-house structure in the hospital, i.e., a 3D surgical planning and design laboratory (3D-LAB) or office. This laboratory will be the core of the project and will allow for the integration of all the stages of the PS process in our hospital. Specialist surgeons, engineers and technicians will work in the office and collaborate throughout the PS process. Thus, a multidisciplinary team will be created, professionals will work in a hub and knowledge dispersion will be avoided.

The existence of an in-house knowledge hub where cases can be managed among the various specialists involved and where doctors and engineers can closely cooperate may be particularly useful in such a complex field as that of maxillofacial surgery. Even apparently minor aspects of the process may negatively affect its outcomes if approaches from the medical and the engineering fields do not work seamlessly. By way of example, a study by Lo Giudice et al. analyzed the accuracy of a semiautomatic segmentation method in the detection of the volumetric and morphological characteristics of the mandible in comparison with manual segmentation (the gold standard). The study revealed that the area of mismatch between manual segmentation and semiautomatic segmentation was mainly located at the condyle level, with an underestimation of this anatomical region. As stated by the authors, if digital segmentation of the mandible is not accurate, the physical model obtained by 3D printing will not reliably reproduce the anatomy of the mandible, therefore generating discordance between the treatment plan and the clinical outcomes. The authors suggest partnering with companies specialized in 3D imaging technology whenever clinicians need help during the refinement process [20]. In our opinion, the PS service we describe will be very helpful with respect to avoiding having to resort to industry whenever technical issues arise. Some pioneering groups have described digital networks in navigation-guided surgery and the advantages they provide in terms of data exchange, as well as the constant flow of information created by various professionals, which acts as a feedback method for the system [16,17].

In this regard, Guijarro-Martínez et al. describe a navigation-assisted multidisciplinary network solution for head and neck cancer that was implemented in their center. According to the authors, the network model stores all the relevant information necessary for each of the involved medical fields in a central server and allows for interactive, multidirectional data flow between all implicated participants [16].

Similarly, Rana et al. describe a language-independent and multidisciplinary imaging-guided navigation technique used in their center for head and neck oncologic surgery. The platform provides intraoperatively collected data to the surgeon, oncologist, radiotherapist, pathologist and radiologist; according to the authors, the platform provides a precise, controlled, safe and minimally invasive surgical method with excellent real-time anatomic orientation [17].

Nevertheless, few studies have been published to date with respect to the introduction of PS units in tertiary healthcare centers or hospitals, as shown by the literature review described above.

Recently, a thought-provoking study fostered by the British Association of Oral and Maxillofacial Surgeons (BAOMS) was published [9,21]. The study examines the barriers to the use of printed titanium and digital planning in maxillofacial surgery in the UK. Results showed that a high percentage of maxillofacial surgeons in the UK (88%) use CAD-CAM technology and design. However, design and manufacturing workflows were found to be highly variable, as were funding opportunities and access to technology. The study highlights the absence of a standardized design pathway for the NHS (National Health Service) in terms of in-house hospital implants, with individual roles and responsibilities. Key barriers include costs, delivery time and the logistical process related to the PS process.

In this sense, we believe that our centralized, comprehensive model for PS could offer significant advantages as compared to current models used to perform PS in most public healthcare tertiary hospitals both in our country and in other countries, such as the UK, as shown in the aforementioned article. In our opinion, these advantages would benefit all stakeholders, including patients, professionals and the hospital.

Patients will benefit from safer, more precise surgeries with improved control of quality indicators and of customized products. The possibility of performing an exhaustive evaluation of the obtained results will also benefit patients.

In our opinion, our PS model could benefit hospital professionals in multiple ways. First, the existence of well-established protocols and circuits managed in a multidisciplinary environment would aid in the professional decision-making process. Decision making would not have to rely so heavily on a single individual but would involve reaching an agreement among different professionals. Secondly, PS would foster learning and training among professionals, which is relevant, considering that new technologies are becoming increasingly relevant and are constantly evolving. Such learning and training would be particularly important in tertiary hospitals that place heavy training burdens on specialists. Thirdly, the potential of establishing a cross-disciplinary collaboration with engineers and specialized technicians could promote concentration of know-how and progress toward research and innovation, in addition to facilitating the creation of new technological developments.

We believe that this model would also provide benefits for the hospital; given that information would be obtained regarding the process, the resources used and the generated costs, the hospital would be provided with an opportunity to achieve improved global management of the PS process. Furthermore, the information obtained with respect to service quality, workflows and time devoted to each stage of the process would allow for the introduction of measures to improve the treatment of various pathologies, including those that are most urgent. From this point of view, the involvement of the hospital in the PS project has made it possible to work with a funding route instead of an individual funding request (IFR), as was done in the past. Whereas when using an IFR inequalities may arise from the free interpretation of what the appropriate route to treat a patient might be, when using a funding route such inequalities are avoided, as the appropriate route to treat a patient is expected to fit into previously established protocols.

As an additional advantage, the new model could provide guidance on the latest regulations regarding new devices and implantable material used in PS, which is an area of concern with respect to quality control. Despite the absence of a standardized in-house implant design pathway with individual roles and responsibilities until recently, recent regulations (ISO 13485) with respect to medical devices (MDR) issued in May 2021 may better bridge the interface between in-house designers and external manufacturers, as the MDR guides the creation of a quality management system for designers and manufacturers of implantable devices [22–25].

As shown by a study published by Goodson [9], most centers with in-house planning facilities have resin 3D printers (not titanium printers), and they can produce sterilizable resin surgical guides and models that are required for the placement of CAD-CAM implants or for the use of pre-bent plates. In our 3D-LAB laboratory, we will also perform 3D prototyping of several elements considered necessary for case diagnosis and planning, including resin surgical guides and models that could be required for the placement of CAD-CAM implants or for the use of pre-bent plates. For the time being, the printing of customized elements made of titanium or other materials (such as PEEK) will be outsourced to industry. A carefully designed workflow will be followed in our interactions with industry, and we cannot rule out the possibility of printing elements in our laboratory in the future, considering the regulations in place and the potential costs generated.

Finally, we believe that this model would have a positive impact on our healthcare system. The office described above would enable the healthcare system to plan for the provision of PS in all medical specialties, reducing the variability between procedures and allowing for improved control of costs. In turn, these advantages would make it possible to scale up the use of a technology that is steadily on the rise.

5. Conclusions

PS is increasingly used in several surgical specialties, in particular in maxillofacial surgery, where it has achieved the highest level of development. However, some published studies have evidenced the current lack of standardization in the PS process in hospitals, which could have negative repercussions with respect to the logistics and costs involved in the PS process.

The creation of a PS service with an internal structure, a clear definition of functions and the establishment of indicators that allow for the assessment of the global process and for the integration of all professionals involved could offer significant advantages in comparison with the PS models that are currently in place in most tertiary hospitals.

Among the advantages of the new model are improved patient safety and a support system for professionals, both in terms of decision making and as a powerful resource when training others specialists. There would also be advantages for the hospital, such as improved global management of the PS process and additional guidance on the latest regulations with respect to new devices and implantable material used in PS (an area of concern for quality control).

Given the lack of publications (based on our systematic review of the literature) describing the creation of PS units or services in tertiary hospitals, we consider our work to be innovative and to have the potential to contribute to the creation of PS units in other hospitals so that they can introduce this ever-growing technology in their daily work.

Author Contributions: Conceptualization, C.B.-A. and J.P.-R.; methodology, C.B.-A. and J.P.-R.; software, not applicable.; validation, C.B.-A. and J.P.-R.; formal analysis, not applicable; investigation, C.B.-A., J.P.-R., J.M.-P., M.S.-B., A.d.-P.-G.-C., S.S.-M., A.S.-C. and V.V.-C.; resources, not applicable; data curation, R.P.-P.; writing—original draft preparation, C.B.-A. and R.P.-P.; writing—review and editing, C.B.-A., J.P.-R., A.S.-C. and V.V.-C.; visualization, C.B.-A. and J.P.-R.; supervision, C.B.-A. and J.P.-R.; project administration, C.B.-A. and J.P.-R.; funding acquisition, not applicable at this stage. All authors have read and agreed to the published version of the manuscript.

Funding: Whereas FEDER funds (Programa Operatiu FEDER 2014–2020: Convocatòria 2017 per a projectes de compra pública d'innovació en l'àmbit de la salut dins del marc del (Resolució SLT/1913/2017, de 2 d'agost, ref. BDNS 358200) SA51-006903 "3D-LAB-Servei de Cirurgia Personalitzada" d'Hospital Universitari Vall d'Hebron-Institut Català de la Salut. Resolució del Servei Català de la Salut; concessió provisional realitzada pel Director del Servei Català de la Salut el 09/11/2018) were awarded for the implementation of the personalized surgery service described in this article, no funds were received for analysis of the situation in the hospital and devising and designing a new service.

Institutional Review Board Statement: Not applicable.

Informed Consent Statement: Not applicable.

Data Availability Statement: Further data may be obtained at https://contractaciopublica.gencat.cat/ecofin_pscp/AppJava/es_ES/notice.pscp?idDoc=71544976&reqCode=viewCtn (accessed on 11 August 2022).

Conflicts of Interest: The authors declare no conflict of interest.

Appendix A. Search Criteria and Strategy for the Systematic Review

Table A1. MeSH terms, definitions and keywords used in the systematic review of the literature.

Mesh Term	Definition	Keywords
Image Processing, Computer-Assisted	A technique of inputting two-dimensional or three-dimensional images into a computer and then enhancing or analyzing the imagery into a form that is more useful to the human observer. Year introduced: 1987	"3D printing *" OR "3D-printing *" OR 3-dimensional OR "in-house 3D-printing" OR "custom-made implant *"
Printing, Three-Dimensional	Process for making, building or constructing a physical object from a three-dimensional digital model by laying down many successive thin layers of building material. Year introduced: 2015	"Three-Dimensional Printing *"
Fiducial Markers	Materials used as reference points for imaging studies. Year introduced: 2011	"Fiducial Marker *" OR "Fiducial Target *" OR "Anatomic Fiducial *" OR "Implanted Fiducial *"
Surgery, Computer-Assisted	Surgical procedures conducted with the aid of computers; used in various types of surgery for implant placement and instrument guidance. Image-guided surgery interactively combines prior CT scans or MRI images with real-time video. Year introduced: 2002	"Computer-Assisted Surger *" OR "Computer-Aided Surger *" OR "Surgical Navigation" OR "Image-Guided Surger *"
Patient-Specific Modeling	The development and application of computational models of human pathophysiology that are individualized according to patient-specific data. Year introduced: 2015	"personalized surger *" OR "personalized reconstruction"
Microsurgery	The performance of surgical procedures with the aid of a microscope. Year introduced: 1972 (1969)	

Table A1. *Cont.*

Mesh Term	Definition	Keywords
Precision Medicine	Clinical, therapeutic and diagnostic approaches to optimal disease management based on individual variations in a patient's genetic profile. Year introduced: 2010	"precision medicine" OR "Individualized Medicine" OR P-Health OR "Predictive Medicine" OR Theranostic *
Tissue Engineering	Generating tissue in vitro for clinical applications, such as replacing wounded tissues or impaired organs. The use of tissue scaffolding enables the generation of complex, multi-layered tissues and tissue structures. Year introduced: 2002	"Tissue Engineering"

* An asterisk represents any group of characters, including no character.

Table A2. Search Strategy used in the systematic review of the literature.

Query	Search Strategy	Filters
1	Image Processing, Computer-Assisted [MeSH Terms]	
2	"3D printing *" [Title/Abstract]	
3	"3D-printin *" [Title/Abstract]	
4	3-dimensional [Title/Abstract]	
5	"in-house 3D-printing" [Title/Abstract]	
6	"custom-made implant *" [Title/Abstract]	
7	Printing, Three-Dimensional [MeSH Terms]	
8	"Three-Dimensional Printing *" [Title/Abstract]	
9	Fiducial Markers [MeSH Terms]	
10	"Fiducial Marker *" [Title/Abstract]	
11	"Fiducial Target *" [Title/Abstract]	
12	"Anatomic Fiducial *" [Title/Abstract]	
13	"Implanted Fiducial *" [Title/Abstract]	
14	Surgery, Computer-Assisted [MeSH Terms]	
15	"Computer-Assisted Surger *" [Title/Abstract]	
16	"Computer-Aided Surger *" [Title/Abstract]	
17	"Surgical Navigation" [Title/Abstract]	
18	"Image-Guided Surger *" [Title/Abstract]	
19	(((((((((((((((Image Processing, Computer-Assisted[MeSH Terms]) OR ("3D printing *"[Title/Abstract])) OR ("3D-printing *"[Title/Abstract])) OR (3-dimensional[Title/Abstract])) OR ("in-house 3D-printing"[Title/Abstract])) OR ("custom-made implant *"[Title/Abstract])) OR (Printing, Three-Dimensional[MeSH Terms])) OR ("Three-Dimensional Printing *"[Title/Abstract])) OR (Fiducial Markers[MeSH Terms])) OR ("Fiducial Marker *"[Title/Abstract])) OR ("Fiducial Target *"[Title/Abstract])) OR ("Anatomic Fiducial *"[Title/Abstract])) OR ("Implanted Fiducial *"[Title/Abstract])) OR (Surgery, Computer-Assisted[MeSH Terms])) OR ("Computer-Assisted Surger *"[Title/Abstract])) OR ("Computer-Aided Surger *"[Title/Abstract])) OR ("Surgical Navigation"[Title/Abstract])) OR ("Image-Guided Surger *"[Title/Abstract])	
20	Patient-Specific Modeling [MeSH Terms]	
21	"personalized surger *" [Title/Abstract]	
22	"personalized reconstruction" [Title/Abstract]	

Table A2. *Cont.*

Query	Search Strategy	Filters
23	Microsurgery [MeSH Terms]	
24	Precision Medicine [MeSH Terms]	
25	"precision medicine" [Title/Abstract]	
26	"Individualized Medicine" [Title/Abstract]	
27	P-Health [Title/Abstract]	
28	"Predictive Medicine" [Title/Abstract]	
29	Theranostic *[Title/Abstract]	
30	Tissue Engineering [MeSH Terms]	
31	"Tissue Engineering" [Title/Abstract]	
32	((((((((((Patient-Specific Modeling[MeSH Terms]) OR ("personalized surger *"[Title/Abstract])) OR ("personalized reconstruction"[Title/Abstract])) OR (Microsurgery[MeSH Terms])) OR (Precision Medicine[MeSH Terms])) OR ("precision medicine"[Title/Abstract])) OR ("Individualized Medicine"[Title/Abstract])) OR (P-Health[Title/Abstract])) OR ("Predictive Medicine"[Title/Abstract])) OR (Theranostic *[Title/Abstract])) OR (Tissue Engineering[MeSH Terms])) OR ("Tissue Engineering"[Title/Abstract])	
33	"Tertiary Care Centers" [Mesh]	
34	Hospital *[Title/Abstract]	
35	"Operating Rooms" [Mesh]	
36	"Operating Room *" [Title/Abstract]	
37	((("Tertiary Care Centers" [Mesh]) OR (hospital *[Title/Abstract])) OR ("Operating Rooms" [Mesh])) OR ("Operating Room *"[Title/Abstract])	
38	((((((((((((((((((Image Processing, Computer-Assisted[MeSH Terms]) OR ("3D printing *"[Title/Abstract])) OR ("3D-printing *"[Title/Abstract])) OR (3-dimensional[Title/Abstract])) OR ("in-house 3D-printing"[Title/Abstract])) OR ("custom-made implant *"[Title/Abstract])) OR (Printing, Three-Dimensional[MeSH Terms])) OR ("Three-Dimensional Printing *"[Title/Abstract])) OR (Fiducial Markers[MeSH Terms])) OR ("Fiducial Marker *"[Title/Abstract])) OR ("Fiducial Target *"[Title/Abstract])) OR ("Anatomic Fiducial *"[Title/Abstract])) OR ("Implanted Fiducial *"[Title/Abstract])) OR (Surgery, Computer-Assisted[MeSH Terms])) OR ("Computer-Assisted Surger *"[Title/Abstract])) OR ("Computer-Aided Surger *"[Title/Abstract])) OR ("Surgical Navigation"[Title/Abstract])) OR ("Image-Guided Surger *"[Title/Abstract])) AND ((((((((((((Patient-Specific Modeling[MeSH Terms]) OR ("personalized surger *"[Title/Abstract])) OR ("personalized reconstruction"[Title/Abstract])) OR (Microsurgery[MeSH Terms])) OR (Precision Medicine[MeSH Terms])) OR ("precision medicine"[Title/Abstract])) OR ("Individualized Medicine"[Title/Abstract])) OR (P-Health[Title/Abstract])) OR ("Predictive Medicine"[Title/Abstract])) OR (Theranostic *[Title/Abstract])) OR (Tissue Engineering[MeSH Terms])) OR ("Tissue Engineering"[Title/Abstract]))) AND (((("Tertiary Care Centers"[Mesh]) OR (hospital *[Title/Abstract])) OR ("Operating Rooms"[Mesh])) OR ("Operating Room *"[Title/Abstract]))	

Table A2. *Cont.*

Query	Search Strategy	Filters
39	((((((((((((((((((Image Processing, Computer-Assisted[MeSH Terms]) OR ("3D printing *"[Title/Abstract])) OR ("3D-printing *"[Title/Abstract])) OR (3-dimensional[Title/Abstract])) OR ("in-house 3D-printing"[Title/Abstract])) OR ("custom-made implant *"[Title/Abstract])) OR (Printing, Three-Dimensional[MeSH Terms])) OR ("Three-Dimensional Printing *"[Title/Abstract])) OR (Fiducial Markers[MeSH Terms])) OR ("Fiducial Marker *"[Title/Abstract])) OR ("Fiducial Target *"[Title/Abstract])) OR ("Anatomic Fiducial*"[Title/Abstract])) OR ("Implanted Fiducial *"[Title/Abstract])) OR (Surgery, Computer-Assisted[MeSH Terms])) OR ("Computer-Assisted Surger *"[Title/Abstract])) OR ("Computer-Aided Surger *"[Title/Abstract])) OR ("Surgical Navigation"[Title/Abstract])) OR ("Image-Guided Surger *"[Title/Abstract])) AND (((((((((((Patient-Specific Modeling[MeSH Terms]) OR ("personalized surger *"[Title/Abstract])) OR ("personalized reconstruction"[Title/Abstract])) OR (Microsurgery[MeSH Terms])) OR (Precision Medicine[MeSH Terms])) OR ("precision medicine"[Title/Abstract])) OR ("Individualized Medicine"[Title/Abstract])) OR (P-Health[Title/Abstract])) OR ("Predictive Medicine"[Title/Abstract])) OR (Theranostic *[Title/Abstract])) OR (Tissue Engineering[MeSH Terms])) OR ("Tissue Engineering"[Title/Abstract]))) AND (((("Tertiary Care Centers"[Mesh]) OR (hospital *[Title/Abstract])) OR ("Operating Rooms"[Mesh])) OR ("Operating Room *"[Title/Abstract]))	in the last 10 years
40	((((((((((((((((((Image Processing, Computer-Assisted[MeSH Terms]) OR ("3D printing *"[Title/Abstract])) OR ("3D-printing *"[Title/Abstract])) OR (3-dimensional[Title/Abstract])) OR ("in-house 3D-printing"[Title/Abstract])) OR ("custom-made implant *"[Title/Abstract])) OR (Printing, Three-Dimensional[MeSH Terms])) OR ("Three-Dimensional Printing *"[Title/Abstract])) OR (Fiducial Markers[MeSH Terms])) OR ("Fiducial Marker *"[Title/Abstract])) OR ("Fiducial Target *"[Title/Abstract])) OR ("Anatomic Fiducial *"[Title/Abstract])) OR ("Implanted Fiducial *"[Title/Abstract])) OR (Surgery, Computer-Assisted[MeSH Terms])) OR ("Computer-Assisted Surger *"[Title/Abstract])) OR ("Computer-Aided Surger *"[Title/Abstract])) OR ("Surgical Navigation"[Title/Abstract])) OR ("Image-Guided Surger *"[Title/Abstract])) AND (((((((((((Patient-Specific Modeling[MeSH Terms]) OR ("personalized surger *"[Title/Abstract])) OR ("personalized reconstruction"[Title/Abstract])) OR (Microsurgery[MeSH Terms])) OR (Precision Medicine[MeSH Terms])) OR ("precision medicine"[Title/Abstract])) OR ("Individualized Medicine"[Title/Abstract])) OR (P-Health[Title/Abstract])) OR ("Predictive Medicine"[Title/Abstract])) OR (Theranostic *[Title/Abstract])) OR (Tissue Engineering[MeSH Terms])) OR ("Tissue Engineering"[Title/Abstract]))) AND (((("Tertiary Care Centers"[Mesh]) OR (hospital *[Title/Abstract])) OR ("Operating Rooms"[Mesh])) OR ("Operating Room *"[Title/Abstract]))	in the last 10 years, Humans

* An asterisk represents any group of characters, including no character.

References

1. Goodson, A.M.; Kittur, M.A.; Evans, P.L.; Williams, E.M. Patient-specific, printed titanium implants for reconstruction of mandibular continuity defects: A systematic review of the evidence. *J. Cranio-Maxillofac. Surg.* **2019**, *47*, 968–976. [CrossRef]
2. Dérand, P.; Rännar, L.-E.; Hirsch, J.-M. Imaging, Virtual Planning, Design, and Production of Patient-Specific Implants and Clinical Validation in Craniomaxillofacial Surgery. *Craniomaxillofac. Trauma Reconstr.* **2012**, *5*, 137–143. [CrossRef] [PubMed]
3. Bell, R.B.; Weimer, K.A.; Dierks, E.J.; Buehler, M.; Lubek, J.E.; Berrone, M.; Aldiano, C.; Pentenero, M.; Berrone, S.; Choi, J.W.; et al. A CAD/CAM-prototyped anatomical condylar prosthesis connected to a custom-made bone plate to support a fibula free flap. *J. Cranio-Maxillofac. Surg.* **2015**, *43*, 45. [CrossRef]
4. Seruya, M.; Fisher, M.; Rodriguez, E.D. Computer-Assisted versus Conventional Free Fibula Flap Technique for Craniofacial Reconstruction: An outcomes comparison. *Plast. Reconstr. Surg.* **2013**, *132*, 1219–1228. [CrossRef] [PubMed]
5. Mazzoni, S.; Marchetti, C.; Sgarzani, R.; Cipriani, R.; Scotti, R.; Ciocca, L. Prosthetically guided maxillofacial surgery: Evaluation of the accuracy of a surgical guide and custom-made bone plate in oncology patients after mandibular reconstruction. *Plast. Reconstr. Surg.* **2013**, *131*, 1376–1385. [CrossRef]
6. Kaariainen, M.; Kuuskeri, M.; Gremoutis, G.; Kuokkanen, H.; Miettinen, A.; Laranne, J. Utilization of Three-Dimensional Computer-Aided Preoperative Virtual Planning and Manufacturing in Maxillary and Mandibular Reconstruction with a Microvascular Fibula Flap. *J. Reconstr. Microsurg.* **2016**, *32*, 137–141. [CrossRef]

7. Fan, B.; Chen, H.; Sun, Y.J.; Wang, B.F.; Che, L.; Liu, S.Y.; Li, G.Y. Clinical effects of 3-D printing-assisted personalized reconstructive surgery for blowout orbital fractures. *Graefe's Arch. Clin. Exp. Ophthalmol.* **2017**, *255*, 2051–2057. [CrossRef]
8. Day, K.M.; Gabrick, K.S.; Sargent, L.A. Applications of computer technology in complex craniofacial reconstruction. *Plast. Reconstr. Surg.—Glob. Open* **2018**, *6*, 1–8. [CrossRef]
9. Goodson, A.M.C.; Parmar, S.; Ganesh, S.; Zakai, D.; Shafi, A.; Wicks, C.; O'Connor, R.; Yeung, E.; Khalid, F.; Tahim, A.; et al. Printed titanium implants in UK craniomaxillofacial surgery. Part I: Access to digital planning and perceived scope for use in common procedures. *Br. J. Oral Maxillofac. Surg.* **2021**, *59*, 312–319. [CrossRef]
10. Lopez, C.D.; Witek, L.; Torroni, A.; Flores, R.L.; Demissie, D.B.; Young, S.; Cronstein, B.N.; Coelho, P.G. The role of 3D printing in treating craniomaxillofacial congenital anomalies. *Birth Defects Res.* **2018**, *110*, 1055–1064. [CrossRef]
11. Levesque, J.N.; Shah, A.; Ekhtiari, S.; Yan, J.R.; Thornley, P.; Williams, D.S. Three-dimensional printing in orthopaedic surgery: A scoping review. *EFORT Open Rev.* **2020**, *5*, 430–441. [CrossRef] [PubMed]
12. Papotto, G.; Testa, G.; Mobilia, G.; Perez, S.; Dimartino, S.; Giardina, S.M.C.; Sessa, G.; Pavone, V. Use of 3D printing and pre-contouring plate in the surgical planning of acetabular fractures: A systematic review. *Orthop. Traumatol. Surg. Res.* **2022**, *108*, 103111. [CrossRef] [PubMed]
13. Servei Català de la Salut (Generalitat de Catalunya, Barcelona, Catalonia, Spain). Programa Operatiu FEDER 2014–2020: Convocatòria 2017 per a projectes de compra pública d' innovació en l'àmbit de la salut dins del marc del (Resolució SLT/1913/2017, de 2 d'agost) SA51-006903 "3D-LAB-Servei de Cirurgia Personalitzada" d'Hospital Universitari Vall d'Hebron—Institut Català de la Salut. 2018; unpublished work.
14. Tellisi, N.; Ashammakhi, N.A.; Billi, F.; Kaarela, O. Three dimensional printed bone implants in the clinic. *J. Craniofac. Surg.* **2018**, *29*, 2363–2367. [CrossRef]
15. Liu, A.; Xue, G.H.; Sun, M.; Shao, H.F.; Ma, C.Y.; Gao, Q.; Gou, Z.R.; Yan, S.G.; Liu, Y.M.; He, Y. 3D Printing Surgical Implants at the clinic: A Experimental Study on Anterior Cruciate Ligament Reconstruction. *Sci. Rep.* **2016**, *6*, 21704. [CrossRef] [PubMed]
16. Guijarro-Martínez, R. Optimization of the interface between radiology, surgery, radiotherapy and pathology in head and neck tumor surgery: A navigation-assisted multidisciplinary network. *Int. J. Oral Maxillofac. Surg.* **2014**, *43*, 156–162. [CrossRef] [PubMed]
17. Rana, M.; Essig, H.; Eckardt, A.M.; Tavassol, F.; Ruecker, M.; Schramm, A.; Gellrich, N.-C. Advances and innovations in computer-assisted head and neck oncologic surgery. *J. Craniofac. Surg.* **2012**, *23*, 272–278. [CrossRef]
18. Dindo, D.; Demartines, N.; Clavien, P.A. Classification of Surgical Complications. A New Proposal With Evaluation in a Cohort of 6336 Patients and Results of a Survey. *Ann. Surg.* **2004**, *240*, 205–213. [CrossRef]
19. Nazar, G.; Garmendia, M.L.; Royer, M.; McDowell, J.A.; Weymuller, E.A.; Yueh, B. Spanish validation of the University of Washington Quality of Life questionnaire for head and neck cancer patients. *Otolaryngol.—Head Neck Surg.* **2010**, *143*, 801–807. [CrossRef]
20. Lo Giudice, A.; Ronsivalle, V.; Grippaudo, C.; Lucchese, A.; Muraglie, S.; Lagravère, M.; Isola, G. One Step before 3D Printing—Evaluation of Imaging Software Accuracy for 3-Dimensional Analysis of the Mandible: A Comparative Study Using a Surface-to-Surface Matching Technique. *Materials* **2020**, *13*, 2798. [CrossRef]
21. Goodson, A.M.C.; Parmar, S.; Ganesh, S.; Zakai, D.; Shafi, A.; Wicks, C.; O'Connor, R.; Yeung, E.; Khalid, F.; Tahim, A.; et al. Printed titanium implants in UK craniomaxillofacial surgery. Part II: Perceived performance (outcomes, logistics, and costs). *Br. J. Oral Maxillofac. Surg.* **2021**, *59*, 320–328. [CrossRef]
22. Popular Standards: Devices. International Organization for Standardization (ISO), 2016. Available online: https://www.iso.org/iso-13485-medical-devices.html (accessed on 28 July 2020).
23. *Medical Devices: EU Regulations for MDR and IVDR*; Updated 2021; Medicines and Healthcare Products Regulatory Agency: London, UK, 2017; Available online: https://eur-lex.europa.eu/eli/reg/2017/745/2020-04-24 (accessed on 27 March 2020).
24. European Union. Regulation (EU) 2017/745 of the European Parliament and of the Council of 5 April 2017 on Medical Devices, Amending Directive 2001/83/EC, Regulation (EC) No 178/2002 and Regulation (EC) No 1223/2009 and Repealing Council Directives 90/385/EEC and 93/42/EE. *Off. J. Eur. Union.* **2017**, *117*, 139–145. Available online: https://eur-lex.europa.eu/legal-content/EN/TXT/PDF/?uri=CELEX:32017R0745 (accessed on 11 July 2022).
25. *Guidance for Products without an Intended Medical Purpose (Annex XVI) under the New Medical Device Regulation (EU 2017/745)*; Medicines & Healthcare Products Regulation Agency (MHRA): London, UK, 2018. Available online: https://assets.publishing.service.gov.uk/government/uploads/system/uploads/attachment_data/file/748131/Guidance_leaflet_on_Annex_XVI_products_.pdf (accessed on 11 August 2020).

Journal of
Clinical Medicine

MDPI

Article

Benefits of Patient-Specific Reconstruction Plates in Mandibular Reconstruction Surgical Simulation and Resident Education

Khanh Linh Tran, Matthew Lee Mong, James Scott Durham and Eitan Prisman *

Division of Otolaryngology, Department of Surgery, Faculty of Medicine, University of British Columbia, Vancouver, BC V6T 1Z4, Canada
* Correspondence: eitan.prisman@ubc.ca; Tel.: +1-604-875-4111

Abstract: Poorly contoured mandibular reconstruction plates are associated with postoperative complications. Recently, a technique emerged whereby preoperative patient-specific reconstructive plates (PSRP) are developed in the hopes of eliminating errors in the plate-bending process. This study's objective is to determine if reconstructions performed with PSRP are more accurate than manually contoured plates. Ten Otolaryngology residents each performed two ex vivo mandibular reconstructions, first using a PSRP followed by a manually contoured plate. Reconstruction time, CT scans, and accuracy measurements were collected. Paired Student's t-test was performed. There was a significant difference between reconstructions with PSRP and manually contoured plates in: plate-mandible distance (0.39 ± 0.21 vs. 0.75 ± 0.31 mm, $p = 0.0128$), inter-fibular segment gap (0.90 ± 0.32 vs. 2.24 ± 1.03 mm, $p = 0.0095$), mandible-fibula gap (1.02 ± 0.39 vs. 2.87 ± 2.38 mm, $p = 0.0260$), average reconstruction deviation (1.11 ± 0.32 vs. 1.67 ± 0.47 mm, $p = 0.0228$), mandibular angle width difference (5.13 ± 4.32 vs. 11.79 ± 4.27 mm, $p = 0.0221$), and reconstruction time (16.67 ± 4.18 vs. 33.78 ± 8.45 min, $p = 0.0006$). Lower plate-mandible distance has been demonstrated to correlate with decreased plate extrusion rates. Similarly, improved bony apposition promotes bony union. PSRP appears to provide a more accurate scaffold to guide the surgeons in assembling donor bone segments, which could potentially improve patient outcome and reduce surgical time. Additionally, in-house PSRP can serve as a low-cost surgical simulation tool for resident education.

Keywords: virtual surgical planning; CAD/CAM; mandibular reconstruction; patient-specific reconstruction plates; medical education; surgical simulation

Citation: Tran, K.L.; Mong, M.L.; Durham, J.S.; Prisman, E. Benefits of Patient-Specific Reconstruction Plates in Mandibular Reconstruction Surgical Simulation and Resident Education. *J. Clin. Med.* **2022**, *11*, 5306. https://doi.org/10.3390/jcm11185306

Academic Editors: Alexandre Bozec and Mark L. Urken

Received: 16 July 2022
Accepted: 31 August 2022
Published: 9 September 2022

Publisher's Note: MDPI stays neutral with regard to jurisdictional claims in published maps and institutional affiliations.

1. Introduction

The human mandible is an important anatomical structure that functions in respiration, deglutition, and mastication [1]. Conditions that affect the mandible, such as oral cancer, osteoradionecrosis, or osteomyelitis, can affect patients' oral functioning and quality of life [2]. Mandibular resection and subsequent reconstruction with donor fibular free flap is a technique to manage oral disease and restore aesthetic and functional outcomes for head and neck cancer patients. The surgery involves resecting the diseased portion of the mandible, harvesting the fibular flap, contouring the fibula segments, securing the flap to the mandible, and vascular anastomosis [3]. To secure the fibular free flap segments to the non-resected area of the mandible, a titanium plate is typically employed [2]. In the traditional fashion, in order to faithfully restore the mandible contour, the plate is bent intraoperatively to the native mandible. It serves as a template for the shaping and placement of the fibula reconstruction. This is a time-consuming step and could take up to 60 min in the operating room [4]. Consequences of a poorly bent plate include plate fracture, plate exposure, and malunion/nonunion of the reconstruction [5]. These complications can severely affect patients' quality of life and may involve costly and invasive treatment such as antibiotics or additional surgeries [6–8].

Alternatively, customized titanium reconstruction plates for a patient-specific reconstruction (patient-specific reconstruction plate, or PSRP) can be designed, optimized for overall strength, and manufactured using selective layer melting or computer numerical control milling [9]. These customized plates and cutting guides are often provided by a commercial medical device company and are associated with incremental costs of up to 3000–8200 USD per case [10,11]. Through a comparative case series, Sieira-Gil et al. demonstrate that reconstructions using VSP with custom titanium plates result in better dental occlusion, lower plate exposure rate, and lower operative time compared with traditional, un-guided surgeries without custom plates [12]. Wilde et al. determined through a multicenter clinical study that the cost associated with plate manufacture can be offset by the time saved in the operating room [13]. However, the specific effect of PRSP versus traditional manual contouring of reconstruction plates for VSP in reducing the gap distance between fibula segment as well as the distance between the plate and reconstruction, which are associated with nonunion and plate exposure, respectively, has not been clearly demonstrated. Furthermore, the ability to generate in-house PSRP has, to the authors' knowledge, never been demonstrated.

The purpose of this study is three-fold: (1) to demonstrate a proof-of-concept design for PSRP using in-house VSP software, (2) to compare PSRP with manually contoured plates in mandibular reconstruction, and (3) to report on the use of customized plates in resident education.

2. Materials and Methods

This study was approved by the clinical research ethics board at the author's institution (H21-00205). Surgical trainees in the Division of Otolaryngology at a tertiary care center were recruited and consented to the study. The participants performed a simulation of mandibular reconstruction with the fibular bone. The mandibular defect chosen involves the mandible ramus and body and crosses the midline to the contralateral side. The in-house VSP software developed at the authors' institution was utilized to plan for a three-piece reconstruction [14]. In order to isolate the specific effect of the preprinted PSRP on the reconstruction, the two remaining segments of the mandible and the three pieces of the fibula and the reconstruction model were 3D-printed in acrylonitrile butadiene styrene. The participants first viewed a demonstration by the senior authors, then performed two reconstructions: first with a 2.0 mm patient-specific, pre-printed vinyl plate (PSRP) and then with a standard, straight 2.0 mm titanium plate that requires manual contouring to the printed reconstruction model. (Stryker, reference number 55-15719). To avoid confounding results, reconstructions with PSRP were performed first to limit any potential advantages over manually contoured plates. In the PSRP component, participants performed the reconstructions in the following steps: drilled holes on the mandible corresponding to the PSRP, arranged the fibula segments, and secured the mandible and fibula segments using the reconstruction plate. In the manual contouring group, this process was preceded by manually contouring the titanium plate to the reconstruction model.

Time to perform each step of the reconstruction was recorded. CT scans of the participants' reconstruction were obtained and segmented using a 3D Slicer, where the following measurements were also performed: volumetric overlap and Hausdorff-95 distance of the reconstructive segments and the entire mandible [15]. Volumetric overlap is calculated as twice the volume of the intersection between the actual and planned reconstructions divided by the sum of the volumes between the two models [15]. Hausdorff-95 is the 95th percentile of the Hausdorff distance, which is the maximum distance of the minimum distances between each vertex on the actual and planned reconstructions [15]. In CloudCompare, a 3D mesh model processing platform that supports computations such as the distance between different models, the distances between the reconstructive plate and mandible, between each fibula segment, and between the mandible and fibula segments were obtained. Each measurement is illustrated in Figure 1. Statistical analyses were performed in Microsoft Excel. A paired Student's t-test was performed to compare the measurements between the reconstruction groups, with each participant acting as their own control. A p-value of <0.05 was considered significant.

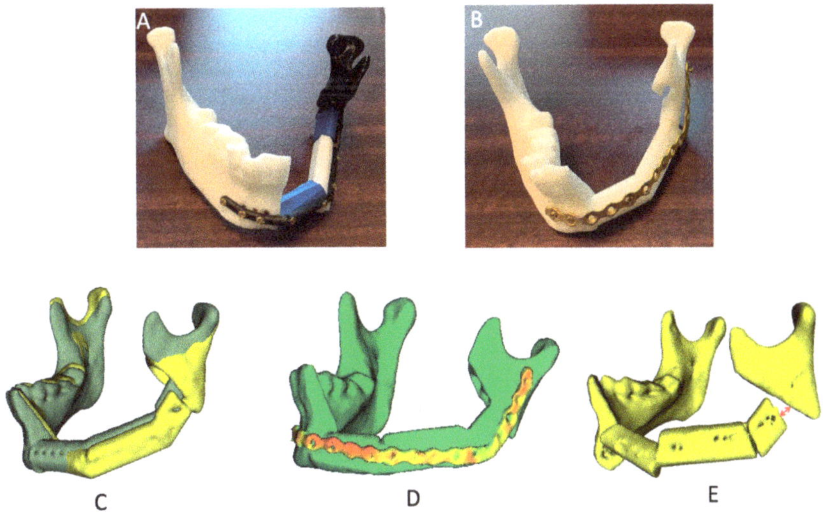

Figure 1. Reconstructions and structural accuracy variables. (**A**) Reconstruction with a customized, patient-specific, pre-printed plate. (**B**) Reconstruction with a manually contoured plate. (**C**) Volumetric overlap and Hausdorff-95 between reconstruction (yellow) and plan (green) were measured in 3D Slicer. (**D**) Distance between reconstruction plate and mandible was measured in CloudCompare. (**E**) Distance at each apposition was measured in 3D Slicer (red arrow).

3. Results

In total, ten Otolaryngology residents in training, two from each year one to year five of training, consented and participated in this study. Six male and four female participants were included in the study. Junior residents are those who are in years one to three of training, and senior residents are in years four and five. They have observed, on average, 18.8 ± 7.0 free flap reconstruction surgeries and have assisted in 11.7 ± 5.5 cases.

3.1. Reconstruction Time

The total time to assemble the reconstruction and time to contour the plate in the two groups is recorded in Table 1. There is a significant decrease in reconstructive time in the PSRP group for all participants and junior residents, as well as senior residents, to a non-significant degree.

Table 1. Comparison of time to perform reconstructions in each group. Significant *p*-values are indicated with a (*).

	Manual Contour Plate (n = 10)	Patient-Specific, Reconstruction Plate (PSRP) (n = 10)	*p*-Value
Time to perform reconstruction (min)	33.78 ± 8.45	16.67 ± 4.18	<0.001 *
(a) Junior residents (min)	39.4 ± 3.78	17.8 ± 3.35	<0.001 *
(b) Senior residents (min)	29.25 ± 8.54	15.25 ± 5.19	0.119
Time to contour plate (min)	13.33 ± 3.97	N/A (Not applicable)	
(a) Junior residents (min)	15.2 ± 2.49	N/A	
(b) Senior residents (min)	11.0 ± 4.55	N/A	

3.2. Reconstruction Accuracy

Lower HD-95 distance of the fibula segments, the lower distance between reconstructive plate and mandible, the lower gap distance between each fibula segment and between the mandible and fibula segments, and lower mandible angle width deviation were observed in the 3D-printed plate group to a significant degree (Table 2). There were also non-significant improvements in volumetric overlap, HD-95 for the reconstructed mandible, and difference in mandible ramus-condyle height.

Table 2. Average accuracy measurements of the reconstructions in each group. Significant p-values are indicated with a (*).

	Manual Contour Plate Plate (n = 10)	PSRP Plate (n = 10)	p-Value
Volumetric overlap of reconstructed mandible (%)	65.70 ± 11.33	70.40 ± 8.62	0.310
Volumetric overlap of fibula segments (%)	51.70 ± 14.61	63.00 ± 12.56	0.080
Hausdorff-95 of reconstructed mandible (mm)	2.40 ± 1.14	1.75 ± 0.90	0.175
Hausdorff-95 of fibula segments (mm)	3.41 ± 1.47	2.10 ± 1.12	0.038 *
Plate-mandible gap distance (mm)	0.75 ± 0.31	0.39 ± 0.21	0.007 *
Gap distance between fibula segments (mm)	2.24 ± 1.03	0.90 ± 0.32	0.001 *
Gap distance between mandible and fibula segments (mm)	2.87 ± 2.38	1.02 ± 0.39	0.026 *
Difference in mandible angle width (mm)	11.79 ± 4.27	5.13 ± 4.32	0.003 *
Difference in mandible ramus-condyle height (mm)	1.26 ± 1.52	1.19 ± 0.93	0.902

4. Discussion

Mandible reconstruction is a challenging procedure, even for experienced surgeons. Complications of the surgery range from reconstructive plate extrusion, non-union or malunion of the flap segments, to free flap failure, all with devastating consequences to patients' cosmetic, oral functioning, and quality of life [5]. Virtual surgical planning has been successfully applied to improve these outcomes. However, they remain a challenge. At the authors' center, an in-house VSP software has been developed and used for oromaxillofacial surgical reconstruction since 2017 [14,16–20]. The platform has been adapted to allow for patient-specific reconstruction plate modeling. To the authors' knowledge, there has not been an evaluation of the utility of in-house designed reconstruction plates in the context of resident training. As such, this study investigates the potential of applying an open-source, in-house VSP platform to generate PSRP by comparing mandible reconstructions with PSRP versus manually contoured plates.

Inaccurate plate contouring could result in additional tensional and torsional forces being placed on the temporomandibular (TMJ) joint, leading to malocclusion or injury to the TMJ [21–23]. Malocclusion could severely impact patients' quality of life and may require additional surgery to remove the plate and realign the position of the reconstruction [24]. The results of this study, including higher volumetric overlap (p = 0.080), lower Hausdorff-95 distance (p = 0.038), and lower difference in mandible angle width (p = 0.003), suggest that employing PSRP can potentially improve reconstructive accuracy as compared with manually bent plates. Manual contouring of reconstructive plates can also introduce residual stress to the plate, leading to postoperative plate fracturing [25]. In a series of biomechanical tests, Gutwald et al. have shown that preprinted plates present an opportunity for customization to reduce stress [26]. Overall, preprinted plates can withstand stronger force than manually bent plates as they avoid deformity introduced during the contouring process [26].

Plate exposure is a common hardware-related complication in head and neck reconstruction with a free vascularized flap. The rate of plate exposure is reported to be between 9–20% [6–8]. Management of plate exposure ranges from antibiotics to hardware removal and surgical debridement of the flap. Treatment not only affects patients' long-term quality of life but can also present a significant cost to patients and the healthcare system [8]. Although flap selection and radiation therapy contribute to the rate of plate extrusion, plate-to-bone gap distance is hypothesized to be an important factor [7,27,28]. Chepeha et al. suggest that the dead space between the plate and bone induces the contraction of tissue lateral to the plate to fill in the void, resulting in eventual flap necrosis [29]. Furthermore, in a clinical study of 94 patients who underwent mandibular reconstruction, Davies et al. demonstrate an association between lower plate-to-bone gap distance and lower rates of plate exposure and intraoral dehiscence [30]. In our study, patient-specific reconstruction plates are shown to reduce the gap between the mandible and plate compared with manually contoured plates. Since the study controls for variability in mandible defect and fibula segment sizes, the difference in the two groups is likely attributable to the type of plate used. Although further clinical studies are required to confirm the effect of printed plates in lowering plate-to-bone gap distance in vivo, the results of this study show a promising utility in designing and manufacturing PSRP.

Reconstruction plates secure the mandible and reconstruction segments to each other to promote union [31]. If the bone does not fully heal, the segments may either not fuse or inadequately fuse together, resulting in nonunion or malunion, respectively [32]. Incomplete osseointegration is associated with a higher rate of wound complications and could lead to bone fracture, osteonecrosis, or reabsorption. If malunion or nonunion is detected, patients may undergo surgical plate refixation or a secondary bone graft [6]. The rate of nonunion is reported to be between 5–23% for mandible reconstruction [6,7,32–37]. Swenseid et al. demonstrate that a gap distance of 1 mm or greater significantly increases the likelihood of malunion or nonunion developing [32]. In the present study, the reconstructions with hand-bent plates resulted in a gap of over 2 mm, on average. Significantly, both the gap distances between mandible-fibula and fibula-fibula in the hand-bent group are more than twice as large as that of the group with PSRP. In the former group, errors introduced by inaccurate manual contouring of the reconstruction plate propagated in later stages of assembling and securing the fibula segments, leading to significant gaps in the final reconstruction. Although our study is ex vivo by nature, the average gap distance measured suggests that PSRP have the potential to improve the osseointegration rate of mandible reconstructions.

The time taken to perform a reconstruction is twice as long for the group with manually contoured plates compared with the group with PSRP. This result represents potential cost savings in the operating room as well as a reduction in complications, which has been shown to be associated with lower operation time [38]. Simulation has been increasingly used as a training tool for otolaryngology surgical residents [21,39]. VSP represents an opportunity for residents to learn and practice complicated procedures such as mandible reconstructions in a controlled environment outside the operating room. The high cost of surgical titanium plates, estimated at 800 CAD per plate, prevents them from being used for routine training purposes. Therefore, in the study, vinyl was explored as a cheaper alternative for this particular reconstruction simulation that does not require the longevity and biocompatibility of in vivo use. Moreover, the reconstruction time is reduced for both junior and senior residents when using PSRP compared with manually contoured plates. Thus, this result suggests that PSRP can benefit residents with differing experience levels.

There are several limitations to the study. Since the participants are surgical trainees, the benefits of using 3D-printed PSRP with respect to time-saving and higher accuracy may not be replicated in more experienced head and reconstructive neck surgeons. However, 3D-printed PSRP may still be used as an educational and training tool in mandibular reconstruction surgical simulation by lowering the learning curve associated with plate contouring. Another limitation is that the 3D-printed PSRP is manufactured with vinyl as opposed to titanium. Although further in vivo studies with patient-specific titanium plates need to be carried out to definitively compare their benefits with manually contoured plates, vinyl plates could be used as a low-cost training tool alternative to titanium plates.

5. Conclusions

Customized mandibular reconstruction plates can be readily designed with open source, in-house software. These customized reconstruction plates improve the accuracy of executing VSP for mandible reconstruction compared with manually contoured mandible reconstruction plates for less experienced surgeons. Finally, this in-house design can be used in mandible reconstruction training as a low-cost simulation tool. Potential clinical benefits of utilizing patient-specific reconstruction plates include surgical time reduction, improved reconstructive accuracy, and lower complication rates, which warrants further clinical studies.

Author Contributions: Conceptualization, K.L.T., M.L.M., J.S.D. and E.P.; methodology, K.L.T., M.L.M., J.S.D. and E.P.; software, M.L.M.; validation, M.L.M., J.S.D. and E.P.; formal analysis, K.L.T.; investigation, K.L.T., M.L.M., J.S.D. and E.P.; resources, K.L.T., M.L.M., J.S.D. and E.P.; data curation, K.L.T. and M.L.M.; writing—original draft preparation, K.L.T.; writing—review and editing, K.L.T., M.L.M., J.S.D. and E.P.; visualization, K.L.T.; supervision, J.S.D. and E.P.; project administration, K.L.T., M.L.M., J.S.D. and E.P.; funding acquisition, E.P. All authors have read and agreed to the published version of the manuscript.

Funding: This research was funded by the Canadian Institutes of Health Research, grant number 163974, and Michael Smith Foundation for Health Research, grant number 17632.

Institutional Review Board Statement: The study was conducted in accordance with the Declaration of Helsinki and approved by the Clinical Research Ethics Board of the University of British Columbia (H21-00205 and date of approval: 2 February 2021).

Informed Consent Statement: Informed consent was obtained from all subjects involved in the study.

Data Availability Statement: Data sharing is not applicable.

Conflicts of Interest: The authors declare no conflict of interest. The funders had no role in the design of the study, in the collection, analyses, or interpretation of data, in the writing of the manuscript, or in the decision to publish the results.

References

1. Kumar, B.P.; Venkatesh, V.; Kumar, K.A.J.; Yadav, B.Y.; Mohan, S.R. Mandibular Reconstruction: Overview. *J. Maxillofac. Oral Surg.* **2015**, *15*, 425–441. [CrossRef] [PubMed]
2. Urken, M.L.; Buchbinder, D.; Costantino, P.D.; Sinha, U.; Okay, D.; Lawson, W.; Biller, H.F. Oromandibular Reconstruction Using Microvascular Composite Flaps: Report of 210 Cases. *Arch. Otolaryngol. Head Neck Surg.* **1998**, *124*, 46–55. [CrossRef] [PubMed]
3. Pellini, R.; Mercante, G.; Spriano, G. Step-by-step mandibular reconstruction with free fibula flap modelling. *Acta Otorhinolaryngol. Ital.* **2012**, *32*, 405–409. [PubMed]
4. Prisman, E.; Haerle, S.K.; Irish, J.C.; Daly, M.; Miles, B.; Chan, H. Value of preoperative mandibular plating in reconstruction of the mandible. *Head Neck* **2013**, *36*, 828–833. [CrossRef] [PubMed]
5. Farwell, D.G.; Kezirian, E.J.; Heydt, J.L.; Yueh, B.; Futran, N.D. Efficacy of small reconstruction plates in vascularized bone graft mandibular reconstruction. *Head Neck* **2006**, *28*, 573–579. [CrossRef]
6. Yeh, D.H.; Lee, D.J.; Sahovaler, A.; Fung, K.; MacNeil, D.; Nichols, A.C.; Yoo, J. Shouldering the load of mandible reconstruction: 81 cases of oromandibular reconstruction with the scapular tip free flap. *Head Neck* **2018**, *41*, 30–36. [CrossRef]
7. Prasad, J.; Sahovaler, A.; Theurer, J.; Yeh, D.H.; Fung, K.; MacNeil, S.D.; Yoo, J.; Nichols, A.C. Predictors of plate extrusion in oromandibular free flap reconstruction. *Microsurgery* **2018**, *38*, 682–689. [CrossRef]
8. Wood, C.B.; Shinn, J.; Amin, S.N.; Rohde, S.; Sinard, R.J. Risk of plate removal in free flap reconstruction of the mandible. *Oral Oncol.* **2018**, *83*, 91–95. [CrossRef]
9. Wilde, F.; Hanken, H.; Probst, F.; Schramm, A.; Heiland, M.; Cornelius, C.-P. Multicenter study on the use of patient-specific CAD/CAM reconstruction plates for mandibular reconstruction. *Int. J. Comput. Assist. Radiol. Surg.* **2015**, *10*, 2035–2051. [CrossRef]
10. Barr, M.L.; Haveles, C.S.; Rezzadeh, K.S.; Nolan, I.T.; Castro, R.; Lee, J.C.; Steinbacher, D.; Pfaff, M.J. Virtual Surgical Planning for Mandibular Reconstruction with the Fibula Free Flap: A Systematic Review and Meta-analysis. *Ann. Plast. Surg.* **2019**, *84*, 117–122. [CrossRef]

11. Fatima, A.; Hackman, T.G.; Wood, J.S. Cost-Effectiveness Analysis of Virtual Surgical Planning in Mandibular Reconstruction. *Plast. Reconstr. Surg.* **2019**, *143*, 1185–1194. [CrossRef] [PubMed]
12. Gil, R.S.; Roig, A.M.; Obispo, C.A.; Morla, A.; Pagès, C.M.; Perez, J.L. Surgical planning and microvascular reconstruction of the mandible with a fibular flap using computer-aided design, rapid prototype modelling, and precontoured titanium reconstruction plates: A prospective study. *Br. J. Oral Maxillofac. Surg.* **2015**, *53*, 49–53. [CrossRef] [PubMed]
13. Wilde, F.; Cornelius, C.-P.; Schramm, A. Computer-Assisted Mandibular Reconstruction using a Patient-Specific Reconstruction Plate Fabricated with Computer-Aided Design and Manufacturing Techniques. *Craniomaxillofac. Trauma Reconstr.* **2014**, *7*, 158–166. [CrossRef] [PubMed]
14. Wang, E.; Durham, J.S.; Anderson, D.W.; Prisman, E. Clinical evaluation of an automated virtual surgical planning platform for mandibular reconstruction. *Head Neck* **2020**, *42*, 3506–3514. [CrossRef]
15. Abdi, A.H.; Pesteie, M.; Prisman, E.; Abolmaesumi, P.; Fels, S. Variational Shape Completion for Virtual Planning of Jaw Recon-structive Surgery. *Lect. Notes Comput. Sci.* **2019**, *11768*, 227–235. [CrossRef]
16. Luu, K.; Pakdel, A.; Wang, E.; Prisman, E. In house virtual surgery and 3D complex head and neck reconstruction. *J. Otolaryngol. Head Neck Surg.* **2018**, *47*, 75. [CrossRef]
17. Wang, E.; Tran, K.L.; D'Heygere, E.; Prisman, E. Predicting the Premorbid Shape of a Diseased Mandible. *Laryngoscope* **2020**, *131*, E781–E786. [CrossRef]
18. Tran, K.L.; Wang, E.; Fels, S.; Hodgson, A.; Prisman, E. Versatility of a single piece scapular tip and lateral border free flap for mandibular reconstruction: A virtual study on angle correspondence. *Oral Oncol.* **2021**, *121*, 105379. [CrossRef]
19. Nguyen, S.; Tran, K.L.; Wang, E.; Britton, H.; Durham, J.S.; Prisman, E. Maxillectomy defects: Virtually comparing fibular and scapular free flap reconstructions. *Head Neck* **2021**, *43*, 2623–2633. [CrossRef]
20. Shkedy, Y.; Howlett, J.; Wang, E.; Ongko, J.; Durham, J.S.; Prisman, E. Predicting the Number of Fibular Segments to Reconstruct Mandibular Defects. *Laryngoscope* **2019**, *130*, E619–E624. [CrossRef]
21. Dziegielewski, P.T.; Zhu, J.; King, B.; Grosvenor, A.; Dobrovolsky, W.; Singh, P.; Ansari, K.; Al-Qahtani, K.H.; Harris, J.R.; Seikaly, H. Three-dimensional biomodeling in complex mandibular reconstruction and surgical simulation: Prospective trial. *J. Otolaryngol. Head Neck Surg.* **2011**, *40*, S70–S81. [PubMed]
22. Wong, R.; Tideman, H.; Kin, L.; Merkx, M. Biomechanics of mandibular reconstruction: A review. *Int. J. Oral Maxillofac. Surg.* **2010**, *39*, 313–319. [CrossRef] [PubMed]
23. Mavili, M.E.; Canter, H.I.; Aydinatay, B.S.; Kamaci, S.; Kocadereli, I. Use of Three-Dimensional Medical Modeling Methods for Precise Planning of Orthognathic Surgery. *J. Craniofacial Surg.* **2007**, *18*, 740–747. [CrossRef]
24. Chang, Y.-M.; Chana, J.S.; Wei, F.-C.; Tsai, C.-Y.; Chen, S.H.T. Osteotomy to Treat Malocclusion following Reconstruction of the Mandible with the Free Fibula Flap. *Plast. Reconstr. Surg.* **2003**, *112*, 31–36. [CrossRef] [PubMed]
25. Martola, M.; Lindqvist, C.; Hänninen, H.; Al-Sukhun, J. Fracture of titanium plates used for mandibular reconstruction following ablative tumor surgery. *J. Biomed. Mater. Res. Part B Appl. Biomater.* **2006**, *80B*, 345–352. [CrossRef]
26. Gutwald, R.; Jaeger, R.; Lambers, F.M. Customized mandibular reconstruction plates improve mechanical performance in a mandibular reconstruction model. *Comput. Methods Biomech. Biomed. Eng.* **2016**, *20*, 426–435. [CrossRef]
27. Onoda, S.; Kimata, Y.; Yamada, K.; Sugiyama, N.; Onoda, T.; Eguchi, M.; Mizukawa, N. Prevention points for plate exposure in the mandibular reconstruction. *J. Cranio-Maxillofac. Surg.* **2012**, *40*, e310–e314. [CrossRef]
28. Nicholson, R.E.; Schuller, D.E.; Forrest, L.A.; Mountain, R.E.; Ali, T.; Young, D. Factors Involved in Long- and Short-term Mandibular Plate Exposure. *Arch. Otolaryngol.-Head Neck Surg.* **1997**, *123*, 217–222. [CrossRef]
29. Chepeha, D.B.; Teknos, T.N.; Fung, K.; Shargorodsky, J.; Bs, A.G.S.; Nussenbaum, B.; Jones, L.; Eisbruch, A.; Bradford, C.R.; Prince, M.E.; et al. Lateral oromandibular defect: When is it appropriate to use a bridging reconstruction plate combined with a soft tissue revascularized flap? *Head Neck* **2008**, *30*, 709–717. [CrossRef]
30. Davies, J.C.; Chan, H.H.L.; Yao, C.M.K.L.; Ziai, H.; Dixon, P.R.; Chepeha, D.B.; Goldstein, D.P.; Almeida, J.R.; Gilbert, R.W.; Irish, J.C. Association of Plate Contouring with Hardware Complications Following Mandibular Reconstruction. *Laryngoscope* **2021**, *132*, 61–66. [CrossRef]
31. Goh, B.T.; Lee, S.; Tideman, H.; Stoelinga, P.J. Mandibular reconstruction in adults: A review. *Int. J. Oral Maxillofac. Surg.* **2008**, *37*, 597–605. [CrossRef] [PubMed]
32. Swendseid, B.; Kumar, A.; Sweeny, L.; Zhan, T.; Goldman, R.A.; Krein, H.; Heffelfinger, R.N.; Luginbuhl, A.J.; Curry, J.M. Natural History and Consequences of Nonunion in Mandibular and Maxillary Free Flaps. *Otolaryngol. Neck Surg.* **2020**, *163*, 956–962. [CrossRef] [PubMed]
33. Brown, J.; Lowe, D.; Kanatas, A.; Schache, A. Mandibular reconstruction with vascularised bone flaps: A systematic review over 25 years. *Br. J. Oral Maxillofac. Surg.* **2017**, *55*, 113–126. [CrossRef]
34. May, M.M.; Howe, B.M.; O'Byrne, T.J.; Ms, A.E.A.; Morris, J.M.; Moore, E.J.; Kasperbauer, J.L.; Janus, J.R.; Van Abel, K.M.; Bs, H.J.D.; et al. Short- and long-term outcomes of three-dimensional printed surgical guides and virtual surgical planning versus conventional methods for fibula free flap reconstruction of the mandible: Decreased nonunion and complication rates. *Head Neck* **2021**, *43*, 2342–2352. [CrossRef]
35. Yla-Kotola, T.M.; Bartlett, E.; Armstrong, K.; Gilbert, R.W.; Hofer, S.O.P.; Goldstein, D.P. Union and Bone Resorption of Free Fibular Flaps in Mandibular Reconstruction. *J. Reconstr. Microsurg.* **2013**, *29*, 427–432. [CrossRef]

36. Chang, E.I.; Jenkins, M.P.; Patel, S.A.; Topham, N.S. Long-Term Operative Outcomes of Preoperative Computed Tomography–Guided Virtual Surgical Planning for Osteocutaneous Free Flap Mandible Reconstruction. *Plast. Reconstr. Surg.* **2016**, *137*, 619–623. [CrossRef] [PubMed]
37. Claiborne, S.; Kademani, D.; Patel, K.; Idle, M. Non-Union Rates in Fibula Free-Flap Reconstruction of Head and Neck Oncologic Defects. *J. Oral Maxillofac. Surg.* **2017**, *75*, e335. [CrossRef]
38. Cheng, H.; Clymer, J.W.; Chen, B.P.-H.; Sadeghirad, B.; Ferko, N.C.; Cameron, C.G.; Hinoul, P. Prolonged operative duration is associated with complications: A systematic review and meta-analysis. *J. Surg. Res.* **2018**, *229*, 134–144. [CrossRef]
39. Mehrotra, D.; Markus, A. Emerging simulation technologies in global craniofacial surgical training. *J. Oral Biol. Craniofacial Res.* **2021**, *11*, 486–499. [CrossRef]

Journal of
Clinical Medicine

MDPI

Article

Assessment of Quality of Life in Head-and-Neck Oncologic Patients with Intraoral Soft-Tissue Defects Reconstructed with Buccinator Myomucosal Flap

Marc Agea Martínez [1], Raúl Antúnez-Conde [1], Carlos Navarro Cuéllar [1,*], Manuel Tousidonis Rial [1], Ignacio Navarro Cuéllar [1], Ana María López López [1], Dafne Gascón Alonso [1], Ángela Sada Urmeneta [1] and José J. Zamorano-León [2]

1 Maxillofacial Surgery Department, Hospital General Universitario Gregorio Marañón, 28007 Madrid, Spain
2 Public Health and Maternal & Child Health Department, School of Medicine, Universidad Complutense, 28040 Madrid, Spain
* Correspondence: cnavarrocuellar@gmail.com

Abstract: The aim of this study is to evaluate the functional outcomes and quality of life (QoL) in oncologic patients with intraoral defects reconstructed with the buccinator myomucosal flap. A retrospective study was performed involving 39 patients with intraoral soft-tissue defects, reconstructed with a buccinator myomucosal flap during a six-year period. Patients completed the European Organization for Research and Treatment of Cancer questionnaires, the standard questionnaire (QLQ-C30) and the head-and-neck specific module (QLQ-H&N35). Thirty-nine patients with a mean age of 61.23 ± 15.80 years were included in the study. Thirty-three patients were diagnosed with an oncological condition (84.61%). Six patients (15.38%) developed orosinusal communication and underwent extensive debridement. The median global-health-status score was 79.27 and emotional performance was the lowest scoring, with a mean score of 76.93. As for the symptom items, the most outstanding were dental problems (33.33), oral opening (31.62) and dry mouth (37.61), followed by sticky saliva (24.79), problems with social eating (21.15) and pain (19.87). The most significant symptoms were radiotherapy-related adverse effects such as pain, fatigue, dental problems and dry mouth. Patients reconstructed with the buccinator myomucosal flap develop a good quality of life for all types of activities, and a correct function and aesthetics. Postoperative radiotherapy is associated with a poorer quality of life, and can lead to impairment of several symptoms such as swallowing, oral opening and dry mouth.

Keywords: quality of life; EORTC QLQ-C30; EORTC QLQ-H&N35; head and neck; buccinator flap; reconstructive surgery

Citation: Agea Martínez, M.; Antúnez-Conde, R.; Navarro Cuéllar, C.; Tousidonis Rial, M.; Navarro Cuéllar, I.; López López, A.M.; Gascón Alonso, D.; Sada Urmeneta, Á.; Zamorano-León, J.J. Assessment of Quality of Life in Head-and-Neck Oncologic Patients with Intraoral Soft-Tissue Defects Reconstructed with Buccinator Myomucosal Flap. *J. Clin. Med.* **2022**, *11*, 7458. https://doi.org/10.3390/jcm11247458

Academic Editor: Gunnar Wichmann

Received: 19 October 2022
Accepted: 13 December 2022
Published: 15 December 2022

1. Introduction

The surgical management of oncologic patients may lead to intraoral soft-tissue defects that require immediate reconstruction to reestablish form and function. The ablative and reconstructive surgery can be challenging, and can be approached with different techniques, depending on the extension of the tumor, the nodal staging, and the involvement of other structures [1]. Small defects are usually reconstructed by primary closure or secondary-intention wound healing. Extensive or complex defects are usually reconstructed with free flaps, depending on patient morbidity and technical limitations. Medium-sized defects are usually reconstructed with local flaps that provide similar tissue, with low morbidity [1–4].

Disorders resulting from ablative and reconstructive surgery can significantly affect the quality of life in oncologic patients. Quality of life (QoL) is a wide and multidimensional concept that comprises many aspects of life: physiological, emotional and psychological [5]. It is considered a system that represents the individual's general perception of well-being [6]. Concern in this area is now a key issue that can be reflected in increased research interest.

The aim of this study was to evaluate the functional outcomes and quality of life (QoL) in oncologic patients with intraoral soft-tissue defects, reconstructed with a buccinator myomucosal flap [6], by means of verified questionnaires. Therefore, the QLQ questionnaire of the European Organization for Research and Treatment of Cancer (EORTC) was implemented and analyzed. It is an integrated system for assessing patients' health-related quality of life [7,8]. It includes a general module of 30 questions (QLQ-C30) and a specific module for the head-and-neck area with 35 questions (QLQ-H&N35) [9]. To date, this is the first study to report EORTC-verified QLQ questionnaires to assess the functionality, health and well-being among patients with intraoral soft-tissue reconstruction with the buccinator myomucosal flap.

2. Materials and Methods

A single-center retrospective study was designed to include 49 patients treated in the Oral and Maxillofacial Surgery Department at Gregorio Marañón General Hospital in Madrid, Spain, from January 2015 to September 2021. The study and review of the medical records and data collection, and the subsequent analysis of the data collected is endorsed by the Hospital Ethics Committee. Informed consent was obtained from all subjects involved in the study.

Inclusion criteria were: (1) reconstruction of intraoral defects with buccinator flap; (2) patients free of oncological disease or recovery from previous pathology, and follow-up of at least 6 months after successful treatment; (3) the interviewer was a different physician than the one who performed the usual follow-up.

Exclusion criteria were: (1) inability to understand or inability to complete the questionnaires; (2) failure to complete the questionnaires; (3) more than one local or regional surgical- procedure prior to surgical reconstruction with buccinator flap; (4) radiotherapy prior to surgical reconstruction. Ten patients were excluded: five patients refused to participate, three patients underwent previous radiotherapy and two patients had undergone two surgical procedures prior to surgical reconstruction.

2.1. Questionnaires

Since its first publication in 1993, the QLQ-C30 has been modified three times. Currently, version 3.0 of the QLQ-C30 and version 1.0 of the head-and-neck specific module (QLQ-H&N35) are implemented. The QLQ-C30 comprises five functioning scales (physical, role, emotional, cognitive and social functioning), nine symptom-scales (fatigue, nausea and vomiting, pain, dyspnea, insomnia, loss of appetite, constipation, diarrhea and economic difficulties) and a global-health-status scale. The first 28 questions provide four answer options measured on a Likert scale (not at all: 1, a little: 2, quite a lot: 3, a lot: 4), while the last two questions concern overall health, and are scored from 1 to 7 (with 1 being poor health and 7 being excellent health).

The QLQ-H&N35 module is designed to be a complement to the QLQ-C30 in order to increase the scope, sensitivity and specificity of the assessments. It includes 35 questions measuring symptoms and related problems in the head-and-neck area (pain, swallowing, coughing, dental problems, oral opening, dry mouth, sticky saliva, sensory problems, feeling sick, speech, social eating, social contact, sexuality, need for nutritional supplements or analgesics, and weight changes). The first 30 questions are scored according to a Likert scale, while the last five questions are answered in a dichotomous model (no: 1; yes: 2).

The scores of the questionnaires are calculated according to the instructions of the EORTC scoring manual. The score obtained for each item is a linear transformation from 0 to 100, whereby higher scores represent a higher level of response. Thus, high scores on symptom scales represent more symptomatology and a worse QoL, while high scores on functioning and global-health-scales represent a high QoL [7,8].

2.2. Reliability

The reliability of the questionnaires was evaluated by means of Cronbach's alpha coefficient, obtaining a total score of 0.95, which is considered an excellent and internally-consistent result, with a value above 0.9.

2.3. Data Recording

The following sociodemographic and clinical data were included at the time of surgery: age, sex, comorbidity, smoking, alcohol consumption, primary diagnosis, and tumor-stage, according to the American Joint Committee on Cancer (AJCC) guidelines in the cases of oncologic disease, location and size of the defect, whether the defect included the resection of soft tissue or was combined with bone tissue, the need for another flap, postoperative complications, treatment with radiotherapy (RT), the need for readaptation of the flap and pedicle section, implant rehabilitation and edentulism. Patients completed the Spanish versions of both questionnaires at a follow-up without any influence on their responses to minimize measurement bias.

2.4. Statistical Analysis

A comparison method based on known comparative groups was performed, due to the absence of a gold standard [9]. Scores of the QLQ-C30 and QLQ-H&N35 questionnaires according to different sociodemographic and clinical parameters and lifestyle-related issues, were compared. Quantitative values were expressed as mean $\pm$ standard deviation (D.S) or median and interquartile range as well as total range, while qualitative variables were reported as frequencies and percentages. The Kruskal–Wallis and Mann–Whitney tests were used to compare differences between groups of quantitative variables. The statistical analysis was performed using the software SPSS 25.0. (IBM Corp. in Armonk, NY, USA). A two-tailed p-value of lower than 0.05 was considered statistically significant.

3. Results

A total of 39 patients with a mean age of 61.23 $\pm$ 15.80 years at the time of surgery (48.7% men, 51.3% women) were included in the study. Sociodemographic and clinical characteristics are summarized in Table 1.

Thirty-three were diagnosed with oncological disease (84.6%). A total of 81.8% corresponded to squamous cell carcinoma, 6% to other malignant tumors, such as embryonal rhabdomyosarcoma and polymorphous adenocarcinoma, and 12.1% to benign lesions, such as pleomorphic adenoma, giant cell granuloma and ossifying fibroma. Oncologic patients underwent resection with clear margins and neck dissection when indicated. Six patients presented (15.38%) orosinusal communication and underwent extensive debridement. All patients were immediately reconstructed with the buccinator flap.

In terms of tumor stage, according to AJCC guidelines, the majority of patients were stage I (72.4%). The location of the defect varied, with the most frequent being the tongue (33.3%). The area of the defect showed a mean size of 9.2 $\pm$ 4.9 cm^2. A soft-tissue defect was reconstructed in 64.10% of patients, while in 35.9% of patients the reconstructed defect included soft tissue and bone. In 66.7% of the patients, no other flaps were necessary to perform the reconstruction of the defect. In patients in whom an additional flap was necessary, the Bichat fat pad flap was the most common technique used for reconstruction (92.3%). Fourteen patients (35.9%) required a second surgical procedure to readapt the flap.

The incidence of patients with postoperative radiotherapy (RT) was 38.5%, with a mean dose of 60Gy. Complications were reported in 38.46%: the most common were partial flap necrosis (six patients) and trismus (five patients), although only 32% required a subsequent procedure.

Table 1. Description of the socio-demographic and clinical characteristics.

Variable	Category	Frequency	
		n	%
Age	≤60	20	51.3
	>60	19	48.7
Gender	Male	19	48.7
	Female	20	51.3
Smoking	No	20	51.3
	Yes	19	48.7
Alcohol consumption	No	30	76.9
	Yes	9	23
Diagnosis	Oncologic (Primary tumor)	31	79,5
	Oncologic (Recurrence)	2	5,1
	Iatrogenic sequelae	5	12.8
	Congenital sequelae	1	2.6
Tumor site	Tongue	13	33.3
	Mouth floor	9	23
	Lower jaw gingiva	3	7.7
	Upper jaw gingiva	6	15.4
	Palate	8	20.5
Resection	Soft tissue	25	64.1
	Combined tissue	14	35.9
Need for another flap	No	26	66.7
	Yes	13	33.3
	Bichat's flaps	12	92.3
	Other	1	7.7
Stage (AJCC)	None	10	25.6
	I	9	23
	II	12	30.8
	III	6	15.4
	IVa	1	2.6
	IVb	1	2.6
Radiotherapy	No	24	61.5
	Yes	15	38.5
Complications	None	24	61.5
	Partial necrosis	6	15.4
	Complete necrosis	1	2.6
	Trismus	5	12.8
	Infection/dehiscence	2	5.1
	Neuropatic pain	1	2.6
Edentulism	Partial	21	53.9
	Complete	16	41
	No	2	5.1
Dental rehabilitation	No	12	30.8
	Yes *	16	41
	In process	11	28.2
Follow-up	≤3	23	59
	>3	16	41

* Two patients were rehabilitated with removable mucosa-supported prostheses (without osseointegrated implants).

Sixteen (41%) patients were completely edentulous and twenty-one (53.9%) were partially edentulous, as a consequence of previous tooth loss or the need for extractions to avoid occlusal trauma to the pedicle. Osseointegrated implants have represented a significant advance in the reconstructive treatment of oncological patients. Because of this, patients can achieve an optimal reconstruction ensuring a fully esthetic and functional rehabilitation. Fourteen patients were rehabilitated with osseointegrated implants, and two patients were rehabilitated with mucosa-supported removable prostheses, because they declined dental-implant treatment. A total of 131 osseointegrated implants were placed. The implants were immediately placed in the same surgical procedure as the buccinator flap reconstruction. In edentulous patients, implants were placed in both the mandible and maxilla to achieve optimal functional reconstruction. In dentate patients who required extraction of the last molars to avoid flap damage, dental implants were placed at the same time as tooth extraction. In non-irradiated patients, prosthetic rehabilitation was performed 4 months after reconstructive surgery. In irradiated patients, dental rehabilitation was performed 8 months after the end of radiotherapy. The follow-up time was 2.9 years, with a range of 6.5 months to 6.2 years.

The questionnaires took between 15 and 20 min to complete. The scores of the QLQ-C30 and the specific module QLQ-H&N35 are shown in Tables 2 and 3, respectively.

Table 2. Total scores for QLQ-C30 questionnaire (Version 3.0).

QLQ-C30 Scale Name	Mean Score	SD	Median Score	IQR	Range
Functional scales					
Physical function	78.6	21	83.3	(66.7–100)	(33.3–100.00)
Role function	85	23.5	100.	(83.3–100)	(0–100)
Emotional function	76.9	23	83.3	(66.7–91.7)	(0–100)
Cognitive function	90.2	21.9	100	(83.3–100)	(0–100)
Social function	85.5	27.4	100	(83.3–100)	(0–100)
Symptom scales/items					
Fatigue	17.7	16.7	11.1	(0–22)	(0–55.6)
Nausea and vomiting	2.1	7.8	0	(0–0)	(0–33.3)
Pain	20.1	19.6	16.7	(0–33.3)	(0–66.7)
Dyspnea	11.1	20.7	0	(0–33.3)	(0–66.7)
Insomnia	13.7	21.2	0	(0–33.3)	(0–66.7)
Appetite loss	8.6	18.3	0	(0–0)	(0–66.7)
Constipation	12	24.8	0	(0–33.3)	(0–100)
Diarrhea	3.4	10.3	0	(0–0)	(0–33.3)
Financial difficulties	9.4	22.9	0	(0–0)	(0–100)
Global health status/qol					
Global health status	79.3	19.8	83.3	(75–91.7)	(16.7–100)

Abbreviations: QLQ = quality of life; SD = standard deviation; IQR = interquartile range.

The median global-health-status score was 79.3, with an interquartile range between 75 and 91.7, with 100 being the highest score. Among the functional scales, emotional functioning was the lowest, with a median score of 76.9. The other items showed high scores, with interquartile ranges between 83.3 and 100. The lowest scores on the symptom scale, with 100 being the lowest score, were fatigue (17.7), pain (20) and insomnia (13.7). Despite this, all items had a mode of 0 and an interquartile range between 0 and 33.3 as a maximum.

As for the symptom items of the specific head-and-neck module (QLQ-H&N35), low scores were obtained, all being below 40 points. The most outstanding were dental problems (33.3), trismus (31.6) and dry mouth (37.6), followed by sticky saliva (24.8), problems with social eating (21.1), and pain (19.9). In addition, it is remarkable that almost half of the patients needed pain medication and that 89.7% used a temporary feeding tube in the first days after surgery.

Table 3. Total scores for QLQ-H&N35 questionnaire.

Scale Name	Mean Score	SD	Median Score	IQR	Range
Symptom scales/items					
Pain	19.9	18.8	16.7	(8.3–25)	(0–75)
Swallowing	12.8	18.3	8.3	(0–25)	(0–75)
Teeth	33.3	34.2	33.3	(0–66.7)	(0–100)
Opening mouth	31.6	31.5	33.3	(0–66.7)	(0–100)
Dry mouth	376	38.4	33.3	(0–66.7)	(0–100)
Sticky saliva	24.8	29.3	0	(0–33.3)	(0–100)
Sense problems	9.8	23.5	0	(0–0)	(0–100)
Coughing	14.5	22.7	0	(0–33.3)	(0–100)
Feeling ill	8.6	19.8	0	(0–0)	(0–100)
Speech problems	14.5	19.1	11.1	(0–22.2)	(0–100)
Troubles with social eating	21.2	22.2	16.7	(0–33.3)	(0–100)
Troubles with social contact	10.6	19.2	0	(0–13.3)	(0–73.3)
Less sexuality	16.2	26.4	0	(0–33.3)	(0–100)
Pain killers	46.2	50.5	0	(0–100)	(0–100)
Nutritional supplements	5.1	22.4	0	(0–0)	(0–100)
Feeding tube	89.7	30.7	100	(100–100)	(0–100)
Weight loss	30.8	46.8	0	(0–100)	(0–100)
Weight gain	43.6	50.2	0	(0–100)	(0–100)

Abbreviations: QLQ = quality of life; SD = Standard deviation; IQR = interquartile range.

As illustrated in Tables 4 and 5, a comparison of the quality-of-life scales according to gender, shows that men showed more fatigue, pain and analgesic consumption than women. In terms of age, significant differences were found only in insomnia, and were more frequent in patients >60 years. No differences were found in smoking, alcohol consumption, aggressiveness and size of resection, dental rehabilitation or post-surgical follow-up.

Table 4. Comparison of groups of the QLQ-C30 questionnaire.

Variable	Categories	QLQ-C30 Questionnaire					
		Functional Scale		Symptom Scale		Global Health Status	
		Score (Mean ± SD)	*p* Value	Score (Mean ± SD)	*p* Value	Score (Mean ± SD)	*p* Value
Gender	Male Female	80.6 ± 18.8 85.7 ± 19.1	0.139	11.8 ± 11.1 10.2 ± 10.9	0.513	77.6 ± 21.4 80.8 ± 18.6	0.629
Age	≤60 >60	82.1 ± 21.2 84.4 ± 16.6	0.933	11.9 ± 11.5 10 ± 10.4	0.855	77.5 ± 21.1 81.1 ± 18.6	0.528
Smoker	Yes No	80.6 ± 26.2 85.8 ± 20.5	0.373	12.2 ± 19.7 9.6 ± 15.7	0.537	82.1 ± 15.6 76.3 ± 23.5	0.403
Alcohol consumption	Yes No	80.4 ± 26.5 84.1 ± 22.4	0.557	12.8 ± 19.3 10.3 ± 16.8	0.34	79.4 ± 18 78.7 ± 26.1	0.741
Diagnosis	Primary tumour Recurrence Sequelae	80.3 ± 20 92.5 ± 0.7 95.3 ± 7.6	0.030	12.6 ± 11.7 5 ± 1.4 4.7 ± 3.3	0.218	76.9 ± 20.9 83.3 ± 11.8 90.3 ± 11.1	0.250
Tumour site	Tongue Floor of the mouth Lower jaw gingiva Upper jaw gingiva Palate	80.2 ± 21.9 75.1 ± 24.2 78.3 ± 11.6 91.5 ± 4.6 93 ± 10.3	0.077	10.4 ± 11 15.2 ± 11.2 18.3 ± 21.4 6.5 ± 5.4 7.5 ± 8.1	0.302	74.4 ± 14.6 71.3 ± 33.1 77.8 ± 9.6 87.5 ± 7 90.6 ± 10.4	0.081
Defect Size	<5 cm 5–10 cm 10–15 cm >15 cm	84.2 ± 19 78.8 ± 30.1 84.9 ± 20.3 91.7 ± 10.9	0.713	13 ± 21.1 11.2 ± 16.5 11.7 ± 20.1 5.1 ± 5.7	0.585	88.5 ± 13.3 72.8 ± 27.7 81.82 ± 11.1 78.3 ± 7.5	0.426

Table 4. *Cont.*

Variable	Categories	QLQ-C30 Questionnaire					
		Functional Scale		Symptom Scale		Global Health Status	
		Score (Mean ± SD)	*p* Value	Score (Mean ± SD)	*p* Value	Score (Mean ± SD)	*p* Value
Stage (AJCC)	No malignant	93.2 ± 9.5	0.144	5.7 ± 7.4	0.260	89.2 ± 9.7	0.217
	I	76.8 ± 2.4		11.6 ± 8.8		72.2 ± 28	
	II	78.3 ± 22.1		14.3 ± 12.4		79.2 ± 22.9	
	III	82.8 ± 12.1		12.2 ± 15.2		76.4 ± 8.2	
	IVA	93		4		66.7	
	IVB	93		4		75	
RT	Yes	81.1 ± 17.7	0.139	11.3 ± 10.6	0.409	75.6 ± 14.6	0.034
	No	84.6 ± 19.8		10.8 ± 11.3		81.6 ± 22.4	
Dental rehabilitation	Yes	85.5 ± 19.3	0.650	10.2 ± 17.7	0.420	85.4 ± 12	0.256
	No	81.6 ± 26.9		11 ± 16.9		74.6 ± 24.1	
Follow-up	</=3 years	81.1 ± 26.5	0.629	10.7 ± 17	0.690	75.4 ± 23.5	0.270
	>3 years	86.4 ± 18.6		11.2 ± 18.9		84.9 ± 11.1	

Remarkably, the comparison of lesion location found no significant differences on the functional scale. Tumors located on the tongue and floor of the mouth scored high on functionality, although not as high as those on the palate or maxilla. In terms of global health and symptoms, although there were no significant differences, good scores were found in the maxillary and palatal regions. In terms of diagnosis, there were better scores for sequelae compared with the other two groups, although there were higher scores for functionality, global health and symptomatology in the recurrences compared with the primary diagnoses, although none of the comparisons were significant.

When compared in accordance with the AJCC staging guidelines (with the "No" category representing non-malignant tumors), it was observed that with increasing stage there was a decrease in functionality and health, and an increase in symptomatology. Despite the above, significant differences were only found in swallowing problems.

As a final comparison, quality of life was evaluated according to the application of RT. Worse functionality and increased symptomatology, such as difficulty in oral opening or thick saliva, were observed in the group treated with RT, but significant differences were found only in global health status, swallowing problems, dental problems, pain, and dry mouth.

Table 5. Comparison of groups of QLQ-H&N35 questionnaire.

Variable	Categories	QLQ-H&N35 QUESTIONNAIRE													
		Pain		Swallowing		Teeth		Opening Mouth		Dry Mouth		Sticky Saliva		Pain Killers	
		Score (M ± SD)	p Value	Score (M ± SD)	p Value	Score (M ± SD)	p Value	Score M ± SD)	p value	Score (M ± SD)	p Value	Score (M ± SD)	p Value	Score (M ± SD)	p Value
Gender	Male	26.3 ± 18.9	0.009	12.7 ± 19.1	0.722	33.3 ± 33.3	0.917	35.1 ± 34.2	0.572	36.8 ± 39.9	0.858	28.1 ± 31.9	0.560	73.7 ± 45.2	0.001
	Female	13.8 ± 16.9		12.9 ± 18		33.3 ± 35.9		28.3 ± 29.2		38.3 ± 37.9		21.7 ± 27.1		20 ± 41	
Age	≤60	19.2 ± 18	0.558	10.4 ± 18.3	0.219	28.3 ± 31.1	0.405	33.3 ± 30.6	0.647	46.7 ± 28.1	0.141	28.3 ± 24.8	0.209	5 ± 22.4	0.435
	>60	20.6 ± 20.1		15.4 ± 19.5		38.6 ± 37.3		29.8 ± 33.1		28.1 ± 37.3		21.1 ± 33.7		52.6 ± 51.3	
Smoker	Yes	20.4 ± 17.6	0.585	12.9 ± 18	0.847	35 ± 33.3	0.645	28.3 ± 32.9	0.396	38.3 ± 43.6	0.976	25 ± 30.4	0.988	55 ± 51	0.262
	No	19.3 ± 20.4		12.7 ± 19.1		31.6 ± 36		35.1 ± 30.4		36.9 ± 33.1		24.6 ± 29.1		36.8 ± 49.6	
Alcohol consumption	Yes	20 ± 17.7	0.670	14.4 ± 20.2	0.574	33.3 ± 35	0.916	32.2 ± 30.9	0.737	38.9 ± 39.2	0.738	27.8 ± 29.1	0.173	50 ± 50.9	0.385
	No	19.4 ± 23.2		7.4 ± 8.8		33.3 ± 33.3		29.6 ± 35.1		33.3 ± 37.3		14.8 ± 29.4		33.3 ± 50	
Diagnosis	Primary tumour	21.8 ± 20.3	0.45	13.2 ± 16.4	0.523	33.3 ± 33.3	0.983	34.4 ± 32.8	0.587	40.9 ± 30.2	0.518	25.8 ± 29.5	0.719	51.6 ± 50.8	0.298
	Recurrence	8.3		4.2 ± 5.9		33.3 ± 47.1		16.7 ± 23.8		33.3 ± 47.1		33.3 ± 47.1		0	
	Sequelae	13.9 ± 10.1		13.9 ± 30.1		33.3 ± 42.2		22.2 ± 27.2		22.2 ± 34.4		16.7 ± 27.9		33.3 ± 51.6	
Tumour site	Tongue	18.6 ± 21	0.390	19.9 ± 18.2	0.089	35.9 ± 34.6	0.879	38.5 ± 32.9	0.664	61.5 ± 35.6	0.071	30.8 ± 28.7	0.546	30.8 ± 48	0.252
	Floor of the mouth	24.1 ± 23.7		6.5 ± 9.1		33.3 ± 33.3		33.3 ± 33.3		3.3 ± 37.3		22.2 ± 28.7		55.6 ± 52.7	
	Lower jaw gingiva	38.9 ± 21		19.4 ± 26.8		44.4 ± 50.9		44.4 ± 50.9		33.3 ± 57.7		44.4 ± 50.9		100	
	Upper jaw gingiva	12.5 ± 4.6		2.8 ± 4.3		33.3 ± 29.8		16.7 ± 18.3		22.2 ± 27.2		22.2 ± 27.2		33.3 ± 51.6	
	Palate	15.6 ± 11.3		13.5 ± 26.3		25 ± 38.8		25 ± 29.6		16.7 ± 30.9		12.5 ± 24.8		50 ± 53.5	
Defect Size	<5 cm	20.8 ± 13.4	0.143	14.6 ± 17.7	0.565	29.2 ± 37.5	0.836	33.3 ± 35.6	0.693	25 ± 38.8	0.651	16.7 ± 35.6	0.586	75 ± 46.3	0.243
	5–10 cm	28.3 ± 24.8		14.4 ± 24.7		33.3 ± 39.8		40 ± 38.2		37.8 ± 35.3		28.9 ± 30.5		40 ± 50.7	
	10–15 cm	12.9 ± 10.1		7.6 ± 10.2		36.4 ± 23.4		24.2 ± 21.6		39.4 ± 38.9		27.3 ± 25		45.5 ± 52.2	
	>15 cm	8.3 ± 8.3		16.7 ± 11.8		33.3 ± 40.8		20 ± 18.3		53.6 ± 50.6		20 ± 29.8		20 ± 44.7	
Stage (AJCC)	No malignant	15 ± 8.6	0.613	8.3 ± 23.6	0.040	30 ± 36.7	0.581	30 ± 29.2	0.552	20 ± 28.1	0.079	20 ± 23.3	0.395	40 ± 51.6	0.816
	I	29.6 ± 21.7		13 ± 21.7		33.3 ± 37.3		33.3 ± 33.3		29.6 ± 38.9		22.2 ± 28.9		55.6 ± 52.7	
	II	18.1 ± 20.4		9 ± 10.9		22.8 ± 27.8		25 ± 32.2		33.3 ± 34.8		16.7 ± 26.6		50 ± 52.2	
	III	19.4 ± 25.1		26.4 ± 14.4		55.6 ± 40.4		50 ± 35		72.2 ± 39		44.4 ± 40.4		50 ± 54.8	
	IVA	16.7		25		33.3		33.3		100		33.3		0	
	IVB	8.3		8.3		0		0		66.7		66.7		0	
RT	Yes	26.7 ± 16.4	0.046	26.1 ± 22.5	0.000	46.7 ± 37.4	0.043	42.2 ± 32	0.103	53.3 ± 43.3	0.039	33.3 ± 35.6	0.052	60 ± 50.7	0.176
	No	16 ± 20.6		4.5 ± 7.8		25 ± 29.9		25 ± 29.9		27.8 ± 32.1		19.4 ± 23.9		37.5 ± 49.5	
Dental rehabilitation	Yes	15.1 ± 14.3	0.259	14.6 ± 20.1	0.606	33.3 ± 32.3	0.872	25 ± 25.8	0.362	33.3 ± 34.4	0.593	18.8 ± 27.1	0.292	43.8 ± 51.2	0.817
	No	23.8 ± 21.8		12.3 ± 13		36.5 ± 36.4		35.5 ± 34.8		41.3 ± 42		28.6 ± 30.3		47.6 ± 51.2	
Follow-up	</=3 years	20.7 ± 19.8	0.849	16.3 ± 21.5	0.278	37.7 ± 39.3	0.576	37.7 ± 35.3	0.221	44.9 ± 37.1	0.123	27.5 ± 32.8	0.663	39.1 ± 60	0.298
	>3 years	18.8 ± 17.9		7.8 ± 11.2		27.1 ± 25		22.9 ± 23.5		27.1 ± 38.9		20.8 ± 24		56.3 ± 51.2	

Abbreviations: QLQ = quality of life; H&N = Head and neck; SD = Standard deviation; RT = Radiotherap; M = Mean.

4. Discussion

The buccinator flap comprises mucosa, submucosa and muscle. It is limited superiorly by the Stenson's duct, inferiorly by the mandibular vestibule, anteriorly by the oral commissure and posteriorly by the pterygomandibular raphe [4,10]. It has a wide vascular supply from both the facial artery and the buccal artery. Venous drainage is achieved through the submucosal venous plexus, the pterygoid venous plexus and the facial vein [1,11] (Figure 1). There are different options to harvest this flap. Rahpeyma [1] described in 2013 a classification based on its pedicle:

(a) Posterior buccinator myomucosal flap: based on the buccal artery (branch of the maxillary artery) and the posterior buccal artery (branch of the facial artery), which can be a pedicled flap or an island flap.
(b) Superior buccinator myomucosal flap: based on the angular artery (branch of the facial artery) with retrograde flow, which can be harvested as a pedicle flap or island flap.
(c) Inferior buccinator myomucosal flap: based on the facial artery with anterograde flow, which can be pedicled (facial artery myomucosal flap or FAMM flap) or dissected as an island flap (Zhao flap) [12].
(d) Anterior buccinator myomucosal flap: pedicled over the anterior buccal artery (branch of the facial artery).

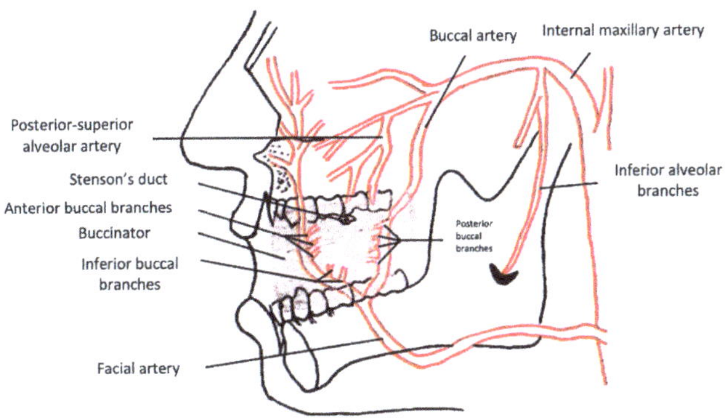

Figure 1. Vascular supply of the buccinator myomucosal flap.

The buccinator flap is very versatile, safe and reliable. It provides a wide arc of rotation for reconstruction of different locations such as the nasal cavity, palate, maxilla, tongue, floor of the mouth, mandible, oropharynx and lips [2,10]. In addition, it provides optimal thickness with a mucosa of similar color and texture to the rest of the intraoral soft tissues and the ability to secrete saliva, which allows for an excellent functional result [13,14]. Nevertheless, functional and aesthetic restoration remains a major challenge for head and neck surgeons [15]. It is not only the coverage of soft-tissue defects that is important, but also the functional outcome.

Restoration of functionality, esthetics and quality of life after oncologic surgery or intraoral sequelae are some of the main challenges of head and neck surgery. Optimal functionality requires good lingual mobility and adequate lip competence, to allow adequate swallowing, breathing, and speech, to perform basic daily needs [2].

Although the buccinator flap provides a limited width and requires a second-stage procedure in many patients, it offers many benefits: (1) it is a thin and pliable flap with a wide arc of rotation and length; (2) it is a myomucosal flap, ideal for reconstruction of mucosal defects because of the lack of hair; (3) it is a safe and reliable flap that allows postoperative radiotherapy; (4) it is easy to harvest; (10) it enables primary closure of the donor site under 3 cm^2; (11) it can be harvested simultaneously with neck dissection;

(12) previous neck dissection and radiation therapy are not contraindications for its use [12–14]; it can be superiorly or inferiorly pedicled, depending on the defect to be reconstructed [14]; it can be used as a reconstructive technique simultaneously with the immediate placement of osseointegrated implants for both aesthetic and functional rehabilitation.

The EORTC questionnaires, version 3.0 of the general module together with the H&N-35 module, have been implemented in this manuscript. These questionnaires are comprehensive, and their validity, internal consistency and reliability have been tested in large groups of patients [5,7–9]. However, it is a general head-and-neck-cancer quality-of-life scoring system, and may have some limitations for the evaluation of study patients.

The design of this study, being cross-sectional, implies that quality of life is measured once for each patient, which represents a limitation of the study. To assess changes over time, patients should be evaluated using a longitudinal study, in which quality of life is measured before, during and after treatment, for each patient. The scale scores of our patients are comparable to the results of previous studies [5,16,17].

Patients reported a good quality of life, showing values above 75 on the functioning scales and a global health status of 79.3, which indicates a good ability to perform daily activities, sociability and an overall high quality-of-life. The most significant symptoms were pain and fatigue in the general questionnaire. In the specific head-and-neck questionnaire, the patients reported more difficulties, which is consistent with previous studies [5,18]. Difficulty in oral opening, dry mouth and thick saliva obtained a higher mean score (<38). These problems were associated with the adverse effects of radiotherapy [19]. A total of 89.7% of the patients used a nasogastric feeding-tube in the postoperative period temporarily and, therefore, the quality of life was not influenced.

In general terms, the researchers highlight the absence of significant differences on the scales of physical, social, cognitive, emotional and role functioning, which allows us to suggest an adequate quality of life in spite of the buccinator flap reconstruction. The investigators also highlight the absence of differences in financial difficulties, presumably due to the fact that these patients experienced short hospital stays without significant impairment of their functionality. Furthermore, it is surprising that no differences were observed in sociability problems, both in social contact and social eating, nor in speech problems.

The gender of the patients is not an important parameter: the only anecdotal evidence obtained was that men presented greater pain than women. As for age, the differences obtained for insomnia seem to be more related to age itself than to the surgical procedure, since older people are more likely to have problems harmonizing their sleep.

The absence of differences in smoking and alcohol consumption is surprising to researchers, since both are the main oncologic risk factors for head and neck cancer. It is true that researchers find as an explanation the fact that most patients have tumors diagnosed in early stages, and this may influence the absence of significant differences. Something similar can be found with the follow-up period, and the size and the extension of the resection. Because they are tumors diagnosed in the early stages or they have benign pathologies, their resection is not usually extensive, and the average defect-area created is small (9.2 ± 4.9 cm^2).

No differences in diagnosis were found, either. The investigators highlight the results in relation to the relapse group, which shows better functionality, better overall health and fewer symptoms than the other two groups. Presumably this is due to a sample-size bias (the relapse group consists of two patients), and therefore the results are not representative in this item.

In terms of AJCC stages, significant differences were found in swallowing. The results highlight worse symptoms from Stage III onwards, a stage which, according to clinical guidelines, implies the performance of adjuvant radiotherapy.

In terms of location, the maxilla and palate region showed better functional results than other locations. In the rest of the scales, although no significant differences were found, the maxilla and palate group obtained better results in global health and symptoms. The researchers explain these data by the fact that 71% of diagnoses in these regions were benign pathologies or non-oncological sequelae. In addition, it has been found that tumors located in the tongue and mandibular gingiva are more likely to develop swallowing and dry-mouth problems. This is due to the effect of radiotherapy and the possibility of these locations reaching stages that require adjuvant treatment, since 66.7% have undergone postoperative radiotherapy. It is surprising that the maxillary gingiva is not similar to the mandibular gingiva, although this could be explained by the low incidence of malignant neoplasms in the study sample.

As for the radiotherapy group, it is the only group in which overall health was significantly compromised. Surprisingly, no differences were found in the oral-opening and thick-saliva scales, due to a lack of statistical strength of the sample size. The highest symptom scores were fatigue, pain, dry mouth, oral-opening difficulties, dental problems, and swallowing. These side effects have been shown to be mainly due to radiotherapy and the consequences of irradiation on salivary glands, scar tissues, temporomandibular joint, teeth, and masticatory muscles. This leads us to conclude that buccinator-flap reconstruction surgery may result in greater morbidity and worse quality of life if adjuvant radiotherapy is subsequently considered.

Finally, no differences were found in patients rehabilitated with dental implants. The reason suggested by the researchers is that, despite the use of a flap that often requires tooth extraction and the immediate placement of dental implants, patients are rehabilitated with implant-supported prostheses in a short period of time, and most patients attach more importance to their oncological process than to the provisional absence of teeth.

5. Conclusions

Patients reconstructed with the buccinator myomucosal flap develop a good quality of life for all types of activities, and adequate functionality and aesthetics. The buccinator flap is an accurate and reliable reconstructive alternative for the reconstruction of medium-sized intraoral defects. It is a predictable flap that allows a like-for-like reconstruction of the oral cavity, with minimal morbidity. It is accepted that postoperative radiotherapy in itself is associated with a poorer quality of life, and that this type of surgery can lead to the impairment of several symptoms such as swallowing, oral opening and dry mouth. With this study the researchers conclude, using validated EORTC questionnaires, that patients reconstructed with the buccinator myomucosal flap obtain a good quality of life for all types of activities, and adequate functionality and aesthetics.

Author Contributions: Conceptualization, M.A.M. and C.N.C.; methodology, M.A.M. and C.N.C.; software, J.J.Z.-L.; validation, I.N.C. and J.J.Z.-L.; formal analysis, J.J.Z.-L.; investigation, R.A.-C., Á.S.U. and D.G.A.; resources, A.M.L.L. and M.T.R.; data curation, J.J.Z.-L.; writing—original draft preparation, M.A.M.; writing—review and editing, C.N.C.; visualization, I.N.C. and A.M.L.L.; supervision, C.N.C.; project administration, C.N.C. All authors have read and agreed to the published version of the manuscript.

Funding: This research received no external funding.

Institutional Review Board Statement: The study was conducted in accordance with the Declaration of Helsinki, and approved by the Hospital Ethics Committee at Gregorio Marañón General, Hospital, Madrid, Spain (protocol code maxilohgugm 02/2021).

Informed Consent Statement: Informed consent was obtained from all subjects involved in the study.

Data Availability Statement: The data presented in this study are available on request from the corresponding author. The data are not publicly available, due to data-protection regulations.

Conflicts of Interest: The authors declare no conflict of interest.

References

1. Khajehahmadi, S.; Rahpeyma, A. Buccinator-based myomucosal flaps in intraoral reconstruction: A review and new classification. *Natl. J. Maxillofac. Surg.* **2013**, *4*, 25–32. [CrossRef] [PubMed]
2. Navarro, C.; Rial, M.T.; Agea, M. Functional Outcomes with Facial Artery Musculo-Mucosal (FAMM) Flap and Dental Implants for Reconstruction of Floor of the Mouth and Tongue Defects in Oncologic Patients. *J. Clin. Med.* **2021**, *10*, 3625. [CrossRef] [PubMed]
3. Szeto, C.; Yoo, J.; Busato, G.; Franklin, J.; Fung, K.; Nichols, A. The buccinator flap: A review of current clinical applications. *Curr. Opin. Otolaryngol. Head Neck Surg.* **2011**, *19*, 257–262. [CrossRef] [PubMed]
4. Ayad, T.; Xie, L. Facial artery musculomucosal flap in head and neck reconstruction: A systematic review. *Head Neck* **2015**, *37*, 1375–1386. [CrossRef] [PubMed]
5. Khandelwal, A.; Neeli, A.; Gadiyar, A.; Khandelwal, A. Assessment of quality of life of patients 1–5 years after treatment for oral cancer. *Indian J. Dent. Res.* **2017**, *28*, 538–544. [CrossRef] [PubMed]
6. Cengiz, M.; Ozyar, E.; Esassolak, M.; Altun, M.; Akmansu, M.; Sen, M.; Uzel, O.; Yavuz, A.; Dalmaz, A.; Uzal, C.; et al. Head and neck assessment of quality of life of nasopharyngeal carcinoma patients with eortc qlq-c30 and h & n-35 modules. *Int. J. Radiaton Oncol. Biol. Phys.* **2005**, *63*, 1347–1353.
7. Aaronson, N.K.; Ahmedzai, S.; Bergman, B.; Bullinger, M.; Cull, A.; Duez, N.J.; Filiberti, A.; Flectner; Fleishman, S.B.; de Haes, J.C.J.M.; et al. The European Organisation for Research and Treatment of Cancer QLQ-C30: A quality-of-life instrument for use in interntional clinical trials in oncology. *J. Natl. Cancer Inst.* **1993**, *85*, 365–376. [CrossRef] [PubMed]
8. Bjordal, K.; Hammerlid, E.; Ahlner-Elmqvist, M.; De Graeff, A.; Boysen, M.; Evensen, J.F.; Kaasa, S. Quality of life in head and neck cancer patients: Validation of the European organization for research and treatment of cancer quality of life questionnaire-H&N35. *J. Clin. Oncol.* **1999**, *17*, 1008–1009. [PubMed]
9. Bjordal, K.; de Graeff, A.; Fayers, P.; Hammerlid, E.; van Pottelsberghe, C.; Curran, D.; Ahlner-Elmqvist, M.; Maher, E.; Meyza, J.; Brédart, A.; et al. A 12 country field study of the EORTC QLQ-C30 (version 3.0) and the head and neck cancer specific module (EORTC QLQ-H&N35) in head and neck patients. *Eur. J. Cancer* **2000**, *36*, 1796–1807. [PubMed]
10. Jowett, N.; Hadlock, T.A.; Sela, E.; Toth, M.; Knecht, R.; Lo, B.B. Facial mimetic, cosmetic, and functional standardized assessment of the facial artery musculomucosal (FAMM) flap. *Auris Nasus Larynx* **2016**, *44*, 220–226. [CrossRef] [PubMed]
11. Rahpeyma, A.; Khajehahmadi, S. Donor site morbidity in buccinator-based myomucosal flaps: A retrospective study. *Asian J. Surg.* **2017**, *40*, 210–214. [CrossRef] [PubMed]
12. Zhao, Z.; Zhang, Z.; Li, Y.; Li, S.; Xiao, S.; Fan, X.; Li, Y.; Liu, P.; He, M.; Deng, C. The buccinator musculomucosal island flap for partial tongue reconstruction. *J. Am. Coll. Surg.* **2003**, *196*, 753–760. [CrossRef] [PubMed]
13. Ferrari, S.; Copelli, C.; Bianchi, B.; Ferri, A.; Sesenna, E. The Bozola flap in oral cavity reconstruction. *Oral Oncol.* **2011**, *48*, 379–382. [CrossRef] [PubMed]
14. Bardazzi, A.; Beltramini, G.A.; Autelitano, L.; Bazzacchi, R.; Rabbiosi, D.; Pedrazzoli, M.; Biglioli, F. Use of Buccinator Myomucosal Flap in Tongue Reconstruction. *J. Craniofacial Surg.* **2017**, *28*, 1084–1087. [CrossRef] [PubMed]
15. Massarelli, O.; Vaira, L.; Gobbi, R.; Biglio, A.; Orabona, G.D.; De Riu, G. Soft palate functional reconstruction with buccinator myomucosal island flaps. *Int. J. Oral Maxillofac. Surg.* **2018**, *47*, 316–323. [CrossRef] [PubMed]
16. Kerlinger, F. *Foundations of Behavioural Research*; Holt, Rinehart and Winston: New York, NY, USA, 1973.
17. Aarstad, H.J.; Østhus, A.A.; Aarstad, H.H.; Lybak, S.; Aarstad, A.K.H. EORTC Quality of Life Questionnaire Head and Neck (H&N)-35 scores from H&N squamous cell carcinoma patients obtained at diagnosis and at 6, 9 and 12 months following diagnosis predict 10-year overall survival. *Eur. Arch. Oto-Rhino-Laryngol.* **2019**, *276*, 3495–3505.
18. Konstantinović, V.S. Quality of life after surgical excision followed by radiotherapy for cancer of the tongue and floor of the mouth: Evaluation of 78 patients. *J. Cranio-Maxillofac. Surg.* **1999**, *27*, 192–197. [CrossRef] [PubMed]
19. Langendijk, J.A.; Doornaert, P.; Leeuw, I.V.-D.; Leemans, C.R.; Aaronson, N.K.; Slotman, B. Impact of Late Treatment-Related Toxicity on Quality of Life Among Patients with Head and Neck Cancer Treated with Radiotherapy. *J. Clin. Oncol.* **2008**, *26*, 3770–3776. [CrossRef] [PubMed]

Journal of
Clinical Medicine

MDPI

Communication

Full Digital Workflow for Mandibular Ameloblastoma Management: Showcase for Technical Description

Vincenzo Abbate [1,*], Giulia Togo [1], Umberto Committeri [1] Fernando Zarone [2], Gilberto Sammartino [2], Alessandra Valletta [2], Andrea Elefante [3], Luigi Califano [1] and Giovanni Dell'Aversana Orabona [1]

1 Maxillofacial Surgery Operative Unit, Department of Neurosciences, Reproductive and Odontostomatological Sciences, Federico II University of Naples, 80131 Naples, Italy
2 Dentistry Unit, Department of Neurosciences, Reproductive and Odontostomatological Sciences, Federico II University of Naples, 80131 Naples, Italy
3 Neuroradiology Unit, Department of Advance Biomedical Sciences, Federico II University of Naples, 80131 Naples, Italy
* Correspondence: vincenzo.abbate@unina.it; Tel.: +39-081-746-2175

Abstract: This is a showcase for technical description of a full digital workflow aimed to reconstruct and prosthetically rehabilitate the mandible after surgical resection. The surgery was performed following a computer-aided design and computer-aided manufacturing (CAD-CAM) guided workflow, using 3D reconstruction of the mandible and the fibula. After 2 years, when the ossification of the flap was reached and verified by a computed tomography (CT) scan, surgery was performed using a two-step implant rehabilitation, with successful outcomes.

Keywords: ameloblastoma; dental prosthetic rehabilitation; fibula flap; CAD-CAM

Citation: Abbate, V.; Togo, G.; Committeri, U.; Zarone, F.; Sammartino, G.; Valletta, A.; Elefante, A.; Califano, L.; Dell'Aversana Orabona, G. Full Digital Workflow for Mandibular Ameloblastoma Management: Showcase for Technical Description. *J. Clin. Med.* **2023**, *12*, 5526. https://doi.org/10.3390/jcm12175526

Academic Editors: Alexandre Bozec and Boban M. Erovic

Received: 28 July 2023
Revised: 18 August 2023
Accepted: 24 August 2023
Published: 25 August 2023

1. Introduction

Maxilla and mandible are critical components of the facial skeleton, with several functional and aesthetic attributes. Total or subtotal resection can lead to severe impairment of the patient's quality of life. The goal of reconstructive surgery is to restore patient symmetry and functionality as close as possible to their premorbid state. This is particularly important because the jaws represent the only toothed portion of the skeleton, with multiple functions such as mastication, breathing, swallowing, speech and lip competency, located in a cosmetically demanding region of the head and neck district.

Ameloblastoma is a rare aggressive odontogenic epithelial tumor: it is a slow-growing but locally invasive benign neoplasm involving the mandible (80%) and maxilla [1]. The most common presentation for ameloblastoma is a painless swelling of the mandible, occasionally associated with tooth displacement.

Surgery is the gold standard treatment for ameloblastomas, but the type of resection depends on tumor size and location. According to Dell'Aversana Orabona et al. [2], gross total tumor resection may be considered the gold standard treatment for a large or recurrent lesion and includes en bloc resection with 1–2 cm bone margins and immediate bone reconstruction to help with speech and swallowing.

Several donor sites of vascularized bone free flaps for head and neck reconstruction have been described in the literature. The fibula free flap is considered one of the main surgical option for mandibular reconstruction after tumor resection [3].

Dental prosthetic rehabilitation of large maxillofacial defects using free tissue transfer and endosseous implants is considered the standard of care and the fibula flap provides favorable bone quality and quantity to receive and integrate dental implants to facilitate prosthetic rehabilitation [4–6]. Usually, the implants are placed after the oncological resection and reconstruction to facilitate a better positioning of the implants on the fibula flap and to facilitate better control of its vitality [7].

Until recently, the results of the surgical restoration relied on surgical skills and it was an operator-dependent procedure with unpredictable results. Today, the application of computer-aided design (CAD) and computer-aided manufacturing (CAM) in the medical field allows surgeons to plan cases virtually and create personalized surgical devices, reducing surgical time and minimizing the chance of failure during the reconstruction. The free fibula flap has some limitations due to the height and contour of the fibula, but the rise in VSP (virtual surgical planning) and the progression in the prototypization techniques of surgical guides and implants helps overcome the challenges of the procedure to maximize functional and aesthetic results.

This is a showcase for the technical description of a full digital workflow aimed to reconstruct and prosthetically rehabilitate the mandible after surgical resection.

2. Materials and Methods

A 41-year-old woman was admitted in our unit for an ameloblastoma of the left mandible. Clinical examination revealed a swelling of the alveolar region from 3.2 to 3.8 with irregular edges and firm consistency. The orthopantomography (OPT) and the head and neck computer tomography (CT) scan with thin slices of 1 mm showed an osteolytic lesion, with multilocular radiolucency extending from 3.2 to the ascending ramus of the left side (Figure 1).

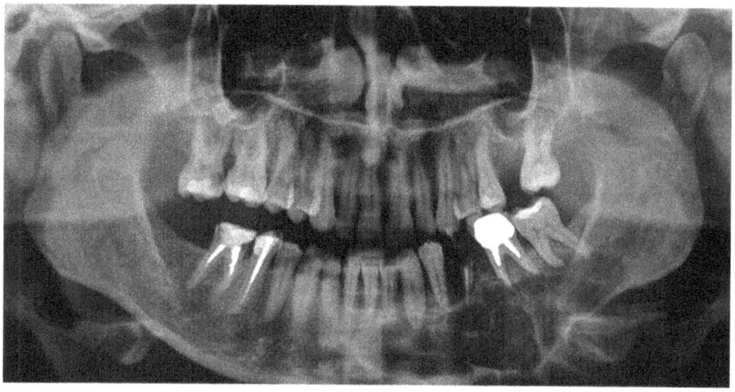

Figure 1. Preoperative Rx-OPT showing a multilocular radiolucency (from 3.2 to 3.8), suggesting an ameloblastoma.

Incisional biopsy of the lesion was performed and showed a solid ameloblastoma. A CT angiography of the lower extremities was performed to evaluate the vessels and bone for the FFF.

The patient underwent a partial mandibulectomy (chin, body and mandibular angle): a full digital workflow for the microsurgical reconstruction with free fibula flap and prosthetic implant rehabilitation is described below.

2.1. *Preoperative Workflow*

2.1.1. Mandibular and Fibula Processing Data from DICOM to STL

CT data acquisition of the mandible and fibula were performed and were processed using Horos software (https://horosproject.org/). On the basis of the digital imaging (DICOM) data acquired from the CT scan, the mandible was reconstructed in 3D using InVesalius software (https://invesalius.github.io/) (Technology of Information Renato Archer Center of the Ministry of Science and Technology, Campinas, Brazil) to produce a standard triangulation language (STL) file of the patient's mandibular and fibular bones (Figure 2).

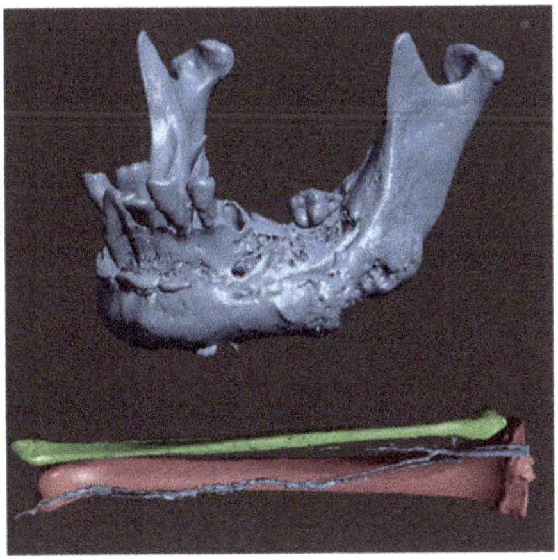

Figure 2. CT data acquisition of the mandible ad fibula.

2.1.2. Meshmixer Processing

The STL file was initially uploaded into the open source software Meshmixer by Autodesk in San Rafael, CA. The lesion was then virtually resected using the "plane-cut" tool. Subsequently, the intact side of the mandible underwent processing with the "mirror" function, generating a virtual guide for the defective side. The goal was to replicate the pre-resection state as closely as possible by superimposing the 3D fibular image onto the mandibular defect, ensuring the best orientation.

To achieve this, various tools such as "extrusion" and "thread" were utilized to model the guides according to the selected design. Measurements, including linear distance and gonial angle from the osteotomized portion of the mandible, were calculated through the "measure" function. These measurements were then applied to the fibular segment to create osteotomy guides for the specific bony portions required for mandibular reconstruction. Furthermore, the virtual design also entailed developing fibula osteotomy guides for any necessary bone divisions. In such cases, osteotomy planes were set and virtually cut for each aspect of the fibula (Figure 3).

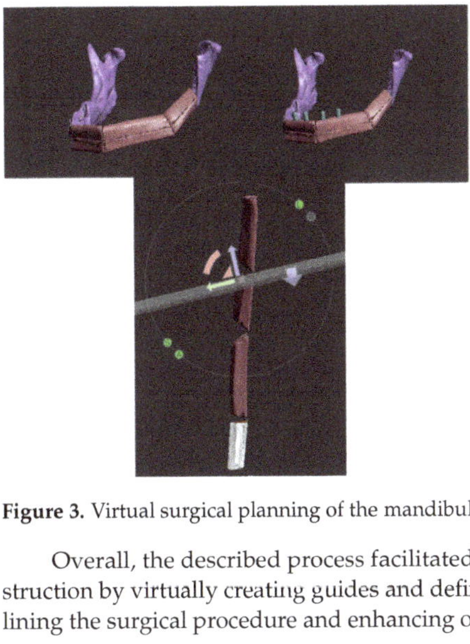

Figure 3. Virtual surgical planning of the mandibular resection and fibula osteotomy guides.

Overall, the described process facilitated the precise planning of mandibular reconstruction by virtually creating guides and defining osteotomy points on the fibula, streamlining the surgical procedure and enhancing overall accuracy.

Through the "Boolean subtraction" tool, mandibular and fibular volumes were subtracted from the guide device to obtain the perfect fitting at the bone–guide interface.

2.1.3. Rapid Prototyping

The digital models were printed in a stereolithography (SLA) 3D printer (Form 2, Formlabs, Somerville, MA, USA) with surgical guide resin (Formlabs) at a 0.1 mm printing resolution. After printing, the models were removed from the build platform and washed for 20 min in a Form Wash (Formlabs) filled with 99% isopropyl alcohol to clean the parts and remove the liquid resin. Then they were post-cured at 60 °C for 30 min in a Form Cure (Formlabs) to achieve biocompatibility and optimal mechanical properties.

Prior to the surgery, the physic models were used to model the titanium reconstruction plates; then, the osteotomy surgical guides and the titanium plates underwent a sterilization using a low temperature hydrogen peroxide plasma technology (STER-RAD; Advanced Sterilization Products, Division of Ethicon US, LLC) (Figure 4).

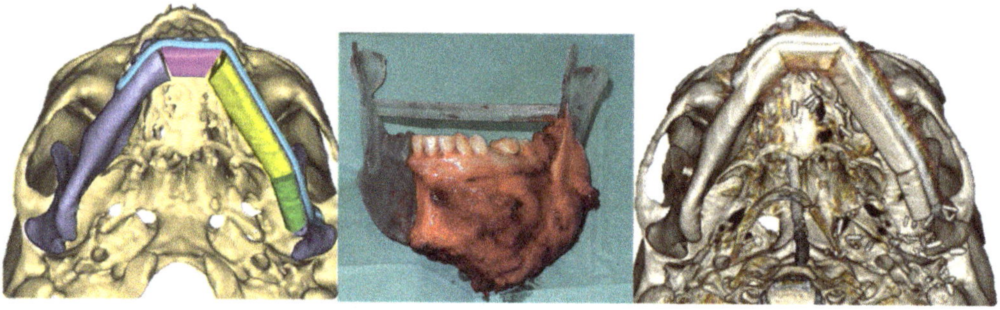

Figure 4. Mandibular resection inserted in the 3D printed model to verify the accuracy of the CAD-CAM guided presurgical planning and postoperative CT scan.

2.2. *Performing Surgery*

The surgery was performed under general anesthesia. A mucosal incision from 3.8 to 4.3 was performed and after the jaw exposure, the surgical osteotomy guides were fixed to the bones with titanium screws (Synthes, West Chester, PA). Mandibular and fibula osteotomies were performed using a surgical saw and a piezoelectric device (Piezosurgery Plus, Mectron s.p.a. 2014). The bony segments were connected using the titanium plates designed and modeled on the digitally planned model. Microvascular anastomoses were performed inside the neck, the peroneal artery was anastomosed end-to-end to the facial artery, while meanwhile one of the peroneal vein was anastomosed end-to-end to a major tributary of the internal jugular vein. A skin paddle was used to cover the mucosal gap.

2.3. *Postoperative Implant Rehabilitation*

At 2 years of follow-up, a CT scan was performed to time the optimal placement of the implant rehabilitation.

Implant rehabilitation was carried out using a guided CAD-CAM technique to avoid interference with the reconstruction plate. The procedure was performed under local anesthesia: an intraoral incision in the buccal vestibule was performed and the alveolar ridge was exposed. Four endosseous implants (Tekka In-Kone) were positioned, as programmed in the virtual plan, through a dental- and crestal-supported surgical guide.

One month later, after a radiographic confirmation of osseointegration, the final implant-retained prosthesis was placed to complete the oral rehabilitation. There was no need for a flap thinning prior to the implant placement. (Figure 5).

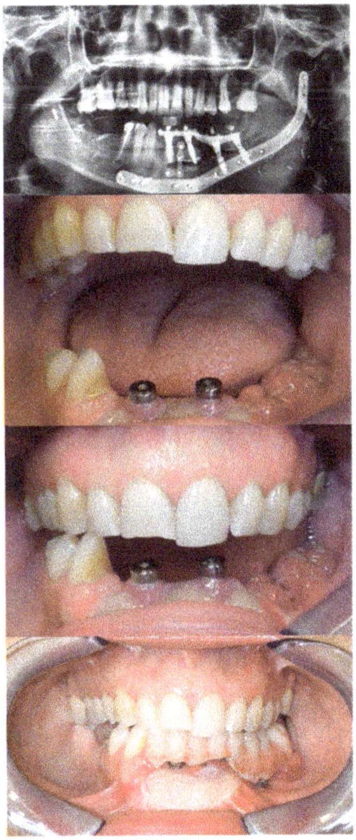

Figure 5. Dental implant rehabilitation after 2 years from surgery.

3. Results

After obtaining the radical resection, the histological diagnosis confirmed the initial ameloblastoma suspect. A significant bone defect of 33 cm in length was identified and subsequently removed, followed by successful reconstruction. The surgery and immediate postsurgical care were uneventful, and no complications such as allergies or infections were observed.

The removal of plates and screws was not performed. The patient did not report any discomfort related to the plates and screws; moreover, the CAD/CAM workflow allowed the implants to be positioned without interfering with the reconstruction plate and its screws.

The mandibular reconstruction procedure achieved a positive outcome, with the digitally planned 3D models demonstrating excellent alignment with the final surgical results. To produce the model and guide, the total cost incurred was about EUR 4.6; meanwhile, the complete service for the start-up process of a CAD/CAM system costs between EUR 4000 and EUR 6000. Overall, the surgical intervention and reconstruction proved successful, providing an effective solution for the ameloblastoma-related bone defect and the expenses associated with manufacturing the 3D models and guides were reasonable.

4. Discussion

The reconstruction of mandibular defects is a complex procedure due to the anatomic and functional features of the bone.

The fibula free flap (FFF) has become the gold standard for surgical reconstruction of mandibular bony defects since Hidalgo first used it in 1989 [8].

The FFF is the most used vascularized bone graft (VBG) used in orofacial reconstructions because it provides adequate bone length, long vascular pedicle and bicortical architecture, increasing primary implant fixation. Implant failure rates in fibula free flaps are higher compared to the native mandibular bone; in any case, a success rate exceeding 91% has been reported [9].

The main difficulty of a FFF in a mandibular reconstruction is represented by the modeling and reshaping of the fibula to achieve proper volume and height for the future dental implant rehabilitation. Another critical step is the intra-surgical correct modeling of the titanium plate, in order to avoid a plate breakage after improper adjustments and reshaping. Since Hirsch et al. [10] first described the computer-assisted surgery (CAS) or computer-aided design and computer-aided manufacturing (CAD/CAM) for mandibular reconstruction in 2009, this technology has gained popularity and has been applied successfully even for the challenging secondary mandibular reconstruction.

The advantages of surgical CAD/CAM reconstructive procedures include ideal presurgical planning for tumor resection and surgical reproducibility for site and orientation osteotomies. The main disadvantages are the cost and the product delivery time.

As showed by this case, CAD/CAM prototypization allowed modeling of the titanium plate prior to surgery, minimizing the stress and the bending fatigue of the plate and reducing the risk of fracture. Moreover, the digital creation of osteotomy guides offered a good bone-to-bone contact between the distal fibula segment and the residual mandible, maximizing the post-reconstruction facial symmetry. The digital surgical planning offers a noticeable reduction in operation time, reducing both the blood loss and the risks of ischemia of the fibula flap [11].

In order to reduce the ischemic time of the fibular flap, the donor pedicle should not be dissected from the lower leg until the harvested fibula has already been shaped and the recipient vessel prepared [12].

Dental implants are one of the important factors involved in the multidisciplinary rehabilitation of patients who have undergone a surgical resection of the maxillofacial district. Improving the optimal aesthetic and functional outcomes for patients with mandible ameloblastoma can be achieved using dental implants. A successful dental restoration can be more challenging on these particular types of patients because of the surgical resection of bone and the damage of the soft tissue, mostly the oral mucosa.

A functional and stable prosthetic rehabilitation after tumor resection can only be achieved using osseointegrated implants; due to the retention of bone height, they provide a reliable long-term stability, whereas removable partial dentures retained by clasps to the remaining teeth are associated with gradual bone loss.

A possible drawback of the fibular flap is a relative lack of bone height, but this limitation can be overcome by double-barreling the fibular flap for the mandibular reconstruction.

The CAD/CAM workflow allows for a highly accurate implant placement, allowing the insertion of implants to ensure maximum resistance to masticatory forces based on the thickness of FFF and minimizing the angular deviation between the central axes of the planned and final position of the implant.

As reported by Ch'ng et al., it is difficult to define an appropriate protocol for the placement of implants in patients with head and neck cancer [9] and most of the previous studies reported a very low rate of dental implant placement in mandibular reconstruction [13]. Moreover, not every patient is eligible for FFF: donor site availability, morbidity, ease of flap dissection and the status of the recipient vessels in the neck, as well as the patient's overall medical condition may also influence the final decision. As well, not every patient can be a candidate for oral rehabilitation because of factors such as oral hygiene, prognosis and patient cooperation. In this case, the patient agreed to reposition the implants 2 years after surgery.

Several factors must be considered for the timing of a postsurgical dental implant rehabilitation in a VBG; among these, the donor site morbidity is paramount.

Placing the osseointegrated implants with a 6–24 months delay after the reconstructive surgery allows for optimum control of the fibula flap vitality, reducing the possibility of a flap failure after the implant rehabilitation.

A proper healing time before the implant's placement ensures a good bone regeneration, which should be evaluated by an OPT and should include an appropriate remodeling and adaptation of the intraoral soft tissue surrounding the reconstructed segment [14]. Hence, a delayed approach allows for a far more comprehensive assessment of the disease status, oral function and patient motivation, as well as more precise prosthetic planning [15].

5. Conclusions

The fibula free flap is considered to be one of the main surgical options for mandibular reconstruction after large bone resections, especially in cases of a benign lesion, such as ameloblastomas. The CAD-CAM presurgical planning can provide optimal bone healing, ensuring the vitality of the free flap and allowing for the anatomical and functional rehabilitation of the mandible, using dental implants, and improving the patient's quality of life. Appropriate timing of the placement of dental implants is critical to guarantee the successful outcome in patients who need this type of reconstruction.

Author Contributions: Conceptualization, G.D.O. and G.T.; methodology, F.Z.; software, U.C. and V.A.; validation, G.D.O. and V.A.; formal analysis, U.C.; investigation, G.S.; resources, A.V.; data curation, L.C.; writing—original draft preparation, G.T.; writing—review and editing, V.A.; visualization, A.E.; supervision, G.D.O.; project administration, G.S. All authors have read and agreed to the published version of the manuscript.

Funding: This research received no external funding.

Institutional Review Board Statement: We complied with the principles stated in the Declaration of Helsinki "Ethical Principles for Medical Research Involving "Human Subjects", adopted by the 18th World Medical Assembly, Helsinki, Finland, June 1964, and as amended most recently by the 64th World Medical Assembly, Fontaleza, Brazil, October 2013.

Informed Consent Statement: Informed consent was obtained from all subjects involved in the study. Patients signed informed consent regarding publishing their data and photographs.

Data Availability Statement: Data sharing is not applicable to this article.

Acknowledgments: Thanks to ANEMA ONLUS for the free donation of the piezoelectric device (Piezosurgery Plus, Mectron s.p.a.).

Conflicts of Interest: The authors declare no conflict of interest.

References

1. Ghai, S. Ameloblastoma: An Updated Narrative Review of an Enigmatic Tumor. *Cureus* **2022**, *14*, e27734. [CrossRef] [PubMed]
2. Dell'Aversana Orabona, G.; Abbate, V.; Maglitto, F.; Bonavolontà, P.; Salzano, G.; Romano, A.; Califano, L. Low-cost, self-made CAD/CAM-guiding system for mandibular reconstruction. *Surg. Oncol.* **2018**, *27*, 200–207. [CrossRef] [PubMed]
3. Fang, W.; Liu, Y.P.; Ma, Q.; Liu, B.L.; Zhao, Y. Long-term results of mandibular reconstruction of continuity defects with fibula free flap and implant-borne dental rehabilitation. *Int. J. Oral. Maxillofac. Implant.* **2015**, *30*, 169–178. [CrossRef] [PubMed]
4. Chang, Y.M.; Wallace, C.G.; Hsu, Y.M.; Shen, Y.F.; Tsai, C.Y.; Wei, F.C. Outcome of osseointegrated dental implants in double-barrel and vertically distracted fibula osteoseptocutaneous free flaps for segmental mandibular defect reconstruction. *Plast. Reconstr. Surg.* **2014**, *134*, 1033–1043. [CrossRef] [PubMed]
5. Jackson, R.S.; Price, D.L.; Arce, K.; Moore, E.J. Evaluation of clinical outcomes of osseointegrated dental implantation of fibula free flaps for mandibular reconstruction. *JAMA Facial Plast. Surg.* **2016**, *18*, 201–206. [CrossRef]
6. Urken, M.L.; Roche, A.M.; Kiplagat, K.J.; Dewey, E.H.; Lazarus, C.; Likhterov, I.; Buchbinder, D.; Okay, D.J. Comprehensive approach to functional palatomaxillary reconstruction using regional and free tissue transfer: Report of reconstructive and prosthodontic outcomes of 140 patients. *Head Neck* **2018**, *40*, 1639–1666. [CrossRef] [PubMed]
7. Carini, F.; Francesconi, M.; Saggese, V.; Monai, D.; Porcaro, G. Implant-supported rehabilitation of a patient with mandibular ameloblastoma. *Ann. Stomatol.* **2012**, *3* (Suppl. S2), 21–25.
8. Hidalgo, D.A. Fibula free flap: A new method of mandible reconstruction. *Plast. Reconstr. Surg.* **1989**, *84*, 71–79. [CrossRef]

9. Ch'ng, S.; Skoracki, R.J.; Selber, J.C.; Yu, P.; Martin, J.W.; Hofstede, T.M.; Chambers, M.S.; Liu, J.; Hanasono, M.M. Osseointegrated implant-based dental rehabilitation in headand neck reconstruction patients. *Head Neck* **2016**, *38* (Suppl. S1), E321–E327. [CrossRef]
10. Hirsch, D.L.; Garfein, E.S.; Christensen, A.M.; Weimer, K.A.; Saddeh, P.B.; Levine, J.P. Use of computeraided design and computer-aided manufacturing to produce orthognathically ideal surgical outcomes: A paradigm shift in head and neck reconstruction. *J. Oral. Maxillofac. Surg.* **2009**, *67*, 2115–2122. [CrossRef] [PubMed]
11. Rodríguez-Arias, J.P.; Tapia, B.; Pampín, M.M.; Morán, M.J.; Gonzalez, J.; Barajas, M.; Del Castillo, J.L.; Navarro Cuéllar, C.; Cebrian, J.L. Clinical Outcomes and Cost Analysis of Fibula Free Flaps: A Retrospective Comparison of CAD/CAM versus Conventional Technique. *J. Pers. Med.* **2022**, *12*, 930. [CrossRef] [PubMed]
12. Chang, S.Y.; Huang, J.J.; Tsao, C.K.; Nguyen, A.; Mittakanti, K.; Lin, C.Y.; Cheng, M.H. Does ischemia time afect the outcome of free fibula flaps for head and neck recontruction? A review of 116 cases. *Plast. Reconstr. Surg.* **2010**, *126*, 1988–1995. [CrossRef] [PubMed]
13. Ooi, A.; Feng, J.; Tan, H.K.; Ong, Y.S. Primary treatment of mandibular ameloblastoma with segmental resection and free fibula reconstruction: Achieving satisfactory outcomes with low implant prosthetic rehabilitation uptake. *J. Plast. Reconstr. Aesthet. Surg.* **2014**, *67*, 498–505. [CrossRef] [PubMed]
14. Zoghbi, S.A.; de Lima, L.A.; Saraiva, L.; Romito, G.A. Surgical experience influences 2-stage implant osseointegration. *J. Oral. Maxillofac. Surg.* **2011**, *69*, 2771–2776. [CrossRef] [PubMed]
15. Kildal, M.; Wei, F.C.; Chang, Y.M.; Chen, H.C.; Chang, M.H. Mandibular reconstruction with fibula oosteoseptocutaneous free flap and osseointegrated dental implants. *Clin. Plast. Surg.* **2001**, *28*, 403–410. [CrossRef]

Journal of
Clinical Medicine

MDPI

Systematic Review

Applications of CAD/CAM Technology for Craniofacial Implants Placement and Manufacturing of Auricular Prostheses—Systematic Review

Waqas Tanveer [1,*], Angela Ridwan-Pramana [2], Pedro Molinero-Mourelle [3] and Tymour Forouzanfar [4]

1 Department of Oral and Maxillofacial Surgery, Amsterdam University Medical Center, 1081 HV Amsterdam, The Netherlands
2 Center for Special Care in Dentistry, Department of Maxillofacial Prosthodontics, Stichting Bijzondere Tandheelkunde, 1081 LA Amsterdam, The Netherlands; a.ridwan@amsterdamumc.nl
3 Department of Reconstructive Dentistry and Gerodontology, School of Dental Medicine, University of Bern, CHE 3012 Bern, Switzerland; pedro.molineromourelle@zmk.unibe.ch
4 Department of Oral and Maxillofacial Surgery, Leiden University Medical Center, 2333 ZA Leiden, The Netherlands; t.forouzanfar@lumc.nl
* Correspondence: w.tanveer@amsterdamumc.nl; Tel.: +31-644-200-096

Abstract: This systematic review was aimed at gathering the clinical and technical applications of CAD/CAM technology for craniofacial implant placement and processing of auricular prostheses based on clinical cases. According to the Preferred Reporting Items for Systematic Reviews and Meta-Analysis (PRISMA) guidelines, an electronic data search was performed. Human clinical studies utilizing digital planning, designing, and printing systems for craniofacial implant placement and processing of auricular prostheses for prosthetic rehabilitation of auricular defects were included. Following a data search, a total of 36 clinical human studies were included, which were digitally planned and executed through various virtual software to rehabilitate auricular defects. Preoperative data were collected mainly through computed tomography scans (CT scans) (55 cases); meanwhile, the most common laser scanners were the 3dMDface System (3dMD LLC, Atlanta, Georgia, USA) (6 cases) and the 3 Shape scanner (3 Shape, Copenhagen, Denmark) (6 cases). The most common digital design software are Mimics Software (Mimics Innovation Suite, Materialize, Leuven, Belgium) (18 cases), Freeform software (Freeform, NC, USA) (13 cases), and 3 Shape software (3 Shape, Copenhagen, Denmark) (12 cases). Surgical templates were designed and utilized in 35 cases to place 88 craniofacial implants in auricular defect areas. The most common craniofacial implants were Vistafix craniofacial implants (Entific Medical Systems, Goteborg, Sweden) in 22 cases. A surgical navigation system was used to place 20 craniofacial implants in the mastoid bone. Digital applications of CAD/CAM technology include, but are not limited to, study models, mirrored replicas of intact ears, molds, retentive attachments, customized implants, substructures, and silicone prostheses. The included studies demonstrated a predictable clinical outcome, reduced the patient's visits, and completed the prosthetic rehabilitation in reasonable time and at reasonable cost. However, equipment costs and trained technical staff were highlighted as possible limitations to the use of CAD/CAM systems.

Keywords: auricular prosthesis; digital planning; surgical template; guided implant surgery; craniofacial implants

Citation: Tanveer, W.; Ridwan-Pramana, A.; Molinero-Mourelle, P.; Forouzanfar, T. Applications of CAD/CAM Technology for Craniofacial Implants Placement and Manufacturing of Auricular Prostheses—Systematic Review. *J. Clin. Med.* **2023**, *12*, 5950. https://doi.org/10.3390/jcm12185950

Academic Editors: José Luis Cebrián-Carretero, Mark L. Urken and Carlos Navarro Cuéllar

Received: 3 August 2023
Revised: 26 August 2023
Accepted: 11 September 2023
Published: 13 September 2023

1. Introduction

Morphological deformity of the external ear, referred to as an auricular defect, can arise from surgical intervention following tumor resection, trauma, or congenital malformation [1–4]. There are two approaches to manage these defects: surgical reconstruction of the external ear or fabrication of auricular prostheses. Auricular prostheses are artificial, removable devices that replicate the morphology of the external ear and are customized to address the cosmetic and psychological challenges posed by auricular defects [3,4]. In principle, the surgical reconstruction of the ear is performed through the use of rib cartilage, which is carved intra-operatively to provide the auricular matrix, or by using a synthetic material framework [5]. Surgical reconstruction comprises multiple surgical revisions to obtain an acceptable outcome [6]. However, reconstruction of the ear through surgical procedures is generally difficult and often fails to provide a satisfactory outcome [3].

A failed autogenous reconstruction is one of the major indications for prosthetic rehabilitation, as fibrosis from previous surgeries makes it difficult to reconstruct the external ear surgically [7]. Prosthetic rehabilitation for auricular defects has been carried out for decades for cosmetic reasons; however, the development of the craniofacial implant (CI) was the milestone that provided optimum retention, support, and stability to the auricular prosthesis [8,9]. The bone thickness in the mastoid region varies between 2.5 mm and 5.5 mm; therefore, the length of craniofacial implants is usually selected between 3 mm and 5 mm to retain the auricular prostheses [10,11]. Upon osseointegration, CI can be used in combination with various types of retentive attachments (clip bar attachment, magnet attachment, locator attachment, or combination of these types of attachments, i.e., bar with locator attachments or bar with ERA attachment) to retain the auricular prostheses [11–13].

Successful auricular defect rehabilitation depends on comprehensive preoperative planning. The presence of mastoid air cells and the proximity of facial nerves and cranial structures make it challenging for maxillofacial surgeons [14]. The use of non-contact and non-invasive medical imaging (CT scan, CBCT, and MRI) has provided the solution to plan preoperatively and thereby prevent damage to the adjacent anatomical structures [14,15]. These imaging techniques provide detailed hard and soft tissue details to plan the precise location of implants in relation to the prosthesis [14,15]. Furthermore, laser scanners can record the surface details; however, the sharp groves and skin folds could be missing in these scan images [16]. CT scans can provide a complete image, but at the expense of X-ray radiation. Similarly, MRI can also provide complete images for 3D models; however, the resolution is low as compared to CT scan images.

Digital planning software have further accelerated the planning and designing stages of rehabilitation procedures in the last couple of decades [17,18]. This digital workflow requires the hard and soft tissue details of the affected and non-affected areas, which can be acquired through CT scans, MRIs, and laser scans [15]. The scanned images from radiographic techniques are in DICOM format, which is converted into STL format for modeling software [19]. Digital designing software uses these data to mirror the structures from the normal side to the defect side to construct the retentive attachments, molds, models, and surgical templates for implant placement [20,21]. Following the computer-aided design (CAD) step, physical models, molds, surgical templates, and even prostheses can be printed through the computer-aided manufacturing (CAM) process by using various materials, i.e., resins, acrylics, thermoplastic waxes, plastics, and metals [17,20,21].

Additionally, surgical navigation systems have added a dynamic approach to the digital workflow for rehabilitation procedures by enabling the surgeons to precisely control the position of instruments during the surgical procedures through multi-planner medical imaging views [10,22]. Once the navigation pointer touches the tissues on the surgical site, the virtual pointer recognizes the exact location on radiographic images, providing the surgeon with the ability to navigate through the anatomical structures while keeping the tract on the virtual anatomical map [22].

The cosmetic limitations of surgical auricular reconstruction paved the way for prosthetic rehabilitation by means of auricular prostheses [3,6]. In recent years, advances in digital technology, specifically Computer-Aided Design and Computer-Aided Manufacturing (CAD/CAM), have emerged as promising tools for enhancing preoperative planning, design, and fabrication of auricular prostheses. The application of digital technology for the fabrication of facial prostheses has reduced the patient's visits, the clinical and laboratory time spent on each visit, and the steps of the fabrication of prostheses with a predictable outcome [23]. Patients can visualize the proposed plan before undergoing the surgical or prosthetic phases. Overall, CAD/CAM systems have been used for the preoperative planning, fabrication of surgical templates, models, molds, substructures, customized implants, and surgical navigation for prosthetic rehabilitation of auricular defects. This systematic review aims to comprehensively examine the clinical and technical applications of CAD/CAM technology in the preoperative planning, designing, and manufacturing processes of auricular prostheses for individuals with auricular defects. To our knowledge, while various studies have discussed the individual components of CAD/CAM technology and auricular prostheses, a comprehensive analysis of their integrated application in clinical practice remains scarce. By synthesizing available clinical data, this review seeks to offer insights into the effective utilization of CAD/CAM technology for enhancing prosthetic rehabilitation outcomes.

2. Materials and Methods

A systematic review was performed based on the protocol of Preferred Reporting Items for Systematic Reviews and Meta-Analyses (PRISMA) [24] to determine the PICO (patients (P), investigations (I), comparison (C), and outcomes (O)) question.

Patients: Patient having an auricular defect

Interventions: Applications of CAD/CAM-based systems for planning, designing, and manufacturing of auricular prostheses and craniofacial implant placement.

Comparison: Not applicable.

Outcome: Fabrication of auricular prostheses.

Therefore, the established question was adapted to the PIO question: "In patients with auricular defects (P), what are the technical and clinical applications of CAD/CAM technology for craniofacial implant placement (I) and the manufacturing of auricular prostheses (O)?". This was performed while also considering that comparison (C) was not applicable in this systematic review.

2.1. Search Strategy

The electronic search was executed by using the following combinations of terms: (Prostheses AND Planning AND Guide).

Prosthesis: (auricular prostheses OR ear prostheses OR silicone auricular prosthesis) AND Planning: (software planning OR scanning OR CAD/CAM OR digital OR navigation OR 3D) AND Guide: (implants OR extraoral implants OR craniofacial implants OR surgical template OR surgical guide OR printed guide OR guided surgery OR navigation system).

2.2. Eligibility Criteria

Clinical human studies published in the English language between January 2000 and May 2023 were reviewed. The inclusion criteria were comprised of randomized control trials, case control studies, case reports, cohort studies, and case series utilizing digital software and CAD/CAM technology for orbital implant placement and manufacturing of auricular prostheses. The exclusion criteria included systematic reviews, animal studies, case reports, in vitro studies, and finite element analysis (FEA) studies executed without the use of digital software and CAD/CAM systems (Figure 1).

2.3. Source of Information

An electronic search was conducted for published articles between January 2000 and May 2023 in the National Library of Medicine (MEDLINE/PubMed) database.

Furthermore, a manual search of the published articles between January 2000 and May 2023 was also executed: The Journal of Prosthodontics, The Journal of Oral Rehabilitation, the International Journal of Prosthodontics, The Journal of Prosthetic Dentistry, The Journal of Oral Implantology, The Journal of Prosthodontic Research, The International Journal of Oral and Maxillofacial Implants, Clinical Oral Implants Research, International Journal of Oral and Maxillofacial Surgery, Journal of Stomatology, Journal of Oral and Maxillofacial

Surgery, British Journal of Oral and Maxillofacial Surgery, Journal of Cranio-maxillo-facial surgery, Oral and Maxillofacial Surgery, Implant Dentistry, and Related Research.

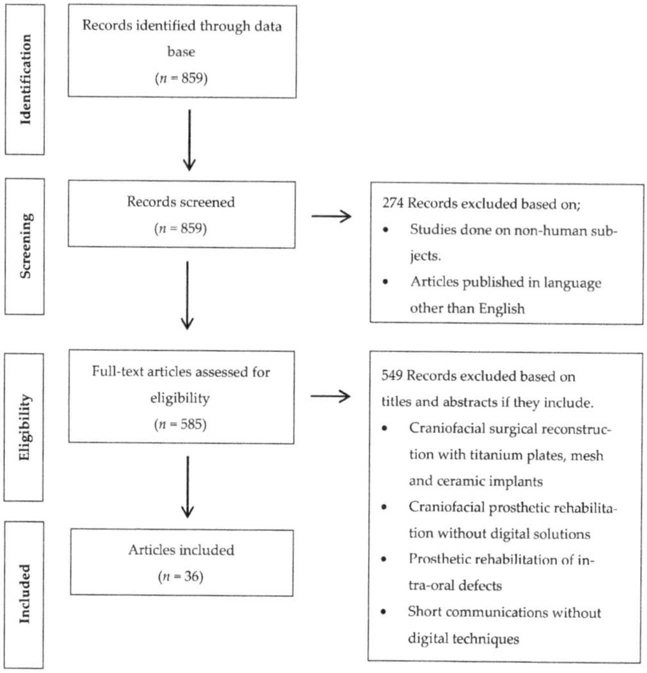

Figure 1. Flow chart of the study's selection process and screening methodology.

2.4. *Study Selection*

The studies were reviewed by two independent reviewers (W.T. and P.M.M.) and selected on the basis of their titles and abstracts from the electronic search. Those studies that fulfilled the inclusion criteria or contained limited data in the abstract to reach the final decision were collected and reviewed. Disagreements among the authors were rectified after discussion.

2.5. *Data Extraction*

The useful data from the included studies were transferred to the standard designed form: authors, publication year, purpose of the digital planning, preoperative data, software used, printers utilized, materials for printing, number of implants placed, and implant systems in each case (Table 1). Authors were contacted for possible missing data.

2.6. *Risk of Bias in Individual Studies*

Two independent reviewers (W.T. and P.M.M.) evaluated the quality of the included studies. In case of a conflict of agreement regarding any publication, a third reviewer (A.R.P.) was contacted. For evaluation, the critical tools of the Joanna Briggs Institute [25] (JBI) for case series and case reports were utilized based on the type of included articles. The bias was evaluated on the basis of the list of 10 questions for case series and 8 questions for case reports, respectively. The questions listed in Tables 2a–c and 3a,b concern the risk of bias. Eventually, an assessment was performed through an overall appraisal to determine if the risk of bias was low (inclusion of the study), high (exclusion of the study), or uncertain (more information was needed). We refer to it as a low risk of bias if the answer "yes" was $\geq$50%, an uncertain risk of bias if the answer "unclear" was $\geq$50%, and a high risk of bias if the answer "no" was $\geq$50%.

Table 1. Digital planning for the prosthetic rehabilitation of auricular defects.

Publications	No. of Cases	Purpose of Software Planning	Pre-Op Data for Digital Planning	Software	Printer/Miller	Printing Materials	Navigation System (Yes/No)	Location & No. of Implants	Implants System
Ciocca L., Scotti R. 2004 [26]	1	Fabrication of ear model	Minolta VIVID 900 3D laser scanner (Konica Minolta, Osaka, Japan)	Polygone editing tool (Minolta Co, Osaka, Japan), Rapidform CAD software (INUS Technology, Seoul, South Korea)	Z Printer 310 (Z Corp, Cambridge, MA, USA)	Powder and sealant from Z Corp. (Z Corp., Cambridge, MA, USA)	No	No	No
Sykes et al., 2004 [27]	1	Fabrication of ear model	Breuckmann OptoTOP scanner system (Breuckmann OptoTOP, Germany)	Polyworks software (InnovMetric Software), Freeform software (Freeform, NC, USA)	Thermojet printer	Wax material	No	No	No
Jiao et al., 2004 [28]	1	Fabrication of ear model	CT scan	Magics RP image ware (Materialise, Leuven, Belgium), Freeform software (Freeform, NC, USA)	Zippy-I RP machine (Kinergy Mechatronics, Singapore)	NM	No	No	No
Ciocca L et al., 2007 [29]	1	Fabrication of mold for auricular prosthesis and acrylic substructure	Minolta VIVID 900 3D laser scanner (Konica Minolta, Osaka, Japan)	Rapidform CAD software (INUS Technology, Seoul, South Korea), Software, Polygone editing tool (Minolta Co., Osaka, Japan)	Z Printer 310 (Z Corp, Cambridge, MA, USA)	Powder and sealant from Z Corp. (Z Corp., Cambridge, MA, USA)	No	No	No

Table 1. *Cont.*

Publications	No. of Cases	Purpose of Software Planning	Pre-Op Data for Digital Planning	Software	Printer/Miller	Printing Materials	Navigation System (Yes/No)	Location & No. of Implants	Implants System
Kurtulmus et al., 2009 [17]	1	Virtual implant planning	CT Scan	Implant 3D, Media Lab Software, 3D-Doctor software (Able Coorporation, Lexington, MA, USA)	NM	NM	No	No	No
Ciocca L et al., 2009 [30]	1	Surgical template for implant placement	CT, NextEngine Desktop 3D Scanner (NextEngine, Santa Monica, CA, USA)	Rapidform CAD software (INUS Technology, Seoul, South Korea)	Rapid prototyping machine (Z310Plus; Z Corp., Burlington, MA, USA)	NM	No	Right mastoid bone; 3 implants	NM
Turgut et al., 2009 [31]	10	Fabrication of ear model	CT scan	Modeling software (FreeForm Modeling Plus System, SensAble, Boston, MA)	Selective laser sintering (SLS) system (DTM Corp., Austin, TX, USA)	NM	No	No	No
Ciocca. L et al., 2010 [32]	1	Fabrication of mold for auricular prosthesis	NextEngine Desktop 3D Scanner (NextEngine, Santa Monica, CA, USA)	NextEngine Scan studio software (NextEngine, CA, USA)	3D printer (Stratasys, Eden Prairie, MN, USA)	ABS P400 jet (Stratasys, Eden Prairie, MN, USA)	No	No	No

Table 1. *Cont.*

Publications	No. of Cases	Purpose of Software Planning	Pre-Op Data for Digital Planning	Software	Printer/Miller	Printing Materials	Navigation System (Yes/No)	Location & No. of Implants	Implants System
Verma et al., 2010 [22]	2	Virtual planning and intraoperative navigation for implant placement	CT scan	Navigation system, Stryker iNtellect Cranial (Stryker Navigation system, MI, USA)	NM	NM	Yes	Left and Right mastoid regions; 4 implants	Vistafix implants (Cochlear, Lone Tree, USA)
De Crescenzio F et al., 2011 [33]	1	Fabrication of mold for auricular prosthesis	NextEngine Desktop 3D Scanner (NextEngine, Santa Monica, CA, USA)	Rapidform CAD software (INUS Technology, Seoul, South Korea), Rhinoceros Software v. 4.0 (Robert McNeel & Associates, USA)	3D printer (Stratasys, Eden Prairie, MN, USA)	ABS P400 jet (Stratasys, Eden Prairie, MN, USA)	No	Right mastoid bone; 2 implants	Straumann implants (Institut Straumann AG, Basel, Switzerland)
Liacouras et al., 2011 [34]	1	Designing and creation of digital model and mold fabrication	CT scan, 3D photography/imaging (3dMD cranial System; 3dMD, Atlanta, GA, USA)	Mimics Software (Mimics Innovation Suite, Materialise, Leuven, Belgium), Freeform software (Freeform, NC, USA) (14 cases), Geomagics Studio software (3D Systems, Rock Hill, SC, USA)	ZPrinter 450, using zp130 Powder and zb59 Binder; (Z Corp., Cambridge, MA, USA)	NM	No	No	No

Table 1. *Cont.*

Publications	No. of Cases	Purpose of Software Planning	Pre-Op Data for Digital Planning	Software	Printer/Miller	Printing Materials	Navigation System (Yes/No)	Location & No. of Implants	Implants System
Kolodney et al., 2011 [35]	1	Surgical template for implant placement	CT scan	Mimics Software (Mimics Innovation Suite, Materialise, Leuven, Belgium), SurgiCase software (Materialise LLC, Ann Arbor, MI, USA)	NM	Somos DMX 100 Resin material (Somos DSM, Desotech Inc., Elgin, Illinois, USA)	No	Right mastoid bone; 3 implants	NM
Karatas MO et al., 2011 [36]	2	Fabrication of ear models	CT scans	Mimics Software (Mimics Innovation Suite, Materialise, Leuven, Belgium)	3D ink-jet FDM printer (Z Corp, Cambridge, MA, USA), Perfactory Standard SXGA+ stereolithography printer (Envisiontec Inc., Germany)	Acrylic material	No	No	No
Bai et al., 2012 [37]	1	Surgical template for implant placement	CT scan	Geomagics Studio software (3D Systems, Rock Hill, SC, USA), Mimics Software (Mimics Innovation Suite, Materialise, Leuven, Belgium)	Rapid Prototyping machine AFS-360 printer (Long yuan Technology Ltd., Beijing, China)	Resin material (Details NM)	No	Left mastoid region, 3 implants	NM
Reitemeier et al., 2012 [38]	1	Surgical template for implant placement	CT scan	Software (VoXim v6.1; IVS Solutions AG, Chemnitz, Germany)	FDM Vantage S; (Stratasys, Eden Prairie, MN, USA)	Acrylic resin template	No	Right mastoid region, 2 implants	Straumann implants (Straumann GmbH, Freiburg, Germany)

Table 1. *Cont.*

Publications	No. of Cases	Purpose of Software Planning	Pre-Op Data for Digital Planning	Software	Printer/Miller	Printing Materials	Navigation System (Yes/No)	Location & No. of Implants	Implants System
Hatamleh and Watson. 2013 [39]	1	Fabrication of ear model	3Shape R700 scanner (3 Shape, Copenhagen, Denmark)	3 Shape software (3 Shape, Copenhagen, Denmark)	Z-Corp Printer (Z Corp, Cambridge, MA, USA)	NM	No	2 craniofacial implants	Vistafix craniofacial implants (Cochlear, Surrey, UK)
Bai et al., 2014 [40]	6	Fabrication of mold for auricular prosthesis	CT scan, structured-light 3D scanner (3DSS-STD-II, Digital Manu, Shanghai, China)	Mimics Software (Mimics Innovation Suite, Materialise, Leuven, Belgium)	Rapid Prototyping machine AFS-360 printer (Long yuan Technology Ltd., Beijing, China)	Resin material	No	No	No
Tam CK et al., 2014 [8]	6	Fabrication of ear model	CT scan, 3dMDFace (3dMD, Atlanta, USA)	Mimics Software (Mimics Innovation Suite, Materialise, Leuven, Belgium), Surgical navigation system (BrainLAB, Feldkirchen, Germany)	Fused Deposition Modeling (FDM)	NM	Surgical navigation system (BrainLAB, Feldkirchen, Germany)	12 implants were placed in mastoid bone	Dental implants (Friadent, Dentsply, Mannheim, Germany)
Watson and Hatamleh 2014 [41]	3	Fabrication of ear model	3Shape R700 scanner (3 Shape, Copenhagen, Denmark)	Software Z-Build (Z Corp, Cambridge, MA, USA)	3D printer (Z Corp., Cambridge, MA, USA).	Gypsum (150 Powder) (Z Corp, Cambridge, MA, USA)	No	No	No
Wang et al., 2015 [42]	1	Fabrication of model for implant placement planning	EBCT scan	Geomagics Studio software (3D Systems, Rock Hill, SC, USA)	SLS machine (AFS-360; (Long yuan Technology Ltd., Beijing, China)	Resin material	No	3 implants in right mastoid bone	Implants (MDIC; FMMU, China)

Table 1. *Cont.*

Publications	No. of Cases	Purpose of Software Planning	Pre-Op Data for Digital Planning	Software	Printer/Miller	Printing Materials	Navigation System (Yes/No)	Location & No. of Implants	Implants System
Nuseir et al., 2015 [43]	1	Surgical template for implant placement	CT scan	Mimics Software (Mimics Innovation Suite, Materialise, Leuven, Belgium)	3D printer (Z Corp, Cambridge, MA, USA)	NM	No	Left mastoid region, 2 implants	Vistafix craniofacial implants (Cochlear, Surrey, UK
Choi et al., 2016 [44]	2	Planning for craniofacial implant placement	CT scan	BrainLAB software (BrainLAB AG, Munich, Germany)	No	No	Image guidance systems (IGS) (Brainlab AG, Munich, Germany).	4 implants in mastoid bone	Vistafix craniofacial implants (Cochlear, Surrey, UK)
Weissler et al., 2017 [45]	1	Virtual planning and intraoperative navigation for implant placement	CT scan, Laser scan	iPlan Cranial 3.0 BrainLAB software (BrainLAB AG, Munich, Germany)	NM	NM	Yes	Left & Right mastoid region; 4 implants	Vistafix craniofacial implants (Cochlear, Surrey, UK)
Yadav et al., 2017 [46]	1	Fabrication of mold for auricular prosthesis	CT scan	3D modeling software	NM	NM	No	No	No
Nafij Bin Jamayet et al., 2018 [47]	1	Fabrication of ear model	NextEngine Desktop 3D Scanner (NextEngine, Santa Monica, CA, USA)	NextEngine Scan studio software (NextEngine, CA, USA), Rapidworks 64 version 4.1.0. (3D system, Inc., Rock Hill, USA)	Objet30 Scholar 3D Printer (Stratasys, Eden Prairie, MN, USA)	NM	No	No	No

Table 1. *Cont.*

Publications	No. of Cases	Purpose of Software Planning	Pre-Op Data for Digital Planning	Software	Printer/Miller	Printing Materials	Navigation System (Yes/No)	Location & No. of Implants	Implants System
Unkovskiy et al., 2018 [48]	1	Fabrication of mold for auricular prosthesis	Artec Color 3D scanner (Artec 3D, Luxembourg)	Artec Studio Software (Artec 3D, Luxembourg), Z brush software (Pixologic, Inc., Los Angeles, CA, USA)	ProJet 3510 CPXPlus (3D Systems, Rock Hill, SC, USA), SPro 60 HD (3D Systems, Rock Hill, SC, USA)	VisiJet M3 Hi-Cast printer (3D Systems, Rock Hill, SC, USA)	No	No	No
Sanghavi, et al., 2018 [49]	1	Fabrication of ear model	CT scan	Freeform software (Freeform, NC, USA)	3D printing technology (Stereolithography)	Acrylic photopolymeric material	No	No	No
Ferreira R, Vives P. 2019 [50]	2	Fabrication of custom titanium plate for locator attachments	CT scan	Materialise 3-matic software 9.0 (Materalise, Leuven, Belgium)	Selective laser melting	Titanium grade 2	No	No	No
Vijverberg MA et al., 2019 [51]	11	Surgical template for implant placement	CT scan	3 Shape software (3 Shape, Copenhagen, Denmark)	NM	Polyamide material (Oceanz BV, Ede, The Netherlands)	No	31 VXI300 implants in mastoid bone	Vistafix implants (Cochlear Bone Anchored Solutions AB, Mölnly-cke. Sweden)
Cevik and Kocacikli. 2020 [52]	1	Fabrication of mold for auricular prosthesis	Artec Color 3D scanner (Artec 3D, Luxembourg)	Artec studio 16 software (Artec 3D, Luxembourg)	FDM technology printer; MakerBot Replicator 2 (MakerBot Industries, Brooklyn, NY, USA)	Polylactic acid material (PLA)	No	No	No

Table 1. *Cont.*

Publications	No. of Cases	Purpose of Software Planning	Pre-Op Data for Digital Planning	Software	Printer/Miller	Printing Materials	Navigation System (Yes/No)	Location & No. of Implants	Implants System
McHutchion and Aalto. 2021 [53]	5	Fabrication of scan bodies and molds for auricular prosthesis	3dMD flex System (3dMD LLC, Atlanta, Georgia, USA), 3Shape R700 scanner (3 Shape, Copenhagen, Denmark)	Geomagics Studio software (3D Systems, Rock Hill, SC, USA)	Stereolithography 3D printer Form2 (Formlabs Inc., Somerville, Massachusetts, USA)	Clear resin, white resin (Formlabs Inc., Somerville, Massachusetts, USA)	No	No	No
Domingue D. et al., 2021 [54]	1	Surgical template for implant placement	CBCT scan	Meshmixer (Autodesk Inc., USA), Blue Sky Plan software (Blue Sky Bio, LLC, USA)	CEL Robox 3D printer (CEL, Bristol, UK)	nGen colorFabb polymer material (Eastman Chemical Company, Belfeld, Netherlands)	No	4 implants in right mastoid bone	Vistafix craniofacial implants (Cochlear, Surrey, UK)
Unkovskiy et al., 2021 [55]	1	Fabrication of ear model and substructure and printing of silicone auricular prosthesis	Pritiface 3D photogrammetry system (pritiface; pritidenta GmbH, Germany), 3Shape R700 scanner (3 Shape, Copenhagen, Denmark)	Exocad software (Exocad, GmbH, Darmstadt, Germany), Z brush software (Pixologic, Inc., USA)	Stereolithography (SLA) (Form 2; Formlabs) (Formlabs Inc., Somerville, Massachusetts, USA)	Resin material (Flexible; Formlabs) (Formlabs Inc., Somerville, Massachusetts, USA), ACEO silicone material (Drop-on-Demand ACEO; Wacker Chemie AG, Munich, Germany)	No	No	No

Table 1. *Cont.*

Publications	No. of Cases	Purpose of Software Planning	Pre-Op Data for Digital Planning	Software	Printer/Miller	Printing Materials	Navigation System (Yes/No)	Location & No. of Implants	Implants System
Dashti et al., 2022 [56]	1	Fabrication of working cast and bar	Artec Color 3D scanner (Artec 3D, Luxembourg), 3Shape R700 scanner (3 Shape, Copenhagen, Denmark)	Z brush software (Pixologic, Inc., USA), Exocad software (Exocad, GmbH, Darmstadt, Germany)	Stereolithography printer	PowerDent resin material (ProTech Transfer Co., Ltd., Bangkok, Thailand)	No	No	No
Hatamleh MM et al., 2022 [57]	3	Surgical template for implant placement	CT scan	CMF Pro Plan; Materialise	Form 2; Formlabs GmbH	NM	No	Patient 1: Right mastoid bone. 2 implants of 4 mm Patient 2: 2 implants on each side	Branemark; Cochlear Europe Ltd.
Heydenrych A et al., 2023 [58]	1	Surgical template for implant placement	CT scan	Materialise 3-matic software 9.0 (Materalise, Leuven, Belgium)	Selective laser sintering printer	Nylon PA 2200	No	Right mastoid bone. 3 implants	No

Abbreviations: CT: computed tomography; CBCT: cone-beam computed tomography; EBCT: electron beam computed tomography; Pre-op: preoperative; and NM: not mentioned.

Table 2. (a) Risk of bias for the case reports. (b) Risk of bias for the case reports. (c) Risk of bias for the case reports.

(a)

Assessment	Author and Year							
	Ciocca L, Scotti R. 2004 [26]	**Sykes et al., 2004** [27]	**Jiao et al., 2004** [28]	**Ciocca L et al., 2007** [29]	**Kurtulmus et al., 2009** [17]	**Ciocca L et al., 2009** [30]	**Ciocca. L et al., 2010** [32]	**De Crescenzio F et al., 2011** [33]
Were patient's demographic characteristics clearly described?	No	No	Yes	No	Yes	No	Yes	No
Was the patient's history clearly described and presented as a timeline?	No	No	Yes	No	Yes	No	Yes	No
Was the current clinical condition of the patient on presentation clearly described?	No	Yes	Yes	No	Yes	Yes	Yes	Yes
Were diagnostic tests or assessment methods and the results clearly described?	Unclear	Unclear	Unclear	Unclear	Unclear	Unclear	Unclear	Unclear
Was the intervention(s) or treatment procedure(s) clearly described?	Yes	Yes	Yes	Yes	Yes	Yes	Yes	Yes
Was the post-intervention clinical condition clearly described?	Yes	Yes	Yes	Yes	Yes	Yes	Yes	Yes
Were adverse events (harms) or unanticipated events identified and described?	Yes	No	No	Yes	No	No	No	No
Does the case report provide takeaway lessons?	Yes	Yes	Yes	Yes	Yes	Yes	Yes	Yes
Overall appraisal	Included	Included	Included	Included	Included	Included	Included	Included

Table 2. *Cont.*

(b)								
	Author and Year							
Assessment	**Liacouras et al., 2011** [34]	**Kolodney et al., 2011** [35]	**Bai et al., 2012** [37]	**Reitemeier et al., 2012** [38]	**Hatamleh and Watson. 2013** [39]	**Wang et al., 2015** [42]	**Nuseir et al., 2015** [43]	**Weissler et al., 2017** [45]
Were patient's demographic characteristics clearly described?	Yes	Yes	No	Yes	Yes	Yes	Yes	Yes
Was the patient's history clearly described and presented as a timeline?	Yes	Yes	No	Yes	Yes	Yes	Yes	Yes
Was the current clinical condition of the patient on presentation clearly described?	Yes	Yes	No	Yes	Yes	Yes	Yes	Yes
Were diagnostic tests or assessment methods and the results clearly described?	Unclear	Unclear	Unclear	Unclear	Unclear	Unclear	Unclear	Unclear
Was the intervention(s) or treatment procedure(s) clearly described?	Yes	Yes	Yes	Yes	Yes	Yes	Yes	Yes
Was the post-intervention clinical condition clearly described?	Yes	Yes	Yes	Yes	Yes	Yes	Yes	Yes
Were adverse events (harms) or unanticipated events identified and described?	No	No	Yes	No	No	No	No	No
Does the case report provide takeaway lessons?	Yes	Yes	Yes	Yes	Yes	No	Yes	Yes
Overall appraisal	Included	Included	Included	Included	Included	Included	Included	Included

Table 2. *Cont.*

(c)

Assessment	Author and Year								
	Yadav et al., 2017 [46]	**Nafij Bin Jamayet et al., 2018** [47]	**Unkovskiy et al., 2018** [48]	**Sanghavi, et al., 2018** [49]	**Cevik and Kocacikli. 2020** [52]	**Domingue D. et al., 2021** [54]	**Unkovskiy et al., 2021** [55]	**Dashti et al., 2022** [56]	**Heydenrych A et al., 2023** [58]
Were patient's demographic characteristics clearly described?	Yes	No	Yes	Yes	Yes	Yes	No	No	No
Was the patient's history clearly described and presented as a timeline?	Yes	No	Yes	Yes	Yes	Yes	No	No	No
Was the current clinical condition of the patient at presentation clearly described?	Yes	No	Yes	Yes	Yes	Yes	No	Yes	Yes
Were diagnostic tests or assessment methods and the results clearly described?	Unclear	Unclear	Unclear	Unclear	Unclear	Unclear	Unclear	Unclear	Yes
Was the intervention(s) or treatment procedure(s) clearly described?	Yes	Yes	Yes	Yes	Yes	Yes	Yes	Yes	Yes
Was the post-intervention clinical condition clearly described?	Yes	Yes	Yes	Yes	No	Yes	Yes	Yes	Yes
Were adverse events (harms) or unanticipated events identified and described?	No	Yes	No	No	No	No	Yes	Yes	No
Does the case report provide takeaway lessons?	Yes	Yes	Yes	Yes	Yes	Yes	Yes	Yes	Yes
Overall appraisal	Included	Included	Included	Included	Included	Included	Included	Included	Included

Table 3. (a) Risk of bias for the case series. (b) Risk of bias for the case series.

(a)							
Assessment	**Author and Year**						
	Turgut et al., 2009 [31]	**Verma et al., 2010 [22]**	**Karatas MO et al., 2011 [36]**	**Bai et al., 2014 [40]**	**Tam CK et al., 2014 [8]**	**Watson and Hatamleh 2014 [41]**	**Choi et al., 2016 [44]**
Were there clear criteria for inclusion in the case series?	Yes	Yes	Yes	Yes	Yes	Yes	Yes
Was the condition measured in a standard, reliable way for all participants included in the case series?	Yes	Yes	Yes	Yes	Yes	Yes	Yes
Were valid methods used for identification of the condition for all participants included in the case series?	Yes	Yes	Yes	Yes	Yes	Yes	Yes
Did the case series have consecutive inclusion of participants?	Unclear	Unclear	Unclear	Unclear	Unclear	Unclear	Unclear
Did the case series have complete inclusion of participants?	Yes	Yes	Yes	Yes	Yes	Yes	Yes
Was there clear reporting of the demographics of the participants in the study?	Yes	Yes	No	Yes	Yes	Yes	Yes
Was there clear reporting of clinical information of the participants?	No	Yes	Yes	Yes	Yes	No	Yes
Were the outcomes or follow-up results of cases clearly reported?	Yes	Yes	Yes	Yes	Yes	Yes	Yes
Was there clear reporting of the presenting site(s)/clinic(s) demographic information?	No	No	No	Yes	Yes	Yes	Yes
Overall appraisal	Included	Included	Included	Included	Included	Included	Included

Table 3. *Cont.*

(b)				
Assessment	**Author and Year**			
	Ferreira R, Vives P. 2019 [50]	**Vijverberg MA et al., 2019** [51]	**McHutchion and Aalto. 2021** [53]	**Hatamleh MM et al., 2022** [57]
Were there clear criteria for inclusion in the case series?	Yes	Yes	Yes	Yes
Was the condition measured in a standard, reliable way for all participants included in the case series?	Yes	Yes	Yes	Yes
Were valid methods used for identification of the condition for all participants included in the case series?	Yes	Yes	Yes	Yes
Did the case series have consecutive inclusion of participants?	Unclear	Yes	Yes	Yes
Did the case series have complete inclusion of participants?	Yes	Yes	Yes	Yes
Was there clear reporting of the demographics of the participants in the study?	Yes	Yes	Yes	Yes
Was there clear reporting of clinical information of the participants?	Yes	No	Yes	Yes
Were the outcomes or follow up results of cases clearly reported?	Yes	Yes	Yes	Yes
Was there clear reporting of the presenting site(s)/clinic(s) demographic information?	No	Yes	Yes	Yes
Overall appraisal	Included	Included	Included	Included

3. Results

3.1. Study Selection

The term was searched in the PubMed database. The literature search and the selection process have been summarized in Figure 1. Since most of the digital planning and designing developments have been noticed in the past two decades, the search strategy was decided to gather data within the time frame of January 2000 to May 2023, which yielded 806 studies. Two hundred and sixty-six (266) studies were excluded through the language (English) and human-based studies filters. Thereby, 540 studies were thoroughly screened based on their titles and abstracts in accordance with the inclusion and exclusion criteria, which led to the further exclusion of 504 studies on the basis of their study design and rehabilitation techniques (rehabilitation of auricular defects performed through surgical reconstruction and prosthetic rehabilitation performed through conventional procedures without digital planning and designing procedures). A total of 36 studies were included after reading full-text papers, which involved clinical cases digitally planned and processed for prosthetic rehabilitation of auricular defects. (Table 1) Due to the quality and data heterogeneity of the included studies, a meta-analysis could not be executed.

3.2. Study Characteristics

3.2.1. CAD/CAM Technology Applications for Prosthetic and Surgical Purposes

The included studies discussed the following applications of digital technology for prosthetic rehabilitation of auricular defects: surgical templates (27 cases), fabrication of ear models (30 cases), fabrication of molds for silicone packing (17 cases), customized scan bodies (1 case), and custom titanium plates for locator attachments fabricated with grade 2 titanium (1 case). A surgical navigation system was used to place craniofacial implants for prosthetic rehabilitation of auricular defects (2 cases).

3.2.2. Preoperative Record for Digital Planning

Digital planning requires preoperative data for surgical and prosthetic procedures. The following modalities were used to gain virtual data for preoperative planning: non-contact medical images (CT scans, CBCT, and EBCT), laser scans, 3D structured light scans, and 3D photogrammetry systems.

Non-contact medical imaging systems: computed tomography scan (CT scan) (55 cases), cone-beam computed tomography scan (CBCT scan) (1 case), and an electron beam computed tomography scan (EBCT) (1 case).

3D structured light scanning systems: 3dMDface System (3dMD LLC, Atlanta, GA, USA) (6 cases), 3dMD flex System (3dMD LLC, Atlanta, GA, USA) (5 cases) Artec Color 3D scanner (Artec 3D, Luxembourg) (3 cases), 3dMD cranial system (3dMD LLC, Atlanta, GA, USA) (1 case), and a Breuckmann OptoTOP scanner system (Breuckmann OptoTOP, Germany) (1 case).

Laser scanners: 3 Shape scanner (3 Shape, Copenhagen, Denmark) (6 cases), NextEngine Desktop 3D Scanner (NextEngine, Santa Monica, CA, USA) (4 cases), and a Minolta VIVID 900 3D laser scanner (Konica Minolta, Osaka, Japan) (2 cases).

3D photogrammetry system: Pritiface 3D photogrammetry system (pritiface; pritidenta GmbH, Germany) (1 case).

3.2.3. Preoperative Record for Digital Designing

The digital software utilized by the included studies were Mimics Software (Mimics Innovation Suite, Materialise, Leuven, Belgium) (18 cases), Freeform software (Freeform, NC, USA) (13 cases), 3 Shape software (3 Shape, Copenhagen, Denmark) (12 cases), Geomagics Studio software (3D Systems, Rock Hill, SC, USA) (6 cases), Rapidform CAD software (INUS Technology, Seoul, South Korea) (5 cases), Software Z-Build (Z Corp, Cambridge, MA, USA) (3 cases), Polygone editing tool (Minolta Co, Osaka, Japan) (2 cases), NextEngine Scan studio software (NextEngine, CA, USA) (2 cases), Magics Materialise software (2 cases), Artec studio software (Artec 3D, Luxembourg) (2 cases), Materialise

3-matic software 9.0 (Materalise, Leuven, Belgium) (3 cases), Z brush software (Pixologic, Inc., USA) (1 case), Exocad software (Exocad, GmbH, Darmstadt, Germany) (I case). Navigation system: Stryker iNtellect Cranial (Stryker Navigation system, MI, USA) (2 cases), and BrainLAB cranial navigation software (BrainLAB AG, Munich, Germany) (9 cases).

3.2.4. Printing Systems Utilized for Surgical and Prosthetic Phases

Stereolithography (SLA), selective laser sintering (SLS), and fused deposition modeling (FDM) were the modalities used following the digital planning and designing phases to print the required models, molds, substructures, custom plates for retentive attachments, and surgical templates for craniofacial implants.

Fused deposition modeling (FDM) printers: MakerBot Replicator 2 (MakerBot Industries, Brooklyn, NY, USA), Zprinter 450 (Z Corp., Cambridge, MA, USA), ZPrinter® 310 Plus (Z Corp., Cambridge, MA, USA), Stratasys 400mc (Stratasys, Eden Prairie, MN, USA), 3D ink-jet Z printer (Z Corp., Cambridge, MA, USA), Stratasys FDM Vantage printer (Stratasys, Eden Prairie, MN, USA), Objet30 Scholar 3D Printer (Stratasys, Eden Prairie, MN, USA), and a CEL Robox 3D printer (CEL, Bristol, UK).

Selective laser sintering (SLS) printers: selective laser sintering (SLS) system (DTM Corp., Austin, TX), Zippy-I RP machine (Kinergy Mechatronics, Singapore), VisiJet M3 Hi-Cast printer (3D Systems, Rock Hill, SC, USA), and an AFS-360 printer (Long yuan Technology Ltd., Beijing, China).

Stereolithography (SLA): Perfactory Standard SXGA+ stereolithography printer (Envisiontec Inc., Germany), and a Form2 printer (Formlabs Inc., Somerville, MA, USA).

Printing materials: Z-corp powder sealant material (Z Corp, Cambridge, MA, USA), Acrylonitrile butadiene styrene plastic material ABS—P400 Jet (Stratasys, Eden Prairie, MN, USA), Polyamide material (Oceanz BV, Ede, The Netherlands), Clear Resin, white resin (Form2labs) (Formlabs Inc, Somerville, MA, USA), Somos DMX 100 Resin material (Somos DSM, Desotech Inc, Elgin, IL, USA), nGen colorFabb polymer material (Eastman Chemical Company, Belfeld, The Netherlands), PowerDent resin material (ProTech Transfer Co. Ltd., Bangkok, Thailand), Polylactic acid material (PLA) (MakerBot Industries, Brooklyn, NY, USA), and a Nylon PA 2200 (3DPRINTUK, London, UK).

3.2.5. Guided Implant Surgery

A total of 88 craniofacial implants for auricular defects were placed in 77 clinical cases after the digital planning, designing, and manufacturing of surgical templates. A total of 51 Vistafix craniofacial implants (Entific Medical Systems, Goteborg, Sweden) were placed in 22 clinical cases, 3 implants (MDIC; FMMU, China) were placed in 1 case, 4 Straumann implants (Straumann GmbH, Freiburg, Germany) were placed in 2 cases, and 12 dental implants (Friadent, Dentsply, Mannheim, Germany) were placed in 6 cases, respectively, to rehabilitate with silicone auricular prostheses. Meanwhile, 20 implants were placed with the help of surgical navigation systems: Stryker iNtellect Cranial (Stryker Navigation system, MI, USA) and BrainLAB software (BrainLAB AG, Munich, Germany) to rehabilitate 9 patients with auricular prostheses. Only one study mentioned the postoperative accuracy of 3D-planned implant placement. According to the results, 3 implants were deviated by 3.814 mm, 5.747 mm, and 4.463 mm, respectively, with mean a value of 4.675 mm.

3.3. *Risks of Bias in Individual Studies*

The JBI criteria were followed to assess the risk of bias in the individual studies. As illustrated by Table 2a–c, the case reports were authored by the following: Ciocca L, Scotti R. 2004 [26], Sykes et al., 2004 [27], Jiao et al., 2004 [28], Ciocca L et al., 2007 [29], Kurtulmus et al., 2009 [17], Ciocca L et al., 2009 [30], Ciocca. L et al., 2010 [32], De Crescenzio F et al., 2011 [33], Liacouras et al., 2011 [34], Kolodney et al., 2011 [35], Bai et al., 2012 [37], Reitemeier et al., 2012 [38], Hatamleh and Watson 2013 [39], Wang et al., 2015 [42], Nuseir et al., 2015 [43], Weissler et al., 2017 [45], Yadav et al., 2017 [46], Nafij Bin Jamayet et al., 2018 [47], Unkovskiy et al., 2018 [48], Sanghavi, et al., 2018 [49], Cevik and Kocacikli

2020 [52], Domingue D. et al., 2021 [54], Unkovskiy et al., 2021 [55], Dashti et al., 2022 [56], Heydenrych A et al., 2023 [58] showed a low risk of bias. Meanwhile, Table 3a,b showed that the case series authored by Turgut et al., 2009 [31], Verma et al., 2010 [22], Karatas MO et al., 2011 [36], Bai et al., 2014 [40], Tam CK et al., 2014 [8], Watson and Hatamleh 2014 [41], Choi et al., 2016 [44], Ferreira R, Vives P 2019 [50], Vijverberg MA et al., 2019 [51], McHutchion and Aalto 2021 [53], and Hatamleh MM et al., 2022 [57] presented a low risk of bias.

In Figure 2, most studies had a low risk of bias (≤50%), except for the specific question, "Were adverse events (harms) or unanticipated events identified and described?", where more than 75% of the included studies had not mentioned any adverse events or unanticipated events. For another question, "Were the diagnostic tests or assessment methods and the results clearly described?", more than 75% of the studies had not clearly mentioned the diagnostic tests, assessment methods, or results of the investigations.

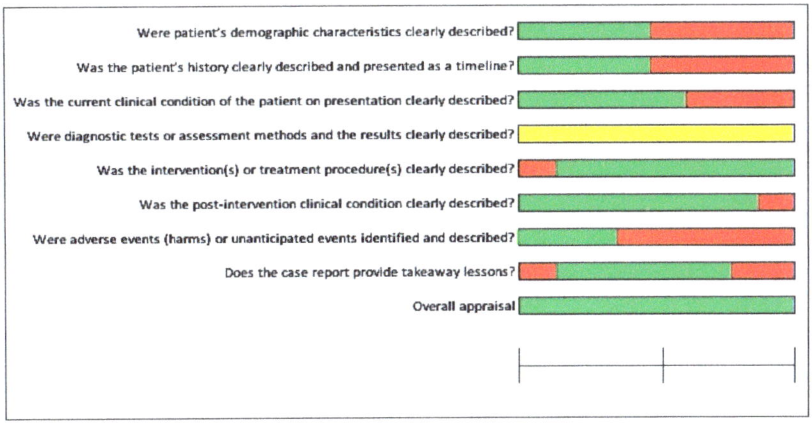

Figure 2. Risk of bias across the included studies for case reports.

Furthermore, Figure 3 illustrates the risk of bias for four case series studies. Most questions were in favor of a low risk of bias. For two questions, the details were unclear: "Were valid methods used for identification of the condition for all participants included in the case series?" and "Was there clear reporting of clinical information of the participants?". Furthermore, it was not possible to perform a meta-analysis due to the quality of the included studies, case series, and case reports.

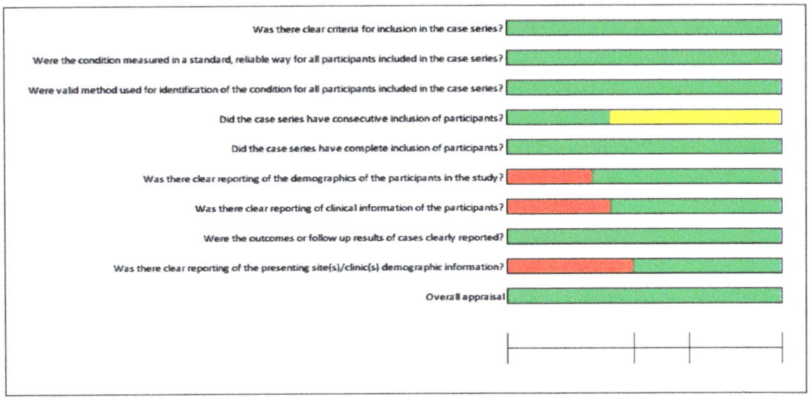

Figure 3. Risk of bias for the case series.

4. Discussion

Digitally assisted design and digitally assisted manufacturing (CAD/CAM) systems have been utilized for the design and manufacturing of medical devices for the last couple of decades. The digital planning software were first utilized for intraoral implant placement in 1997 [59,60]. Further digital and technical advancements led clinicians and dental technologists to plan guided implant surgeries, the manufacturing of custom implants, retentive attachments, digital wax-ups, molds, and prostheses [61,62]. With the CAD/CAM applications, virtual surgical planning and its application in surgical procedures became more predictable, reduced the laboratory and clinical time for the procedures, reduced the patient's appointments, and enabled the patients to virtually observe the proposed outcome prior to invasive procedures [61,62]. Various clinical case studies have documented the applications of digital technology for the fabrication of auricular prostheses; therefore, the aim of this paper was to gather the clinical studies involving the clinical and technical applications of CAD/CAM technology for craniofacial implant placement and the fabrication of auricular prostheses.

Three-dimensional imaging has added an extra dimension to the conventionally available preoperative radiographs, with the additional advantage of low radiation doses and detailed information about the bone quantity, bone volume, and proximity of adjacent critical anatomical structures [63,64]. The obtained data from computed tomography (CT), magnetic resonance imaging (MRI), or cone-beam computed tomography (CBCT) can be used in conjunction with digital planning software for preoperative planning [65,66]. The obtained data from tomographic images in combination with digital planning software help guide the implant placement in the optimum position and angulation according to the surgical and prosthetic plan [65,67]. Various factors such as tube current, slice thickness, voltage, pitch, the reconstruction algorithm for image slices, minor patient movement, and artifacts from metal objects can induce significant errors [68]. Among these factors, the slice thickness can influence the volume measurement, thus it should be set at <1.25 mm [68,69]. A total of seven included studies mentioned the slice thickness of CT scans ranging from 1 to 1.25 mm [28,34,35,37,40,44,49], while two included studies made use of a slice thickness less than 1 mm [31,50]. Furthermore, the voxel size affects the quality and reconstruction time of the CBCT images. None of the included clinical studies mentioned the voxel size.

The integration of 3D radiographic images and laser scans enabled the preoperative planning for guided implant surgeries. These two entities, when incorporated into the digital designing software, provided the possibility for maxillofacial surgeons and prosthodontists to plan the surgeries in chronological sequence (prosthesis-driven implant placement), from prosthetic design and position downwards to the implant position and angulation [70]. In this study, 77 cases were planned and executed by utilizing CT scans, CBCT scans, EBCT scans, MRIs, and laser scanners; however, only 14 cases were planned by the combined use of 3D radiographic images and laser scans for preoperative planning and designing of auricular prostheses.

Virtual planning has been mainly dependent on computer-aided design systems (CAD). These designing systems combine laser scans of intact and defect sides as well as 3D tomographic images to estimate the exact location and angulation of implants, to design the surgical templates, to plan and design the retentive attachments, and to design the molds, frameworks, customized implants, and provisional and definitive prostheses. In the current study, Meshmixer (Autodesk Inc., USA), Geomagics Studio software (3D Systems, Rock Hill, SC, USA), 3 Shape software (3 Shape, Copenhagen, Denmark), iPlan Cranial 3.0 BrainLAB software (BrainLAB AG, Munich, Germany), BrainLAB software (BrainLAB AG, Munich, Germany), Mimics Software (Mimics Innovation Suite, Materialise, Leuven, Belgium), Rapidform CAD software (INUS Technology, Seoul, South Korea), Rhinoceros Software v. 4.0 (Robert McNeel & Associates, USA), and Stryker iNtellect Cranial (Stryker Navigation system, MI, USA) were used in a total of 77 cases to plan and place 88 implants in auricular defects for prosthetic purposes. These implants were guided by surgical templates to be placed between 9 and 11 o'clock positions on the right side and between 1 and 3 o'clock positions on the left side, respectively [10]. Meanwhile, Z brush software (Pixologic, Inc., USA), Exocad software (Exocad, GmbH, Darmstadt, Germany), Geomagics Studio software (3D Systems, Rock Hill, SC, USA), Artec studio 16 software (Artec 3D, Luxembourg), Materialise 3-matic software 9.0 (Materalise, Leuven, Belgium), Freeform software (Freeform, NC, USA), NextEngine Scan studio software (NextEngine, CA, USA), Rapidworks 64 version 4.1.0. (3D system, Inc. Rock Hill, USA), Mimics Software (Mimics Innovation Suite, Materialise, Leuven, Belgium), and Polygone editing tool (Minolta Co, Osaka, Japan) designing software were used in 42 cases to design the scan bodies, customized implants, retentive attachments, models, molds, substructures for silicone auricular prostheses.

The computer-aided designing (CAD) step ultimately leads to the computer-aided manufacturing (CAM) step in order to convert the virtually planned and designed models, molds, templates, and prostheses to physical form by utilizing 3D printing systems [71–73]. Currently, six prototyping technologies can be used to convert virtually planned and designed objects into physical reality: stereolithography, laminated object manufacturing, selective laser sintering, solid ground curing, 3D ink-jet printing, and fused deposition modeling [36]. However, stereolithography (SLA), selective laser sintering (SLS), and fused deposition modeling (FDM) are the most frequently used 3D printing technologies. The FDM technology makes use of plastic filament, which is heated and extruded through the extrusion head onto the platform. As soon as extruded filament drops on the platform, it hardens due to the controlled temperature. In this way, layer-by-layer deposition builds up a physical model. To construct more complex models, multiple extrusion heads are required [73]. Plastics used for FDM technology are mainly acrylonitrile butyric styrene (ABS), polycarbonates, and polysulfides. The SLA technology utilizes ultraviolet light to polymerize the photosensitive resin. Following each layer of resin deposition on the platform, ultraviolet light cures successive layers, and photopolymerization helps to build up complex structures [73]. SLA-based printing technology utilizes a monomer resin that converts into a polymer upon photopolymerization. FDM printers are usually used to print models, molds, and provisional prostheses, while SLA printers are mainly used to print surgical templates for guided implant placement surgeries [74]. In the current review, SLA printing technology was used for 10 cases, SLS printers were used for 22 cases, and FDM printers were used for 40 cases. The most common printing materials were resin powders, polylactic acid (PLA), polyamide, titanium grade 2, gypsum powder, and ABS material.

Craniofacial implants were virtually planned for precise placement in the mastoid bone for the support and retention of auricular prostheses. A total of 88 implants were placed in right and left auricular defects in 35 cases following digital planning. Surgical templates and navigation systems were used to guide the implants in the planned locations. Due to various factors such as the anatomical morphology, radiation therapy, chemotherapy, and morphology of the tissue bed, two to four implants were placed in each auricular defect for prosthetic rehabilitation. Retention of auricular prostheses was mainly gained by clip bar and magnet attachments; however, locator attachment with a customized bone plate was also reported in one study [50]. Postoperative data to assess the accuracy of digitally planned extraoral implant placement for facial prosthetic rehabilitation are very limited [61,62]. Only one included study mentioned the postoperative accuracy of digitally planned auricular implant placement. Three implants had deviated by an average of 4.67 mm. However, the case was successfully rehabilitated by using an orientation guide for an auricular prosthesis [58].

Digital planning and design systems have reduced the patient's visits to a minimum of two to three visits. [29,33,40] Table 4. Furthermore the included studies showed satisfactory clinical outcome for the prosthetic rehabilitation of auricular defects (Table 5). Mirroring the intact ear to the defect side helps to obtain the digital model, which can be printed to replicate the ear wax pattern [27–29,32,33,40,41]. The time required to plan, design, and manufacture the wax pattern through CAD/CAM systems ranged from 40 min to 4 h, which if processed conventionally would require more than 6 h [27,41] (Table 4). The systematic reviews from Tanveer, W. et al. [61,62] further provided the expected time and cost for the digital workflow involved in the processing of facial prostheses for the readers to obtain a general overview of the time and cost involved in the digital planning, designing, and manufacturing of facial prostheses. Navigation systems have further paced the surgical planning and placement of implants. According to Verma et al., 2010 [22], the navigation system for guiding the craniofacial implants had reduced the clinical and laboratory time by 10 h. Additionally, digital workflow has enabled patients to visualize the proposed plan prior to invasive procedures, thereby giving the option to the patients to either accept or reject the proposed plan based on the expected outcome. Once the clinician and patient decide to proceed, the planning and designing software helps to construct surgical templates, models, molds, customized implants, retentive attachments, and even direct silicone prostheses (Figure 4).

Table 4. Efficiency of digital workflow verses conventional processing of auricular prostheses.

Studies	Purpose	Digital Process				Convencional Process
		Material	Cost	Time	No. of Appointments	Time
Sykes et al., 2004 [27]	Digitization of ear model and processing in Freeform software for rapid prototyping of mirrored ear model	Wax	NM	4 h	NM	6 h
Jiao et al., 2004 [28]	Printing and finishing of ear prosthesis	NM	NM	1.5 h	NM	NM
Ciocca L et al., 2007 [29]	Computer-aided design and rapid prototyping of auricular mold and substructure	Resin	15$	NM	3	NM
Ciocca. L et al., 2010 [32]	Computer-aided design and rapid prototyping of auricular molds and substructures for bilateral auricular prostheses	—ABS	36.58€	10 h 42 min	NM	NM
De Crescenzio F et al., 2011 [33]	Computer -aided design and rapid prototyping of auricular mold and substructure	ABS	23.79€	6 h 39 min	3	NM
Watson and Hatamleh 2014 [41]	Scanning, manipulation, RP build, and finishing time for wax prototype	Wax	58$	40 min	NM	2 h
Bai et al., 2014 [40]	Clinical time spentComputer-aided design and rapid prototyping of auricular molds	Resin	NM	4 h10 h	2	NM

Abbreviations: NM—Not mentioned; H—hour; Mins—minutes.

Table 5. Enlisted are the clinical outcomes, recommendations, and limitations mentioned in the included clinical studies.

Included Articles	Outcome	Recommendations	Limitations
Ciocca L, Scotti R. 2004 [26]	The stone cast of existing ears was scanned and mirrored with the help of software to the affected side. A 3D printer helped print the resin model of the ear for the affected side.	The technique utilized in this clinical case is faster; it takes about 8 h. Once the equipment is available, the cost of individual procedures can be less expensive as compared to the anaplastologist's work.	The limitation of this clinical technique is the inability to reciprocate the color information, and the equipment cost can be expensive.
Sykes et al., 2004 [27]	Digital technology provided the way to obtain an accurate wax model in a reasonable short time as compared to conventional methodology for the rehabilitation of auricular defects.	External imaging methods can provide better accuracy than CT scan images, especially in cases of complex ear anatomy. Additionally, it does not require volumetric modeling interpolation between the slices.	High cost of equipment and a trained laboratory technician for digital designing and printing procedures.
Jiao et al., 2004 [28]	The shape, dimension, and anatomic contour of the ear prosthesis matched the normal side and fitted well on the defect side.	The Magics RP (Materilise) program permits the mirrored ear position to move anteroposterior superioinferior, projections from the surface to match the unaffected side precisely.	According to the authors, improvement of the technique is required.
Ciocca L et al., 2007 [29]	The described protocol enabled the fabrication of an ear prosthesis in three appointments through the construction of a virtual CAD/CAM model, a mold, and digitization of the implant location.	This protocol allows the scanning and replacement of a lost ear virtually without the need for a diagnostic wax pattern.	The limitations are the technical skills required to use CAD/CAM technology and the relevant costs of laboratory equipment, including 3D scanners and rapid prototyping machines.
Kurtulmus et al., 2009 [17]	The prosthetically driven implant's location was determined by mirroring the normal ear to the defect side and the virtual construction of the model. The prosthesis was processed and fitted in a conventional way.	NM	NM
Ciocca L et al., 2009 [30]	The prosthetically driven implant's locations were determined. A surgical template was printed to place the implants in the planned locations.	The location of landmarks during a CT scan and the duplication of the diagnostic template can induce errors; therefore, the authors recommend their protocol for the correct diagnosis of available bone and the precise transfer of planning to the surgical template.	NM
Turgut et al., 2009 [31]	Auricular prostheses were manufactured through mirroring of the contralateral normal ear and rapid prototyping of a 3D ear model. Digital technology helped complete the prosthetic rehabilitation with only one trial session.	The auricular prosthesis procedure was cost-effective, required fewer patient visits, and eliminated the chances of sculpturing errors by utilizing rapid prototyping methodologies.	The protocol described here is only applicable to patients with one missing ear. According to the authors, in the case of bilateral auricular atresia, esthetic ratios of facial features can be used as a guideline to design prostheses.

Table 5. *Cont.*

Included Articles	Outcome	Recommendations	Limitations
Ciocca. L et al., 2010 [32]	Bilateral auricular defects were rehabilitated by selecting a reference ear from the digital ear and nose library. The mold and substructure were designed virtually and rapidly prototyped for silicone packing to obtain bilateral auricular prostheses.	The Ear and Nose Digital Library is a useful tool if the patient has bilateral auricular defects. Mirroring a selected reference ear from a digital library can provide identical bilateral auricular prostheses.	The presence of a stair-case effect on the superficial surface is one limitation that can be minimized by using thin printing layers or using surface finishers conventionally, following construction of models or molds.
Verma et al., 2010 [22]	A surgical navigation system was used to plan and place the craniofacial implants in two patients without any reported complications. Prostheses were fabricated in a conventional way.	The authors recommend this technique as it is virtually possible to visualize future prostheses, which helps surgeons alter the soft tissues prior to or during surgery without the necessity to keep a soft tissue profile for soft tissue registered surgical templates.	NM
De Crescenzio F et al., 2011 [33]	A three-piece mold was designed and 3D-constructed by means of CAD/CAM technology. Precise positioning of the substructure was attained in the prototype mold. Molds are fitted precisely with silicone packing.	This technique reduced the time and cost considerably when compared to conventional procedures and anaplastologist services. To reduce the stair-case effect, mold parts were oriented along the vertical axis of the prosthesis (from bottom to top).	NM
Liacouras et al., 2011 [34]	A mold for an auricular prosthesis was designed and printed using rapid prototyping technology for silicone packing. A three-piece mold fitted well to the fabricated silicone auricular prosthesis.	Rapid prototyping material is usually devoid of color; therefore, it prevents contamination, which is the issue with colored stone molds. A three-piece mold is recommended for ease of recovery, positioning of the seam at a favorable spot, and ease of placement of the retentive substructure.	Laboratory technicians can induce very limited surface texture in 3D printed molds; therefore, it is difficult to produce that surface texture in a finished prosthesis. Furthermore, the cost and technical skills required to use CAD/CAM technology are the limiting factors.
Kolodney et al., 2011 [35]	Cephalometric analysis was used to plan the implant's locations digitally and transferred into a physical ear model by rapid prototyping. The planned implant locations were then copied into a surgical template for craniofacial implant placement.	The authors recommend this technique of using cephalometric analysis to locate the implant's location in patients who are facially symmetric. It is not applicable to craniofacial anomaly cases.	Despite the advantages of this technique, it is still necessary to place the physical wax pattern on the patient to verify the shape and position before proceeding to process it with silicone to fabricate a prosthesis.
Karatas MO et al., 2011 [36]	Intact ears were mirrored onto the defect side. Rapid prototyping technology was used to construct the ear models. Following the duplication of models, auricular prostheses were fabricated in a conventional way.	The authors suggest scanning and mirroring the intact side to the defect side, as these steps eliminate the potential errors from impression and wax carving.	The skilled laboratory technologist and cost of designing and printing equipment pose limitations to this technique.

Table 5. *Cont.*

Included Articles	Outcome	Recommendations	Limitations
Bai et al., 2012 [37]	The surgical template was digitally designed to place the auricular implants. A maxillary occlusal splint was connected to a surgical template to stabilize it, and implants were placed through flapless surgery.	The authors recommend this technique to design the surgical template for implant placement as it permits flapless surgery and precise implant placement, reducing the procedure time and morbidity.	This technique can only be used on dentate patients, as the surgical template needs to be stabilized with an occlusal splint.
Reitemeier et al., 2012 [38]	The surgical template for implant placement was designed by mirroring the intact ear to the defect side. The glabella and nose were used to stabilize the surgical template during the surgical procedure.	This approach facilitates the design of a surgical template for implant placement, which guides the symmetrical positioning of an auricular prosthesis.	The additional cost of a surgical template for implant placement can pose a limitation to this technique.
Hatamleh and Watson. 2013 [39]	The surgical template for implant placement was designed by mirroring the intact ear to the defect side. The ear model was printed and duplicated to adapt to the working cast for precise positioning during implant placement. Two implants were placed at the planned position in the mastoid bone.	Digital mirroring and printing the ear saved time, which is usually spent on wax carving. Mirrored images were saved in a computer system, which can be used to reprint the ear model for future prostheses, thus saving the patient's visit and storage space.	NM
Bai et al., 2014 [40]	Intact ears were mirrored on the defect side and used to create a negative three-piece mold for silicone packing. Prostheses fitted well in all cases, and patients showed thorough satisfaction.	With this technique, the try-in step can be eliminated, thereby reducing the patient's visits. Furthermore, by eliminating manual flasking and investing procedures. The overall time of fabrication was significantly reduced.	An objective investigation of patient satisfaction is required to evaluate the acceptance of prostheses following this digital technique.
Tam CK et al., 2014 [8]	The intact ear was mirrored on the defect side to obtain the prototyped model. A surgical navigation system was utilized to place the craniofacial implants. The delivered prostheses had good retention, stability, and a symmetrical position. Psychological assessment showed decreased depressive symptoms and positive emotions.	Computer-assisted planning and surgical navigation systems have been recommended by the authors. CAD software helps in preoperative planning, while surgical navigation systems improve intraoperative safety and prevent damage to critical anatomic structures.	The authors encountered problems with reduced retention of prostheses and discoloration or color mismatch of silicone auricular prostheses.
Watson and Hatamleh 2014 [41]	The intact ear was mirrored on the defect side and prototyped to obtain a 3D model. The obtained model was copied into a wax pattern and adjusted in a trial session on the patient. Mirroring the ear model produced an accurate shape and form, comparable to the intact normal ear.	The presented technique required less clinic time. Scanning, manipulation, rapid prototyping, and finishing the wax prototype took 40 min, while an average ear wax pattern requires 2 h.	The limitation of this technique is the cost of software and hardware use, maintenance, and trained staff to operate these digital systems.

Table 5. *Cont.*

Included Articles	Outcome	Recommendations	Limitations
Wang et al., 2015 [42]	The normal ear was mirrored on the defect side, and a surgical template was designed to place three implants on the defect side. The ear model was printed and duplicated into a wax pattern for trial and laboratory processing.	Remnants of the malformed ear should be removed to facilitate the correct position and enhance the stability of the prosthesis.	NM
Nuseir et al., 2015 [43]	The normal ear was mirrored on the defect side, and a surgical template was designed to place two implants on the defect side. The ear model was printed and duplicated into a wax pattern for trial and laboratory processing.	This technique saved time and reduced the patient's visits. Additionally, current data would be useful for future fabrication of prostheses without the patient's physical presence.	NM
Choi et al., 2016 [44]	An intraoperative navigation system was used to place two craniofacial implants at the auricular defect location. The trajectory of the implants was confirmed at the planned location by using a navigation probe. An implant-retained ear prosthesis was fabricated without complications.	The intraoperative navigation system provides real-time navigation into the localized anatomy on the backdrop of multiplanar views. This system is recommended by the authors for patients with altered anatomy and limited bone availability.	According to the authors, this study is limited by the number of cases and the study design. The goal of this study was to highlight management principles for patients with altered anatomy only.
Weissler et al., 2017 [45]	The father's ear was scanned and mirrored on the defect side for implant planning. An intraoperative navigation system was used to place three implants bilaterally, while two implants on each side were used for prostheses retention without any reported complications.	The intraoperative navigation system helps to execute the planned cases precisely, especially in failed auricular reconstruction attempts or complex cases with limited bone availability.	NM
Yadav et al., 2017 [46]	The normal ear was mirrored on the defect side and used to design the mold for silicone packing. The prosthesis recovered from a 3D-printed mold was adjusted and delivered. The patient was satisfied with the final outcome.	The scanning of soft tissues prevents the distortion that is inevitable with conventional impression techniques. A digitally designed prosthesis is a more accurate procedure. The mold prepared by using this reported technique can be used multiple times to pack silicone.	The technique used in this case requires expensive equipment and a trained computer graphic designer, which ultimately increases the cost of a prosthesis.
Nafij Bin Jamayet et al., 2018 [47]	The intact ear was mirrored on the defect side and printed to obtain a 3D ear model. The model was duplicated into a wax pattern and processed with conventional techniques to fabricate an auricular prosthesis.	The digital system used in this study was portable, easy to use, saved clinic time, and produced an exact replica of a normal ear for the defect side.	According to the authors, this technique lacks the ability to procedure silicone prostheses with proper color match with adjacent skin.

Table 5. *Cont.*

Included Articles	Outcome	Recommendations	Limitations
Unkovskiy et al., 2018 [48]	The normal ear was mirrored on the defect side and processed with two different techniques: direct mold making (DMM) and indirect mold making (IMM). The authors concluded that IMM is the preferred technique, as the 3D-printed model, being an exact replica of a normal ear, can be duplicated for the trial step before laboratory processing.	According to the authors, the IMM technique is preferred over the DMM technique, as the 3D-printed model, being an exact replica of a normal ear, can be duplicated for a trial step before laboratory processing. Hence, a more predictable outcome can be achieved.	Anterior marginal fit was compromised following the DMM-derived prosthesis and the IMM-derived prototype model. However, following the IMM technique, the duplicated wax pattern was well adapted during the trial session, which improved the final outcome.
Sanghavi, et al., 2018 [49]	The intact ear was scanned and mirrored on the defect side to obtain the 3D-printed model. The model was duplicated into a wax pattern for the trial phase and processed conventionally.	This technique provides an accurate shape and form of the ear, which can be duplicated and processed in a conventional way, thereby making it an economical solution when compared to other 3D printing techniques.	According to the authors, the duplication step can induce errors such as distortion of the wax pattern, which would limit the accuracy and esthetics of the final prosthesis.
Ferreira R, Vives P. 2019 [50]	Custom plates with three locator attachment positions were designed digitally and printed with grade two titanium material. During the surgical procedure, the plates were screwed on the mastoid bone and used to retain ear prostheses without any reported complications.	The use of customized titanium plates can eliminate the problem of limited bone availability for craniofacial implants. This surgical procedure is safe and faster when compared to the placement of implants to retain facial prostheses.	NM
Vijverberg MA et al., 2019 [51]	A total of 31 implants were placed in 12 patients after digital planning and the design of a surgical template. None of these implants failed. GBI displayed positive scores from patients' responses.	By digitally planning and designing surgical templates, higher accuracy and precise placement of craniofacial implants can be achieved. It further helps anaplastologists design the auricular prosthesis without compromising the retentive attachment position.	The study was from retrospective data; therefore, there might be missing data from patients' records. Furthermore, Holger's scores were not mentioned in two cases.
Cevik and Kocacikli. 2020 [52]	The intact ear was mirrored on the defect side. A negative mold was designed digitally and printed for silicone packing. This procedure reduced the fabrication steps, and the fabricated prosthesis fit well on the patient.	This technique saves a number of laboratory and clinical steps by mirroring the intact ear to the defect side and fabricating the mold without conventional wax and flasking procedures.	NM

Table 5. *Cont.*

Included Articles	Outcome	Recommendations	Limitations
McHutchion and Aalto. 2021 [53]	A total of five patients were scanned for ear defects, and scan bodies were designed and printed to fit on the implants. The intact ear model was scanned and mirrored on the defect side. Molds were designed and printed for silicone packing to obtain auricular prostheses. Two prostheses fit well, while the remaining prostheses had open margins against adjacent tissues.	This digital workflow can be used as the starting point for future planning and design of facial prostheses, following some improvements.	Two prostheses had a poor fit against the tissues. The third prosthesis fit well in some areas; however, a large gap was noticed along the upper edge of the prosthesis. Test prostheses exerted less pressure on underlying tissues, and surface details were lacking.
Domingue D. et al., 2021 [54]	Craniofacial implants were planned with digital planning software to be placed in the right mastoid location for an auricular prosthesis. Implants were precisely placed at the planned location with no clinically reported complications.	This technique prevents damage to the critical underlying tissues and optimizes the prosthetically driven approach to implant placement with precise angulation and depth.	NM
Unkovskiy et al., 2021 [55]	A silicone auricular prosthesis was printed with various shore A hardness of the silicone. External staining, sealing, and finishing were performed conventionally. The anterior margin was further adjusted with conventional silicone to blend with adjacent skin.	Through proper digital workflow and mirror imaging techniques, the precise size, shape, and position of the auricular prosthesis can be achieved.	The printed silicone prosthesis lacked surface details due to limited printing resolution. Furthermore, grinding with abrasive paper to create a staircase effect further made the silicone surface smooth.
Dashti et al., 2022 [56]	The intact ear was mirrored on the defect side to obtain the exact size and shape of the contralateral ear. Stereolithographic casts, substructures, and milled bars were obtained following virtual planning and design. The wax pattern was copied and processed conventionally to fabricate an auricular prosthesis.	This technique provides a stable working cast without the need for convectional impression steps.	The limitation of this technique was the scanner's inability to record functional movements. It did not affect the outcome in the present study, but it can be a limitation in cases of excessive tissue movement during function.
Hatamleh MM et al., 2022 [57]	Implants were guided through surgical templates produced by using 3D planning software.	Symmetry is relatively easier to achieve using 3D planning software in cases of bilaterally missing ears.	NM
Heydenrych A et al., 2023 [58]	A surgical template to guide the implants and a template to orient the auricular prosthesis were designed and manufactured with rapid prototyping techniques.	The authors recommend this technique as it eases implant placement, saves time, and helps in the orientation of the auricular prosthesis in relation to the implants.	Implants were deviated in relation to the planned implant position by an average of 4.67 mm. The orientation guide helped overcome the discrepancy in implant position.

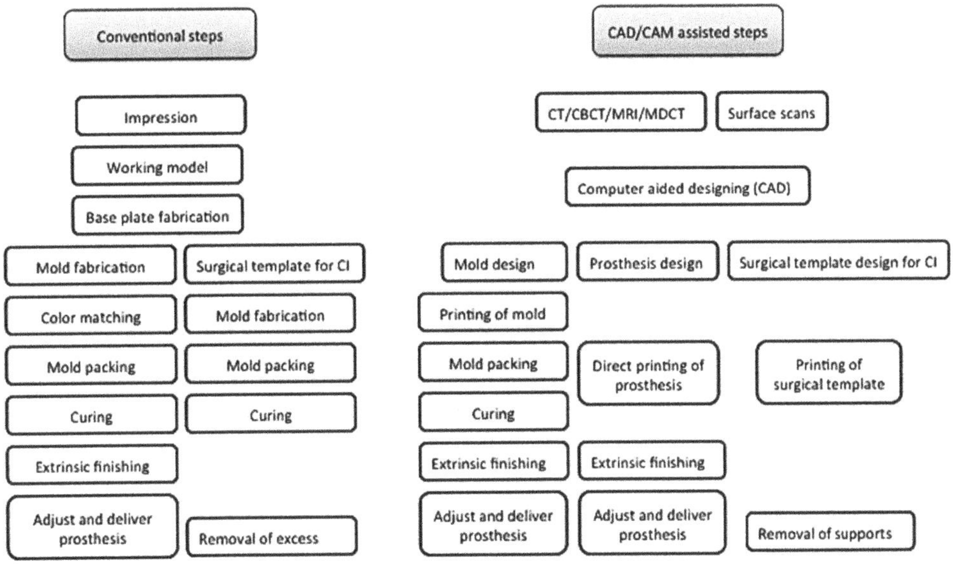

Figure 4. Comparison between conventional and digital planning and designing of surgical templates and prostheses fabrication.

The current systematic review includes clinical studies that were planned and executed from data acquisition to the virtual designing and printing of surgical templates, molds, substructures, implants, retentive attachments, and auricular prostheses. CAD/CAM systems have provided numerous advantages over conventional processing, such as predictability, reduced clinical and laboratory time, reduced patient visits, and the ability to view and discuss the end outcome before invasive procedures. However, studies about the accuracy of these digital planning software and printing systems are not yet available. Therefore, clinical trials are needed to assess the precision and accuracy of these CAD/CAM systems, especially for guided implant surgeries. Furthermore, the cost of equipment, maintenance, and trained technical staff pose limitations; therefore, these facilities are only accessible in high-end centers. Printing of color-matched prostheses, direct printing of prostheses with medical-grade silicone, and controlled fine thickness of the margins of prostheses are the other limitations that need to be addressed with further digital and technical advancements.

5. Conclusions

CAD/CAM systems have been used for maxillofacial prosthetics in the planning, designing, and manufacturing stages for the last couple of decades. Clinical and technical applications of CAD/CAM technology include data acquisition, planning and designing surgical templates, models, molds, retentive attachments, customized implants, and the manufacturing of prostheses. These CAD/CAM systems have shown a predictable clinical outcome, reduced the clinical and technical time to fabricate auricular prostheses, and reduced the patient's appointments when compared to conventional processing techniques. However, the availability of trained technical staff and the equipment cost limit the use of CAD/CAM in most parts of the world. Despite the digital advancements, direct printing of silicone auricular prostheses, production of featheredge thin margins, and direct printing of color-matched prostheses are the few current limitations of CAD/CAM-assisted techniques that need to be addressed. Furthermore, human clinical trials are needed to determine the precision and accuracy of these CAD/CAM systems for craniofacial implant placement and the fabrication of auricular prostheses.

Author Contributions: Conceptualization, W.T., A.R.-P. and T.F.; methodology, W.T., A.R.-P. and T.F.; validation, W.T., A.R.-P. and T.F.; formal analysis, W.T. and P.M.-M.; resources, W.T. and P.M.-M.; writing—original draft preparation, W.T.; writing—review and editing, W.T.; supervision, A.R.-P. and T.F. All authors have read and agreed to the published version of the manuscript.

Funding: This research received no external funding.

Institutional Review Board Statement: Ethical review and approval were waived for this study due to the retrospective data, which were readily available through published papers. Therefore, no direct human or animal contact was involved in gathering these data.

Informed Consent Statement: Not applicable for this systematic review.

Data Availability Statement: Not applicable for this systematic review.

Conflicts of Interest: The authors declare no conflict of interest.

References

1. Nishimura, R.D.; Roumanas, E.; Sugai, T.; Moy, P.K. Auricular prostheses and osseointegrated implants: UCLA experience. *J. Prosthet. Dent.* **1995**, *73*, 553–558. [CrossRef] [PubMed]
2. Guo, G.; Schwedtner, O.; Klein, M. A retrospective study of implant-retained auricular prostheses. *Int. J. Oral Maxillofac. Implant.* **2008**, *23*, 539–543.
3. Visser, A.; Raghoebar, G.M.; Van Oort, R.P.; Vissink, A. Fate of implant-retained craniofacial prostheses: Life span and aftercare. *Int. J. Oral Maxillofac. Implant.* **2008**, *23*, 89–98.
4. Aydin, C.; Karakoca, S.; Yilmaz, H.; Yilmaz, C. Implant-retained auricular prostheses: An assessment of implant success and prosthetic complications. *Int. J. Prosthodont.* **2008**, *21*, 241–244. [PubMed]
5. Brent, B. Auricular repair with autogenous rib cartilage grafts: Two decades of experience with 600 cases. *Plast Reconstr. Surg.* **1992**, *90*, 355–374. [CrossRef] [PubMed]
6. Tanzer, R.C. Total reconstruction of the external ear. *Plast. Reconstr. Surg. Transplant Bull.* **1959**, *23*, 1–15. [CrossRef]
7. Thorne, C.H.M.; Brecht, L.E.D.; Bradley, J.P.M.; Levine, J.P.M.; Hammerschlag, P.M.; Longaker, M.T.M. Auricular Reconstruction: Indications for Autogenous and Prosthetic Techniques. *Plast. Reconstr. Surg.* **2001**, *107*, 1241–1251. [CrossRef]
8. Tam, C.K.; McGrath, C.P.; Ho, S.M.Y.; Pow, E.H.N.; Luk, H.W.K.; Cheung, L.K. Psychosocial and Quality of Life Outcomes of Prosthetic Auricular Rehabilitation with CAD/CAM Technology. *Int. J. Dent.* **2014**, *2014*, 393571. [CrossRef]
9. Gumieiro, E.H.; Dib, L.L.; Jahn, R.S.; Junior, J.F.d.S.; Nannmark, U.; Granström, G.; Abrahão, M. Bone-anchored titanium implants for auricular rehabilitation: Case report and review of literature. *Sao Paulo Med. J.* **2009**, *127*, 160–165. [CrossRef]
10. Girod, S.C.; Rohlfing, T.; Maurer, C.R. Image-Guided Surgical Navigation in Implant-Based Auricular Reconstruction. *J. Oral Maxillofac. Surg.* **2008**, *66*, 1302–1306. [CrossRef]
11. Williams, B.H.; Ochiai, K.T.; Baba, T.; A Caputo, A. Retention and load transfer characteristics of implant-retained auricular prostheses. *Int. J. Oral Maxillofac. Implant.* **2007**, *22*, 366–372.
12. Lemon, J.C.; Chambers, M.S. Locking retentive attachment for an implant-retained auricular prosthesis. *J. Prosthet. Dent.* **2002**, *87*, 336–338. [CrossRef] [PubMed]
13. Waqas, T.S.; Shrestha, B.; Srithavaj, M.L.T.; Chotprasert, N. A two-step functional impression technique for the fabrication of an implant-retained silicone auricular prosthesis. *J. Prosthet. Dent.* **2017**, *117*, 444–447. [CrossRef] [PubMed]
14. Van Der Meer, W.J.; Vissink, A.; Raghoebar, G.M.; Visser, A. Digitally designed surgical guides for placing extraoral implants in the mastoid area. *Int. J. Oral Maxillofac. Implant.* **2012**, *27*, 703–707.
15. Datarkar, A.; Daware, S.; Dande, R.; Datarkar, U. Rehabilitation of unilateral congenital microtia by implant-retained prosthesis. *Ann. Maxillofac. Surg.* **2017**, *7*, 291–295. [CrossRef] [PubMed]
16. Ballo, A.M.; Nguyen, C.T.; Lee, V.S. Digital Workflow of Auricular Rehabilitation: A Technical Report Using an Intraoral Scanner. *J. Prosthodont.* **2019**, *28*, 596–600. [CrossRef]
17. Kurtulmus, H.; Cotert, H.S.; Guneri, P. Computed tomography-based planning and three-dimensional modeling for craniofacial implant placement: A technical note. *Int. J. Oral Maxillofac. Implant.* **2009**, *24*, 943–946.
18. Elbashti, M.; Sumita, Y.; Kelimu, S.; Aswehlee, A.; Awuti, S.; Hattori, M.; Taniguchi, H. Application of Digital Technologies in Maxillofacial Prosthetics Literature: A 10-Year Observation of Five Selected Prosthodontics Journals. *Int. J. Prosthodont.* **2019**, *32*, 45–50. [CrossRef]
19. Kernen, F.; Kramer, J.; Wanner, L.; Wismeijer, D.; Nelson, K.; Flügge, T. A review of virtual planning software for guided implant surgery—Data import and visualization, drill guide design and manufacturing. *BMC Oral Health* **2020**, *20*, 251. [CrossRef]
20. Ciocca, L.; Scotti, R. Oculo-facial rehabilitation after facial cancer removal: Updated CAD/CAM procedures: A pilot study. *Prosthet. Orthot. Int.* **2014**, *38*, 505–509. [CrossRef]
21. Liu, H.; Bai, S.; Yu, X.; Zhao, Y. Combined use of a facial scanner and an intraoral scanner to acquire a digital scan for the fabrication of an orbital prosthesis. *J. Prosthet. Dent.* **2019**, *121*, 531–534. [CrossRef] [PubMed]

22. Verma, S.N.; Schow, S.R.; Stone, B.H.; Triplett, R.G. Applications of surgical navigational systems for craniofacial bone-anchored implant placement. *Int. J. Oral Maxillofac. Implants* **2010**, *25*, 582–588. [PubMed]
23. Nuseir, A.; Hatamleh, M.M.; Alnazzawi, A.; Al-Rabab'Ah, M.; Kamel, B.; Jaradat, E. Direct 3D Printing of Flexible Nasal Prosthesis: Optimized Digital Workflow from Scan to Fit. *J. Prosthodont.* **2019**, *28*, 10–14. [CrossRef]
24. Moher DL, A.; Tetzlaff, J.; Altman, D.G. Preferred reporting items for systematic reviews and meta-analyses: The PRISMA statement. *PLoS Med.* **2009**, *6*, e1000097. [CrossRef] [PubMed]
25. Moola SA, E.; Sears, K.; Sfetcu, R.; Currie, M.; Lisy, K.; Qureshi, R.; Mattis, P.; Mu, P. Chapter 7: Systematic reviews of etiology and risk. In *Joanna Briggs Institute Reviewer's Manual*; Aromataris, E., Munn, Z., Eds.; JBI: Adelaide, Australia, 2017. [CrossRef]
26. Ciocca, L.; Scotti, R. CAD-CAM generated ear cast by means of a laser scanner and rapid prototyping machine. *J. Prosthet. Dent.* **2004**, *92*, 591–595. [CrossRef] [PubMed]
27. Sykes, L.M.; Parrott, A.M.; Owen, C.P.; Snaddon, D.R. Applications of rapid prototyping technology in maxillofacial prosthetics. *Int. J. Prosthodont.* **2004**, *17*, 454–459. [PubMed]
28. Jiao, T.; Zhang, F.; Huang, X.; Wang, C. Design and fabrication of auricular prostheses by CAD/CAM system. *Int. J. Prosthodont.* **2004**, *17*, 460–463. [PubMed]
29. Ciocca, L.; Mingucci, R.; Gassino, G.; Scotti, R. CAD/CAM ear model and virtual construction of the mold. *J. Prosthet. Dent.* **2007**, *98*, 339–343. [CrossRef]
30. Ciocca, L.; Mingucci, R.; Bacci, G.; Scotti, R. CAD-CAM construction of an auricular template for craniofacial implant positioning: A novel approach to diagnosis. *Eur. J. Radiol.* **2009**, *71*, 253–256. [CrossRef]
31. Turgut, G.; Sacak, B.; Kiran, K.; Bas, L. Use of rapid prototyping in prosthetic auricular restoration. *J. Craniofac. Surg.* **2009**, *20*, 321–325. [CrossRef]
32. Ciocca, L.; De Crescenzio, F.; Fantini, M.; Scotti, R. CAD/CAM bilateral ear prostheses construction for Treacher Collins syndrome patients using laser scanning and rapid prototyping. *Comput. Methods Biomech. Biomed. Engin.* **2010**, *13*, 379–386. [CrossRef]
33. De Crescenzio, F.; Fantini, M.; Ciocca, L.; Persiani, F.; Scotti, R. Design and manufacturing of ear prosthesis by means of rapid prototyping technology. *Proc. Inst. Mech. Eng. H.* **2011**, *225*, 296–302. [PubMed]
34. Liacouras, P.; Garnes, J.; Roman, N.; Petrich, A.; Grant, G.T. Designing and manufacturing an auricular prosthesis using computed tomography, 3-dimensional photographic imaging, and additive manufacturing: A clinical report. *J. Prosthet. Dent.* **2011**, *105*, 78–82. [CrossRef]
35. Kolodney, H., Jr.; Swedenburg, G.; Taylor, S.S.; Carron, J.D.; Schlakman, B.N. The use of cephalometric landmarks with 3-dimensional volumetric computer modeling to position an auricular implant surgical template: A clinical report. *J. Prosthet. Dent.* **2011**, *106*, 284–289. [CrossRef] [PubMed]
36. Karatas, M.O.; Cifter, E.D.; Ozenen, D.O.; Balik, A.; Tuncer, E.B. Manufacturing implant supported auricular prostheses by rapid prototyping techniques. *Eur. J. Dent.* **2011**, *5*, 472–477. [CrossRef] [PubMed]
37. Bai, S.; Bi, Y.; Dong, Y.; Feng, Z.; Zhao, Y. Computer-aided design/computer-aided manufacturing implant guide used in flapless surgery for auricular prosthesis. *J. Oral Maxillofac. Surg.* **2012**, *70*, 1338–1341. [CrossRef] [PubMed]
38. Reitemeier, B.; Schöne, C.; Schreiber, S.; Stockmann, F.; Ullmann, K.; Eckelt, U. Planning implant positions for an auricular prosthesis with digital data. *J. Prosthet. Dent.* **2012**, *107*, 128–131. [CrossRef]
39. Hatamleh, M.M.; Watson, J. Construction of an implant-retained auricular prosthesis with the aid of contemporary digital technologies: A clinical report. *J. Prosthodont.* **2013**, *22*, 132–136. [CrossRef]
40. Bai, S.-Z.; Feng, Z.-H.; Gao, R.; Dong, Y.; Bi, Y.-P.; Wu, G.-F.; Chen, X. Development and application of a rapid rehabilitation system for reconstruction of maxillofacial soft-tissue defects related to war and traumatic injuries. *Mil. Med. Res.* **2014**, *1*, 11. [CrossRef]
41. Watson, J.; Hatamleh, M.M. Complete integration of technology for improved reproduction of auricular prostheses. *J. Prosthet. Dent.* **2014**, *111*, 430–436. [CrossRef]
42. Wang, S.; Leng, X.; Zheng, Y.; Zhang, D.; Wu, G. Prosthesis-guided implant restoration of an auricular defect using computed tomography and 3-dimensional photographic imaging technologies: A clinical report. *J. Prosthet. Dent.* **2015**, *113*, 152–156. [CrossRef] [PubMed]
43. Nuseir, A.; Hatamleh, M.; Watson, J.; Al-Wahadni, A.M.; Alzoubi, F.; Murad, M. Improved Construction of Auricular Prosthesis by Digital Technologies. *J. Craniofac. Surg.* **2015**, *26*, e502–e505. [CrossRef]
44. Choi, K.J.; Sajisevi, M.B.; McClennen, J.; Kaylie, D.M. Image-Guided Placement of Osseointegrated Implants for Challenging Auricular, Orbital, and Rhinectomy Defects. *Ann. Otol. Rhinol. Laryngol.* **2016**, *125*, 801–807. [CrossRef]
45. Weissler, J.M.; Sosin, M.; Dorafshar, A.H.; Garcia, J.R. Combining Virtual Surgical Planning, Intraoperative Navigation, and 3-Dimensional Printing in Prosthetic-Based Bilateral Microtia Reconstruction. *J. Oral. Maxillofac. Surg.* **2017**, *75*, 1491–1497. [CrossRef] [PubMed]
46. Yadav, S.; Narayan, A.I.; Choudhry, A.; Balakrishnan, D. CAD/CAM-Assisted Auricular Prosthesis Fabrication for a Quick, Precise, and More Retentive Outcome: A Clinical Report. *J. Prosthodont.* **2017**, *26*, 616–621. [CrossRef]
47. Jamayet, N.B.; Abdullah, J.Y.; Rahman, A.M.; Husein, A.; Alam, M.K. A fast and improved method of rapid prototyping for ear prosthesis using portable 3D laser scanner. *J. Plast. Reconstr. Esthet. Surg.* **2018**, *71*, 946–953. [CrossRef]
48. Unkovskiy, A.; Brom, J.; Huettig, F.; Keutel, C. Auricular Prostheses Produced by Means of Conventional and Digital Workflows: A Clinical Report on Esthetic Outcomes. *Int. J. Prosthodont.* **2018**, *31*, 63–66. [CrossRef]

49. Sanghavi, R.V.; Shingote, S.D.; Abhang, T.N.; Thorat, P.R.; Vathare, A.S. An innovative technique for fabricating a mirror image wax pattern using three-dimensional printing technology for an auricular prosthesis. *J. Res. Dent. Sci.* **2018**, *9*, 91. [CrossRef]
50. Ferreira, R.; Vives, P. Two auricular epithesis surgical cases retained by a custom titanium implant: Result at four years. *J. Stomatol. Oral Maxillofac. Surg.* **2019**, *120*, 147–151. [CrossRef]
51. Vijverberg, M.A.; Verhamme, L.; van de Pol, P.; Kunst, H.P.M.; Mylanus, E.A.M.; Hol, M.K.S. Auricular prostheses attached to osseointegrated implants: Multidisciplinary work-up and clinical evaluation. *Eur. Arch. Otorhinolaryngol.* **2019**, *276*, 1017–1027. [CrossRef]
52. Cevik, P.; Kocacikli, M. Three-dimensional printing technologies in the fabrication of maxillofacial prosthesis: A case report. *Int. J. Artif. Organs.* **2020**, *43*, 343–347. [CrossRef]
53. McHutchion, L.; Aalto, D. Simulation of tissue-prosthesis margin interface by using surface scanning and digital design for auricular prostheses. *J. Prosthet. Dent.* **2021**, *125*, 361–372. [CrossRef]
54. Domingue, D.; Glenn, N.C.; Vest, A.; White, J.R. Osseointegrated implant-retained auricular prosthesis constructed using cone-beam computed tomography and a prosthetically driven digital workflow: A case report. *Clin. Case Rep.* **2021**, *9*, 37–45. [CrossRef]
55. Unkovskiy, A.; Wahl, E.; Huettig, F.; Keutel, C.; Spintzyk, S. Multimaterial 3D printing of a definitive silicone auricular prosthesis: An improved technique. *J. Prosthet. Dent.* **2021**, *125*, 946–950. [CrossRef]
56. Dashti, H.; Rajati Haghi, H.; Nakhaei, M.; Kiamanesh, E. A combined digital technique to fabricate an implant-retained auricular prosthesis for rehabilitation of hemifacial microsomia. *J. Prosthet. Dent.* **2022**, *127*, 807–810. [CrossRef]
57. Hatamleh, M.M.; Watson, J.; Nuseir, A. Successful prosthetic salvage of a suboptimal autogenous auricular reconstruction with digital technologies: A report of 3 challenging treatments. *J. Prosthet. Dent.* **2022**, *128*, 1103–1108. [CrossRef] [PubMed]
58. Heydenrych, A.; van der Walt, J.G.; van den Heever, H.J. Auricular prosthesis positioning using virtual planning in combination with additive manufacturing. *J. Stomatol. Oral Maxillofac. Surg.* **2023**, *124*, 101258. [CrossRef] [PubMed]
59. Ewers, R.; Schicho, K.; Truppe, M.; Seemann, R.; Reichwein, A.; Figl, M.; Wagner, A. Computer-aided navigation in dental implantology: 7 years of clinical experience. *J. Oral Maxillofac. Surg.* **2004**, *62*, 329–334. [CrossRef]
60. Mupparapu, M.; Singer, S.R. Implant imaging for the dentist. *J. Can. Dent. Assoc.* **2004**, *70*, 32. [PubMed]
61. Tanveer, W.; Ridwan-Pramana, A.; Molinero-Mourelle, P.; Koolstra, J.H.; Forouzanfar, T. Systematic Review of Clinical Applications of CAD/CAM Technology for Craniofacial Implants Placement and Manufacturing of Nasal Prostheses. *Int. J. Environ. Res. Public Health* **2021**, *18*, 3756. [CrossRef]
62. Tanveer, W.; Ridwan-Pramana, A.; Molinero-Mourelle, P.; Forouzanfar, T. Systematic Review of Clinical Applications of CAD/CAM Technology for Craniofacial Implants Placement and Manufacturing of Orbital Prostheses. *Int. J. Environ. Res. Public Health* **2021**, *18*, 11349. [CrossRef]
63. Tahmaseb, A.; Wismeijer, D.; Coucke, W.; Derksen, W. Computer technology applications in surgical implant dentistry: A systematic review. *Int. J. Oral Maxillofac. Implant.* **2014**, *29*, 25–42. [CrossRef]
64. Jacobs, R.; Adriansens, A.; Verstreken, K.; Suetens, P.; van Steenberghe, D. Predictability of a three-dimensional planning system for oral implant surgery. *Dentomaxillofac. Radiol.* **1999**, *28*, 105–111. [CrossRef]
65. Israelson, H.; Plemons, J.M.; Watkins, P.; Sory, C. Barium-coated surgical stents and computer-assisted tomography in the preoperative assessment of dental implant patients. *Int. J. Periodontics Restor. Dent.* **1992**, *12*, 52–61.
66. Basten, C.H. The use of radiopaque templates for predictable implant placement. *Quintessence Int.* **1995**, *26*, 609–612.
67. Mizrahi, B.; Thunthy, K.H.; Finger, I. Radiographic/surgical template incorporating metal telescopic tubes for accurate implant placement. *Pract. Periodontics Aesthet. Dent.* **1998**, *10*, 757–765.
68. Whyms, B.J.; Vorperian, H.K.; Gentry, L.R.; Schimek, E.M.; Bersu, E.T.; Chung, M.K. The effect of computed tomographic scanner parameters and 3-dimensional volume rendering techniques on the accuracy of linear, angular, and volumetric measurements of the mandible. *Oral Surg. Oral Med. Oral Pathol. Oral Radiol. Endod.* **2013**, *115*, 682–691. [CrossRef]
69. Taft, R.M.; Kondor, S.; Grant, G.T. Accuracy of rapid prototype models for head and neck reconstruction. *J. Prosthet. Dent.* **2011**, *106*, 399–408. [CrossRef] [PubMed]
70. Alauddin, M.S.; Baharuddin, A.S.; Mohd Ghazali, M.I. The Modern and Digital Transformation of Oral Health Care: A Mini Review. *Healthcare* **2021**, *9*, 118. [CrossRef] [PubMed]
71. Ishida, Y.; Miura, D.; Miyasaka, T.; Shinya, A. Dimensional Accuracy of Dental Casting Patterns Fabricated Using Consumer 3D Printers. *Polymers* **2020**, *12*, 2244. [CrossRef] [PubMed]
72. Dawood, A.; Marti Marti, B.; Sauret-Jackson, V.; Darwood, A. 3D printing in dentistry. *Br. Dent. J.* **2015**, *219*, 521–529. [CrossRef] [PubMed]
73. Stansbury, J.W.; Idacavage, M.J. 3D printing with polymers: Challenges among expanding options and opportunities. *Dent. Mater.* **2016**, *32*, 54–64. [CrossRef] [PubMed]
74. Nayar, S.; Bhuminathan, S.; Bhat, W.M. Rapid prototyping and stereolithography in dentistry. *J. Pharm. Bioallied Sci.* **2015**, *7* (Suppl. 1), S216–S219. [CrossRef] [PubMed]

Journal of
Clinical Medicine

Case Report

Custom CAD/CAM Peek Implants for Complex Orbitocranial Reconstruction: Our Experience with 15 Patients

Cristina Cárdenas-Serres [1,2,*], Fernando Almeida-Parra [1,2,*], Anna María Simón-Flors [1,2], Patricia de Leyva-Moreno [1,2], Álvaro Ranz-Colio [1,2], Luis Ley-Urzaiz [3] and Julio Acero-Sanz [1,2]

1 Department of Oral and Maxillofacial Surgery, Ramón y Cajal University Hospital, IRYCIS, 28034 Madrid, Spain; patricia.leyva@salud.madrid.org (P.d.L.-M.); jacero@salud.madrid.org (J.A.-S.)
2 Department of Oral and Maxillofacial Surgery, Puerta de Hierro University Hospital, 28222 Majadahonda, Spain
3 Department of Neurosurgery, Ramón y Cajal University Hospital, Instituto Ramón y Cajal de Investigación Sanitaria (IRYCIS), 28034 Madrid, Spain
* Correspondence: ccardenass@salud.madrid.org (C.C.-S.); fernando.almeida@salud.madrid.org (F.A.-P.)

Abstract: Bone defects within the cranio-orbital complex present unique challenges in terms of surgical planning and reconstruction. This article presents a novel approach using PEEK material and advanced surgical technologies to address these challenges. A retrospective analysis of 15 patients who underwent craniofacial reconstruction using patient-specific polyetheretherketone (PEEK) implants between 2016 and 2021 was carried out. Comprehensive preoperative planning was performed, utilizing advanced imaging techniques and specialized software for virtual surgical planning. Patient-specific PEEK PSIs were designed and manufactured based on the preoperative plan. Intraoperative navigation was used to guide the surgical procedure, enabling precise osteotomy and optimal implant placement. This article describes the step-by-step process and the tools utilized in each phase. The etiologies were as follows: meningioma in seven cases, benign lesions in five cases, malignant tumors in two cases, and trauma sequelae in one case. In all cases, 3D-printed PEEK implants were utilized to achieve precise reconstruction. No major complications were described. In one case, an implant replacement was needed with successful outcomes. Our study demonstrates the feasibility and effectiveness of using PEEK patient-specific implants for personalized craniofacial reconstruction. The combination of advanced imaging, virtual planning, and CAD-CAM technology contributes to improved surgical outcomes in terms of oncologic margin control, functional restoration, and aesthetic results.

Keywords: cranio-orbital complex; bone defects; PEEK; virtual surgical planning; intraoperative navigation; osteotomy; reconstruction; patient-specific implants

Citation: Cárdenas-Serres, C.; Almeida-Parra, F.; Simón-Flors, A.M.; de Leyva-Moreno, P.; Ranz-Colio, Á.; Ley-Urzaiz, L.; Acero-Sanz, J. Custom CAD/CAM Peek Implants for Complex Orbitocranial Reconstruction: Our Experience with 15 Patients. *J. Clin. Med.* **2024**, *13*, 695. https://doi.org/10.3390/jcm13030695

Academic Editor: Mikio Suzuki

Received: 14 October 2023
Revised: 14 December 2023
Accepted: 18 January 2024
Published: 25 January 2024

1. Introduction

The aesthetic and functional reconstruction of complex cranio-maxillofacial defects can be challenging, especially involving deformity and tissue loss as a result of trauma, oncologic resection, and craniofacial syndrome.

The cranio-orbital region serves as a vital support and protective structure for various components, including the eyeball, orbital cavity, brain, internal carotid artery, and cranial nerves. Comprising a pyramid-shaped framework with a quadrangular base, the orbit remains to be a complicated 3D structure which presents a significant challenge for surgical reconstruction and the correction of deformities in this area. Conventional techniques frequently employed for orbital reconstruction involve the use of standard titanium meshes, or polymeric implants, which need pre- or intraoperative bending and contour correction. The precise location of implants and their adaptability to the individual anatomy of the affected structures (in terms of size and shape) are critical factors for the overall success rate in cranio-orbital reconstruction.

With the development of computer-aided design/computer-assisted manufacturing (CAD/CAM), and the advancement of virtual surgical planning and 3D printing, the emergence of patient-specific implants (PSIs) has enabled the precise design, production, and fitting of implants tailored to individual anatomical defects with much more predictable postoperative results [1].

Although reconstruction with autologous tissue (such as bone grafting) was traditionally considered the best option for craniofacial bone repair, the introduction of synthetic materials has allowed further development in the field of reconstructive surgery [2]. In light of the limitations observed with metallic and ceramic biomaterials, there has been a recent introduction of polymers as a viable alternative. Numerous polymers, including polymethyl methacrylate (PMMA), polylactide (PLA), and polyglycolide (PGA), have found wide applications in the field of biomedicine. PMMA is a bone cement that is easy to shape and is relatively inexpensive compared to some other materials, but there is a higher risk of infection associated with this biomaterial, especially in long-term applications. PLA and PGA are biodegradable, which means they gradually break down in the body, become eventually replaced by natural tissue, and carry a lower risk of infection compared to non-biodegradable materials, but may not offer the same immediate stability and strength as other materials. Biodegradable polymers are radiolucent, ensuring that they do not interfere with X-rays or CT scans for accurate postoperative assessment. These polymer materials can be used for various reconstructive procedures, including orbital floor and zygomatic arch reconstruction, and they can be combined with other materials when necessary.

Among the various alloplastic materials, polyether ether ketone (PEEK) has emerged as an appealing choice for PSIs. PEEK is a polyaromatic semi-crystalline thermoplastic polymer that contains ether and ketone linkages. In recent years, it has increased in popularity due to its bone-like strength and elasticity, and other characteristics such as lower thermal conductivity and lower infection rates compared to other biomaterials [3]. PEEK is a lightweight material, making it suitable for facial bone reconstruction, and is radiolucent, allowing for better postoperative imaging. Surgeons should also consider that PEEK is less malleable than metals, which can make it more challenging to shape during the procedure, and can be relatively costly compared to other materials.

The utilization of advanced imaging techniques for the design of PSIs and preoperative planning has become standard practice in complex craniofacial procedures. While the use of imaging data for device design is well established, in our study, we aimed to highlight the specific workflow and considerations related to zygomatic–orbital complex reconstruction, with an emphasis on addressing the complexities and challenges of this procedure. There is currently a lack of systematic reporting on clinical studies regarding the implementation of patient-specific individual PEEK implants for cranio-orbital-zygomatic reconstruction. Hence, the objective of this article is to evaluate our approach for addressing bone defects within the orbito-zygomatic complex using PEEK and share our firsthand experience in employing virtual surgical planning and intraoperative navigation to conduct precise osteotomy and achieve accurate reconstruction through the utilization of custom-made prefabricated PEEK PSIs.

2. Materials and Methods

2.1. Patient Data

This study included 15 patients who underwent craniofacial reconstruction using PEEK PSIs in our department between 2016 and 2021. All the patients enrolled presented with either a benign or malignant lesion that needed complex cranioorbital resection or the subsequent reconstruction of the resulting defect. The variables analyzed were the sex, age, medical history, etiology, size, and location of the defect. The type of reconstruction performed, i.e., primary or secondary, and any postoperative complications were also recorded. Preoperative demographic data, as well as clinical and radiological findings, are presented. After obtaining informed consent, preoperative clinical images were taken of all patients with the intention of attaining an outcome closely resembling their preoperative state (Figure 1). Data were obtained retrospectively from hospital, clinical, and surgical records. The mean follow-up was 2.5 years, and ranged between 2 and 7 years.

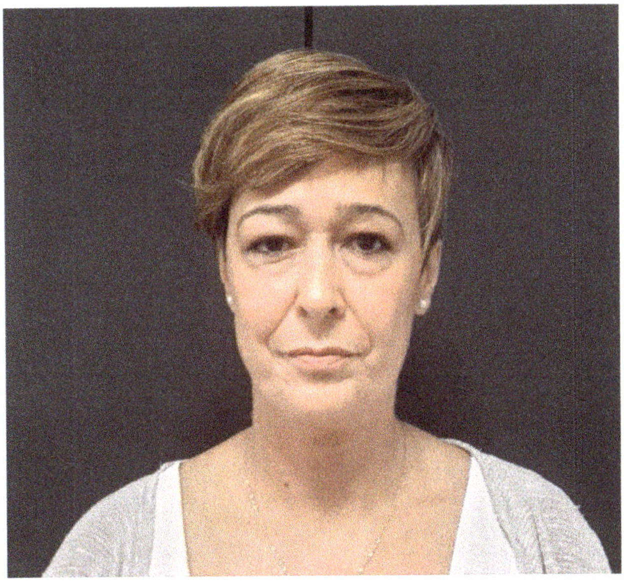

Figure 1. Preoperative imaging of Patient 5 reveals noticeable right ocular proptosis.

2.2. Preoperative Study and Virtual Surgical Planning

Multislice computed tomography (slices < 1 mm) was performed in all patients as part of a preoperative study (Figure 2). A 3D study of the patient was obtained using the Digital Imaging and Communications in Medicine (DICOM) viewer and was imported to computer software (Brainlab I-plan 3.0®, Munich, Germany) where virtual surgery was performed. The PSI design process was a collaborative effort, closely involving both the surgical team and biomedical engineers, with the primary objective of achieving precise and optimal outcomes. Preoperative CT data in DICOM format were used, ensuring that the files were uncompressed to maintain the highest possible quality and accuracy of anatomical information. These images served as the foundation for our PSI design process. The interdisciplinary collaboration between biomedical engineers and the surgical team allowed us to leverage the expertise of both parties. Surgeons provided critical insights into the anatomical requirements, the specifics of the craniofacial defects, and the desired placement of the implant to achieve optimal functional and aesthetic results. This collaboration ensured that the implants were tailored to each patient's unique anatomy and needs.

The biomedical engineers utilized the preoperative CT data to design the PSI, considering factors such as implant size, shape, and optimal positioning within the orbit. In one-step reconstructions, a combination of multiplanar two-dimensional (2D) slices and three-dimensional (3D) volume-rendering models was utilized to meticulously delineate the lesion and establish surgical bone resection margins with precision before the PSI was designed. For secondary delayed reconstructions, software was employed to transform and manipulate the CT data, enabling the generation of an anatomically appropriate implant. In instances of unilateral cases, whenever feasible, a mirroring technique was applied.

Once the design was finalized and approved by the surgical team, the PSI was manufactured through a milling process from radio-opaque PEEK blocks. The use of this material, which resembles bone in terms of density, provided an additional advantage in terms of the radiographic monitoring and assessment of implant positioning.

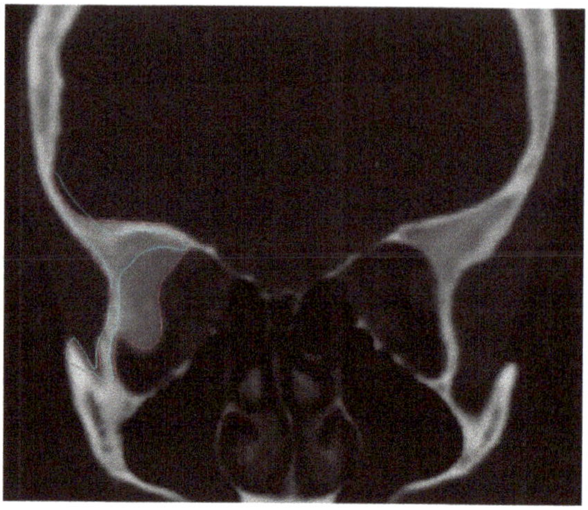

Figure 2. The preoperative CT scan of Patient 5 indicates a lesion consistent with meningioma in the fronto-orbital region (highlighted in red). The virtual design of the PEEK PSI is represented in blue.

The collaborative design and manufacturing process ensured that the PSI was tailored to each patient's specific needs, taking into account the intricacies of their craniofacial defects. This approach not only improved the accuracy of implant placement but also enhanced the overall outcomes in terms of aesthetics, functionality, and postoperative quality control.

Virtual planning was transferred into the surgical field through navigation (Brainlab I-plan) or surgical guides, performing the planned resection and the immediate insetting of the custom-made implant. Figure 3 shows the virtual surgery planned for Patient 5, focusing on meningioma excision. The planned procedure involved a fronto-orbital craniectomy, and to facilitate this, a surgical cutting guide was meticulously designed through collaboration between the surgical team and biomedical engineers. This cutting guide was instrumental in ensuring precision during the craniectomy, aligning with the patient's unique anatomy and the requirements of the surgical plan.

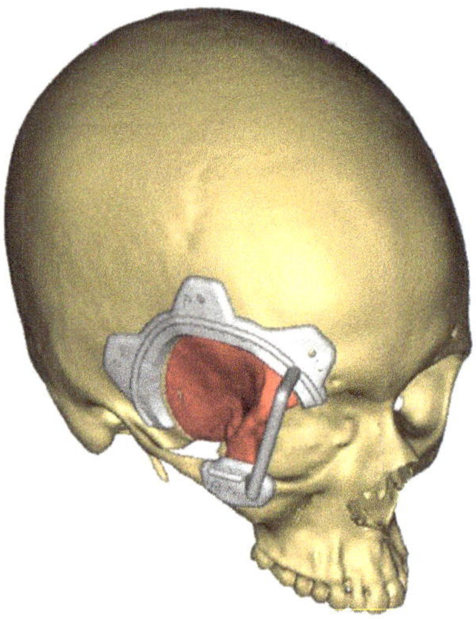

Figure 3. The virtual surgical planning for Patient 5 involved a fronto-temporal craniectomy (red), assisted by a designed and manufactured cutting guide (white).

Using intraoperative navigation, a non-invasive registration process for correlating anatomical references to digitalized CT was performed. Skin markers at various points of the face or surface matching were alternatively used, and the register was performed preoperatively.

2.3. Surgical Procedure

All the procedures were performed under general anesthesia. An extraorbital–transcranial approach was used for all the patients. Bicoronal, hemicoronal, and intraoral incision types were used to expose the orbital rim and zygoma region. According to the location of the lesion, different approaches were performed, classified into four groups: the anterior approach (fronto-orbital craniotomy), the lateral approach (temporo-orbito-zygomatic), the anterolateral approach (fronto-temporal and fronto-orbito-zygomatic), and combined approaches (orbito-malar). Neither the endoscopic approach nor the transfacial approach was needed. For Patient 5, a hemicoronal incision was executed to facilitate the fronto-temporal craniectomy. Figure 4 shows the surgical field after tumor resection, revealing the defects. The entire process was guided by surgical guides designed beforehand, ensuring precision and adherence to the planned resection margins. Following the tumor resection, the previously manufactured PEEK implant was placed into the defect and securely fixed to the adjacent bone with titanium miniplates. In this instance, the noticeable gap between the implant and the underlying bone surface can be attributed to the neurosurgeon executing a craniotomy that was wider than initially planned, driven by technical considerations (Figure 5). Intraoperative complications were recorded retrospectively.

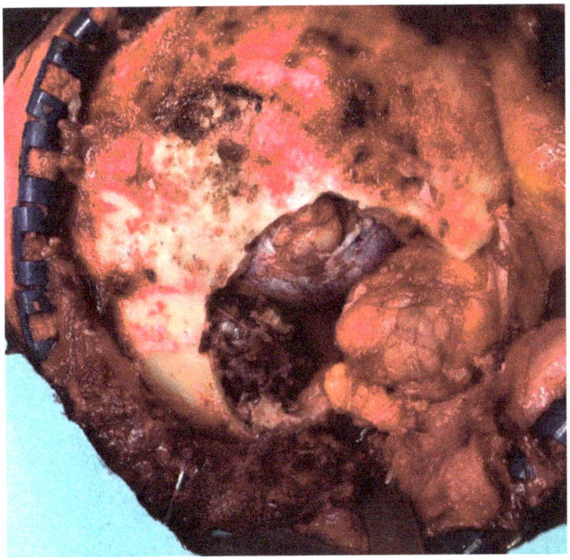

Figure 4. In the case of Patient 5, a right hemicoronal incision was meticulously carried out to provide optimal exposure for the subsequent fronto-temporal craniectomy, and surgical field post-tumor resection can also be observed.

Intraoperative or postoperative cranial CT examination was performed in all cases to check the planned tumor resection and the correct PEEK PSI position. The expected resection and planned reconstruction were compared with the radiological results.

All the resected lesions were sent for the histopathological study and the results were collected.

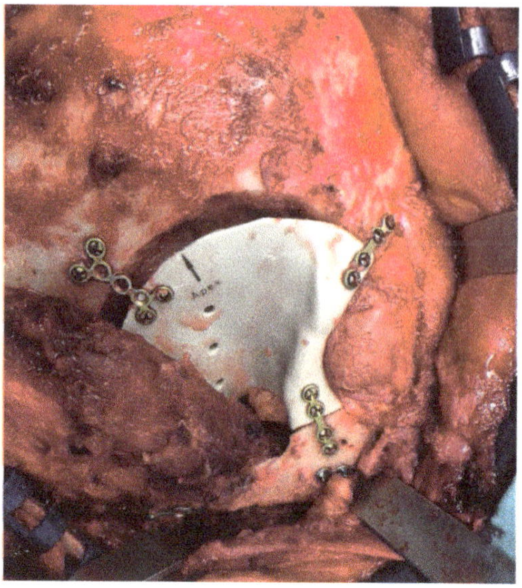

Figure 5. After the successful resection of the tumor in Patient 5, the pre-fabricated PEEK implant was placed as planned.

2.4. Follow-Up

All patients were submitted to regular follow-up examinations in the first month after the procedure and subsequently every 6 months to evaluate potential recurrence, functionality, and aesthetic outcomes through clinical assessments (Figure 6). A CT scan was performed during the 12-month follow-up to assess tumor recurrence and the PEEK PSI position. Any postoperative complications, including ocular mobility restrictions, diplopia, allergic reactions, etc., were also recorded.

Figure 6. Patient 5 after 6-month follow-up.

The analyzed data are presented descriptively, with a review of the scientific literature on the topic.

3. Results

The reconstruction of cranio-orbital defects using virtual surgical planning and custom-made PEEK PSI was performed on 15 patients (12 female and 3 male), with an average age of 46.13 years (ranging between 18 and 66 years). The genders, ages, preoperative clinical findings, and pathological diagnosis are shown in Table 1.

Table 1. Patient data, etiologies, locations, and surgical approaches.

N	Age	Gender	Etiology	Clinical Findings	Location	Surgical Approach	Reconstruction
1	18	F	Parry–Romberg syndrome	Asymmetry	Fronto-orbitary	Anterior (FO) [1]	Immediate
2	66	F	Fibrous dysplasia	Asymmetry	Fronto-Orbitary	Anterior (FO) [1]	Immediate
3	46	M	Squamous cell carcinoma	Surgical defect; pain	Ethmoid bone	Anterior (F) [2]	Delayed
4	25	F	Treacher Collins syndrome	Asymmetry	Fronto-orbitomalar	Combined (FOM) [3]. IO [4]	Delayed
5	46	F	Meningioma	Ocular proptosis	Greater sphenoid wing	Lateral (TZ) [5]	Immediate
6	59	F	Meningioma	Hypoacusia; pain	Temporal fossa	Lateral (TZ) [5]	Immediate
7	47	M	Pleomorphic adenoma	Ptosis; pain	Lacrimal gland	Antero lateral (FT) [6]	Immediate
8	61	F	Meningioma	Ocular proptosis	Fronto-orbitary	Antero lateral (FOT) [7]	Immediate
9	50	F	Meningioma	Ocular proptosis	Fronto-orbitary	Lateral (TOZ) [8]	Immediate
10	34	F	Meningioma	Ocular proptosis; loss of visual acuity	Greater sphenoid wing	Combined (OTM) [9]	Immediate
11	52	F	Hemangioma	Asymmetry	Orbitomalar	Combined (TZM) [10]	Immediate
12	53	F	Meningioma	Ocular proptosis	Greater sphenoid wing	Antero lateral (FOZ) [11]	Immediate
13	63	F	Meningioma	Asymmetry	Temporal fossa	Lateral (TZ) [5]	Immediate
14	36	F	Liposarcoma	Ocular proptosis; [pain]	Temporo-orbital	Lateral (TOZ) [8]	Immediate
15	36	M	Trauma sequelae	Asymmetry	Orbitomalar	Combined (TZM) [10]. IO [4]	Delayed

[1] FO: fronto-orbitary. [2] F: frontal. [3] FOM: fronto-orbito-malar. [4] IO: intraoral. [5] TZ: temporo-zygomatic. [6] FT: fronto-temporal. [7] FOT: fronto-orbito-temporal. [8] TOZ: temporo-orbito-zygomatic. [9] OTM: orbito-temporo-malar. [10] TZM: temporo-zygoma-malar. [11] FOZ: fronto-orbito-zygomatic.

Meningioma was the most frequent etiology (seven cases—46%), followed by benign bone lesions (three cases—20%), other benign tumors (two cases—13.33%), malignant tumors (two cases—13.33%), and trauma sequelae (one case—6.66%). The extension of the defect measured in the preoperative CT scan after virtual surgical planning ranged from 10.01 cm^3 to 256.5 cm^3 (mean surface 61.37 cm^3).

An extraorbital–transcranial approach was selected in all patients, using hemicoronal incision (10 cases—66.6%), coronal incision (3 cases—20%), and combined hemicoronal-intraoral approach (2 cases—13.33%). In 12 patients, the lesion resection was performed with immediate reconstruction using PEEK PSIs, and in the other 3 patients, a delayed reconstruction was performed. The mean operative time was 369 min. Wound healing was observed in all patients with no complications. The median hospital stay of the patients included in this study was 4.9 days (range: 2–11 days).

The aesthetic outcomes in our study were good, characterized by the absence of cranial convexities and orbital rim asymmetries. During the first three months, temporal asymmetry could be observed in most of the patients due to postoperative edema, but it spontaneously resolved during follow-up. In a single case, our study encountered less favorable outcomes, primarily stemming from an inadequate relationship between the soft tissue cover and the volume of the implant. Lipo-filling was performed one year after primary reconstruction was performed with successful outcomes.

Only one intraoperative complication was recorded: one of the patients (6.66%) showed malposition in the implant due to failed navigation relating to the setting of the stereotactic system. A second surgical procedure was needed to replace the implant in the correct position with favorable outcomes. In the two cases, including the one discussed in the article, the implant's contour deviated from the planned surgical defect as a result of the necessity for an expanded craniotomy performed by the neurosurgeon. Postoperative complications were also analyzed. During the first 6-month postoperative, mild complications were registered, mostly edema (10 cases—66.6%), ecchymosis (8 cases—53.3%), and diplopia (3 cases—20%), with complete resolution and without the need of reintervention. PEEK PSI infection only occurred in one patient (6.66%), presenting wound dehiscence and exposure of the osteosynthesis material used for the fixation of PEEK PSIs in the superior orbital rim. The osteosynthesis material was removed in a second surgical procedure conserving PEEK PSIs with no further complications. There was no surgical mortality. No recurrence of the lesion was observed during the follow-up. Postoperative complications are shown in Table 2.

Table 2. Postoperative complications during the follow-up.

Postoperative Complications	N	Patient Number	%
Edema	10	1, 2, 3, 5, 7, 9, 11, 12, 14, 15	66.6%
Ecchymosis	8	1, 2, 4, 5, 7, 8, 9, 11	53.3%
Diplopia	3	1, 8, 9	20%
Reintervention needed			
1. PSI misposition	1	10	6.66%
2. PSI infection	1	3	6.66%
3. Refinements	2	9	13.33%
Life-threatening complications	0		0%

Patients reported high levels of satisfaction with the aesthetic results achieved through the utilization of patient-specific PEEK implants. They expressed relief and contentment with the improved appearance of their craniofacial region. Beyond aesthetic improvements, patients also noted that the restoration of their facial appearance positively influenced their overall quality of life. They reported feeling more confident and self-assured in social and professional settings.

Long-term follow-up revealed that the aesthetic benefits of patient-specific PEEK implants remained stable over time. This element of sustainability added to the overall satisfaction, as patients could enjoy lasting improvements.

4. Discussion

Trauma, chronic infections, and malformation syndromes are the main causes of defects in the cranio-orbital region, with benign and malignant tumors representing the most frequent type of etiology in our series. Orbito-cranial neoplasms can be of primary origin, and secondary tumors and metastasis tumors, being primary orbit lesions, are the most frequently described in the literature [4]. In our case series, the majority of cases showed the secondary origin of tumors arising from surrounding anatomical regions. This can be attributed to this study's inclusion of only large tumors that required an aggressive approach and extensive resection, including craniofacial bone osteotomies.

Meningioma is the most frequently observed lesion in our series. It is the most common primary tumor of the central nervous system (CNS) and constitutes up to 55% of non-malignant primary CNS tumors [5]. Despite being a benign lesion, meningiomas can lead to certain morbidity, particularly those with an aggressive growth pattern.

To thoroughly assess each case, imaging tests such as computed tomography (CT) and magnetic resonance imaging (MRI) with axial, coronal, and sagittal plane reconstruction should be performed. Obtaining 3D images will provide us with a deeper understanding of the anatomical relationships between the lesion to be resected and other structures, such as eye globes, cavernous sinus lesions, or internal carotid arteries [1,6].

4.1. Surgical Approach

When selecting the optimal surgical approach for adequate resection and reconstruction, factors such as the anatomical location, size, and type of the tumor must be carefully considered. Numerous surgical approaches have been well documented in the literature [1]. For benign or smaller tumors located in the midline of the anterior skull base, a transnasal endoscopic approach can be a viable option. However, for major benign lesions or malignant tumors, as presented in our study, alternative surgical approaches should be chosen, including the coronal approach, the lateral approach, the anterolateral approach, or a combination of these approaches [4,7].

In order to achieve wide surgical exposure, one or more osteotomies may be necessary. For instance, in the coronal approach, frontal craniotomies are typically performed, minimizing neural tissue retraction. When dealing with tumors superolateral, superomedial, or inferolateral to the optic nerve, a lateral approach with temporo-orbital-zygomatic osteotomy is often preferred [8]. Additionally, if required, transfacial or transmandibular approaches can also be considered.

4.2. Surgery Virtual Planning: CAD CAM Technology

Advances in CAD/CAM technology have led to an evolution in cases involving the reconstruction of cranio-maxillofacial defects. By utilizing CAD/CAM technology, surgeons can establish accurate pre-operative plans, conduct virtual ablations, and plan osteotomy and reconstruction procedures. This advancement has allowed for improved aesthetics and functionality through more precise surgical procedures and reduced operation times [9,10].

At our institution, three-dimensional facial analysis and virtual surgical planning were incorporated into all of our cases involving orbito-craniomaxillofacial reconstruction and ablation over the past few years. CT scan multislice images were transformed into three-dimensional (3D) digital imaging and were then converted into a standard triangle language (STL) format using CAD technology. Through the 3D study, we could accurately delineate the lesion to be resected and establish safe oncologic margins prior to surgical intervention [11–13]. Additionally, it was feasible to conduct preoperative virtual surgery, incorporating the surgical approach, resection osteotomies, and the manufacture of computer-generated cutting guides based on the planned procedure. The collaborative process between biomedical engineers and the surgical team was integral to ensuring precise implant design and optimal patient outcomes. By transferring virtual surgery to the operating room, either through intraoperative navigation or the utilization of cutting guides, we could achieve the desired outcomes, as shown during the planning phase.

Over the past decade, there has been a notable increase in the use of intraoperative navigation applications in head and neck surgery. This trend can be attributed to the intricate anatomy of this region and the imperative for precise outcomes. These stereotaxy systems enable the accurate localization of anatomical landmarks or implants with a margin of error ranging from less than 1 to 2 mm [14]. This heightened surgical precision enhances safety by allowing us to effectively manage the anatomical relationships between the tumor and vital structures (like the cavernous sinus or the internal carotid artery) [15]. One potential drawback of intraoperative navigation is that if the stereotactic system becomes displaced during the surgical procedure, it can lead to an error during the resection or placement of the custom implant, as occurred in one of our cases.

Although further prospective studies with larger patient cohorts are necessary, the use of intraoperative navigation appears to contribute to the improved control of surgical margins, particularly in tumors situated within complex anatomical regions, like the cranio-orbital region or the skull base [13,16].

Surgical guides can be designed and manufactured according to our virtual surgery. By combining the use of cutting guides and intraoperative navigation, it is possible to achieve safer resection margins, enhance intraoperative precision, and reduce overall operative times [1,9,11,15].

4.3. Reconstruction with Patient-Customized Implants (PSIs)

Other advantages of CAD/CAM technology include enhanced accuracy in achieving aesthetic results and the ability to restore large and geometrically complex anatomical defects through the design and creation of patient-specific implants. The design process of patient-specific implants (PSIs) in our center involves a series of essential steps. The process starts with an in-depth preoperative assessment of the patient's cranio-maxillofacial defects, typically utilizing various diagnostic modalities, such as CT scans and three-dimensional (3D) imaging. These images provide precise information about the extent and shape of the defect and any surrounding structures that must be considered [8,17,18]. Collaboration among the surgical team, including craniofacial and maxillofacial surgeons, as well as biomedical engineers, is essential. The surgical team's expertise guides the implant's functional and anatomical requirements, while the engineers contribute their knowledge of materials and design techniques. The implant design process involves sculpting a prosthetic piece that precisely matches the patient's unique defect. The implant should not only be anatomically accurate, but also capable of restoring lost functionality, such as providing structural support or maintaining occlusion in the maxillofacial region.

The implant's design incorporates safe margins, ensuring that it extends beyond the edges of the defect to guarantee complete coverage. This margin is typically a few millimeters and aids in preventing any potential complications or adjacent tissue exposure. The design should also account for any surgical hardware, such as screw holes or attachment points. These facilitate the fixation of the implant during surgery to ensure stability. The designed implant should undergo rigorous validation to confirm its fit and accuracy. This may involve 3D-printing a prototype of the implant to ensure that it aligns precisely with the patient's defect. Once the design is validated and approved, the final implant is manufactured. The design data are sent to a specialized manufacturing facility, where the implant is fabricated with precision using computer-aided machining techniques. Quality control procedures are applied to the manufactured implant to ensure it meets the required specifications. This may involve rigorous testing to guarantee its structural integrity and biocompatibility.

A primary constraint associated with preoperative customized implants is the potential need to deviate from the initially planned approach during surgery. This deviation may arise due to various factors, including the surgeon's technical considerations, the necessity for a broader resection prompted by intraoperative requirements, or challenges encountered during osteotomy. Surgeons should be mindful of these possibilities, aiming to execute the operation as closely as possible to the initial plan. Nevertheless, the paramount objectives remain, ensuring appropriate oncologic resection margins and prioritizing patient safety.

The complex three-dimensional anatomy of the orbito-cranial region contributes to technical challenges in surgical reconstruction. The gold standard for the bone reconstruction of this region has been conventionally autologous bone due to its biocompatibility and strength, aligning well with native bone characteristics. However, limitations in shaping the graft, potential donor site complications, the lack of predictability, and the time-consuming harvesting process pose difficulties in the reconstruction of defects, especially those that are large or irregular in the orbito-maxillofacial region [1,19]. As a result, alloplastic materials are currently preferred due to their absence of donor site morbidity, intraoperative adaptability, and the advantage of prefabrication through computer design that allows better morphological results to be achieved [8,20,21].

For this purpose, a wide range of materials, including titanium, hydroxyapatite, poly-DL-lactic acid (PDLLA), and polyether-ether-ketone (PEEK), have been used [6,20]. Among these options, PEEK is preferred by the authors for cranio-facial bone replacement. This biomaterial was first developed in 1978 and has been used for surgical reconstruction since 1998 [22]. Since then, PEEK has been extensively utilized in various applications due to its similar strength and weight to human bone, as well as its low infection and allergic reaction rates. Moreover, PEEK is radiolucent and does not generate artifacts in imaging tests, enabling effective post-surgical oncologic monitoring. PEEK prostheses can be precisely molded to match the size and shape of the defect to be covered [8,23]. When compared to other biomaterials such as titanium, both of them exhibit strength, rigidity, biocompatibility, and non-allergenic properties. They can be easily sterilized through heat or ionizing radiation and can be individually manufactured to fit each patient's needs [24,25]. However, PEEK offers several advantages over titanium. It closely resembles bone in terms of elasticity and density, reducing shielding. PEEK implants can be easily adjusted during surgery, unlike prefabricated titanium implants. PEEK allows increased thickness to restore bone volume and minimize dead space. Unlike titanium, PEEK does not osseo-integrate with bone, requiring fixation, normally using titanium screws to maintain stability and prevent bulging [17,26,27]. PEEK PSIs demonstrated excellent biocompatibility in our series. During the close follow-up of reconstructed patients, no signs of rejection were observed.

According to the related literature, it is essential to acknowledge that PEEK, while offering numerous advantages for cranio-facial bone replacement, is not without its disadvantages. Notably, PEEK can be a relatively costly material which may impact its accessibility and utility in certain healthcare settings. Additionally, one of the notable drawbacks of PEEK is its limited osteointegration potential, which increases the risk of dislodgment and infection, posing challenges in long-term stability [17,26,27]. This is in contrast to materials like titanium which exhibit more favorable osteointegration characteristics [25].

Another concern highlighted in the literature is the comparatively higher infection rate associated with PEEK when compared to titanium implants. This raises concerns about patient safety and long-term outcomes. Furthermore, there have been previous reports of foreign body reactions to PEEK implants, although the incidence remains relatively rare. Such reactions, when they do occur, can complicate the recovery and necessitate additional interventions. In our series, it is noteworthy that only one patient, constituting 6.66% of the cases, experienced an infection related to the PEEK PSI. This isolated incidence of infection is relatively low in the context of our study, and while it represents a potential drawback of using PEEK implants, it is important to consider the specific circumstances and contributing factors that may have led to this outcome.

Moreover, the structural properties of PEEK, including its thickness and lack of porosity, can present challenges in certain clinical scenarios [25]. Specifically, its non-porous nature may impede fluid drainage when required, potentially leading to complications during the healing process.

Despite these limitations, it is important to recognize that the choice of implant material should be based on a thorough evaluation of the specific patient's needs, the nature of the procedure, and the surgeon's expertise. PEEK, with its distinct set of advantages and disadvantages, represents a valuable option in cranio-maxillofacial surgery. Careful consideration of these factors is crucial in achieving the best possible outcomes for patients while minimizing associated risks.

4.4. Intraoperative Imaging

Upon the completion of the reconstruction, whether assisted by a navigation system or not, it is essential to submit the surgical outcome to three-dimensional validation for quality control purposes. Ideally, this validation should take place intraoperatively immediately after the reconstruction is finished in order to identify and correct an implant mispositioning, as this happened in one of our cases [1,28].

Intraoperative CT offers a clear advantage for the control of orbito-cranial reconstruction over other imaging modalities, including MRI, due to its high resolution and the adequate visualization of the thin bony structures of the orbit and the implanted materials [29,30]. However, intraoperative CT has some drawbacks, including relatively high radiation doses and high procurement costs [31].

4.5. Esthetic, Socio-Psychological, and Functional Results

The socio-psychological adaptation of patients to surgery and the changes in their appearance are critical aspects of the overall well-being and recovery process. Patients undergoing cranio-orbitofacial surgery often face significant changes in their facial appearance, which can have profound effects on their psychological and emotional state. Understanding how patients adapt to these changes, their anxiety levels, and pain tolerance is crucial for providing comprehensive care.

Many patients may experience feelings of distress, sadness, or a sense of identity loss. They may fear societal judgment or stigmatization and face altered self-esteem due to their altered appearance. The fear of the unknown, concerns about surgical outcomes, and the anticipation of potential pain or discomfort can contribute to heightened anxiety levels. During our study, we provide psychological support and counseling in order to help patients adapt to their altered appearance.

Patients' pain tolerance can vary significantly. Effective postoperative pain management is a key component in helping patients adapt to their new appearance. The surgeons and healthcare team at our center collaborate to develop pain management strategies tailored to each patient. This may include medications, physical therapy, and psychological interventions to improve pain tolerance and enhance recovery.

The overall satisfaction of our patients following craniofacial reconstruction with PEEK PSIs was a fundamental aspect of our study. Unlike conventional reconstruction techniques, which often lead to noticeable aesthetic changes, patient-specific PEEK implants allowed for subtler and more natural enhancements. Patients included in our study reported minimal psychological distress or discomfort associated with their postoperative appearance. Long-term follow-up revealed that the aesthetic benefits of patient-specific PEEK implants remained stable over time. This element of sustainability added to the overall satisfaction, as patients could enjoy lasting improvements.

5. Conclusions

The use of CAD/CAM technology has significantly enhanced the evaluation and surgical planning of craniofacial complex tumor resections, enabling the precise design of resection and reconstruction procedures. Through the introduction of cutting-guides and intraoperative navigation, virtual surgical plans can be seamlessly translated to the operating room, facilitating improved control over surgical margins and enhanced proximity to vital structures. The use of customized PEEK implants, along with navigation-assisted techniques, allows for the immediate reconstruction of large craniofacial defects while minimizing the occurrence of major complications and avoiding donor site morbidity. Patients' emotional responses, anxiety levels, and pain tolerance must be carefully assessed and managed to ensure a successful recovery.

Author Contributions: C.C.-S.: conceptualization, data collection, methodology, investigation, analysis, interpretation, and writing. F.A.-P.: conceptualization, methodology, investigation, review, and editing. A.M.S.-F.: data collection and investigation. Á.R.-C.: data collection and investigation. P.d.L.-M.: data collection and investigation. L.L.-U.: methodology and review and editing. J.A.-S.: conceptualization, methodology, investigation, software, review and editing, and supervision. All authors have read and agreed to the published version of the manuscript.

Funding: This research received no external funding.

Institutional Review Board Statement: Ethics approval was not required—It was a retrospective study. Only informed consent was obtained.

Informed Consent Statement: Informed consent was obtained from all subjects involved in the study. Written informed consent was obtained from the patients in order to publish this paper.

Data Availability Statement: Data are contained within the article.

Conflicts of Interest: The authors declare no conflicts of interest.

References

1. Acero, J.; de Leyva, P. Computer assisted surgery and navigation in Cranio-orbital resection and reconstruction. In *Innovations and New Developments in Craniomaxillofacial Reconstruction*; Springer Nature Switzerland: Madrid, Spain, 2021; pp. 96–115.
2. Acero, J.; Maza, C.; Salmerón, J.; Ochandiano, S.; Navarro-Vila, C. Reconstruction of the cranio-orbital region. In *Reconstructive Oral and Maxillofacial Surgery*; Springer: New York, NY, USA, 2015; pp. 77–102.
3. Ma, R.; Tang, T. Current strategies to improve the bioactivity of PEEK. *Int. J. Mol. Sci.* **2014**, *15*, 5426–5445. [CrossRef]
4. Kılıç, M.; Özöner, B.; Aydın, L.; Özdemir, B.; Yılmaz, İ.; Müslüman, A.M.; Yılmaz, A.; Çavuşoğlu, H.; Aydın, Y. Cranio-Orbital Tumors: Clinical Results and A Surgical Approach. *Sisli Etfal Hastan. Tip Bul.* **2019**, *53*, 240–246. [CrossRef]
5. Marosi, C.; Hassler, M.; Roessler, K.; Reni, M.; Sant, M.; Mazza, E.; Vecht, C. Meningioma. *Crit. Rev. Oncol. Hematol.* **2008**, *67*, 153–171. [CrossRef]
6. Dubois, L.; Steenen, S.A.; Gooris, P.J.J.; Mourits, M.P.; Becking, A.G. Controversies in orbital reconstruction--II. Timing of post-traumatic orbital reconstruction: A systematic review. *Int. J. Oral. Maxillofac. Surg.* **2015**, *44*, 433–440. [CrossRef]
7. Acero, J.; de Leyva, P.; Almeida, F.; Núñez, J.; Picón, M. The combined coronal-transconjunctival approach: An innovative surgical access for orbital exenteration in craniofacial resection. *Int. J. Oral. Maxillofac. Surg.* **2022**, *51*, 300–306. [CrossRef]
8. Lv, M.; Yang, X.; Gvetadze, S.R.; Gupta, A.; Li, J.; Sun, J. Accurate reconstruction of bone defects in orbital-maxillary-zygomatic (OMZ) complex with polyetheretherketone (PEEK). *J. Plast. Reconstr. Aesthetic Surg.* **2022**, *75*, 1750–1757. [CrossRef]
9. Rudman, K.; Hoekzema, C.; Rhee, J. Computer-assisted innovations in craniofacial surgery. *Facial Plast. Surg. FPS* **2011**, *27*, 358–365. [CrossRef]
10. Levine, J.P.; Patel, A.; Saadeh, P.B.; Hirsch, D.L. Computer-aided design and manufacturing in craniomaxillofacial surgery: The new state of the art. *J. Craniofac. Surg.* **2012**, *23*, 288–293. [CrossRef]
11. Sharaf, B.; Levine, J.P.; Hirsch, D.L.; Bastidas, J.A.; Schiff, B.A.; Garfein, E.S. Importance of computer-aided design and manufacturing technology in the multidisciplinary approach to head and neck reconstruction. *J. Craniofac. Surg.* **2010**, *21*, 1277–1280. [CrossRef]
12. Cevidanes, L.H.C.; Tucker, S.; Styner, M.; Kim, H.; Chapuis, J.; Reyes, M.; Proffit, W.; Turvey, T.; Jaskolka, M. Three-dimensional surgical simulation. *Am. J. Orthod. Dentofac. Orthop.* **2010**, *138*, 361–371. [CrossRef]
13. Ranz-Colio, Á.; Almeida-Parra, F.; De Leyva-Moreno, P.; Cárdenas-Serres, C.; García-Cosío, M.; Acero-Sanz, J. Navigation-guided resection of locally advanced midface malignancies. Does it improve the safety of oncologic resection? *Oral. Oncol.* **2023**, *143*, 106455. [CrossRef]
14. Luebbers, H.T.; Messmer, P.; Obwegeser, J.A.; Zwahlen, R.A.; Kikinis, R.; Graetz, K.W.; Matthews, F. Comparison of different registration methods for surgical navigation in cranio-maxillofacial surgery. *J Cranio-Maxillo-Fac. Surg. Off. Publ. Eur. Assoc. Cranio-Maxillo-Fac. Surg.* **2008**, *36*, 109–116. [CrossRef]
15. Sukegawa, S.; Kanno, T.; Furuki, Y. Application of computer-assisted navigation systems in oral and maxillofacial surgery. *Jpn. Dent. Sci. Rev.* **2018**, *54*, 139–149. [CrossRef]
16. Tarsitano, A.; Ricotta, F.; Baldino, G.; Badiali, G.; Pizzigallo, A.; Ramieri, V.; Cascone, P.; Marchetti, C. Navigation-guided resection of maxillary tumours: The accuracy of computer-assisted surgery in terms of control of resection margins—A feasibility study. *J. Cranio-Maxillo-Fac. Surg. Off. Publ. Eur. Assoc. Cranio-Maxillo-Fac. Surg.* **2017**, *45*, 2109–2114. [CrossRef]
17. Chepurnyi, Y.; Chernogorskyi, D.; Kopchak, A.; Petrenko, O. Clinical efficacy of peek patient-specific implants in orbital reconstruction. *J. Oral. Biol. Craniofacial Res.* **2020**, *10*, 49–53. [CrossRef]
18. Patel, N.; Kim, B.; Zaid, W. Use of Virtual Surgical Planning for Simultaneous Maxillofacial Osteotomies and Custom Polyetheretherketone Implant in Secondary Orbito-Frontal Reconstruction: Importance of Restoring Orbital Volume. *J. Craniofac. Surg.* **2017**, *28*, 387–390. [CrossRef]
19. Järvinen, S.; Suojanen, J.; Kormi, E.; Wilkman, T.; Kiukkonen, A.; Leikola, J.; Stoor, P. The use of patient specific polyetheretherketone implants for reconstruction of maxillofacial deformities. *J. Cranio-Maxillofac. Surg.* **2019**, *47*, 1072–1076. [CrossRef]
20. Honigmann, P.; Sharma, N.; Okolo, B.; Popp, U.; Msallem, B.; Thieringer, F.M. Patient-Specific Surgical Implants Made of 3D Printed PEEK: Material, Technology, and Scope of Surgical Application. *BioMed. Res. Int.* **2018**, *2018*, 4520636. [CrossRef]
21. Kim, M.M.; Boahene, K.D.O.; Byrne, P.J. Use of customized polyetheretherketone (PEEK) implants in the reconstruction of complex maxillofacial defects. *Arch. Facial Plast. Surg.* **2009**, *11*, 53–57. [CrossRef]
22. Eschbach, L. Nonresorbable polymers in bone surgery. *Injury* **2000**, *31* (Suppl. S4), 22–27. [CrossRef]
23. Oh, J.H. Recent advances in the reconstruction of cranio-maxillofacial defects using computer-aided design/computer-aided manufacturing. *Maxillofac. Plast. Reconstr. Surg.* **2018**, *40*, 2. [CrossRef]
24. Zegers, T.; Koper, D.; Lethaus, B.; Kessler, P.; Ter Laak-Poort, M. Computer-Aided-Design/Computer-Aided-Manufacturing Titanium Cranioplasty in a Child: Critical Appraisal. *J. Craniofac. Surg.* **2020**, *31*, 237–240. [CrossRef]
25. Lethaus, B.; Safi, Y.; ter Laak-Poort, M.; Kloss-Brandstätter, A.; Banki, F.; Robbenmenke, C.; Steinseifer, U.; Kessler, P. Cranioplasty with customized titanium and PEEK implants in a mechanical stress model. *J. Neurotrauma* **2012**, *29*, 1077–1083. [CrossRef]
26. Gerbino, G.; Zavattero, E.; Zenga, F.; Bianchi, F.A.; Garzino-Demo, P.; Berrone, S. Primary and secondary reconstruction of complex craniofacial defects using polyetheretherketone custom-made implants. *J. Cranio-Maxillo-Fac. Surg. Off. Publ. Eur. Assoc. Cranio-Maxillo-Fac. Surg.* **2015**, *43*, 1356–1363. [CrossRef]

27. Alonso-Rodriguez, E.; Cebrián, J.L.; Nieto, M.J.; Del Castillo, J.L.; Hernández-Godoy, J.; Burgueño, M. Polyetheretherketone custom-made implants for craniofacial defects: Report of 14 cases and review of the literature. *J. Cranio-Maxillo-Fac. Surg. Off. Publ. Eur. Assoc. Cranio-Maxillo-Fac. Surg.* **2015**, *43*, 1232–1238. [CrossRef]
28. Cuddy, K.; Khatib, B.; Bell, R.B.; Cheng, A.; Patel, A.; Amundson, M.; Dierks, E.J. Use of Intraoperative Computed Tomography in Craniomaxillofacial Trauma Surgery. *J. Cranio-Maxillo-Fac. Surg. Off. Publ. Eur. Assoc. Cranio-Maxillo-Fac. Surg.* **2018**, *76*, 1016–1025. [CrossRef]
29. Strong, E.B.; Tollefson, T.T. Intraoperative use of CT imaging. *Otolaryngol. Clin. N. Am.* **2013**, *46*, 719–732. [CrossRef]
30. Voskuil, F.J.; Vonk, J.; van der Vegt, B.; Kruijff, S.; Ntziachristos, V.; van der Zaag, P.J.; Witjes, M.J.; van Dam, G.M. Intraoperative imaging in pathology-assisted surgery. *Nat. Biomed. Eng.* **2022**, *6*, 503–514. [CrossRef]
31. Chau, A.C.M.; Fung, K. Comparison of radiation dose for implant imaging using conventional spiral tomography, computed tomography, and cone-beam computed tomography. *Oral Surg. Oral Med. Oral Pathol. Oral Radiol. Endod.* **2009**, *107*, 559–565. [CrossRef]

MDPI AG
Grosspeteranlage 5
4052 Basel
Switzerland
Tel.: +41 61 683 77 34

Journal of Clinical Medicine Editorial Office
E-mail: jcm@mdpi.com
www.mdpi.com/journal/jcm

www.ingramcontent.com/pod-product-compliance
Lightning Source LLC
Chambersburg PA
CBHW061621210926
51850CB00009B/2396
* 9 7 8 3 7 2 5 8 1 9 8 1 2 *